Political Sociology

Political Sociology: Structure and Process

George Andrew Kourvetaris
Northern Illinois University

Allyn and Bacon
Boston • London • Toronto • Tokyo • Singapore

Editor-in-Chief, Social Sciences: Karen Hanson
Series Editorial Assistant: Jennifer Jacobson
Marketing Manager: Karon Bowers
Composition Buyer: Linda Cox
Manufacturing Buyer: Aloka Rathnam
Cover Administrator: Suzanne Harbison
Cover Designer: Jennifer Hart
Production Administrator: Deborah Brown
Editorial-Production Service: Susan McNally
Copyeditor: Leslie Brunetta

Library of Congress Cataloging-in-Publication Data

Kourvetaris, George A.
    Political sociology : structure and process / George Andrew
Kourvetaris.
        p.   cm.
    Includes bibliographical references and index.
    ISBN 0-205-14793-3
    1. Political sociology.   I. Title.
JA76.K67   1996
306.2—dc20   96-15327
                                                        CIP

Printed in the United States of America

10 9 8 7 6 5 4 3 2   01 00 99 98

To my brothers Dimitri and Taki; to Taki's wife, Voula, and their three children, Sophia, Andreas, and Dimitri; and also to my three children, Sophia, Andreas, and Nicholas Kourvetaris

Contents

Preface

The end of the Cold War has brought sweeping political and social changes, not only in the former Soviet Union and Eastern Europe, but in other parts of the world as well. It was clear to me that the available books in political sociology were too narrow or outdated to capture these profound changes. This timely, highly readable and comprehensive book on political sociology, I believe, will fill this lacuna. It gives students and teachers of politics and society the opportunity to use the concepts, frameworks, and empirical findings in this important area to understand and analyze the political and social structures and processes not only of the U.S., but also of all societies and nations. Using an interdisciplinary approach, I have examined a number of old and new conceptual and empirical issues in view of new developments and changes taking place around the world. Both the sociohistorical and empirical aspects of politics and society are explored and discussed.

The book is organized in four parts. Part I, "The Field of Political Sociology," consists of an introduction to political sociology and a discussion of some of the major issues and models in this field. The subjects' nature, levels of analysis, and important concepts are introduced. The relationship of political sociology to other disciplines and issues of moral relevance are raised. Part II, "Power and Power Structures," includes five chapters—"The Study of Societal Power and Authority," "Nations and States," "Structure and Behavior of U.S. Elites," "Media Communication and Power," and "Civil–Military Relations"—and emphasizes power and power structures manifested in various institutions and structures of society and polity. Part III, "Electoral Politics and Movements," consists of four chapters—"Political Participation and Voting," "Political Parties," "Political Ideology," and "Social and Political Movements"—and explores partisanship, political ideology, and conventional and nonconventional aspects of politics. Finally, Part IV, "Development and World Politics," includes three chapters—"Democratization and Development," "Social Conflict and Ethnic Nationalism," and "Politics and Society in the Post–Cold War Era." This part is more comparative and international in scope than the others; it deals primarily with ongoing developments in many parts of the world, following the end of the Cold War. The issues of democratization, ethnic nationalism, and the politics of the post–Cold War era are examined and assessed. In the last chapter of Part IV, a number of models and scenarios are suggested for the twenty-first century.

This book, in preparation for the past three years, has been designed as an introduction to political sociology for upper-level undergraduate and graduate students in politics and society. It is the distillation of twenty-five years of teaching experience in political sociology courses, at both the undergraduate and graduate levels. In addition, the *Journal of Political and Military Sociology,* founded in 1973 by the author, has given me a more comprehensive interdisciplinary view of the field of political sociology and the allied field of military sociology. For the past two dozen years the JPMS has been associated with some of the leading scholars in these fields. In the words of Seymour Martin Lipset, "The JPMS is clearly the leading publication in political sociology. Its articles have high standards. It should be read regularly by anyone who wants to keep up with the field."

The book has been strengthened by the suggestions and comments of many colleagues, anonymous reviewers, and specialists in various sub-areas of political sociology, including scholars from political science and communications studies, military sociologists, social and political movement specialists, and neo-Marxists. Some of these individuals have long been affiliated with the *Journal of Political and Military Sociology.* I extend my deepest thanks and appreciation to the following colleagues who read and provided me with invaluable comments: Kevin Anderson, Martha Cooper, Constantine Danopoulos, Thomas R. Dye, Samuel Eldersveld, Ted Goertzel, Eric Goode, Pierre Gravel, John Higley, David Jacobson, Dwight King, Louis Kriesberg, Kurt Lang, Charles Moskos, Clark Neher, Anthony Oberschall, Manny Paraschos, Frances Fox Piven, Mostafa Rejai, and Dan Zirker. In addition, the following reviewers provided insightful commentary on this edition: Carmen Blalock, Calhoun Community College; Edward L. Kick, University of Utah; Rory McVeigh, University of North Carolina, Chapel Hill; and Robert J. S. Ross, Clark University.

Also, I would like to thank my assistant James Rowe and his wife, Pat, both graduate students at Northern Illinois University, for their assistance in compiling the bibliography. I also extend my appreciation to my son Andreas G. Kourvetaris, who holds an M. A. in social sciences from the University of Chicago and he is working toward his Ph.D. in Sociology at Columbia University, who meticulously read the entire manuscript and made very constructive suggestions for stylistic improvement.

Political Sociology

Introduction to Political Sociology

The complex world in which we live constantly requires that we make personal choices, both small and large, that will affect our lives and perhaps the lives of others. But in many important areas of our lives, others make crucial decisions for us. These decisions, made by a handful of powerful individuals and groups, have vast societal consequences. In order to understand the complexity of society and our place in it, we must first comprehend its structures of power and processes of decision making. How are decisions, or nondecisions, made? Who makes important decisions, and why? Who exercises the most power and control over the resources in society? Why are some individuals, groups, or institutions more powerful than others? Who decides whether we will go to war, which job applicant will be hired, or which environmental decisions affecting the health of a whole community will be made? Questions of this nature are the subject matter of political sociology.

Although the United States has never had a hereditary aristocracy, no one can deny the fact that some form of political, social, and cultural elite has always existed here. From the beginning, power and wealth in the United States have been unevenly distributed. The founders of this country and the framers of the Constitution set the norms for the new nation. "We the people of the United States" consisted of a small number of white, male slaveholders and landowners, a wealthy minority, rather than a broader representation of the various segments of early U.S. society. The English Protestant core culture became the basis of U.S. political and social institutions. In this sense, the birth of the United States was an extension of European culture, particularly that of northwestern European countries such as England, Scotland, Germany, and Ireland. Two centuries later, the United States has become an unprecedented example of a pluralistic society.

At the end of the nineteenth century, the main source of immigrants to the United States shifted from Western Europe to southern, central, and eastern Europe. By the mid-1970s, European immigration to the United States had almost come to a standstill. Perhaps for this reason, the United States is no longer described as a melting pot but rather as an ethnic and religious mosaic made up of four main racial and ethnic groups—Caucasian or white, African American, Asian, and Latino. According to

1

J. Gordon Melton (1987) there are at least 1,347 religious groups (churches, sects, cults) in the United States. In the twenty-first century, the makeup of the United States will be more and more nonwhite, or non-European. This change will make the United States a more racially and ethnically diverse society, creating implications for the political and power dynamics of intergroup relations.

The early 1990s ushered in the end of the Cold War and the end of the arms race between the United States and the Soviet Union—rival superpowers for almost fifty years. Yet this decade has also created an air of uncertainty, fueled by a resurgence of ethnic nationalism and the tentative realization of a fledgling international order. The collapse of the Soviet Union, the failure of economic modernization and democratization in the states of the former Yugoslavia, and the hasty decision by the European Economic Community and other countries to recognize the independence of former Yugoslavian republics contributed to the rise of ethnic nationalism and civil war in Bosnia-Herzegovina.

Social scientists failed to predict this dramatic turn of events, and Marxist theoreticians were bewildered by the collapse of state socialism and the bloody events in Bosnia-Herzegovina. It is ironic that while a number of European communities are moving toward political and economic union in Western Europe, Yugoslavia and the republics of the former Soviet Union are undergoing ethnic antagonism, militant neo-nationalism, and "ethnic cleansing." Although the end of the Cold War has diminished the threat of a nuclear holocaust, it would be premature to think that it signals the end of potentially serious conflicts in different regions of the world.

According to Bogdan Denitch (1990), three major developments will shape the end of the twentieth century and the beginning of the twentieth-first century: the end of the Cold War, European unification, and democratic upheavals and reforms in Eastern Europe and the former Soviet Union. These sociopolitical changes will have far-reaching consequences, not only for Europe, but also for the entire world. Coupled with these transformations, international power structures will undergo profound changes. These events fall within the international and comparative perspective of political sociology, and raise questions such as these: Is the process of democratization compatible with the reemergence of ethnic nationalism and self-determination? What kind of political and economic system will replace state socialism and Communist regimes?

Before embarking on a discussion of these broad issues, we should first address some of the important issues that concern the political sociologist: (1) What is the nature of political sociology? (2) What is the relationship between political sociology and other disciplines in the social sciences? (3) What is the relevance of political sociology?

The Nature of Political Sociology

Political sociology is an interdisciplinary field that draws primarily upon political science and sociology. It studies the nexus of society and politics, or the sociology of politics; it examines how society and various social groups, defined by factors such as social class, race, gender, ethnicity, religion, and occupation, affect politics, and vice versa. The beginnings of modern political sociology in the United States date back to the Great Depression (Coser, 1966:2; Lasswell, 1951). However, the concerns of political sociology can be traced to earlier European political and social philosophers, such as Karl Marx and Max Weber, and even to the classical world of the ancient Greeks, especially to the writings of Plato, Aristotle, and Thucydides. Yet as political issues change, so does the subject matter of political sociology. Amid the diverse topics in political sociology, a number of themes recur in research and teaching.[1]

Most political sociologists stress the relationships between polity, society, and the state, focusing on studies of power, power structures, and aspects of institutional (conventional) and extrainstitutional (nonconventional) politics. Many political sociologists are interested in comparative politics, societies, and states, and they often use an economic approach to analyze and explain issues. Only a few, however, concentrate on the interdependence of economy, polity, and the military. Similarly, only a few political sociologists view political sociology as the study of elites and masses. Many of the concepts mentioned above will be discussed in later chapters.[2]

Thus, political sociology is the study of power and power structures at all levels of analysis: individual, group, organizational, societal, regional, national, transnational, and international. This book uses an interdisciplinary and comparative approach, drawing from a variety of social science disciplines, including civil-military relations, history, political science, sociology, communications, and political philosophy. A wide range of examples and perspectives will be reviewed, which seems particularly appropriate in our increasingly interdependent political world. Events in distant regions of the world (for example, the conflict between Arabs and Israelis in the Middle East, or between Protestants and Roman Catholics in Northern Ireland) have consequences for U.S. foreign policy. We cannot attain a broad understanding of politics and political conflict by studying local or national politics alone, although the specific effects of a political decision on individuals and communities must be considered together with its wider consequences.

Political Sociology and Related Disciplines

A definition of the nature and scope of political sociology would be incomplete without comparing it with its parent disciplines of political science and sociology, on the one hand, and with the related disciplines of political economy, political psychology, and political anthropology, on the other. Giovanni Sartori (1969) distinguished political sociology from the sociology of politics and political science by noting that political science deals primarily with political structures and conditions, whereas the sociology of politics selects structural or social psychological conditions for its focus. Political sociology, Sartori argued, can be considered an interdisciplinary hybrid that combines both political and social variables in explaining political behavior and conditions (Tatalovich and Daynes, 1988). In addition, for Sartori, political science starts with the study of the state and government, whereas political sociology focuses on society. At present, political sociology deals mainly with the issues of civil society and the state, or, more broadly, the relationship between society and politics, including the state.

Political science primarily comprises the study of government and the state, highlighting administrative structures and political institutions (such as the executive, legislative, and judicial branches of government) and political parties and interest groups (such as the military as a client of the state). Political scientists mainly study the functions of government machinery and political institutions, whereas political sociologists stress *why* political institutions work the way they do, *who* gains and *who* loses because of such political arrangements, and *what* constitutes the link between political institutions and other social institutions such as the economy, the military, public education, and so on. Furthermore, whereas political sociologists traditionally stress change and conflict, political scientists focus on issues of order, endurance, and stability in political systems; whereas political sociology criticizes society, politics, and the way that power is exercised and distributed in society, political science tends to be less critical and more accommodating, simply describing government functions. At the same time, in its analyses of politics and society, political sociology draws from both the conflict and functionalist perspectives of sociology and political science.

In addition to political science, three more social science disciplines are related to political sociology: political economy, political anthropology, and political psychology (see Table 1.1). Originally, the field of economics was known as political economy. Adam Smith (1776: Book 4) wrote, "Political economy, considered as a branch of the science of a statesman or legislator, proposed two distinct objectives: first, to provide a plentiful revenue or subsistence for the people . . . and secondly, to supply the state . . . with a revenue sufficient for the public services." To the Marxist, political economy is a historical science, or the science of laws governing the production, exchange, and distribution of material means. Following World War II and the emergence of developing nation-states, Marxist political economists revived an interest in political economy.

In recent times, the term *political economy* has come to mean that part of economic theory dealing with the entire socioeconomic system, as well as with politico-economic policies and theories guided by liberal, conservative, and radical approaches. Political economy, then, studies political and economic institutions and how they affect one another. A number of political sociologists, such as Martin Marger (1987) and Berch Berberoglu (1990), used a politico-economic approach to look at some major issues in political sociology. Indeed, political sociology is defined more and more in terms of political economy. Although political philosophy is the oldest prescientific discipline, political economy is considered the oldest of all social science disciplines.

Political psychology considers the subjective or psychological dimensions of political behavior, working with ideas such as personality, political socialization, and political attitudes, feelings, and meanings, including genetic or biological factors. The field of political psychology has become more interdisciplinary, drawing heavily from a variety of sources, including political sociology. Furthermore, political psychology deals with the way psychological and social psychological variables (such as motivation, personality, feelings, and attitudes) affect political behavior and political leadership. It also deals with micropolitics, or the study of individual and small group political attitudes and behavior.

Political anthropology is also related to political sociology and encompasses the comparative study of nonliterate power structures or kinship groups that gave way to states. Of course, different cultures employ different methods to solve political problems and to resolve conflicts. Political anthropology studies mechanisms—such as factions, brokers, and leadership—that guide political behavior in different tradi-

Table 1.71   Nature and Scope of Political Sociology and Related Fields of Study

Nature and Scope	Political Sociology	Political Science	Political Anthropology	Political Economy	Political Psychology
Scope of discipline	The study of power and power structures. The interface of politics and society, including the role of the state. The relationship between political and other social institutions, including military, economic, educational, religious, and kinship groups.	The study of national government; political processes, purposes, and character; and organization of the state.	The political process and solutions to political problems. Power structures of nonliterate societies.	Political and economic issues. The laws governing the production, exchange, and distribution of material means for living. The functioning of the entire socioeconomic system.	The psychological, personal, and subjective aspects of political behavior, political motives. The subconscious, psychopathology and politics, defense mechanisms and politics, and the ego and politics.
(1) Levels of analysis and (2) methods of study	(1) Organizational, communal, state, national, regional, international. (2) Survey, historical study, issue analysis, positional study, reputational study (who's who variety), qualitative and quantitative methods.	(1) State, public administration, government, public opinion polls. (2) Survey, issue analysis, positional study, reputational study and quantitative methods.	(1) Functionalism, structuralism. (2) Survey, participant observation, description of individual cultures (ethnography).	(2) Models, surveys, inductive and deductive approaches.	(2) Interdisciplinary survey, scales, opinion polls.
Key concepts and areas of study	Power, elites, state, class, hegemony, authority, ethnicity. Political elites, ideology, development, electoral politics, democratization, political legitimacy, power structures, community power and decision making, ethnicity and politics, class and politics, social and political movements, voting and political participation, voluntary associations, interest groups.	Government, public policy, public administration, party system, constitutions, political elites. Party structure, legislative behavior, elections and political participation, national government, comparative politics, public administration, international relations, political theory, interest groups, party preference, political recruitment.	Political process, political action, authority, power, political culture, ethnocracies (rule by ethnic groups).	(1) Economic theory, production, exchange, distribution. (2) Public policies, social economics, Marxist economics, economic development. Political systems, modernization.	(1) Personality types, electoral behavior, belief systems, ideology, party preference, political participation. (2) Psychobiography of leaders, political leadership, military conflict, conflict resolution, political views, conflict management, political leadership.

Sources: Based on Kuper and Kuper (1985), Kourvetaris and Dobratz (1980), Dobratz and Kourvetaris (1983), Lipset (1981), and my own surveys and interpretations.

tional societies. Political anthropology also deals with the relationships between cultural factors such as norms, values, customs, traditions, and rituals of primitive societies and their effect on the power structures of these societies.

The Value Relevance of Political Sociology

In addition to its applied, theoretical, and empirical dimensions, political sociology has moral and value relevance for society and for a polity. In practical terms, political sociology helps us understand the nature of society and to solve political and social problems. The empirical components of political sociology help in investigating political questions and collecting data. This research can generate sophisticated theories to help interpret, explain, and resolve political conflicts that may endanger democratic institutions.

Political sociology's moral relevance for our society and moral polity has deep roots within the philosophical and religious traditions of Greek sociopolitical thought, Judaism, and Christianity. Its relevance to modern society can hardly be overstated; today, both domestic and foreign politics cannot be divorced from considerations of ethics, morality, and human rights. To cite only one example, in Somalia the conflict between warlords and other factions plunged the country into anarchy, resulting in mass starvation and death. Some argue that this human tragedy led the United States to intervene for humanitarian reasons in December 1992; others state that the United States entered Somalia to ensure safe passage for oil freighters traveling through the Red Sea.

Such actions affect the lives of many people. The study of political sociology provides us with knowledge to help in making the right decisions concerning global or local political problems. The fields of political sociology and ethics share moral concerns: Is it right for some people to control most of the wealth in a society, while millions go hungry? for some people to remain ill because they do not have medical insurance? for rulers to deny basic human rights to citizens?

Why do some people, groups, and institutions wield more power than others? What is the structure of power and behavior of elites in the United States and the world? Why do these structures persist? What is the relationship between economic and political power? What is the basis of political power and decision making on the levels of the community, the nation, and the world? Questions such as these fall within the purview of political sociology, the study of society and politics aimed at understanding and bettering human civilization and culture.

Summary and Conclusion

In the introduction an effort was made to lay out the major questions and issues that political sociology deals with. In the first three pages some general ideas and background information provided the socio-historical context for the emergence of political sociology as an academic discipline. More specifically, three major issues were discussed: (1) the nature of political sociology, (2) political sociology and related fields, and (3) the analysis of the relevance of political sociology. Regarding our first question, it was argued that while the issues and concerns of political sociology can be traced to earlier European political and social philosophers such as Karl Marx and Max Weber, even to Plato, Aristotle, and Thucydides, for all practical reasons political sociology in the United States emerged during the Great Depression. It was also pointed out that political sociology as a hybrid discipline draws its concepts, theories, and methods both from political science and sociology. While political sociology studies the relationship between political institutions and other social institutions, it focuses on the study of power and power structures at all levels of analysis: individual, group, organizational, societal, regional, national, and international.

With reference to our second question of the relationship of political sociology to its parent and related disciplines three major issues were explored: (a) the scope of each of these disciplines, (b) levels of analysis and methods of study, and (c) key concepts and areas of study. The fields related to political sociology briefly discussed included: political science, political psychology, political anthropology, and political economy. Finally, the value and moral relevance of political sociology and its implications for society and politics were briefly delineated. It was argued that the subject matter of political sociology and the questions it tackles has deep roots in our Western philosophical and moral/religious traditions. Political decisions and exercise of power can affect the lives of individuals and nations. The issues and questions political sociologists raise cannot be business as usual. Politics cannot be divorced from considerations of ethics, morality, and violations of human rights. The relevance of political sociology for democracy and human rights can hardly be overstated.

Endnotes

1. In a 1994 survey of sociological and political science abstracts, I tabulated the following references to topics in political sociology.

voting	8,383	political parties	317
classes	5,542	human rights	283
masses	1,001	religious fundamentalism	244
nationalism	883	power, participation, state	220
racism	521	political sociology	135
social inequality	508	intelligence	120
new world order	501	corporate elites	92
capitalism	500	multinational corporations	90
socialism	473	politics and ecology	69
political movements	366	insurgency	53
self-determination	338	civil–military relations	48

2. For more detailed views on the field of political sociology (by selected sociologists), see Bendix and Lipset (1966), Eisenstadt (1971), Goertzel (1976), Greer and Orleans (1964), Horowitz (1972), Janowitz (1970), Kourvetaris and Dobratz (1980), Lipset (1968, 1881), Marger (1987), Olsen and Marger (1993), Orum (1988, 1989), Segal (1974), Szymanski (1978), and Wasburn (1982).

3. In my survey I asked four questions: (1) What is the scope of political sociology (general and specific)? (2) What are the levels of analysis or approaches? (3) What are the ten key concepts in political sociology, in rank order? and (4) What are the most important areas of study in political sociology? The results from seven political sociologists who returned the questionnaire are as follows:

(a) *Scope of political sociology. General:* Most respondents stressed politics and society, social bases of politics, political change, individuals and communities, class nature of politics and the state, and political institutions. *Specific:* Most respondents emphasized the relationship between the state and various social classes; ethnic, racial, gender, and institutions; and other groups under capitalism—also the effect of the public-policy-making process on these classes, groups, and institutions. In addition, they considered the manner in which class, race, gender, age, and other dimensions of stratification shape political ideas and actions. The social roots of different political ideologies and the relationship between political parties, social movement, and the state were also stressed.

(b) *Levels of analysis and approaches:* The respondents emphasized macrolevel, social structural, systemwide, global, international, cross-cultural, Marxist (historical materialist), and dialectal elements; organizations, nation-states, individuals, social institutions (including the political), social-psychological interpersonal power, community, national and international spheres, and multimethods; macro, meso, micro, and world systems; survey, historical, documentary, participant observation, and experimental and simulation techniques.

(c) *The ten key concepts in rank order:* Respondents most frequently mentioned power, class, hegemony, state, legitimacy, democracy, racism, sexism, elitism, and conflict.

(d) *The ten most important areas of study:* Most areas of political sociology were paralleled with the key concepts in political sociology.

References

Bendix, Reinhard, and Seymour Lipset, eds. 1966. "The Field of Political Sociology." In *Political Sociology,* ed. Lewis Coser, 9–42. New York: Harper & Row.

Berberoglu, Berch. 1990. *Political Sociology: A Comparative/Historical Approach.* Dix Hills, NY: General Hall.

Coser, Lewis, ed. 1966. *Political Sociology: Selected Essays.* New York: Harper & Row.

Denitch, Bogdan. 1990. *The End of the Cold War.* Minneapolis: Univ. of Minnesota Press.

Dobratz, Betty A., and George A. Kourvetaris. 1983. "An Analysis and Assessment of Political Sociology." *Micropolitics.* Vol. 3, no. 1:89–133.

Eisenstadt, S. N., ed. 1971. *Political Sociology.* New York: Basic Books.

Goertzel, Ted George. 1976. *Political Society.* Chicago: Rand-McNally.

Greer, Scott, and Peter Orleans. 1964. "Political Sociology." In *Handbook of Modern Sociology,* ed. Robert E. L. Faris, 808–51. Chicago: Rand-McNally.

Horowitz, Irving. 1972. *Foundations of Political Sociology.* New York: Harper & Row.

Janowitz, Morris. 1970. *Political Conflict.* Chicago: Quadrangle Books.

Kourvetaris, George A., and Betty Dobratz. 1980. *Society and Politics.* Dubuque, IA: Kendall/Hunt.

Kuper, Adam, and Jessica Kuper, eds. 1985. *The Social Science Encyclopedia.* London: Routledge and Kegan Paul.

Lasswell, Harold D. 1951. *The Political Writings of Harold D. Lasswell.* Glencoe, IL: The Free Press.

Lipset, Seymour. 1981. *Political Man: The Social Bases of Politics.* Baltimore: The Johns Hopkins Univ. Press.

———. 1968. "Political Sociology." In *American Sociology: Perspectives, Problems, Methods,* ed. Talcott N. Parsons, 156–700. New York: Basic Books.

Marger, Martin. 1987. *Elites and Masses: An Introduction to Political Sociology.* 2nd ed. Belmont, CA: Wadsworth.

Melton, Gordon J. 1987. *Encyclopedia of American Religions.* Detroit: Gale Research Co.

Olsen, Marvin E., and Martin N. Marger, eds. 1993. *Power in Modern Societies.* Boulder, CO: Westview Press.

Orum, Anthony. 1989. *Introduction to Political Sociology: The Social Anatomy of the Body Politic.* Englewood Cliffs, NJ: Prentice-Hall.

———. 1988. "Political Sociology." In *Handbook of Sociology,* ed. Neil J. Smelser. Newbury Park: Sage.

Sartori, Giovanni. 1969. "From the Sociology of Politics to Political Sociology." In *Politics and the Social Sciences,* ed. Seymour M. Lipset, 65–100. New York: Oxford Univ. Press.

Segal, David. 1974. *Society and Politics: Uniformity and Diversity in Modern Democracy.* Glenview, IL: Scott, Foresman and Co.

Smith, Adam. 1776/1991 edition. *The Wealth of Nations.* New York: Random House.

Szymanski, Albert. 1978. *The Capitalist State and the Politics of Class.* Cambridge: Winthrop.

Tatalovich, Raymond, and Byron W. Daynes. 1988. *Social Regulatory Policy: Moral Controversies in American Politics.* Boulder, CO: Westview Press.

Wasburn, Philo C. 1982. *Political Sociology.* Englewood Cliffs, NJ: Prentice-Hall.

Major Models in Political Sociology

Political sociologists use certain models as methodological and theoretical frameworks to explore and explain specific issues in the interplay between politics and society. Some of these models are not exclusively used by political sociologists. This means that political sociologists borrow a number of methodological and conceptual approaches from other social science disciplines and apply them to their own inquiries. Some of these models become more explanatory of the interplay between society and politics than other ones. The consensus model for example, was a dominant paradigm in political sociology for a long time. However, in the 1960s the conflict model became more dominant. In this chapter, we will discuss some of the major models. First, we will briefly analyze the functionalist and conflict perspectives of society and politics and examine the general issue of social inequality.

Contrasting Views of Society and Politics: The Functionalist Perspective versus the Conflict Perspectives

The structural-functionalist perspective emphasizes order and consensus, viewing society as a system of well-integrated, interdependent parts and units. These various social units (groups, institutions, social classes, ethnic grops, and so on) interact with, mutually influence, and adjust to one another. Whatever contributes to the stability or harmony of the social system is viewed as functional; the reverse is viewed as dysfunctional. Structural functionalists believe that society is held together by the shared values of its citizens, who reach a consensus on major political and social issues. Individualism, independence, freedom of expression, freedom of religion, democracy, and equality of opportunity are just a few values that might be shared. The functionalist perspective views the state and political institutions in general as contributing to the integration of society and helping to maintain stability and order by strengthening common values and beliefs. Many social scientists consider this position to be politically conservative; it is identified primarily with the work of the

preeminent American social theorist Talcott Parsons, although it has earlier antecedents in the work of Émile Durkheim and other classical sociologists.

In contrast to the structural-functionalist model, the power conflict perspective
views society as an arena of competing interests that generate conflicts among different groups vying for power and dominance. Society is held together not by shared
common beliefs and values but by coercion, which leads to conflict. Whereas the
structural functionalists hold stability and shared values to be prerequisites of a
workable social system, conflict theorists emphasize social change and conflict as the
most dynamic aspects of society. Functionalists view the exercise of power and
authority as legitimate and necessary mechanisms to achieve societal goals; conflict
theorists perceive power as a tool used by a stronger group at the expense of a weaker
one, leading to conflict in society: blacks versus whites, men versus women, rich versus poor, and so on.

Studying conflicts can help identify the root causes of problems. By studying
those issues that generate conflict between various social groups it can help us to
identify problems and focus on making changes in social policies and our institutions
in such a manner that we can alleviate the causes of the discontent. For example, in
the 1992 presidential election, both the Republicans and the Democrats were
engaged in pointing out the problems of U.S. society. The Democrats stressed a
domestic agenda—issues such as jobs, health insurance, foreign debt, trade deficit,
and the deterioration of the infrastructure (roads, bridges, environment, schools, and
the like). The Republicans tended to emphasize foreign policy issues and successes,
such as the Gulf War, the end of the Cold War, and so on. The debates between President George Bush and Governor Bill Clinton heightened the conflict, generating
greater interest among the electorate. Ross Perot, the third-party candidate, cam-
paigned at his own expense, asserting his independence from special interests, and
criticized both the Democrats and Republicans. He focused primarily on the economy and the huge national debt. Many believed that the election of Bill Clinton in
1992 was due, to a large extent, to the voters' greater interest in the economy and
other domestic issues than in foreign issues. U.S. citizens seemed to feel that their
quality of life was deteriorating and especially plagued by crime, illicit drugs, the
spread of AIDS, health care costs, pollution, and the persistence of racial conflict and
community violence. Despite Clinton's and the Democrats' capture of the White
House and Congress, voters were not necessarily satisfied with any of the candidates.
Perot captured about 20 percent of the votes, an indication of the general dissatisfaction of the electorate with the two major political parties. While the discussion of
issues during an election year can create conflict among the candidates, it can also
educate the public and help the citizen to make an intelligent voting decision.

Power conflict theories focus on the means by which one group takes advantage
of another group and the outcomes of this dynamic. Various episodes in the continued conflict between African Americans and white Americans can illustrate the
power conflict perspective. African Americans have accused white Americans of
racial discrimination. The conflict between the two groups led to the 1960s Civil
Rights Movement for racial justice and equality, spearheaded primarily by African
Americans. Disenfranchised blacks argued that shared common values and the

American dream of equal opportunity would be meaningless as long as ideals contained in the Constitution and the Bill of Rights did not apply to African Americans. A moral dilemma exists between the ideals of the Constitution and the treatment of minorities, a fact to which Gunnar Myrdal of Sweden referred a half century ago in his *An American Dilemma* (1944).

The roots of conflict theory can be traced to Karl Marx and George Simmel. More recently, political sociologists Louis Coser, Ralph Dahrendorf, William Gamson, Anthony Giddens, C. Wright Mills, Theda Skocpol, Charles Tilly, and Marvin Tumin have furthered the study of the power conflict perspective. This perspective became more prominent as a general theoretical framework in sociology following the Civil Rights Movement and anti–Vietnam War protests during the 1960s in the United States. Presently most sociologists tend to favor the conflict perspective.

However, the most balanced understanding of society and politics incorporates both functionalist and conflict perspectives; both approaches are useful and interconnected. At times, stability is necessary for a society and polity, whereas at other times, change is more desirable. When review and reform in the social and political system follow a period of conflict, the society may function more smoothly and ultimately become more stable.

The Issue of Social Inequality

One way to understand how the functionalist and conflict perspectives operate is to apply both perspectives to the issue of social inequality, the unequal distribution of resources (prestigious jobs, political power, wealth, social status, and so on) in society. Functionalists view social inequality as functional and necessary because resources are finite and excellence needs to be encouraged by a reward structure. Conflict theorists believe that inequality emerges out of exploitation or domination of the society as a whole by powerful, wealthy groups. Whereas functionalists perceive large-scale inequality to be inevitable, conflict theorists view it as an illegitimate source of social tension. Many conflict theorists believe that the state has an obligation to protect the weaker classes from exploitation by the more dominant classes. For example, Native Americans, according to some conflict theorists, should have been protected from the European settlers who appropriated their lands, wiped out their culture, and practiced genocide against them. Other conflict theorists support grassroots movements for social change.

Beth E. Vanfossen (1979) summarized six sources of domination that in her view cause social inequality and conflict: (1) *competition for scarce goods and services*—those who control the surpluses tend to have more power and prestige; (2) *ownership or control of property*—dominance usually emerges out of control and ownership of property; (3) *unequal marketability of occupations*—those who have professional and managerial skills tend to be more marketable than those in unskilled occupations; (4) *inability of the majority to band together for political action*—in contrast to masses, elites and other well-organized small groups know what they want and make every effort to obtain it; (5) *the oligarchical tendency in organizations*—Robert

Michels (1962) pointed out the tendency over time for organizations and political parties to be run by a few individuals; that is, they become oligarchies; (6) *unequal distribution of authority*—authority, an institutionalized form of power, is a source of potential conflict between the old and the young, races, genders, or dominant and subordinate groups in society. If inequality is based on dominance and coercion, the potential for opposition, resistance, and hostility on the part of the subordinate classes is great. Conflict is more likely to occur over the distribution of scarce resources, especially if individuals or groups challenge the legitimacy of power and authority arrangements, or the allocation of resources. For example, conflict has erupted over the fact that some groups or communities receive more federal and state aid for public education than do poorer communities.

Conflict sociologists argue that the shared values pointed to by consensus theorists are usually those of the dominant class or elites who legitimate power arrangements rather than those of society as a whole. Often, members of the dominant classes have difficulty controlling the subordinate classes. How do the dominant classes control the subordinate classes? What kinds of mechanisms do they use?

Vanfossen (1979) mentioned four such mechanisms: (1) *Force:* This mechanism can wield coercion and punishment; often, its penalties are unequally distributed to the dominant and less powerful classes. For example, crimes against property, such as robbery, burglary, and theft, are usually committed by lower classes (many of whom belong to racial or ethnic minorities) and are usually punished severely, whereas "white-collar crimes" committed by elites and dominant classes, such as embezzlement, price fixing, graft, or bribery by government officials, usually are punished less severely. As a rule most white-collar crime is committed by whites (Parenti, 1995). Usually, those who commit white-collar crimes are rarely caught, and even if they are caught are not punished as severely as those who commit blue-collar crimes (Parenti, 1995:120–29). (2) *Value legitimation:* The subordinate classes are more likely to accept the core, or dominant, values of society (as promulgated by the powerful classes) as legitimate. (3) *Social mobility:* According to this principle, anyone can move up in the U.S. social structure, enabling one's children to achieve a better life. Although this promise is in theory extended to all citizens, many members of the new generation feel that it rings hollow because of limited career opportunities and a troubled economy. (4) *Low expectations:* The idea that the United States is a land of opportunity in which anyone can potentially succeed is both fact and fiction. In many ways, subordinate classes are socialized by the educational system, the community, peer groups, and parents to have lower expectations concerning their futures. Although millions have "made it" in the United States, a large number have not, often because they have lacked encouragement and opportunity.

In general, most economic and political elites and the higher classes in most capitalist countries espouse a structural-functionalist view of society and politics. In the United States, traditionally, the conservative segments of society favor this perspective. Usually they vote for less progressive candidates and tend to stress stability and order, whereas those classes on the bottom strata of the system usually advocate a conflict power perspective—they tend to support candidates who endorse change to better the weaker classes. Drawing from both structural functionalist and conflict perspectives of society and politics, political sociologists have over the years formu-lated a number of middle-range models of politics and society.[1]

Political Sociology Models

A number of different sociological and political science perspectives have been applied to politics and society. In this section, I have chosen five different models for discussion and analysis. Each one gives a different interpretation of society and pol-itics; each has its advocates and its critics. Try to become familiar with them all and to understand politics and society from these various points of view. There are no good or bad models; each has something to offer. Together, they reflect the breadth of the sociological perspective, which is diverse in its substantive, theoretical, and methodological dimensions.

The following political sociology models will be discussed: (1) *the elite*, (2) *the pluralist*, (3) *the class*, or *Marxist*, (4) *the realist*, and (5) *the corporatist/consocia-tionalist*. They will be examined in terms of three dimensions: (a) basic tenets and principles, (b) theoretical and historical antecedents, and (c) major shortcomings and critiques. The five models can be used to analyze specific issues in politics and society at the community, national, regional, and international levels. Other more specific frameworks exist for narrower topics in political sociology. Whenever possible, both broad and more specific frameworks will be used throughout this book to make var-ious political issues easier to comprehend.

The Elite Model

Basic Tenets and Principles
The elite model is based on the assumption that power in society is concentrated in the hands of a few people or small groups who make the crucial decisions. Regardless of the nature of society, elites occupy leadership positions in various social, eco-nomic, political, cultural, military, and other institutional settings. According to the elite theory, one political elite may be replaced by another; although the composition of a given elite may change at different times, elite rule remains. Once the elites assume power, they are reluctant to relinquish it. Sometimes, in order to maintain power, elites use all means available to them. The elite perspective, of course, runs contrary to the basic democratic view that leaders are accountable to citizens. Elite theory raises a number of questions. Are elites indispensable to society? How cohe-sive are elite groups? Are elites self-serving, or do they serve the interests of society? What are the social characteristics of elites? How are elites recruited? Many of the findings about elites and classes will be discussed in Chapter 5.

Defining Elites and Classes. In every society, some individuals are better off than others. Although many groups may exert influence in society and politics, some are more influential than others. Eva Etzioni-Halévy (1993:13) provided two basic strategies for understanding the issue of inequality: class and elite analyses. Class analysis focuses on the way resources of society are distributed, whereas elite analysis deals with the way power and influence (as resources) are allocated between elites and non-elites. Although both class and elites can be studied as distinct entities, they are interdependent; one cannot be understood without the other. Although political sociologists deal with both concepts, they mainly focus on the elites. Moshe M. Czudnowski (1982, 1983) believed that when social scientists talk about elites, they mean "those who run things," namely, certain key actors who play important roles not only in the governance of a nation-state but also in economic, military, academic, industrial, religious, cultural, mass media, and other institutional settings within the same nation. Michael Burton and John Higley (1987:296) viewed elites as all those who, because of their positions in powerful organizations, are able to affect political outcomes individually, regularly, and seriously. According to them, elites constitute the nation's top leadership in all institutions, including both "establishment" and "counter-elite" factions.

Despite political sociologists' various viewpoints concerning elites, Higley and Burton (1989:18–19) have found some scholarly agreement on the idea that national elites take three basic forms in the modern world. The first type of elite is called *divided, competitive,* or *disunited,* characterized by ruthless, often violent, inter-elite conflicts. This type may be found in many contemporary societies and polities divided along ethnic, religious, political, racial, or cultural divisions (e.g., the former Yugoslavia). Various factions deeply distrust one another and are unable to cooperate. The second type is termed *totalitarian,* or *ideologically unified.* This type of elite is characterized by unity of purpose, ideology, and policy, exemplified by the fascist, totalitarian elite in Nazi Germany in the 1930s and 1940s, and the Communist elites in the Soviet Union and Eastern Europe. The third type of elite structure is the *pluralistic, competitive,* or *consensually united.* This type of elite displays substantial, but less than monolithic, unity. Its members may take different views concerning public policies but refrain from extreme positions that could lead to violent conflict. This type is more characteristic of pluralistic Western democracies such as England, the United States, and so on.

In contrast, when social scientists discuss social classes, they often disagree. Those who have a Marxist orientation define classes as conflicting groups; each group competes with another for economic advantages. Those who belong to the same socioeconomic class define themselves by their relationship to another socioeconomic class in the system of production. For example, those who control most of the wealth or the means of production are viewed as the ruling classes; they in turn control the working classes. Those of a non-Marxist orientation define social classes as social strata or status groups based on a system of social ranking or social stratification and defined in terms of objective criteria such as income, occupation, and education.

Marxists stress the notions of subjective class consciousness and objective class identification. Class consciousness is more of a political concept, meaning that unless one can develop a class consciousness, one has not become a member of a class. Marx used the concepts of class-in-itelf versus class-for-itself to explain the differences between subjective and objective class. He referred to an aggregate of people having shared economic, political, and cultural interests as a class-for-itself; he called a separate aggregate of people having its own distinct social status in a system of social ranking a class-in-itself. In general, Marxists view classes as economic in nature, as discrete rather than continuous, and as real rather than statistical. Furthermore, the classes are always in conflict (Hurst, 1992:12). Some people use the terms *elites* and *classes* interchangeably. However, although elites are relatively easy to identify in society, classes are more difficult to locate. Elites tend to be institutional or organizational in nature, whereas classes are dispersed throughout society.

Charles E. Hurst (1992:4–5) identified three basic views of social classes in the United States. First, some believe that social classes as antagonistic groups do not exist in the United States. Second, others hold that fairly distinct social classes exist at the extremes of the stratification hierarchy (upper and lower classes) but not in the middle, which is considered a mass of relatively indistinguishable categories of people. Third, some insist that distinct classes have always existed in the United States and continue to cause class conflict among different categories of people.

Theoretical and Historical Dimensions

Two major theoretical and empirical streams of thought exist in the study of elites in general and political elites in particular: *the conservative* and *the radical*. The conservative draws primarily from the writings of classical elite theorists Gaetano Mosca and Vilfredo Pareto and, to some extent, from the writings of Max Weber and Robert Michels. The radical view is represented by radical structuralists such as C. Wright Mills (who was more of a Weberian), Floyd Hunter, and William Domhoff. Domhoff has advanced a somewhat different elite model, which he refers to as the "hegemony class" model.[2]

The conservative version of the elite model, promulgated by Pareto and Mosca, is based on two interrelated assumptions; namely, the belief in the natural superiority of the elites and the indispensability of elites for a stable and ordered life in society and polity. The conservative view sees the masses as untrustworthy and inconsistent in their ability to initiate valuable substantive changes and therefore incapable of ruling themselves. In the political sphere, conservative elite theorists believe that the majority of the people are incapable of ruling themselves, and, therefore, elites are necessary to maintain order and to govern society effectively. Conservative theorists tend to look at the non-elites of the society as a single apathetic and politically alienated mass. This theory applies to different sectors of society—bureaucratic, religious, educational, and so on. Sometimes this elite theory is called the "elitist theory of democracy," a name that suggests not only that elites are inevitable and desirable, but also that they form the basis of a democratic society. According to this view, the social system is kept democratic through competition among elites and the possibility that individuals and groups will influence decision makers through voting and lobbying. This view of elite theory is similar to the pluralist view of society and politics, which we will discuss later.

From a historical perspective, the concept of elites in Western thought can be traced to Plato. In his *Republic,* Plato advocated the idea of the "philosopher king" and "the guardian class" as rulers of the future city-state. The guardian class is an aristocratic elite group made up of those who by training and descent are considered best qualified to become the future rulers of the city-state or political community. However, the theoretical antecedents of the contemporary theory of elites are generally attributed to the contributions of the Italian classical elite theorists Vilfredo Pareto and Gaetano Mosca, and to some extent to the German political sociologist Robert Michels. The latter was a student of Max Weber and is not considered strictly a conservative. He was more of a Marxist, with some anarchist influences. All three, however, are considered advocates of the elite school in political sociology. Among the three, Pareto and Mosca are representative of the political right, whereas Michels is considered to be in the middle and similar to Weber in his political views. Elite conservative theorists believe that social and political change comes from the social elites or those who occupy top positions in society and politics.

Conservative Elite Theory: Vilfredo Pareto and Gaetano Mosca.   Vilfredo   Pareto (1848–1923) defined an elite as "a class of people who have the highest indices in their branch of activity" (Pareto, 1935:1423). He further divided the concept of the elite into two classes: a governing elite, comprising individuals who directly or indirectly play a considerable part in government, and a nongoverning elite, made up of the rest (Pareto, 1935:1423). Furthermore, Pareto identified two major strata in a population: (1) a lower stratum, the non-elite, and (2) a higher stratum, the elite, which is divided into (a) governing elite and (b) a nongoverning elite. The higher stratum usually contains the rulers, and the lower stratum usually contains the ruled. Pareto argued that there is a class, or elite, circulation in history. According to him, history is a graveyard of aristocracies; the governing elite is always in a state of slow and continuous transformation. Pareto held that elites and aristocracies decay both in numbers and quality when they lose power.

Gaetano Mosca (1858–1941) was the founder of political science in Italy. He took an active role in political life, became a conservative member of the Chamber of Deputies (1908 and 1919), and served as a professor of constitutional law and political institutions in Rome. He is well known for his theory of the ruling class; his treatment of the topic was translated into English in 1939. Mosca (1939:50) defined elites as those who occupy positions of preeminence. Whereas Pareto stressed the psychological and irrational aspects of elites, Mosca emphasized the sociological, organizational, and personal characteristics. He argued that in all

> *societies—from societies that are very underdeveloped to the most advanced and powerful societies—two classes of people appear—a class that rules and a class that is ruled. The first class, always the less numerous, performs all of the political functions, monopolizes power, and enjoys the advantages that power brings, whereas the second, the more numerous class, is directed and controlled by the first, in a manner that is now more or less legal, now more or less arbitrary and violent (Mosca, 1939:50).*

Mosca's survey of societies led him to the conclusion that ruling classes exist in all societies. Consequently, according to him democracies do not exist, and it is not necessary to include them in classifications of political regimes. All ruling classes rule by appeal to a political formula or universal moral principle that justifies their rule and has a broad appeal to the masses. Rulers have an advantage over the ruled because they are better organized than the non-elites. At the same time, elites are marked by qualities that give them material, intellectual, or even moral superiority. Below the ruling elite or political class, Mosca recognized another substratum, which he called a sub-elite, composed of intellectuals, technocrats, civil servants, managers, and organizational specialists. Using an analogy from the military, Mosca argued that whereas "the higher stratum in the ruling class corresponds to the general and staff, the second stratum to the officers (sub-elite) or the officers who personally lead the soldiers under fire" (Mosca, 1939:405).

A comparison of these two versions of the elite classical model is given in Figure 1.1.

Moderate Elite Theory: Robert Michels.   Robert   Michels   (1876–1936)   made important contributions to the sociology of organizations and political sociology. In his classic study of *Political Parties* (English translation, 1949), he formulated his famous "iron law of oligarchy," the tendency for most social and political organizations to be run by a few individuals who make most of the decisions. Michels believed that the iron law of oligarchy is inevitable in any organization; an inner circle of participants will take over the organization and run it for their own selfish purposes. Michels's treatment of bureaucracy is detailed; he spoke of both centralized and decentralized tendencies of bureaucracy and viewed it as essential for a modern state, although he referred to it as "the sworn enemy of individual liberty" (Michels, 1959:189; 1962). In his analogy between a modern state and a political party, he noted that both organizations attract a large number of individuals and a strong bureaucracy.

Michels spoke of bureaucracy with distrust, believing that it corrupts character and engenders moral poverty, and that every bureaucracy tends toward self-promotion,

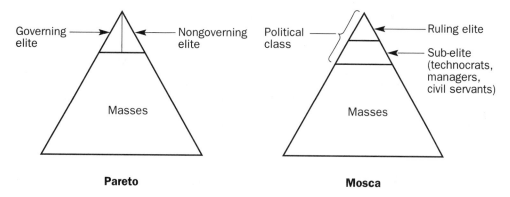

Figure 1.1   Two Versions of the Elite Model

Source: Martin Marger, *Elites and Masses* (1987:53), 2nd ed.; reprinted here by permission of the publisher.

arrogance toward inferiors, and servility toward superiors. He reasoned that the political apathy and lack of interest that characterize the majority of the people lead to the iron law of oligarchy. Michels identified the variables producing oligarchical tendencies in large organizations, including their technical and administrative features, the psychological dependency of the masses on the leaders, and the superior qualities of the leaders (Michels, 1962:401). Figure 1.2 shows the causal relations among Michels's major variables.

The Concept of Bureaucracy: Max Weber.   Max Weber (1864–1920), a German sociologist and contemporary of Émile Durkheim, spoke of bureaucracy as a social mechanism that maximizes efficiency in administration. He conceptualized bureaucracy as a pure form or ideal type made up of a cluster of attributes including precision, speed, subordination, reduction of friction, unity, unambiguity, knowledge of the files, discretion, and continuity (Gerth and Mills, 1958). Weber identified the specific dimensions of bureaucracy as follows: (1) a set of rules or administrative regulations that dictate fixed and official duties or jurisdictions; (2) ways of fulfilling these duties, accompanied by analogous rights; (3) the power of authority for the execution of these duties; (4) a division of labor based on the degree of specialization and competence; and (5) opportunity for a career and a system of promotion based on seniority and achievement. Weber stressed the spirit of formality and impersonality. For him, bureaucracy had a "rational character"; rational discretion must overrule emotional judgment. According to him, bureaucracy involves rules, means, ends, a matter-of-fact approach, a technical superiority over any other form of organization, and utter rationality. Modern corporate enterprises and management are examples of such bureaucracies.

Weber was primarily concerned with the traditional view of bureaucracy, which was and remains more apparent in Europe than in the United States. His formulation of bureaucracy as an ideal type included the following major components: (1) It con-

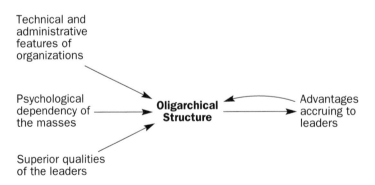

Figure 1.2   Michels's Major Variables of The Law of Oligarchy

Source: Neil Smelser, *Sociological Theory* (1971:53); reprinted here by permission of the publisher.

sists of a continuous *organization of official functions* (offices) bound by rules. (2) Each office has a *specified sphere of competence.* The office is obligated to perform various functions and possesses the authority to carry out these functions and the means of compulsion required to do the job. (3) The offices are organized into *a hierarchical system.* (4) The offices may demand *technical qualifications,* requiring the participants to obtain suitable training. (5) The staff *does not own the means of production* associated with their office. They are provided with the use of the things they need to do the job. (6) An incumbent *cannot appropriate a position;* it always remains part of the organization. (7) *Administrative acts, decisions, and rules* are formulated and recorded in writing (Ritzer, 1988:117). In Europe, during Weber's time, the spirit of oligarchy and monarchy were predominant, and bureaucracy was considered the instrument of an oligarchic, authoritarian central government.

Radical and Power Elite Theory: C. Wright Mills.   In contrast to the conservative elite theorists, the radical elite theorists are troubled by inherent undemocratic and oligarchical tendencies of elites. Unlike the aristocratic elite theorists, C. Wright Mills (1916–1962) and other radical structuralists have viewed elites with displeasure and criticized them. They do not believe in the inevitability of elites, and they do not perceive the masses as inconsistent, incompetent, untrustworthy. Mills, who coined the term *power elite,* was very critical of American society and polity and was a significant representative of the radical elite school. Mills (1956) argued that the "power elite" is not an anti-American conspiracy but a group of families who have dominated the three major sectors of American society: the government, the military, and the economy. Tracing the development of the power elite in U.S. history, he described the origin of the power elite as follows:

> *The conception of the power elite and its unity rests upon the corresponding developments and the coincidence of interests among economic, political, and military organizations. It also rests upon the similarity of origin and outlook, and the social and personal intermingling of the top circles from each of these dominant hierarchies.... As a result, the political directorate of the corporate rich, and the ascendant military have come together as the power elite, and the expanded and centralized hierarchies which they have encroached upon the old balances and have now relegated them to the middle levels of power. (Mills, 1956:292–96)*

Power elite theorists believe that a small group or a few people control most of the important decisions in society. Mills argued that the concentration of power and wealth in a few hands undermined U.S. claims to equality and democracy. Under the power elite thesis, Mills identified other groups of people with a middle range of power who carry out the orders of the power elite. He described the middle levels as a "drifting set of stalemated, balancing forces" that have failed to "link the bottom with the top." The "bottom" of this society is "politically fragmented" and "increasingly powerless," or what he referred to as "mass society" (Mills, 1956:324).

The power elite thesis is depicted in Figure 1.3.

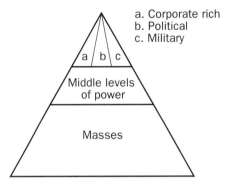

The power elite

Figure 1.3   The Power Elite Model

Source: Drawn by the author from C. Wright
Mills, *The Power Elite* (1956).

The apex of the pyramid shows the power elite, which consists of a top group of military, government, and economic figures. The second level is a diversified group of special interest groups, representing the middle level of power. And the third level is mass society, powerless because it is unorganized and composed of atomized individuals controlled from above.

The theoretical roots of the radical elite model can be traced to Karl Marx. However, contrary to the radical elite theorists, Marx and the Marxists have given greater emphasis to the role of economic classes and the state in politics and society. The empirical roots of the radical elite model can be found in Robert and Helen Lynds's pioneer study (1937) of Muncie, Indiana, which they called Middletown. From that study, the authors discovered that a single family who had amassed a fortune from the manufacture of canning jars controlled most sectors of local institutions, including the bank, the college, and the hospital. In Muncie, the Lynds concluded that power was concentrated in the hands of a single wealthy family. Floyd Hunter's study (1963) of Atlanta, Georgia, is also an example of the elite radical perspective derived from the work of Mills. Hunter found that power was concentrated in the business community, where a small group of leaders informally made social policies. The group consisted of forty industrialists, business owners, and top executives of large enterprises. Still, Mills's study was by far the most widely cited elitist study of the distribution of power on the national level in the United States. The shortcomings of this model will be discussed after we examine the pluralist model.

The Pluralist Model

Basic Tenets and Principles
According to the pluralist model, power is dispersed among many competing interest groups. Pluralists believe that politics is an arena of competing interest groups and

that power has many sources and centers, including wealth, charisma, political office, social status, education, and so on. Phrases such as "government of, by, and for the people," "equality before the law," and "separation of powers" are part of the U.S. political culture and serve to portray power as diffused in the United States. The pluralist model is more fitting in multicultural and ethnically heterogeneous and competitive societies than in traditional, more authoritarian types of societies.

Pluralists do not recognize the existence of an integrated power elite. Instead, they believe that many functional social elites and other special interest groups compete with one another, but no single group is strong enough to monopolize power. Pluralists argue that elites are functional and specialized; their actions and demands are checked by the institutionalized and competing demands of other groups and classes, all of whom represent varying and overlapping constituencies. They recognize that conflict exists but believe it is resolved within the social system. Among the leading advocates of the pluralist perspective are Robert Dahl, Suzanne Keller, Nelson Polsby, David Riesman, Arnold Rose, and David Truman.

Pluralists also believe that pluralism is compatible with the liberal capitalist democracy, which is governed by a system of checks and balances that counterweighs the three branches of government. Dianne Pinderhughes (1987:13) divided pluralist arguments into three distinct types. The first type is associated with the work of Robert Dahl, who maintained that "instead of a single center of sovereign power there must be multiple centers of power, none of which is or can be wholly sovereign." The second type of pluralism is sociological and related to the work of Milton Gordon (1964), who, in analyzing the United States, developed important theories of ethnic pluralism and assimilation. Social pluralism refers to a society comprising diverse ethnic, religious, racial, and other social groups. It arises in response to the decline of assimilation or the convergence of cultures into the dominant Anglo-Saxon model. The third type of pluralism is linked to the ways in which ethnic groups are incorporated into politics. As ethnic solidarity declines, transethnic issues gain prominence and group interests expand, leading to increasing political inclusion.

Theoretical and Historical Dimensions

Pluralism in Western political thought originated in Aristotle's *Politics* (fourth century B.C.) and in the writings of Alexis de Tocqueville (1805–1859), a French statesman and political writer. In *Politics,* Aristotle spoke of a pluralist political community in which autonomy, decentralization, hierarchy, tradition, and locality are key characteristics (Nisbet, 1973:387–390). Unlike Plato, who stressed "unity within conformity" in the city-state, Aristotle emphasized "unity within diversity." And unlike Plato, Aristotle favored a community of diverse elements administered by laws, institutions, and individuals. Unity was sought in the interdependence of diverse social and political units in the *polis* (city-state). In his *Republic,* Plato advocated the rule of a "philosopher king" and a ruling class made up of elites who, by education and background, were superior and destined to be "guardians." Later, in his *Laws,* Plato changed his views and, like Aristotle, stressed the necessity of laws and institutions.

Tocqueville's *Democracy in America* (1835) catalyzed the analysis of political pluralism and democracy in the United States. Writing in the early nineteenth century, Tocqueville saw a diffusion of democracy in the United States that was absent in Europe at that time. He noted an absence of aristocracy and a proliferation of voluntary organizations, which, he believed, could be used as countervailing forces against the abuse of power by the central federal government. However, Tocqueville feared the tyranny of the majority in the United States and the emphasis on equality over individual liberty, and he saw both of them as a threat to democracy. He thought that the decentralization of authority, the separation of powers, and the proliferation of autonomous organizations served as intermediaries between the citizen and the central government, and prevented rise of an all-powerful state. These competing groups, he believed, gave the American democracy its pluralist character.

Studies of ethnic diversity in the United States have led to the introduction of pluralism in political discourse. From the beginning, the United States was a "nation of nations," a phrase coined by Walt Whitman (1812–1892), the U.S. poet, and popularized by Louis Adamic (1899–1951, a Yugoslavian author). In 1915, for example, Horace Kallen, a Harvard-educated philosopher, challenged the notion of assimilation along the Anglo conformity model by publishing a series of articles on democracy and ethnic diversity in *The Nation*. He saw cultural and ethnic pluralism as compatible with American democracy and the tenets of the Declaration of Independence and the Constitution. According to Kallen, ethnic pluralism contributed to the richness of the American society because "creation comes from diversity." Later, Milton Gordon (1964), a sociologist, articulated the theory of assimilation and and identified seven different conditions or subprocesses of types of assimilation: (1) *cultural* or *behavioral assimilation* (change of cultural patterns to those of the host society, also called *acculturation*); (2) *structural assimilation* (large-scale entrance into cliques, clubs, and institutions of the host society on a primary, small, face-to-face group level); (3) *marital assimilation* or *amalgamation* (large-scale intermarriage along ethnic, racial, and religious dimensions); (4) *identificational assimilation* (development of a sense of personhood based exclusively on the host society); (5) *attitude receptional assimilation* (absence of prejudice on the part of the dominant groups); (6) *behavior receptional assimilation* (absence of discrimination on the part of the dominant groups); and (7) *civic assimilation* (absence of power conflict). According to Gordon, unless structural assimilation takes place, no complete assimilation can take place in society (Gordon, 1964:71–84). The assimilation, or Anglo conformity, model was the predominant paradigm up to the 1920s, advocated by the dominant western European groups commonly known as White Anglo Saxon Protestants (WASPs), which included all Protestant Europeans (English, Dutch, Irish, German, Scandinavian) who came to the United States prior to 1910. The cultural ethnic pluralist model was associated mostly with the new immigration from southeastern European, Asian, African, and Latin American countries; it represents a minority utopian model. William M. Newman (1973:67) viewed cultural pluralism as a symbiosis, or peaceful coexistence, of different social, racial, ethnic, and religious groups in pluralist societies. Through such assimilation models, the notion of ethnic pluralism was introduced into political discourse.

Important Political Pluralists.   What do pluralists say about political pluralism? In general, the pluralist model is identified with the works of both political scientists and political sociologists, with the former more interested in studies in political pluralism than the latter; political sociologists identify more with elite studies. Pluralists believe that interest groups articulate different issues, which find their way into the election process and thus negotiate with other groups. Robert Dahl's primary concept of polyarchy purports that power has many centers. Pluralism is a form of polyarchy. Pluralists argue that political resources in a polyarchy or a pluralist society are dispersed. Dispersion, however, does not mean that political resources are equally distributed.

In 1951, David Truman argued that open pluralistic competition among different interest groups guarded against the domination of U.S. society by a single ruling elite. David Riesman (1950) introduced the notion of the "veto groups," or interest groups having an amorphous structure of power. Contrary to C. Wright Mills, Riesman believed no power elite or pyramid of power structure existed. According to Riesman, veto groups, a plurality of interest groups, maintained a balance of power. According to this notion, power on the national scene must be viewed in terms of particular issues. When an issue involves only two or three veto groups, themselves tiny minorities, the official or unofficial broker among the groups can be quite powerful—but only on that issue. However, when the issue involves the country as a whole, no individual or group leadership is likely to be very effective, because the entrenched veto groups cannot be budged: unlike a party that may be defeated at the polls, or a class that may be replaced by another class, the veto groups are always in (Riesman, 1950:254). William Kornhauser (1960) argued that pluralism, with its array of interest groups, is the best safeguard against authoritarian intrusion by the masses into the political arena. By masses, Kornhauser meant the uprooted individuals that characterize modern society. He believed that the established structure in a pluralist democracy was threatened by the rise of mass society. For Nelson Polsby, another pluralist, there is nothing categorical about power in the community; he rejected the stratification thesis, propounding that no single group dominates the community.

In general, pluralists view American society as fractured into special interest groups having overlapping memberships and a diverse basis of power (Polsby, 1963:118). Polsby's version of pluralism stresses issues and the way power is used to arrive at decisions. As the issues change, so does the basis of power and decision making.

Shortcomings and Criticisms of Elite and Pluralist Models

The antiestablishment movement of radical sociology in the 1960s split political sociology into different schools. The mainline political sociologists of the consensus, pluralist, and structural-functionalist schools were attacked by those who held to radical elite, neo-Marxist, and radical sociology, and who challenged the very values upon which the political consensus was based.

C. Wright Mills (1956) gave a new impetus to the radical movement of the 1960s. The critics of the radical elite model argue that the power elite theory is a simplistic, shallow caricature of the American power structure. In addition, a prejudicial bias exists concerning the rich and those engaged in business. Critics of the elite radical school argue that businesspeople and the wealthy do not necessarily control political decisions; rather leaders come from diverse backgrounds, and no one has a monopoly of power. Also, critics point to the fact that power is not a permanent characteristic of any individual or group. However, one cannot dismiss the fact that contributions to political candidates in politics usually come from interest groups and business lobbyists.

Those having a radical elite perspective accuse pluralists of being naive, romantic, and utopian in their conception of politics and power. The pluralist perspective dominated the politics of the 1950s, whereas the radical elite viewpoint gained preeminence during the 1960s and early 1970s. Pluralism has been under attack from all quarters as being nothing more than an apologia for the status quo. In his comprehensive review of pluralism, Grant Jordan (1990:301) concluded that there is no well-elaborated pluralist theory but rather a multiplicity of ideas about interest groups loosely connected under the pluralist tag. Pluralism has been out of academic fashion for the past decade. As R. W. Cox (1981:303) put it, "Pluralism as a concept is not an explanation of anything. On the contrary, pluralism is a description of a political form of the state, in which the question of which interests dominate is an open empirical question."

The Marxist Class Model

Basic Tenets and Principles

The Marxist class model views society as ruled by those who control the means of production. The basic unit of analysis in this model is a class or a group whose members are in direct conflict with another group within the capitalist economic system. The institution of property and the class relations that originate from it become paramount in understanding the relationship between society and the state. In the Marxist view, the state is controlled by the capitalist class or its agents. However, as we pointed out earlier, more recently a number of political sociologists, including those within the Marxist tradition, view the state as being more independent and autonomous; class or economic groups are sometimes unable to affect its policies. The elite theorists differ with the Marxists in their belief that power is not always anchored in possessing the means of production.

Theoretical and Historical Dimensions

The theoretical and historical underpinnings of the class perspective can be traced to Karl Marx (1818–1883) and other European socialist writers. Marx's model consists of (1) *the forces of production* (e.g., natural resources, technology) and (2) *the social relations of production*. Together, these make up the *mode of production* (economic system). The economic mode of production is the material base and the infrastructure of society; they in turn determine the nonmaterial aspects of society, including ideologies, social institutions (the military, politics, education, religion, and the family), and all other concrete forms of social consciousness. This emphasis on the economic (objective, material) base is known in Marxist terminology as *economic determinism,* or the materialist interpretation of history. According to Marx, the mode of production includes (1) the means to satisfy human needs and wants, (2) the institutional arrangements to satisfy these needs, (3) the goods of production, and (4) a set of interpersonal relationships. To explain the origin of the social classes or stratification, Marx turned to the history of society and the mode of production of a particular epoch. His concept of *historical materialism,* or the belief that the primary force in social change is economic, led him and his collaborator Friedrich Engels to issue *The Communist Manifesto* in 1847. In this work, they imposed a pattern on the canvas of history, stipulating that feudalism gave impetus to capitalism by means of the French Revolution, which abolished the landed aristocracy and replaced it with merchants and capitalists, who became the ruling class. They viewed society as divided into two main antagonistic classes, capitalists and the proletariat. Marx predicted an inevitable revolution of the proletariat class because of conflict between the capitalists and the proletarians—that is to say, those who own the means of production and those who own nothing.

A famous passage from Marx's preface to *A Contribution to the Critique of Political Economy* (1970:20–22) summarizes in part some of the basic theoretical aspects of the Marxist class perspective.

> *In the social production of their existence, men inevitably enter into definite relations, which are independent of their will, namely, relations of production appropriate to a given stage in the development of their material forces of production. The totality of these relations of production constitutes the economic structure of society, the real foundation, on which arises a legal and political superstructure and to which correspond definite forms of social consciousness. In broad outline, the Asiatic, ancient, feudal and modern bourgeois modes of production may be designated as epochs marking progress in the economic development of society. The bourgeois mode of production is the last antagonistic form of the social process of production— antagonistic not in the sense of individual antagonism but of an antagonism that emanates from the individuals' social conditions of existence—and the productive forces developing within bourgeois society create also the material conditions for a solution of this antagonism.*

This passage contains some of the essential ideas of Marx's economic interpretation of history, called historical materialism. Marx examined two important issues: (1) the social forces and relations of production, which constitute the economic structure of society, or the substructure/infrastructure of society upon which the entire legal and political superstructure is based. According to Marx the social superstructure (legal, political, religious, cultural, educational institutions) are definite forms of social consciousness or ideologies shaped by the economic forces of production. In other words, Marx believed capitalism or the economic system determines the social system; and (2) the emergence of conflict between material forces of production and relations of production, which will lead to social revolution. Because Marxist thought represents a comprehensive worldview of society and history, a Marxist explanation can be tendered for almost every aspect of individual and social life. More than any other social and political thinker, Marx advanced the ideals of socialism. Marxism must be understood as a critical analysis and interpretation of capitalist society in general and its economy in particular. As a revolutionary, Marx sought to replace capitalism with socialism as an economic system. As a social thinker, he sought to describe the stages of historical and social transformation.

Marx's Critique of Capitalist Society.   Some aspects of Marx's analysis are applicable to any historical epoch, but his writings deal mainly with capitalist society, especially early industrial capitalism (Ollman, 1993). His major critique of the capitalist system revolved around the notion of the production of commodities and the accumulation of capital. Marx accepted the theory of the market value of the commodity, which according to him was determined by the amount of labor required for its production. He introduced the idea of surplus value and the exploitation of labor, and he defined the concepts of *use value* and *exchange value.* Use value is an exchange of mutual benefits between partners in a transaction. For example, a car used as a means of transportation demonstrates use value. Objects are produced for use by oneself or by others. Exchange value is based on the amount of labor power that goes into the production of a commodity (e.g., the price of an old car is only a fraction of the price of a new car on the market). The problem of commodities is central to the capitalist form of production. According to Marx, the *process of exchange* initially involves the metamorphosis of commodities into money and back again into commodities, which he represented by the following formula: commodity → money → commodity, or C-M-C (Turner et al., 1989:151). Marx elaborated on the concepts of labor and purchase of labor. In the market, labor was a commodity to be bought and sold like any other commodity. The price for which the commodity is sold minus the value of the labor and the cost of materials becomes what Marx called *surplus value.* For Marx, the accumulation of capital produces the capitalist exploitation of the workers. For example, the value of a commodity produced in one hour equals the wages a laborer makes when the capitalist sells that commodity. Now, by working eight hours, the worker produces more commodities, which become surplus value, or profit, for the capitalist. The accumulation of surplus values enables an ever smaller number of capitalists to acquire an ever larger percentage of the means of production. Marx's central conviction was that humans, not machines, produce surplus value.

Capitalist Expansion, Competition, and Economic Crisis.   According to Marx, the capitalist expansion for profits leads to competition between capitalists, who introduce labor-saving machinery. In turn, the machinery increases the productive capacity but not the demand. Lack of sales and reduced demand for products lead to unemployment, decreased profits, and reduced investment and growth. The multinational corporation, the epitome of the capitalist organization, is focused on the search for lower costs in commodities and markets to restore profits. The larger companies buy the smaller ones, which leads to monopoly; other small companies can no longer compete. Advanced monopoly capitalism and postindustrial, postcapitalist society have changed from a goods-producing to a service-producing economy, or what economists call a change from secondary, or industrial manufacturing, to the tertiary, or service sector, economy. In an advanced form of multinational corporate capitalism, capitalists are looking for cheap labor to maximize their profits and compete in the global economy. Economic crisis is more likely to occur in terms of unemployment in postindustrial society. By postindustrial/postcapitalist society is meant here the decline of industrial forms of capitalism and the use of the service sector of the economy. Due to the fact most countries produce, there is an abundance of products flooding the market. Most of these commodities are made in less developed countries by multinational corporations, and sold in more economically advanced countries. The service economy needs different types of jobs and occupations such as sales, finance, marketing and the like. Most of the service type jobs are not highly paid, and people are forced to have two jobs or both parents have to work.

Shortcomings and Criticisms
It is true that the early industrial capitalist system of production in Europe and the United States was exploitative and oppressive. But contrary to Marx's predictions, a violent class struggle between the capitalists and the working classes, culminating in revolution, did not occur in Western industrial societies. Revolution took place in agrarian or semifeudal societies (e.g., Russia in 1917, China in 1949, Cuba in 1959, and Vietnam in the 1960s). Marx attempted to explain social and human relationships in society in terms of economics or class antagonisms, classes forming the linkage between economic facts and social facts. In reality, however, not all relationships in society are shaped by class. In most instances, family and kinship relationships transcend class relations and form the basis of legal systems and politics.

The proletarian revolution, Marx believed, would destroy the capitalist class society and establish a classless society wherein harmony and consensus would prevail. In order to achieve this society, Marx thought it was necessary to destroy the capitalist bourgeois society—the source of social conflict. If this could be accomplished, Marx argued, there would be no need for social institutions such as education or religion, nor for the state, organized labor, or specialization. In his words, "It is possible for one person to do one thing today and another tomorrow, to hunt in the afternoon, rear cattle in the evening, criticize after dinner, just as I have in mind, without ever becoming a hunter, shepherd or a critic." In this society, Marx believed there would be no conflict of interests, which to him was the cause of antagonism between the "haves" and the "have-nots." In his writings on revolution, such as *The Civil War in France,* he also seemed to suggest the possibility of a direct democracy without mediating institutions such as political parties or an independent judiciary. This idea has been criticized by political sociologists as utopian and dangerous, carrying within it the seeds of totalitarianism (Anderson, 1994).

In summary, Marx saw a gap between the wealthy capitalists and the mass of impoverished wage earners, and felt that the gulf between them would widen with the decline of the middle class. But he overestimated the extent of antagonisms between the capitalists and the proletarian class. Though these antagonisms may have existed in Europe during Marx's life, in the United States, the working class, which was made up mostly of European immigrants, did not fulfill Marxist predictions. In fact, the American working class embraced the Protestant work ethic and the capitalist ideology. In view of the collapse of Communism in the former Soviet Union and Eastern European countries, Marx's predictions of the collapse of capitalism did not come true. The shape of advanced capitalism in the future is difficult to predict, and it will be discussed in this book's last chapter.

The Realist Model

Basic Tenets and Principles

The realist model of politics and society recognizes the national and international interests of nation-states. *Interest* is defined in terms of power and represents the essence of politics in this model. The Greek political historian Thucydides, who wrote about the causes of the Peloponnesian War (431–413 B.C.), thought that "identity of interests is the surest of bonds whether between states or individuals." Nation-states, as well as individuals, have interests and attempt to defend or enhance those interests. A political realist maintains that (1) nation-states struggle for political power in order to advance their national interests, and (2) politics has its own autonomy and dynamic and cannot be defined in the abstract or by moral or other nonpolitical terms. The realists look at politics "the way it is," not wishing to transform what they perceive to be its basic nature. In many ways, the realist approach to national interests has become the governing principle not only among states and governments but in social and psychological relationships, including interpersonal relations.

Hans J. Morgenthau (1985:4–17) synthesized the work of many writers of the realist school in politics. He set forth six principles of the political realist model: (1) Political realists believe that both politics and society are governed by objective laws that have their roots in human nature, which has not changed much since it was described in the classical philosophies of China, India, and Greece. A theory of politics must be tested by reason and experience. (2) Political realism, especially in international politics, is defined in terms of interest and power. Its main concern is not motives and ideological preferences, which are full of psychological and emotional distortions, but rather the ability to comprehend the essentials of foreign policy and to translate them into political action. A realist must avoid political sympathies and ideological beliefs contrary to the national interests of the country concerned. (3) The key concept of political realism is *interest* defined in terms of power, whether between states or individuals. Each political action must be judged on whether it empowers the state to protect or advance its interests. (4) The realm of moral principles and ethics is separate from the realm of politics. (5) The moral aspirations of a nation are not identical to the moral laws that govern the universe. Therefore, a foreign policy toward another nation cannot be guided by abstract moral principle or the aspiration of a nation to observe a universal moral law. It must be based on political interest, not on moral interest. (6) The political realist maintains a certain objectivity, as other professionals must. For example, the economist asks, "How does this policy affect the wealth of a society or a segment of it?" In the same way, a political realist asks, "How does this policy affect the power and interests of the nation?" Professionals who lack this objectivity, relying instead on emotion and edeology, are not properly doing their jobs. Morgenthau provided a view of the world based on three assumptions: (1) nation-states are the most important players in international relations; (2) international relations are a struggle for power, national interest, and peace; and (3) a distinction exists between domestic and international politics. In the 1950s and 1960s, the realists turned to more empirical analysis and attempted to bring the scientific practices of the field in line with the models of the physical sciences.

Theoretical and Historical Dimensions

Historically, the realist approach to politics is founded upon the ideas of Niccolò Machiavelli (1469–1527) and upon those of Thomas Hobbes (1588–1679), who both linked politics with human psychology. Both writers believed that to understand politics, one must understand human nature; both viewed politics as separate from the realm of ethics and morality. For Machiavelli, the goal of politics is power. Thus, any action or means utilized by a state to achieve or maintain power is legitimate. Hobbes, too, was a champion of absolute power of the state. Similarly, Morgenthau (1985:12) argued that the realist view maintains that any political action by individuals and nation-states cannot be judged by moral or ethical principles.

The realist approach puts conflict at the center of international relations. Nation-states, like individuals, try to promote their own interests against the interests of others. Karl von Clausewitz (1780–1831), a Prussian general and writer, defined war as the continuation of politics by other means. When politics and negotiations between nation-states fail and their contradictory aspirations cannot be reconciled, conflict and war are likely to ensue. Although the realist model promulgates the single-minded pursuit of power, national security, and national interest, starting in the 1960s, students and theoreticians of the "interdependence school," who as neorealists stress the notion of the increasing integration of international economy and trade, have criticized the position's emphasis on national interest. Political realists have become political neorealists the same way as conservatives have become neo-conservatives or liberals become neo-liberals. In many instances, liberals of the 1960s have become neo-conservatives in the 1990s. The realist and neorealist perspectives apply to global economy, which is shaped by the distribution of power among nation-states and the rise and fall of great powers. Thus, the global economy is structured by the richest and most powerful states and exercised through hegemony, or a form of domination. The realist model in international politics is helpful for understanding the struggle for power and influence in many regions and countries of the world, especially following the end of the Cold War, or the earlier bipolar international relations between the United States and the Soviet Union.

Shortcomings and Criticisms

The realist school of thought lacks vigorous theoretical and methodological sophistication; it is general and diverse. This approach has also been attacked because of its position concerning ethics. By advocating a double ethical standard, one for political leaders and another for individuals, or one for domestic and another for international politics, realists embrace a crude Machiavellian ethic. Furthermore, its approach to foreign politics is derived from nationalist doctrines and ignores the global interdependence of nation-states. Following the end of the Cold War and the demise of Communist regimes in the former Soviet Union and Eastern Europe, the realist and the neorealist approaches to international politics have been criticized as reductionist, similar to Marxism. This rational and calculating approach to politics allows the stronger to dictate terms to the weaker and upholds the old Thrasymachean ethic found in Plato's *Republic*: "Might makes right." Thrasymachus defined "justice as the right of the stronger" which much later became the Machiavellian ethic the "end justifies the means." Although the realist approach sounds neat and tough, it is not as simple as that. When the more powerful nation-states constantly vie to dominate the weaker ones, conflict and instability are sown.

This model and its relevance will be further discussed in this book's last chapter.

The Corporatist and Consociationalist Model

Basic Tenets and Principles

Modern corporatism is defined as a partnership between state agencies, business, and unions. Corporatism is a decision-making mechanism that contributes to political stability by reducing the levels of unemployment and inflation. It represents a major challenge to party government, especially in Western Europe (Lane and Ersson, 1991:37). There, since World War II corporatism has been widespread (more so than in the United States), especially in the mixed economies of the Scandinavian democracies (Lane and Ersson, 1991:261–62). The corporatist model is considered a postpluralist model. A number of European scholars have distinguished between *corporate pluralism* and *competitive pluralism*. There are those who believe that corporatist decision-making mechanisms contribute to political stability just as United States' types of pluralist and competitive politics. The former was more prevalent during the 1950s, whereas the latter was more characteristic of the 1970s and 1980s.

Consociationalism is a kind of Madisonian model of democracy in which party government is restrained by various checks and balances and a constitution. A. Lijphart (1974:79) defined *consociational democracy* as that type of government run by "an elite cartel and designed to turn a democracy with a fragmented political culture into a stable democracy." The use of consociational devices, such as consensus rather than majoritarian decision making, is one such device. These devices are effective in unstable democracies having heterogeneous societies. Other consociational devices include grand coalition, mutual veto, proportionality, autonomy, and federalism (Lijphart, 1977:25–52). The decline of consociationalism leads to an increase of corporatism.

P. C. Schmitter (1979:73) distinguished two types of corporatism: state and societal. *State corporatism* is imposed "from above" as public policy and uses corporatism for its own purpose, whereas *societal corporatism* is closer to the pluralist model and comes "from the bottom up," creating a more fragmented type of corporatism. In the case of a federation, for example, a group of independent or sovereign states decide to work together in a cooperative or consociational manner based primarily on some form of consensus rather than majority rule. Ronald J. Glossop (1993:23–24) identified three possible types of federalism. First, some nation-states may give up their separate identities as independent states and become parts of a new central unitary state, as was the case, for example, in the former Soviet Union and in Yugoslavia. In both cases, federalism was imposed by force. The demise of state socialism brought about the end of forced federalism and the resurgence of neonationalism in the former republics, where separate nationalities sought self-determination. Second, some nation-states may decide to maintain their separate identities as sovereign and independent states but agree to form a loose association and cooperate on a number of issues. This is called a *confederation*. Third, there is a middle path between the two extremes. A nation-state may form a federation by delegating certain powers or authority to a new central government, maintaining other powers under its own authority. This new central government, in which decision-making authority is shared between the newly created central government and the member states, is called a federation. The United States is an example of a federation. The conflict of Bosnia-Herzegovina in the former Yugoslavia shows how difficult it is for ethnically and religiously diverse societies to come to a consensus in establishing a nation-state.

Theoretical and Historical Dimensions

Historically, the corporatist model can be traced to the feudal society of the Middle Ages (roughly A.D. 400–1400), which stressed organic solidarity based on reciprocal relationships between lord and vassal. The former granted the latter land, which became the bond between the two. Feudal relationships were asymmetrical, allowing the lord to exploit his economic and political power over the vassal. Feudalism gave way to the absolutist rule of militarized royal power in the fifteenth and sixteenth centuries in most western European countries. The Scientific Revolution of seventeenth century along with the political, intellectual and industrial revolutions in the eighteenth and nineteenth centuries gave way to the rise of corporations. By the early twentieth century the corporation became the most important capitalist institution in the West. Later, corporations evolved as partnerships involving cooperation between government, business, and trade unions, especially during World War I, in countries such as Germany and Austria. In recent times, corporatism and/or neocorporatism have been defined as a tripartite cooperation between state, business, and unions, a device used to bring workers into the mainstream of the capitalist system. According to Lehmbruch (1979:158) "Since 1948, unions and business have collaborated intermittently to restrain wages and prices" in Austrian corporatism. Corporatism is more prevalent in Western Europe and especially in those countries in which organized interests have become legitimate in the policy process. In a corporatist model, the state serves as a bargaining agent with corporations and favors capitalist investment and accumulation. In general, corporatism welcomes state interventionist policies as long as they do not run contrary to capitalist principles (King, 1986:121). The U.S. government's economic assistance to the failing Chrysler Corporation during the 1980s is an example of the corporatist model.

Claus Offe (1975) and A. Cawson and P. Saunders (1983) sought to distinguish a state corporatist model from a market or bureaucratic one (King, 1986:123). Offe purported that in each model, decision making takes a particular form in relation to production: (1) bureaucratic machinery is incapable of generating innovative solutions to problems and thus cannot help business; (2) although pluralist decision making solves the problem of consent, it poses risks to capitalists, allowing more influence to noncapitalists; and (3) although corporatism allows more social groups to take part in decision making, it is biased in favor of capitalists, and this generates opposition from the working class. Cawson and Saunders (1983) and James O'Connor (1973) have extended Offe's analysis by applying it to the idea of state spending. O'Connor (1973) identified three major categories of spending (King, 1986:123–24): (1) *social expenses* (projects and services that ensure social order and legitimation, such as welfare systems), (2) *social investment* (services that provide productivity and profitability, such as land clearance), and (3) *social consumption* (programs such as social insurance).

This model of state expenditures is elaborated by Cawson and Saunders into a theory of different modes of state action (King, 1986:124–25): (1) *The Market Mode:* This refers to mechanisms in the market whereby resources are allocated independently of political authority. In this case the state's role in the market economy is minimal, especially as the guarantor of private property and as a legal enforcer of contracts (King, 1986:124). The invisible mechanisms of market and capital flow with minimal state intervention to maximize the profit of capital investment. This type of market is usually associated with capitalist free market economies of the United States and Western Europe. Social expenses such as welfare are viewed by the state as non-productive but necessary to ensure the legitimation of the capitalist state. (2) *The bureaucratic mode:* In this mode resources are distributed by the state institutions, for example, this was true in the former socialist Soviet and Eastern European state socialism. The allocation process followed explicit rules and guidelines which, in most instances, social investment and services by the state were inefficient, cumbersome, and non-productive. (3) *The corporatist mode:* This mode is somewhat different from the other two. It is based on a bargaining process between corporate interests on one hand and the state on the other. Power is neither pluralistic nor concentrated, but polycentric within an overall hierarchical structure (Cawson and Saunders, 1983:16). The corporatist mode of action usually emerges because of failure of market or bureaucratic modes.

In the last analysis, Cawson and Saunders (1983) believe the different forms of state interventionism and resource allocation are linked to the different types of state spending. For example, social investment such as social security benefits can be administered by the state quite efficiently on the basis of universal criteria. Social investment production, however, can be better operated in a corporatist mode.

Summary and Conclusion

In this chapter, five models in political sociology were discussed—the elite, the pluralist, the Marxist, the realist, and the corporatist and consociationalist models. These models are not the monopoly of political sociologists; they are used in other disciplines as well. Each of these five models explains differently the interface of society, politics, and power. In the elite model, power is concentrated in a few hands. Elites occupy top organizational positions in the structure of the society. Conversely, the pluralist model explains power as being dispersed and having many centers. The Marxists find that power is centered in the economic elites, or ruling classes. The state and classes are key concepts in the Marxist perspective. The realist model stipulates that power lies in states that are able to secure their national interests—it is more applicable to international relations or foreign policy decisions. Finally, the corporatist model is an extension of the pluralist model, forming an alliance of business corporations, government, and labor. The consociationalist model is basically consensual and is based on constitutional checks and balances, which restrain the power of the party government.

Table 1.1 presents a brief summary of the various models and the way they are applied to certain issues: power, state, ideology, authority, and democracy. A student can use these models to analyze a number of other issues on the local, national, regional, and international level.

Endnotes

1. Middle-range theories are based on a lower level of abstraction, from which testable hypotheses can be generated (Merton, 1968). Recently, the society-centered orientation of the study of politics has somewhat shifted to a state-centered approach. The concept of the state is central in the institutionalist approach (Almond, 1988; Evans et al., 1985). In the past, political sociologists, including Bendix and Janowitz, have employed the institutionalist approach to politics (more about this later). However, the state-centered approach to politics cannot be divorced from the society-centered orientation of political processes. Both state and society are interdependent and mutually reinforcing.

The argument whether or not politics can be better understood and examined through a society-centered or state centered-approach is not a crucial issue; both society and state are mutually reinforcing and interdependent. No state or government, no matter how autonomous or independent, can ignore societal forces or social groups. The importance and the influence of such groups can be seen during an election year. Presidents or candidates for political offices are always looking for endorsements and support from powerful individuals, groups, and organizations; Congress, in many ways, represents these various social groups and constituencies. In this book, both approaches will be used as two sides of the same coin. There is not society without a state and no state without society.

2. Although William Domhoff has been inspired by C. Wright Mills's power elite thesis, he has over the years been critical of elite, pluralist, and class models of political sociology. He has advanced the thesis of hegemony and class by looking at who governs, who benefits, and who wins as dimensions of power. Domhoff is considered a leading theorist and researcher in the Mills tradition. His "class hegemony" framework combines the ideas of a capitalist ruling class and Mills's "power elite." For Domhoff, this power elite represents the leadership arm of the ruling class. A ruling class, according to Domhoff, is a privileged social class, which he calls the governing class. Domhoff is critical of Marxist, pluralist, and elitist perspectives, but in general he supports the "class-hegemony" paradigm that views social classes as the focal point in the analysis of power. He draws on both elitist and Marxist perspectives in his work. Unlike the Marxists, however, he stresses the primacy of the ruling class in the capitalist system. According to him, the power elite consists of active, working members of the upper

Table 1.1 The Five Models of Political Sociology as Related to Key Concepts in Politics and Society

Key Issue	Elite	Pluralist	Marxist Class	Realist	Corporatist/ Consociationalist
Power	A means by which small groups run society and politics. Elites exert power by occupying the top positions in all institutions of society.	Dispersed among different interest groups and constituencies. No single group has a monopoly of power. There are as many groups as there are issues.	Held by an economic ruling class in capitalist societies.	Manifests itself in the promotion of national interests and struggle for peace and power among nation-states.	Partnership and cooperation between government, business, and trade unions, maintained by checks and balances defined in a constitution.
State	An overarching political mechanism controlled by a small group of leaders.	One of the many political institutions that coordinate, direct, and serve societal interests. It unites the will of the people.	Run by an economic ruling class. The state primarily serves ruling class interests.	Competes with other nation-states for power and advancement of its national interests.	One of the three major partners (with business and trade unions) that share power.
Ideology	Rationalizations, falsehoods, myths, and distortions used by elites to perpetuate their hegemony and power.	A multiplicity of beliefs and ideas. No single belief system or perspective dominates society and politics.	A form of social consciousness peculiar to a historical epoch. Dominant ideologies are those of the ruling class.	Nationalism and national interests.	A basically capitalist ideology.
Authority	Institutionalized or legitimated power that enables elites to initiate change in society and politics.	No absolute authority. Many groups can take part in this form of institutionalized or legitimated power.	Vested in the economic structures of society.	The power and strength of the national interests.	A joint, cooperative effort.
Democracy	Compatible with democracy. Elites can compete with one another in a democratic system.	Compatible with democracy.	No real democracy in capitalism. The rich dominate the political system; the wealthy few control the many.	May or may not promote the notion of democracy; depending on a nation's interests.	Not always possible in practice. Power is often unevenly distributed.

class and upper-middle-class executive employees in profit and nonprofit institutions. This elite is drawn from the corporate, community, upper class, policy-planning networks employed in government offices, foundations, policy groups, think tanks, and university institutions.

References

Adamic, Louis. 1938. *My America*. New York and London: Harper & Brothers.

Almond, Gabriel. 1988. *Comparative Politics Today: A World View*. Boston: Little, Brown.

Anderson, Kevin. June 15, 1994. Written communication.

Burton, Michael, and John Higley. 1987. "Invitation to Elite Theory." In *Power Elites and Organizations*, ed. G. William Domhoff and Thomas R. Dye, 133–43. Newbury Park, CA: Sage.

Cox, R. W. 1981. "Social Forces, States, and World Order: Beyond International Relations." *Millennium*. Vol. 16, no. 10:126–55.

Cawson, A., and P. Saunders. 1983. "Corporatism, Competitive Politics, and Class Struggle." In *Capital and Politics*, ed. R. King. London: Routledge and Kegan.

Czudnowski, Moshe M. 1982. *Does Who Governs Matter?* DeKalb, IL: Northern Illinois Univ. Press.

———. 1983. *Political Elites and Social Change: Studies of Elite Roles and Attitudes*. xi:255.

Domhoff, William G. 1992. *The Power Elite and the State: How Policy is Made in America*. New York: Aldine DeGruyter.

Evans, Peter B., B. Rueschemeyer, and Theda Skocpol. 1985. *Bringing the State Back In*. Cambridge: Cambridge Univ. Press.

Gerth, H. H., and C. Wright Mills, ed. and trans. *From Max Weber: Essays in Sociology*. New York: Oxford Univ. Press.

Glossop, Ronald J. 1993. *World Federation? A Critical Analysis of Federal World Government*. Jefferson, NC: McFarland & Co.

Gordon, Milton. 1964. *Assimilation in American Life*. New York: Oxford Univ. Press.

Etzioni-Halévy, Eva. 1993. *The Elite Connection: Problems and Potential of Western Democracy*. Oxford, England: Polity Press.

Higley, John, and Michael G. Burton. 1989. "The Elite Variable in Democratic Transitions and Breakdowns." *American Sociology Review*. Vol. 54:17–32.

Hunter, Floyd. 1953. *Community Power Structure*. Chapel Hill, NC: Univ. of North Carolina Press.

Hurst, Charles E. 1992. *Social Inequality: Forms, Causes, and Consequences*. Boston: Allyn & Bacon.

Jordan, Grant. 1990. "The Pluralism of Pluralism: An Anti-theory?" *Political Studies* 38:286–301.

Kallen, Horace. 1915. "Democracy Versus the Melting Pot." Reprinted in *The Nation* (Feb. 18, 25).

King, Roger. 1986. *The State in Modern Society: New Directions in Political Sociology*. Old Greenwich, CT: Chatham House.

Kornhauser, William. 1960. *Politics of Mass Society*. New York: The Free Press.

Lane, Jan Erik, and Svante O. Ersson. 1991. *Politics and Society in Western Europe*. 2nd ed. Newbury Park, CA: Sage.

Lehmbruch, G. 1979. "Liberal Corporatism and Party Government," in Schmitter and Lehmbruch (eds). London: Sage.

Lijphart, A. 1977. *Democracy in Plural Societies: A Comparative Exploration*. New Haven: Yale Univ. Press.

Lynd, Robert S., and Helen M. Lynd. 1937. *Middletown in Transition*. New York: Harcourt, Brace and World.

March, J. G., and J. P. Olsen. 1989. "The New Institutionalism Organizational Factors in Political Life." *American Political Science Review*. 78:734–49.

Marger, Martin N. 1987. *Elites and Masses*. Belmont, CA: Wadsworth.

Marx, Karl. 1970. *A Contribution to the Critique of Political Economy*. New York: International.

Marx, Karl, and Friedrich Engels. 1959. (1848) *The Communist Manifesto*. In *Marx and Engels*, ed. Lewis Feuer, 1–41. New York: Anchor Books.

Merton, Robert. 1968. *Social Theory and Social Structure.* New York: The Free Press.

Michels, Robert. 1962, 1959. *Political Parties.* New York: The Free Press and Dover.

Mills, C. Wright. 1956. *The Power Elite.* New York: Oxford Univ. Press.

Mosca, Gaetano. 1939. *The Ruling Class.* New York: McGraw-Hill.

Morganthau, Hans J. 1985. *Politics Among Nations: The Struggle for Power and Peace.* 6th ed. New York: McGraw-Hill.

Myrdal, Gunnar. 1944. *An American Dilemma.* New York: Harper & Brothers.

Newman, William M. 1973. *American Pluralism: A Study of Minority Group and Social Theory.* New York: Harper & Row.

Nisbet, Robert. 1973. *The Social Philosophers.* New York: Crowell.

O'Connor, James. 1973. *The Fiscal Crisis of the State.* New York: St. Martin's Press.

Offe, Claus. 1975. "The Theory of the Capitalist State and the Problem of Policy Formulation." In *Stress and Contradiction in Modern Capitalism,* ed. Lindberg, Leon N. et al. Lexington, MA: D. C. Heath.

Ollman, Bertell. 1993. *Dialectical Investigations.* London: Routledge.

Parenti, Michael. 1995. *Democracy for the Few.* New York: St. Martin's Press.

Pareto, Vilfredo. 1935. *The Mind and Society: A Treatise on General Sociology.* Vol. 3. New York: Dover.

Polsby, Nelson. 1963. *Community Power and Political Theory.* New Haven: Yale Univ. Press.

Pinderhughes, Dianne M. 1987. "Race and Ethnicity in Chicago Politics: A Reexamination of Pluralist Theory." Urbana: University of Illinois Press, 1987

Riesman, David. 1950. *The Lonely Crowd.* New Haven: Yale Univ. Press.

Ritzer, George. 1988. *Sociological Theory.* 2nd ed. New York: Alfred A. Knopf.

Schmitter, P. C. 1979. "The Century of Corporatism." In *Trends Towards Corporatist Intermediation,* ed. P. C. Schmitter and G. Lehmbruch. Beverly Hills: Sage.

Smelser, Neil. 1971. *Sociological Theory: A Contemporary View.* New York: General Learning Corp.

Tocqueville, Alexis de. 1955. *Democracy in America.* New York: Vintage Books (published originally in 1835).

Turner, Jonathan H., Leonard Beeghley, and Charles Powers. 1989. *The Emergence of Sociological Theory.* 2nd ed. Chicago: The Dorsey Press.

Vanfossen, Beth E. 1979. *The Structure of Social Inequality.* Boston: Little, Brown.

Chapter 2
The Study of Societal Power and Authority

The study of societal power and authority is extremely important in understanding the nature of polities and societies. Before we explore the concepts of power and authority, we must briefly discuss those of polity and politics and study the theoretical debate between society-centered and state-centered models in politics and society.

A polity is a society's overall system of political power. Some of the basic elements of a political system include leadership and decision making, power and authority, structure and process, and political ideology. A polity includes units such as the state or government, political parties, and interest groups, and its functions are to establish goals and direction for the entire society and to allocate and mobilize societal resources. Through taxes and other revenues, for example, politicians distribute societal resources; in the United States, such resources tend to be allocated unequally to the various states and communities, because some communities have more political clout than others. In general, individuals, groups, and communities having more political influence usually receive more societal resources.

Edward Lehman (1988:817) identified four levels of a polity: *public, organization, party,* and *state.* They form a hierarchy of authority, with the public at the bottom and the state at the top. The public is made up of the various groups and individuals who support a spectrum of candidates and issues.

Organization, the next tier of the polity, includes all kinds of affiliations, including voluntary organizations such as churches, fraternal orders, and professional associations. These organizations or interest groups teach and disseminate political attitudes and behaviors, and they exert influence on the political system. Examples of these groups are Common Cause, the National Rifle Association, and the right-to-life movement.

The modern political party represents the link between the public and the government. Most parties are engaged in electoral politics, although some are elite agencies of political systems, such as the Communist Party in China. Other parties do not engage in electoral politics, such as the Black Panther Party in the 1960s. Political parties and mass political parties in modern democracies will be discussed in detail later.

Finally, according to Lehman, although the state is only one part of the polity, it is usually the most powerful and strategically situated unit of the political system. This human institution has a monopoly over the legitimate use of physical force within a given territory, and is thus the sole institution having the right to use violence against its own citizens or against another country.

A current theoretical debate exists in political sociology between the "society-centered" and the "state-centered" camps. Society-centered explanations of policies and governmental activities were especially popular in the 1950s and 1960s. During this period, politics was explained in terms of societal influences, such as social class or social group. In the mid-1960s, however, a series of debates were initiated by the neo-Marxists, concerning the role of the capitalist state in society and politics. The state-centered perspective included neo-Marxists such as Louis Althusser, Fred Block, James O'Connor, Claus Offe, Nicos Poulantzas, Theda Skocpol, and others. They regarded the state as an increasingly independent political organization exempt from external societal influences. However, the state-centered approach to politics cannot entirely discount social groups and socioeconomic class influences. Both state and society tend to be interdependent.

In the past thirty years, the society-centered approach to politics has been the major focus of political sociology. Political and social phenomena are viewed as interdependent. Seymour Lipset (1968, 1981), one of the major architects of political sociology, defined political sociology as the study of the relationship between political institutions (the state, political parties, interest groups, a house of representatives) and other social institutions (the economy, the military, family, religion, education, culture). Political sociology encompasses the application of societal power in its various forms, underlying structures, and processes.

Reinhard Bendix (1968:6) argued that for politics to be possible, four major prerequisites must be present: (1) *social inequality,* (2) *group conflict,* (3) *political decision,* and (4) *the use of force.* In many instances, inequality generates conflict, which may lead to group mobilization for political action. Thus, for Bendix, politics arises when there is social conflict. In this instance, it can be argued that politics is necessary as a mechanism of compromise between collectivities and the state for the purpose of allocating societal resources. When political decisions fail to resolve social conflict between groups and nations, force might be used.

Modern politics is embodied in the state and the government, one of the dominant political and bureaucratic institutions of our times. Political parties, as we will examine, compete for the power to manage or control the machinery of government. In the United States, for example, which of the two major political parties controls the machinery of government greatly affects the kinds of social policies and political decisions the government will forge. The execution of such policies inevitably benefits some individuals or groups and excludes other individuals or groups.

One way to discover the nature of modern politics is to explore its basic elements, activities, and functions. The essence of politics is power, or the capacity to control and influence the actions of others, whether those others wish to cooperate or not. To understand power in its complexity, it must be examined at various levels: How and in what ways do various social organizations, classes, groups (ethnic, racial, religious, cultural, occupational, age, and gender groups), and social institutions (religion, economy, kinship, education, and military) use or exert power in society? Who is responsible for the rules and policies at various levels of government, and in public and private bureaucracies? How do these groups and institutions affect social policy, and how are they, in turn, affected by them?

In the most general sense, politics is a continuous process of human action and reaction. Here, action refers to decisions or the exercise of power by certain individuals and groups; reaction refers to the way other groups react to those decisions. For example, civil rights legislation during the 1960s was perceived by many conservatives as too liberal and too generous to minorities. Hence, politics, and what comprises the political, is constantly defined and redefined by various groups immersed in the political process. The way we perceive and view the world depends on the way we interpret political images and the meanings we attach to various social or political issues. This we refer to as political reality. Political sociologists try to discover who initiates or constructs political reality in a given society.

Defining politics requires both practical and theoretical scope. The practical aspect of politics enables us to solve societal problems and social conflicts, whereas the theoretical helps us conceptualize and explain the dynamics of politics. The two realms are interdependent. A group's perspective on the social world guides the policy decisions made by its political leaders. Modern politics is directed toward solving real problems, resolving issues, generating action, and shaping the distribution of power (raising questions such as who benefits, who loses, who has a surplus of power, and how resources will be allocated).

Max Weber, in his speech at Munich University in 1918, argued that the goal of politics was striving to share power or striving to influence the distribution of power, either among states or among groups within a state (Weber, in Gerth and Mills, 1958:78). He distinguished between those who live "of politics," and thus use politics as a vocation, and those who live "for politics." The latter case includes those who have a passion for politics; they must be economically independent in order to engage in politics full-time. Politics, in this sense, is an avocation and not a source of income. An example would be the candidacy of Ross Perot in the 1992 presidential election. Perot spent millions of dollars of his own money and did not rely on political contributions to support his presidential aspirations; he was thus exercising Weberian "power," the "chance of a man or of a number of men to realize their own will in a communal action even against the resistance of others who are participating in the action" (Weber, in Gerth and Mills, 1958:180). Most modern definitions of power are somewhat similar to Weber's definition. In many respects, the Weberian approach to political structures parallels the Marxian approach to economic structures—Weber recognized the multidimensionality of power (economic, political, and status), whereas Marx stressed the economic aspects of power structures.

The Study of Societal Power

Broadly defined, political sociology is the study of political processes and structures of power. Even a cursory review of the literature on politics and society shows that the overriding preoccupation of political sociologists is the study of societal power and the manifestation of such power in society, or what Harold D. Lasswell (1951) referred to as "the what, how, and why of politics." Although politics deals primarily with the study of power, power is not confined to politics; it pervades all of society. Amos Hawley (1963:433) wrote that "every social act is an exercise of power, every social relationship is a power equation, and every social group or system is an organization of power." Only recently, however, has power become the major focus of political sociology. Because power occupies a strategic position in society and politics, we must understand its nature as well as the systemic relationship and interdependence of society and the polity. We must define the structure of power and how it relates to the overall political and social system.

A social system embraces the entire society and its organization, including its constituent parts: social groups, social institutions, relationships, norms, roles, and positions. Political institutions are part of the total social system. What happens politically has an impact on the entire social system and vice versa. Political sociologists try to understand and explain the nature of the relationship of political institutions and political roles, and their relationship to other social institutions and social groups.

Four questions dealing with the study of societal power will concern us here: (1) What is the nature of power? (2) What are some perspectives on power? (3) What are the social bases of power and power structures? and (4) What are some consequences of and problems concerning power? By answering these questions, we will be in a better position to understand the actual manifestation of power in society: the role of the state and the power of elites, as well as the power of various groups, classes, organizations, corporations, institutions, social and political movements, political parties, interest groups, nations, and states.

The term *social structure* refers to any pattern of stable relationships of social groups, associations, communities, social organizations, and even entire societies. The units or elements of social structure are themselves structures, such as norms (rules), roles (expectations), statuses (positions), and patterns of established relationships among various actors. Actors can be individuals as well as groups, including entire nations. *Social process* as used in sociology, means a series of recurrent events or social activities, including specific forms of interaction. Whereas structure denotes the more static and stable arrangement, social process represents the more dynamic aspects of a social system. For example, a political party can be analyzed as a structure, whereas the political socialization (the learning of political roles) that takes place within a political party can be described as a process. Thus, both social structures and social processes are two sides of the same coin. Usually, we cannot understand one without understanding the other. Sometimes the term *social organization* is used synonymously with *social structure*.

Related to the concepts of social structure and social organization is the concept of social system. The concept is central to sociology. A social system involves a set of interdependent and complex phenomena. The most important of which include: (1) patterns of actions and interactions between two or more individuals organized into a system of roles and statuses (2) boundaries and their environments. A boundary means simply "a difference between structures and processes internal to the system and external to it, exists and tend to be maintained" (Parsons, 1961:36). (3) *Structure, function, process.* The concept of structure focuses on more stable or constant features of the system. Function refers to more dynamic or changing features and processes and involves changes in the structure itself including problems of interchange with cultural and institutional norms. (4) A hierarchy of relations of control or subsystems. A social system consists of various parts of subsystems which interconnect with the whole. For example, society can be analyzed as a social system of interconnected individuals, groups, and institutions which themselves constitute subsystems or parts of the social system.

The Nature of Power

Power is difficult to define, not only because it is abstract, but also because it has been conceptualized in various ways. We speak of economic power, political power, military power, and even divine or spiritual power. We see its results, but we cannot see or touch power. It is analogous to an electric current; we all see the light electricity produces, but electricity itself is invisible.

At the simplest level, two aspects of power can be identified: "power to" and "power over" (NG and Bradac, 1993:3). In a positive sense, "power to" is the realization of personal or collective goals; in a negative sense, it is the power to hinder such goals. "Power over" refers to the relational component of one person or group having power over another person or group. Both aspects of power form an asymmetrical relationship between dominant party and submissive party. This may take place in institutions (e.g., the military), and in noninstitutional settings (e.g., a hostage situation). This asymmetrical relationship may take a legitimate or an illegitimate form between friends or enemies (NG and Bradac, 1993:3).

Power is generally synonymous with ability, capacity, and efficacy. Power can also be thought of as potency, which refers not to actual performance but to the latent ability of an individual or group to act out or produce a particular kind of performance. Mark Philip (1985: 635–36) identified three major sources of power: inherent power, such as wealth, status, knowledge, and charisma; externally focused power, such as influence, coercion, force, control, and domination; and stratified power, such as power at the individual, community, national, political, or economic level. We will discuss some of these sources of power in more detail later. First, let us look at some of the salient features of power.

Power as an Interactive Process

Social power is an interactive process; it is found within relationships of social interaction and social structures, whether small groups, families, communities, or nations. As a relational concept, power can be exercised over someone or some group, or within any type of relationship. An individual actor can command resources such as wealth, knowledge, and status, but power does not exist until the resources are used in a dynamic activity, in which the individual or group uses these resources to pursue goals or influence people. A number of social theorists (Arendt, 1970; Lukes, 1974; Parsons, 1953) define power as a relationship between agents or systems, meaning that individuals, groups, or entire nations act on behalf of others (exerting power by proxy). For example, in many developing countries, the military can be used as an agent by an outside power to take over the government of that country. Robert Dahl (1961:202–3) also described power in relational terms. According to him, "A has power over B to the extent that A makes B do something that B would not otherwise do." To impose one's own will on others, even against resistance, is a basic feature of power as a relationship. Bertrand de Jouvenel (Friedrich, 1958:160) identified three elements of power within a relationship: (1) *extensiveness* (narrow or broad), (2) *comprehensiveness* (number of activities involved, or scope of the power holder's control), and (3) *intensity* (how strongly the power holder is committed to pursuing a goal). All three elements are important ingredients of power as an interactive process.

Power as Social Exchange

Related to the interactive feature of power is the notion of power as social exchange and network. Following George Homan's original work, *Social Behavior* (1961), concerning social exchange and activity, Peter Blau (1967:115) broadly defined power as "all kinds of influence between persons or groups, including those exercised in exchange transactions, where one induces others to accede to his wishes by rewarding them for doing so." Power, in this instance, means that an individual or a group can control the behavior of another individual or group by using either a reward for compliance or a punishment for noncompliance. For example, the United States exercises power in other countries by providing military or economic assistance in exchange for compliance. A number of other social scientists (Cook, 1987; Emerson, 1976; Markowski et al., 1972; Molm, 1990; Stolte and Emerson, 1977) also defined power in terms of social exchange. To be effective, power as an exchange must have a "structural potential" (Emerson, 1976; Wrong, 1979), a "behavioral" or "tactical" influence (Michener and Suchner, 1972), and a "successful outcome of influence" (Dahl, 1961; Simon, 1957). This means that power is somewhat similar to a successful outcome in a social exchange relationship. Structural potential means that power can be energized through a social context or organizational framework; behavioral influence means that power must include an action dimension, and a tactical influence refers to the method or way in which power is exercised. All these dimensions have to be present for power as an exchange to take place.

Power as Space and Constraint

Power provides space to those who possess it and places those who don't at a disadvantage. The idea of constraint is also related to the idea of domination, or the ability to exert power over someone. According to Thomas E. Wartenberg, power as constraint can be viewed as a form of domination, not only over an actor's choices, but also over the structure of those choices (Wartenberg, 1990). In the words of Alan Wolfe (1991:244–45), Wartenberg's most important contribution to understanding the nature of power is the notion of power as a "magnetic field." In other words, the exercise of power over another is not so much the idea of constraint upon an individual or a group as the shaping of the "space" within which others may act. The narrower our fields or spaces, the less power we exert over others; and inversely, the larger the space or field, the more power we exert over others (Wartenberg, 1990). Those in power and elite positions are aware of space as a form of power. Related to the notions of space and constraint is the idea of power as autonomy.

Power as Autonomy

Power is related to one's freedom of movement and independence. For example, professionals are more independent than nonprofessionals. Professionals as opposed to nonprofessionals are those occupations who possess a body of generalized and specialized knowledge. Professionals are typified by careers, i.e. physicians, diplomats, lawyers, etc. They profess to know more and possess more competence and expertise to solve concrete problems. Professions are exclusive occupational groups with special skills and extensive training. Professional or institutional elites have more autonomy than non-elites. Those who consider themselves knowledgeable do not take orders from others. They make their own decisions, and they generate their own ideas. Those who have less control carry out the decisions and ideas of others. They do not possess autonomy; instead, they have heteronomy (a lack of self-determination). Those who are engaged in heteronomous occupations or semiprofessions, such as schoolteachers and social workers, do not have complete control of their jobs. These semiprofessionals are influenced by other groups, such as administrators, parents, or clients. In reality, however, no one is completely autonomous; autonomy is a matter of degree. Those who work in organizational and institutional settings whose actions are scrutinized by the public (e.g., politicians) may feel an inhibiting lack of autonomy.

Power as Ritual and Symbol

A ritual is a symbolic form of behavior that is culturally standardized and repetitively aimed at influencing human and social affairs. A symbol is a powerful sign or token of identity and solidarity (e.g., a flag represents a country; a cross signifies Christianity). A ritual employs many symbols. David I. Kertzer (1988:8) showed that ritual plays an important role in the political life of cultures, nations, and societies, from the smallest tribe to the largest empire. Thus, a ritual is a form of communication used both to make claims to power and to send messages to the public (Kertzer, 1988:104). Hierarchical organizations use it to communicate power relationships (such as in the military). A potent means of legitimization, ritual presents particular images of the universe and develops a strong emotional attachment to them, such as in religion. In addition, rituals structure our cognition, as well as our perceptions, and thus discourage critical thinking.

Kertzer demonstrated how the success of all political forces, whether revolutionary or reactionary, is linked to their successful use of ritual and political symbolism. Politics may be expressed through various forms of symbolism. In his view, without understanding the anthropological concept of rituals, we cannot understand the contemporary concepts of power and politics. We must understand how we use political actions both consciously and unconsciously to manipulate symbols of political legitimacy. Through the manipulation of symbols, the powerful maintain their power. By using highly emotional symbols such as flags, national anthems, patriotic songs, and parades, political leaders manipulate citizens. These symbols, in turn, transmit ideas of nation and political order that give meaning to our lives and connect the past, present, and future. Sometimes political symbols are used as diversionary tactics to win elections or attack a political adversary. For example, in the 1988 national elections, Vice President George Bush used the American flag to symbolize patriotism during his presidential campaign, beginning with his visit to a flag factory. Coupled with his attacks on Michael Dukakis in 1988, Bush focused on this symbol, drawing criticism that it was a means of avoiding discussion of domestic issues such as jobs, health insurance, and the trade deficit.

Power as Construction and Deconstruction of Political Reality

Power as construction and deconstruction of political reality depicts power as the way we create or re-create our social world. Mass media, for example, select certain political issues or political problems to discuss or to communicate to the public, thus directly influencing our political reality. This tendency is exemplified in media coverage of the use of drugs and the violence pervasive in American society. Until such problems began infiltrating suburban, white America, they were dismissed by most politicians and the media (thus skewing the public's social perception and political reality) as poor urban phenomena that did not merit the nation's attention.

Murray Edelman (1987) described politics as a "spectacle" by depicting its use of social psychological interpretations, such as meanings, symbols, situations, sentiments, and so on. According to him, a political spectacle is what the public sees—or the way that news is packaged, selected, interpreted, and presented to the public. It reflects the diverse social situations of its audience, employing familiar language and symbols. Prominent political leaders utilize these expressions and symbols to rationalize and perpetuate political roles, power positions, and favored ideologies. He looked at politics and power as processes that we continually interpret, create, and re-create, depending on the situation, the meaning we derive from it, and the way we view the world of politics.

The nomination of Judge Clarence Thomas to the Supreme Court by former president George Bush in 1992, and the subsequent Senate hearings regarding Thomas's alleged sexual harassment of law professor Anita Hill, was a classic example of political spectacle. The nomination of Thomas became highly sensationalized, largely because both the accused and the accuser were African Americans. Different people perceived different things in this nomination. Some feminists equated the nomination of Clarence Thomas to the nomination of sexual harassment. Others pointed to the fact that the Senate was a bastion of white, male domination, underscored by the fact that the senators who conducted the televised hearings were white males. Others saw it as a conservative versus liberal conflict, each side desiring a majority in the Supreme Court. Judge Thomas's nomination also split the African American leadership: those with more liberal views opposed the Thomas nomination, whereas those with more conservative politics supported it. (Eventually, Thomas became a Supreme Court justice.)

Power as Higher Social and Economic Position

Another feature of power is associated with those who occupy higher political and social positions, commonly known as social elites. Tony Orum (1988) believed that power can be defined in terms of social and economic position; those who hold similar positions share common ideas and join together to act on them. Power thus becomes an aspect of structure, which perpetuates social inequality and stratification. Tony Orum (1988:402) offered a more general definition of power as a "social capacity to make binding decisions that have major consequences over the directions in which a society moves." His definition of power is structural, or institutional in nature.

Power as Potential and Purposeful Activity
Others have emphasized the potential and purposeful features of power. Potential power is simply the *capacity* of an individual or a group to energize and use its resources to exercise power. Power becomes *active* when an individual or a group decides to use its resources against others; it becomes a *purposeful activity* when it is intended to influence others in specific ways. Most political sociologists, however, restrict the concept of power to actions intended to affect the recipient, rather than potential power. An example of power as potential *and* purposeful activity is the possession of nuclear arms, which though actively produced are intended as a deterrent or preventive measure against an enemy, not as an agent of physical destruction.

Power as Promotive or Preventive: As Balanced or Unbalanced and Power Exertion
Marvin Olsen and Martin Marger (1993) believed that the exercise of power can affect actions and ideas in two directions—in a *promotive* or a *preventive* manner. Promotive power entails exercise of power in concert with others to achieve common goals, whereas preventive power refers to the exercise of power over others in order to control them. Although the former is desirable for collective endeavors, the latter is undesirable because it restricts people's freedom of action. The authors also argue that the exercise of power can be either symmetrical or asymmetrical. In a balanced, or symmetrical, power exertion, each actor exerts approximately the same amount of influence or control over the other actor(s), so that everyone receives equal benefits. In highly unbalanced situations, a single actor or a few actors exert much greater influence or control over all others and, therefore, receive most of the benefits. The balanced form of power is more stable and desirable than the unbalanced power; a balanced form of power diminishes inequality among people, producing less conflict.

The late political sociologist Marvin Olsen (1993:29–36) identified four forms of social power exertion and three levels of social power. The four forms of power exertion include: (1) *force* or "the intentional exertion of social pressures on others to achieve desired outcomes," (2) *dominance* or "the performance of established roles or functions," (3) *authority* or "the right to issue directives to others who must accept them," (4) *attraction* or "the ability of an actor to affect others because of who he or she is." In conjunction with these four forms of power exertion, Olsen identified three levels of power: *First level* "actors make decisions and take actions that affect others." *Second level* of power exertion "actors prevent decisions from being made or actions from being taken by others." and *Third level* of power exertion, "actors shape the overall settings in which issues are defined and decisions are made and hence define the parameters for the exercise of power." According to Olsen, all four forms and the three levels of power exertion occur throughout all realms of social life.

In this book, power will be considered both as a structural and a dynamic process and defined as an organizational concept. As a structure, power is not so much a feature of an individual but of an organization. Power as a process means that power is a dynamic element of an organization. It can be changed or redirected. Power as an organizational concept encompasses most of the features of power that we have discussed, including space; autonomy; social, economic and military positions; and social resources (wealth, incomes, positions, jobs, values, and knowledge). Typically, power represents an asymmetrical relationship between two or more individuals, groups, or social structures.

Perspectives on Power

During the 1950s, discussions of power focused on the concept of a power elite. C. Wright Mills (1956), for example, stressed the notion of power as a form of administrative domination exercised by three dominant institutions: the corporate wealthy, the political establishment, and the military establishment. Those who espoused this elitist view saw power as concentrated in the hands of those who occupy top positions in organizations and bureaucracies. The functionalist approach, represented particularly by Talcott Parsons (1960), defined power as the "generalized capacity of a social system to get things done in the interests of collective goals." This definition assumes that all groups in society agree on similar goals or share similar interests. The pluralists (Dahl, Polsby, Riesman) view power as dispersed among different interest groups; no single group possesses a monopoly. The pluralists' theory does not answer the empirical question of who gets more or less from this dispersion of power. After all, not all groups and individuals share the resources of society equally.

Conflict theory expresses another view of power, describing it as a form of coercion or domination of one group by another. Conflict emerges concerning values; one party yields to the other because it fears being deprived of a value that it desires. Peter Bachrach and Morton Baratz (1970) identified two processes of power, decision making and nondecision making. Even making a nondecision is a form of power.

Related to conflict theory, the Marxist interpretation of power cites wealth and property as the major sources of power and conflict. Since the mid-1970s, a number of neo-Marxists (Lukes, 1974; Therborn, 1976) have advanced new perspectives on power. Lukes (1974) presented a three-tiered model of power: The first level pertains to the actions that people take as they attempt to influence others, even against opposition. It involves making and implementing decisions that are directly observable, which usually generate conflict. The second level refers to the control exercised over situations and people that prevents activities from taking place or decisions from being made. The third level of power refers to the ways in which people shape the social contexts in which others act. Sometimes power can be exercised through manipulated consensus or thought control through mass media communication. As Lukes (1974:34) put it, "People's wants may themselves be a product of a system which works against their interests."

Drawing from a number of social scientists (including works by Arendt, Dahl, Gamson, Giddens, Kant, Parsons, Weber, Wrong, and his own work), David Knoke

(1990) offered a structuralist but non-Marxist perspective of power. He explained that almost all political analysts reject the structuralist view because they define social power primarily in relational terms. Structuralists understand power not as an attribute of an individual or a group, but rather as an aspect of the actual or potential interaction between two or more social actors within a structure or organization. Knoke avers that power relationships are asymmetrical; one actor actually or potentially dominates another. Using the concepts of influence and domination, Knoke (1990:5) constructed a typology of four pure types of power (Figure 2.1).

Figure 2.1 shows that an *egalitarian* form of power is not actually a dimension of power because neither party possesses any advantages over the other or commands the resources and means to control the other's behavior (e.g., two close friends or a married couple). *Coercive* power relies on some kind of force, including violence, threats, and sanctions, to make people comply.

For example, in 1991 the United Nations Security Council asked Iraq to allow teams to inspect the country's nuclear facilities and urged Iraq to destroy these facilities, creating the potential for the use of coercive power. If Iraq had failed to comply, more severe sanctions might have been imposed by other powerful nations. Coercive power, however, contrasts sharply with the *persuasive* form of power, which relies only on informational messages and persuasive arguments without the actual or potential threat of sanctions for refusals to cooperate.

Finally, when both influence and domination occur simultaneously, power often evolves into a right or directive, which people usually obey without question. As we mentioned before, the presidency of the United States is an example of a legitimate form of power or authority that people are willing to accept.

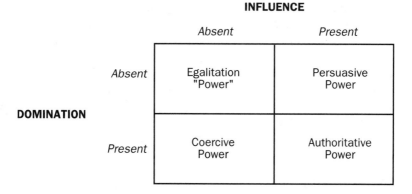

Figure 2.1   Types of Power as Combinations of Influence and Domination

Source: David Knoke, *Political Networks: The Structural Perspective* (1990:5); reprinted here by permission of the publisher.

Social Bases of Power and Power Structures

Social bases of power include collective resources that individuals or groups master or mobilize to promote or to stem change. Social bases of power include matters such as who takes action—which groups, organizations, communities, movements, or even nations succeed in mobilizing their resources for collective actions. Who gets mobilized for political or social action is of central interest to political sociology. Anthony Oberschall (1973:102) defined mobilization as the "process of forming crowds, groups, associations, and organizations for the pursuit of collective goals." An example of this is the ecological or green movement to clean the environment in the 1960s both in the United States and in Europe. The peace and anti-nuclear movements during the 1980s are also examples of social and political mobilization for change.

Power resources also include those tangibles or intangibles that can be used as social bases of power. Tangibles are elements that can be measured, such as natural resources, industrial output, property, agricultural output, money, information cybernetics, good jobs, expert knowledge, military capabilities, and demographic resources (population, people, generations). Intangibles—such as morale, leadership, competence, reputation, respect, honor, and character—cannot be easily measured. The possession of power resources does not always result in the use or application of such resources—some people have tremendous personal or family wealth, yet they fail to use this as a power resource. Furthermore, some talented people are not motivated to use their own talents for self-actualization or to advance the quality of life for the benefit of their community, the nation, or the world. It is not enough to possess resources; one must know how to use them effectively. Whether we use it in positive or negative ways, intentionally or unintentionally, consciously or unconsciously, in small groups or large groups, power constitutes the foundation of social and political life in most societies.

In a political democracy, voters are an important source of power. In the United States almost half of the eligible citizens in a national election do not vote. What would happen in presidential elections with high voter turnouts? Possibly the outcome of an election might change. What does a high voting turnout mean for politicians and the political system? Does it put more pressure on the politicians for political and social change? Does a greater turnout affect the incumbent president and those in power, or those outside? Some of these questions will be discussed in later chapters. Needless to say, politically organized and mobilized groups differ from larger, nonmobilized collectives. The former tend to be more goal- or action-oriented. They want to change things, or stop a particular change.

The Structure of Power

Power is not exercised among individuals or groups by chance. Most societies contain a structure of power. As we mentioned previously, when sociologists talk about social structures, they refer to the regular and stable relations between groups and individuals. The power structure of society refers to a relatively stable system of relationships among various groups and individuals, and the way that power is exercised among them. A social structure consists of various social positions occupied by persons who play certain roles. Positions are often static, whereas roles tend to be more dynamic. Power relations can be either static or dynamic. Those who occupy social positions are expected to play certain social roles. For example, the president of the United States occupies the position of the presidency, and such a position carries authority and entails certain social responsibilities, which shape the president's role. An individual can occupy more than one position at a time and perform different roles. Sometimes, however, those who occupy different positions and roles find themselves in conflict. For example, chaplains in the military might find themselves in conflict when their religious convictions lead them to disagree with a particular military operation.

Power structure is correlated with various groups and institutions and their relationship to one another. What kinds of social groups occupy top, middle, or lower positions of power in society? Who has a surplus or deficiency of power? In general, power is correlated with variables such as economic class, ethnicity, race, gender, age, and religion. In a stratified society, one would expect those who occupy high-status positions to exercise more influence than those who occupy lower positions. What classes or groups benefit most in the United States? Does the tax system benefit the upper class, the middle class, or the working class? Is it an equitable and fair system? Certain tax systems benefit certain classes of people. For example, under Presidents Reagan and Bush during the 1980s, the upper economic or corporate classes received certain tax breaks as incentives for investing, based on the assumption that capitalist investments would create jobs for individuals of all classes. This became known as "trickle-down economics": financial benefits given to big business by the government in terms of tax breaks would pass down to smaller businesses and consumers. Many with a more progressive or liberal political and economic orientation question this type of economic planning and its purported benefits for the lower socioeconomic classes.

Another important issue related to power is the percentage of important political or governmental positions occupied by each class or social group. In 1992, President Bill Clinton appointed a few more African Americans, Latinos, and women to cabinet positions than his Republican predecessors had. This greater representation, however, will not necessarily afford these groups more power. Various other factors, including the type of position, its access to the president, and the decision-making process, might be more significant in determining actual government policies.

Forms of Social Power

Just as we can identify many social bases of power, we can distinguish different forms of social power. Dennis Wrong (1979:24) identified four distinct forms: (1) *force,* (2) *manipulation,* (3) *persuasion,* and (4) *authority,* including five subtypes of authority: (a) *coercive authority* (compliance by coercive force), (b) *induced authority* (compliance by offering rewards), (c) *legitimate authority* (socially or acknowledged right to command, which others are obligated to obey), (d) *personal authority* (compliance in order to please another), and (e) *competent authority* (compliance because of knowledge or skill, as in professional expertise).[1] Figure 2.2 shows Wrong's different forms of power. Somewhat similarly, Marvin Olsen and Martin Marger (1993:29) recognized four forms of social power: (1) *force* (intentional exertion of social pressures on others to achieve desired outcomes), (2) *dominance* (the performance of established roles of functions within any organized activity), (3) *authority* (the right to issue directives to others who must accept them), and (4) *attraction* (the ability of an actor to affect others because of who he or she is).

A brief description of each of these forms of power can help us understand how they are manifested in society. In general, Wrong (1979) looked at power as a form of influence, whether intended or unintended. Force (treating a person like a physical object) can be defined as violence or commission of harm to the person, either physical or psychic, violent or nonviolent. Amitai Etzioni (1993:3) recognized three different types of force: (1) *utilitarian force* (also called inducements or compensation), whereby the recipient is offered desired benefits in return for compliance; (2) *coercive force* (also known as constraint or deprivation), wherein punishments are inflicted or benefits are withheld to obtain compliance; and (3) *persuasive force* (also called information or communication), in which messages are conveyed in a way that alters the recipient's beliefs, values, attitudes, emotions, or motivations, in an attempt to produce compliance. Manipulation, a more concealed, psychological form of power exemplified by commercial advertising or political propaganda, has a sinister reputation.

Persuasion as a form of power denotes the ability of an individual to alter the behavior of another by using convincing arguments. Persuasion involves rhetoric, which Aristotle defined as "the faculty of observing in any given case the available

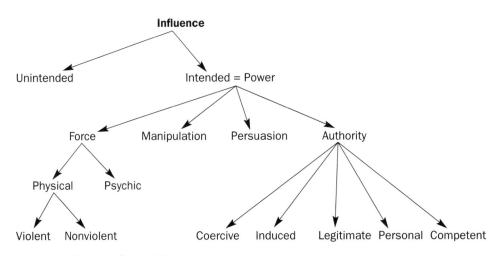

Figure 2.2   Forms of Social Power

Source: Dennis Wrong, *Power* (1979:29); reprinted here by permission of the publisher.

means of persuasion" (Aristotle, *Rhetoric*: 24). He identified three main modes of rhetoric: the speaker's power and personal character, which make the speech credible; the speaker's ability to stir the emotions of the listeners; and the speaker's ability to prove a truth or truths by means of persuasive arguments.

Authority is an institutionalized or legitimated form of power. It is invested in an institution or position, and not in the individual who occupies it. The essence of authority lies in the notion of command. Max Weber in Gerth and Mills (1946) defined authority "as a probability a command will be obeyed" by virtue of legitimate position. It is the right, held by persons who occupy certain positions or offices, to command others. By virtue of occupying the position of presidency, the president of the United States carries a certain power and authority, as defined by the Constitution. However, even presidents must submit to laws and cannot use their authority arbitrarily. Robert MacIver (1926:63) defined *authority* as "the established right, within any social order, to determine policies, to pronounce judgments on relevant issues, and to settle controversies, or more broadly, to act as leader or guide to other men."

Authority, as a socially approved power, entails the attributes of *legitimacy* and *impersonality*. Legitimacy means that people are willing to accept the authority of the incumbent who occupies a position. For example, the president of the United States has authority because historically the office of the presidency is socially and politically accepted. We accept the authority of any leader because of the legitimacy of a given office. The exercise of authority is for the most part impersonal. This means that individuals because of their institutional positions command others, give directions, or allocate social resources not on the basis of personal traits or achievements but rather because they occupy particular positions and roles in the various institutions of society. Those who occupy those positions may change over time but the rights and duties remain the same (Marger, 1987:14). Individuals occupying certain positions, such as teachers, employers, or presidents, are entitled by their position to exercise certain powers.

We think of the state or government as a political institution that exercises authority over its citizens. People are willing to obey laws, pay taxes, or follow the commands of the president as commander in chief in time of war or national crisis. The state itself is the ultimate authority, simply because it has a monopoly of the organized means of violence, the armed forces. Only the state and its agents can coerce, physically harm, or even kill its citizens with impunity. In some cases, for example, a state governor or the president of the United States can decide whether a convicted criminal will live or die. How does authority become legitimate, and why do individuals follow the commands of their leaders and consent to be ruled? To answer this question, we turn to the sources of authority.

Sources of Authority and Legitimacy

Why do people obey authority? Why are citizens in some societies more obedient to the law, whereas citizens in other societies challenge those who rule or those who are said to exercise authority? Max Weber (in Gerth and Mills, 1958:78–79) suggested three major sources of authority or legitimacy, which give those in positions of authority their right to rule. The first one is *traditional authority*, conferred by custom and accepted practice (for example, in a monarchy such as in Saudi Arabia). Traditional authority is the predominant form of authority in most preindustrial societies. Most hereditary and tribal societies also exercise this form of authority.

Legal-rational authority, the second source of authority, is found mostly in modern societies. Here, modern leaders are accorded authority by certain legal and bureaucratic procedures. For example, the presidents of the United States are chosen through the legal, rational procedure of the electoral process. This type of authority is also characteristic of modern organizations and advanced political systems. When traditional societies evolve into modern societies, the source of authority generally changes from traditional to legal-rational.

Charismatic authority is based on the charisma and extraordinary personal qualities of an individual. *Charisma* literally means "gift of grace," which charismatic leaders possess. Religious charismatic leaders include Jesus Christ, Moses, and Muhammad; political and military charismatic leaders include Alexander the Great, Julius Caesar, Cyrus, and Napoleon. Leaders of social and political movements, such as Ho Chi Minh, Martin Luther King, Jr., and Nelson Mandela, are also examples. Their authority comes from their charisma. Charismatic leaders emerge during periods of crisis or profound social and political change. For example, during the decolonization period following World War II, a number of charismatic leaders led the struggle against the colonial powers in Africa. People and nations are inspired by the social, moral, economic, political, military, or spiritual guidance these leaders offer. As a rule, people become emotionally attached to charismatic leaders. For example, during World War II, Prime Minister Winston Churchill of Britain emerged as a charismatic leader, an inspiring force in the victory against the Nazis. However, charismatic leaders do not always solve the problems of society or nations. Skills and expertise are often more important than charisma in solving problems, and in many societies, critical voices in the populace will call the leader to account. If charismatic leaders prove ineffective, they may lose their legitimacy and effectiveness to rule, despite their personal power.

Consequences and Problematics of Power

Power can be used to benefit society or to hurt people, both individuals and collectivities. For example, during the 1960s, some U.S. economic, political, and military institutions were criticized by university students, African Americans, and other minorities for waging an expensive war in Southeast Asia while neglecting the poor and many social problems at home. They felt that an abuse of power had caused widespread negative societal consequences. On a microlevel, power's allure can help or destroy individuals. It may enhance the individual's own selfish motives, or it may serve the collectivity as a means to a beneficial end. Power can become merely ego gratifying, seductive as an end in itself. Popular wisdom tends to look at power, or those who possess power, with suspicion and distrust. Many believe that power, by its very nature, has a corruptive influence on those who possess it.

Power can be used to dominate or control other people or nations, expand and conquer territory, or even exterminate entire populations through genocide: for example, Native Americans by early European settlers, Armenians by the Ottoman Turks during World War I, and Jews by the German Nazis during World War II. Abuse of power abounds in history because individuals and nations alike seem to desire self-glorification and expanded power. The late senator William Fulbright of Arkansas called it the "arrogance of power." As a sophisticated student of history and public affairs, he was a critic of U.S. policies in the Vietnam War and recognized the limit of power even within powerful nations like the United States. Abuse of power was central in the thoughts of the framers of the U.S. Constitution, who limited power through a system of checks and balances, distributed over three branches of government—executive, judiciary, and legislative.

Wrong (1979) used a fourfold classification of power, differentiating power when sought as a means or as an end, and when serving an individual's selfish goals or collective, altruistic aims. Figure 2.3 presents ideal types of attitudes toward political power. Box A represents all those who seek power as a means to secure their own personal satisfaction and comfort. The glory-seeker politician, who cares little for the common good while making a living from holding political office and PAC (political action committee) contributions, belongs to Box A.

Box B includes those who seek power as an end in itself. Some individuals will use all means available simply to attain and enjoy power. This approach is typical among ambitious politicians who would do anything, by any means necessary, to be elected or reelected to an office, or unscrupulous businesspeople who favor employees who will lie or remain silent to protect the boss's position of power.

Box C represents those who seek or wield power in the service of an ideal, value, or the collective interest of a group. The group may be a nation-state, an institution,

	Goals for Which Power Is Sought	
Power Sought As	Individual	Collective
Means	A	C
End in Itself	B	D

Figure 2.3　A Fourfold Classification of Power and
Its Goals

Source: Dennis Wrong, *Power* (1979:231); reprinted by permission of the publisher.

a religious group, an ethnic group, a class, a party, a social movement, or a limited special interest group (Wrong, 1979:233). It can also be used as a means for something negative.

Finally, Box D represents those who seek power for the sake of power and wish to exercise it over a certain group. It includes individuals who exploit people's insecurities and fears to stir up emotions against other groups, which are then cited as scapegoats for the ills of society. For example, during World War II the Nazis blamed the Jews as the root cause of Germany's problems. It must be noted this fourfold classification of power as means versus goals presents ideal types toward power and doesn't always reflect reality.

Another way to understand power is by looking at its use and its consequences. Kenneth Boulding (1989) identified types of power in terms of its use: *destructive* or *threat power, productive* or *economic power,* and *integrative power.* He called these three the "stick," the "carrot," and the "hug," respectively. The first is the power to destroy; the second is the power to create, construct, invent, produce, and exchange; and the third, a productive form of power, binds people together in love, friendship, and respect. In short, the exercise of power has consequences for society and the nation. It can have both positive and negative effects. It can contribute to unity and integration of society or it can destroy that unity. More and more the exercise of power especially by the state is challenged by various groups. The end of the Cold War and the demise of former socialist regimes in the Soviet Union and Eastern Europe brought about the resurgence of ethnonationalism in many parts of the world (more about this later).

Summary and Conclusion

In this chapter the concepts of societal power and its various forms were discussed. The levels of polity including the notions of public, organization, party, and state were examined. It was argued that all four form a hierarchy of authority with the public at the bottom and the state at the top. The state has become the most powerful institution in modern times. Second, the theoretical debate between society-centered versus state-centered views of the polity, the concept of politics, and the prerequisites of politics were critically evaluated. It was pointed out that the state-centered perspective has become more dominant over the society-centered view of polity. The role of the state has increasingly been stressed and recognized more and more as an independent institution in making social policies. Politics is embodied in the state and the government and who controls the machinery of government is the very essence of politics and political parties. Four major prerequisites must be present for politics to emerge—social inequality, group conflict, political decision, and use of force. Politics is about solving societal problems and resolving disputes and conflicts between groups and nations. It is a process of compromise and power between groups and individuals. Third, the nature of societal power along its various features, forms, and perspectives were extensively discussed. Power is above all an interactive process.

This means social power takes place in groups and social organizations. It has its own dynamics. It is both an actual and potential activity. It is the ability of one actor (individual, group, society, nation) to exert influence and dominance over another. It is more of an asymmetrical relationship between groups and individuals. Various forms and dimensions of power exertion were discussed including force, manipulation, persuasion, dominance, attraction, and authority. The three sources of legitimacy suggested by Max Weber were also examined, the charismatic (based on the extraordinary ability or charisma of the individual), the legal-rational (based on bureaucratic and legal criteria), and traditional type (more applicable to those societies ruled by kings and dynasties). Along with the various aspects and forms of power the perspectives of power were examined. These included the functionalist (power as functional and goal attainment for society), the conflict (power as dysfunctional for society), the neo-Marxist (power as serving the capitalist class). The structuralist and instrumentalist views of state power were also briefly discussed. While the former looks at the structures of society and the state to understand the nature and workings of power exertion the latter looks at the types of individuals and groups who manipulate the state. Finally, the consequences of power were briefly discussed. Power can benefit society or can hurt people. It can promote peace or can cause war and destruction. In the last analysis the understanding of the nature of societal power is essential in understanding the process of power and power structures.

Endnotes

1. Wrong's subtypes of authority resemble French and Raven's five-fold typology of power (see Kanter, 1977:174): (1) *reward power* (controlling resources that can be used as reward or induced authority), (2) *coercive power* (controlling resources that could be used to punish), (3) *expert power* or *competent authority* (controlling knowledge or information), (4) *reference power* (having personal attractions that other people identify with or seek a relationship with), and (5) *legitimate power* (authority vested in a position and accepted by others as legitimate).

References

Aristotle. "Rhetoric" in Roberts Phys, 1984, New York: The Ohio State Univ. Press.

Arendt, Hannah. 1970. *On Violence*. New York: Harcourt, Brace and World.

Bachrach, Peter and Morton Baratz. 1970. *Power and Poverty: Theory and Practice,* New York: Oxford University Press.

Bendix, Reinhard. 1968 (ed.) *State and Society: A Reader in Comparative Political Sociology.* Berkeley, CA: University of California Press.

Blau, Peter. 1964. *Exchange and Power in Social Life*. New York: Wiley.

Boulding, Kenneth. 1989. *Three Faces of Power.* Newbury Park: Sage.

Cook, Karen S., ed. 1987. *Social Exchange Theory.* Newbury Park, CA: Sage.

Dahl, Robert. 1961. *Who Governs?* New Haven: Yale Univ. Press.

Edelman, Murray. 1987. *Constructing the Political Spectacle*. Chicago: Univ. of Chicago Press.

Emerson, Richard M. 1976. "Social Exchange Theory." *Annual Review of Sociology.* Vol. 62:

Etzioni, Amitai. 1993. "Power as a Societal Force." In *Power in Modern Societies,* ed. Marvin E. Olsen and Martin N. Marger. Boulder, CO: Westview Press.

Friedrich, Carl J., ed. 1958. "Authority, Reason, and Discretion." In *Authority,* ed. Carl J. Friedrich. Cambridge: Cambridge Univ. Press.

Gerth, H. H., and C. Wright Mills. 1958. *From Max Weber: Essays in Sociology.* New York: Galaxy.

Hawley, Amos. 1963. "Community Power and Urban Renewal Success." In *American Journal of Sociology.* Vol. 68 (January):422–43.

Homans, George C. 1961. *Social Behavior: Elementary Forms.* New York: Harcourt, Brace and World.

Jouvenel, Bertrand de. "Authority: the Efficient Imperative." In *Authority,* ed. Carl J. Friedrich. Cambridge: Cambridge Univ. Press.

Kanter, Rosabeth Moss. 1977. *Men and Women of the Corporation.* New York: Basic Books.

Kertzer, David I. 1988. *Ritual, Politics, and Power.* New Haven: Yale Univ. Press.

Kourvetaris, George A., and Betty A. Dobratz. 1980. *Political Sociology: Readings in Research and Theory.* New Brunswick: Transaction Books.

Knoke, David. 1990. *Political Networks: The Structural Perspective.* New York: Cambridge Univ. Press.

Lasswell, Harold D. 1951. *The Political Writings of Harold D. Lasswell.* Glencoe, IL: The Free Press.

Lehman, Edward. 1988. "The Theory of the State versus the State of Theory." *American Sociological Review.* Vol. 53 (Dec.):807–23.

Lipset, Seymour. 1968. "Political Sociology," pp. 156–170 in Talcott Parsons (ed.) *American Sociology: Perspectives, Problems, Methods,* New York: Basic Books, Inc.

———. *Political Man.* 1981. Second Edition, Baltimore: Johns Hopkins University Press.

Lukes, Steven. 1974. *Power: A Radical View.* London: Macmillan.

MacIver, Robert. 1926. *The Modern State.* Oxford: Oxford Univ. Press.

Marger, Martin. 1987. *Elites and Masses: An Introduction to Political Sociology.* 2nd ed. Belmont: Wadsworth Publ. Co.

Markowski, Barry, David Willer, and Travis Patton. 1988. "Power Relations in Exchange Networks." *American Sociological Review* Vol. 53 (April:220–36).

Michener, H. Andrew, and Robert W. Suchner. 1982. "The Tactical Use of Social Power." In *The Social Influence Processes,* ed. James T. Tedeschi, 239–86. Chicago: Aldine-Atherton.

Mills, C. Wright. 1956. *The Power Elite.* New York: Oxford Univ. Press.

Molm, Linda D. 1990. "Structure, Action, and Outcomes: The Dynamics of Power in Social Exchange." *American Sociological Review.* Vol. 55 (June):427–47.

NG, Sik H. and James J. Bradac. 1993. *Power in Language: Verbal Communications and Social Influence.* Newbury Park, CA: Sage.

Oberschall, Anthony. 1973. *Social Conflict and Social Movement.* Englewood Cliffs: Prentice Hall.

Olsen, Marvin, and Martin Marger. 1993. "Power in Social Organization" in *Power in Modern Societies,* Boulder, CO: Westview Press.

———. 1993. "Forms and levels of Power Exertion" in *Power in Modern Societies,* edited by Marvin Olsen and Martin Marger, Boulder, CO: Westview Press.

Orum, Anthony. 1989. *Introduction to Political Sociology: The Social Anatomy of the Body Politic.* Englewood Cliffs: Prentice Hall.

Parsons, Talcott. 1953. *The Social System.* Glencoe, IL: The Free Press.

Parsons, Talcott. 1961. "An Outline of the Social System" in *Theories of Society* (two volumes in one) edited by Talcott Parsons, Edward Shils, Kaspar D. Naegele, and Jesse R. Pitts, New York: The Free Press.

Philip, Mark. 1985. "Power." In *The Social Science Encyclopedia,* ed. Adam Kuper and Jessica Kuper. London: Routledge and Kegan Press.

Simon, Herbert A. 1957. *Models of Man.* New York: Wiley.

Smith, Adam. 1776. *The Wealth of Nations.*

Stolte, John, and Richard Emerson. 1977. "Structural Inequality: Position and Power in Network Structures." In *Behavioral Theory in Sociology,* ed. R. Hamlin and J. Kunkel. New Brunswick: Transaction Books.

Tatalovich, Raymond and Byron W. Daynes. 1988. *Social Regulatory Policy: Moral Controversies in American Politics.* Boulder: Westview Press.

Therborn, Göran. 1976. "What Does the Ruling Class Do When It Rules? Some Reflections on Different Approaches to the Study of Power in Society." *The Insurgent Sociologist.* Vol. 6 (Spring):3–16.

Wartenberg, Thomas E. 1990. *The Forms of Power: From Domination to Transformation.* Philadelphia: Temple Univ. Press.

Wolfe, Alan. 1991. *America at Century's End.* Berkeley: Univ. of California Press.

Wrong, Dennis. 1979. *Power: Its Form, Bases and Uses.* New York: Harper.

Nations and States

One of the most important developments in modern times is the emergence and expansion of nation-states. Whereas the concept of nation is sociological, the notion of the state is legal, territorial, and political. The composition of most modern nation-states, including the United States, is pluralistic. The concepts of nations and states are linked; they are also related to those of nationality, race, ethnicity, and nationalism. We will try to clarify these concepts in light of the emergence and expansion of modern states. An understanding of nations and states, both historically and in modern times, will help explain relationships among nation-states and why they sometimes go to war against one another.

The importance of the state as a political institution has been of continual interest to political sociologists, especially in the past thirty years. Indeed, from the beginning, the entire Western tradition of political philosophy has dealt extensively with the notions of power, order, and the state. Plato's *Republic* (fourth century B.C.), Niccolò Machiavelli's *The Prince* (A.D. 1513), and Thomas Hobbes's *Leviathan* (1651), to mention only three important works, deal extensively with the themes of order and the state. Since the time of Machiavelli (who introduced the realist approach to politics and separated the study of politics from the study of ethics), politics in the West has been defined as the study of power and the state. In this chapter, four major questions will be addressed: (1) What is the nature and role of the modern state system and its constituent parts? (2) What is the nature of a nation and its relationship to the state, to nationality, and to nationalism? (3) How have modern nation-states developed, and what are their modern roles and functions? and (4) How do we explain the emergence of modern nation-states?

The Nature and Role of the Modern State System

The concept of the state is central to understanding the nature of the modern political system. Indeed, political sociologists and other social scientists have shown a renewed interest in studying the expanded role of the state (Evans et al., 1985). They have raised a number of old and new questions. For example, what is the role of the state in shaping domestic, economic, and social policies in modern societies? Political sociologists for a long time have studied the impact of social classes and ethnic, racial, and religious groups on state policies, as well as the role of the state in class mobilization and ethnic and intergroup conflict.

In modern usage, the term *state* describes that aspect of the political system through which authority is exercised over a given territory. Max Weber defined a state "as a human community that successfully claims the monopoly of the legitimate use of physical force within a given territory...the state is considered the sole source of the right to use violence" (Weber, in Gerth and Mills, 1958:78). Harry Redner (1990:638), however, argued that neither Marx nor Weber ever produced a complete theory of the state. In defining the concept of the state, Michael Mann (1993:314) identified two different levels, one institutional and another functional, an approach originally suggested by Weber. In his words, "The state can be defined in terms of what it looks like as an institution or the way it functions." Mann (1993:314) identified four major elements of the state: (1) a distinct set of institutions and personnel, (2) a centralized authority, (3) a territory, and (4) a monopoly of authoritative rule making, backed up by a monopoly on the means of physical violence. He has also suggested two types of state power: despotic and infrastructural. Despotic power is the power of the state to exercise its will through coercion or force, primarily exercised by the military and the police. This type of state power, Mann argued, has declined. Infrastructural power describes the state's power to coordinate all areas of social life, especially the distribution of economic resources and the protection of life and property. Political authority is exercised by a small group of bureaucratic and other social elites (Mann, 1993:315).

To understand the nature of state power, we must also distinguish the various elements that make up the entire state power system. According to Ralph Miliband (1993:277–80), five elements make up that system: government, administration, military and police, the judiciary, and subcentral government and parliamentary assemblies. Power lies in these institutions and in those who occupy their leadership positions: presidents, prime ministers, cabinet or ministerial colleagues, high-level civil servants, state administrators, top military people, judges of higher courts, and political and administrative leaders of subcentral units of the state elites.

Administration, known also as public administration or civil service, manages state affairs and activities, both those that directly and indirectly involve the state. Administration, by its very nature, has a political and policy-making function. Ideally, politics and administration might be thought to be separate; in reality, however, they are usually allies. Indeed, some administrators and high-level civil servants may have more power in policy making than do political or executive appointees. The power of administrators varies from country to country and even within the same country; a change of government or of party in power may somewhat alter the administration. The view that administrators are simply instruments of government policies, the individuals who carry out the government's decisions, is not always accurate. In general, administrators play an important role as policy advisers to successive governments. Governments come and go, but administrators, especially career civil servants, remain. In the United States, certain administrators are appointed by the president, whereas others are career civil servants and work for a number of successive presidents, both Democrats and Republicans.

Some sociologists consider the military and paramilitary forces (police or militia) to be part of the state system of government, whereas others treat them as a separate institution. The military is nonetheless a powerful institution and its officer corps an elite group that wields tremendous power. We will discuss it more extensively in a separate chapter.

In Western political systems, the judiciary is independent of the political executive. Its role is to protect the rights and liberties of citizens from the abuse of state power. The president of the United States nominates the Supreme Court justices, and the Senate in turn confirms or rejects such nominations. The state system also includes the various subunits and agencies of the government, such as the Federal Bureau of Investigation (FBI), the Central Intelligence Agency (CIA), and of course the representative assembly, known as Congress.[1] (These particular institutions are beyond the scope of our discussion.)

The Nature and Forms of Government

The notion of the state should not be confused or equated with the idea of government. A government, as Robert R. Alford and Roger Friedland (1985:1) have noted, is "merely the specific regime in power at any one moment—the governing coalition of political leaders." The government is simply the political party in power. For example, in the United States there are two major political parties, the Republicans and the Democrats. Every four years they compete to see which will capture the White House. The state, on the other hand, is a permanent political institution that transcends any particular political party, political officials, or civil servants, and as such remains the most important symbol of authority despite frequent changes in government. The president of the United States has authority by virtue of the position occupied, not because of personality or political party. The state power itself grants the president the authority to rule and command public respect. Although in most European countries the president is the head of the state and the prime minister is the head of the government, in the United States the president is both the head of government and the head of state. According to the Constitution, the president of the United States is not only the leader of the party in power but also the chief officer who officially represents the United States to other countries.

One, the Few, and the Many
The questions of who should control the government and what form of government is the best have preoccupied political theorists and philosophers since the days of the ancient Greeks. Aristotle, who may be considered the first political scientist, began his search for the best form of government by examining the people who rule. According to him, good governments are usually those that pursue the common good, whereas bad ones pursue the private good. The common good benefits society as a whole, not a given group or individual. Aristotle posited three alternative sys-

tems that can achieve the common good: the rule of one, or *kingship;* the rule of the few best, or *aristocracy;* and the rule of the many, or *polity.* This list exhausts the alternatives because the rule of none, or *anarchy,* is actually no rule at all—no one is in charge of the government. The number of rulers was not important to Aristotle as long as each ruler was committed to the common good of society. As long as this goal was served by one, the few, or the many, a regime was considered good. Regimes that promoted the private good, however, were considered corrupt or degenerate. According to Aristotle, the degenerate form of kingship becomes *tyranny* (the rule of the unjust), the degenerate form of aristocracy gives way to *oligarchy* (the rule of the few rich), and the degenerate form of polity results in *democracy.*

Aristotle identified five different contenders for the title of ruler: the people, the rich, the few talented, the one best, and the tyrant (Barker, 1961:121–23). Each has something to contribute to the common good: the people, their numbers or human strength; the wealthy, their money; the few talented, their skills; the one best, his or her virtue; and the tyrant, his or her power. Despite the fact that he recognized five claimants, however, Aristotle considered only two: the one best and the people. The problem with the rule of the people, Aristotle reasoned, is whether it can be directed toward the common good—how can it serve its proper purpose? As Aristotle perceived it, this involved reconciling the two most influential factors, wealth and numbers. His answer was a large middle class, made up of the poorer of the rich and the richer of the poor and blending the democratic principle of numbers and the oligarchic principle of wealth. The better the blend, the more likely democrats would mistake it for democracy and oligarchs for oligarchy. Who, then, rules in the best practical regime? The people—specifically, the middle class. Neither rich nor poor, they are likely to favor stability and order in the polity and society. Aristotle's solution to a stable society and polity was empowering the middle class, or what he referred to as the mean. Indeed, this principle is still applicable today.

The state exercises control over society and the nation through the agency of government, known as the political regime. In most societies and nations there is a distinction between a state and its government. In Britain, for example, a constitutional monarch, Queen Elizabeth II, is head of state, but a politically elected leader, the prime minister, is head of government. Likewise, in most European parliamentary systems the president is the head of state and the prime minister is the head of government. In some countries ruled by military dictatorships, especially in Latin America, Asia, and Africa during the 1960s and 1970s, the military dictator is the head of state, the head of government, the legislator, and the commander in chief. Political and military authority are one and the same. We will explore this further in our chapter on civil–military relations.

Varieties of Government

Over the course of history, three varieties of government have been predominant: authoritarian, totalitarian, and democratic. In authoritarian government, ultimate authority is vested in a single individual—a dictator, a monarch, a charismatic leader, or a hereditary ruler—or a few individuals. In authoritarian states, ideology and political parties do not play a major role. Politics is the expression of the devotion of the people to the dominant authority figure. The dictator rules by decree (without a constitution) and by cultivating a personality cult based on charismatic leadership. Since the mid-1970s, thirty or so countries have changed from some form of dictatorship to democracy (Huntington, 1991). Prior to the 1970s, many countries in Latin America were ruled by military dictatorships, and a number of Asian and African countries still are.

Totalitarianism is a form of government run by a single party that controls all aspects of society. Totalitarianism can be traced to Roman imperial times. However, the advent of communications technology in the twentieth century made possible the manipulation of masses through propaganda and ideology, giving rise to modern totalitarian states. In a totalitarian state, the individual and the people are subordinate to the state. No clear distinction exists between state and society, and individual and human rights are of little value. A strong military presence, an active paramilitary and police force, continuous surveillance of citizens, widespread censorship of mass media, and lack of freedom of speech or assembly characterize totalitarian states. No one is allowed to criticize the government, and dissidents are usually imprisoned, exiled, or executed. Examples of totalitarianism include Nazi Germany and Fascist Italy during the 1930s and 1940s, and Communist Party rule of the Soviet Union. According to Carl J. Friedrich et al. (1969), a totalitarian system is characterized by an authoritarian and charismatic leadership, control of the mass media, secret police, militarism, extreme nationalism, a bureaucratized and centralized control of the economy, and an official and highly specific ideology.

With the defeat of the Nazis and Fascists during World War II and, more recently, the fall of state socialism in the former Soviet Union and Eastern Europe, totalitarianism appears to be in decline.[2] However, the collapse of Communism in the former Soviet Union and the former Yugoslavia is creating a political vacuum in which the rise of ethnic nationalism is renewing ancient animosities. Chapter 13 will cover this phenomenon in more detail.

Democracy means "power of the people." The concept originated in ancient Greece in the fifth century B.C. and meant "the power of the *deme*." A *deme* was a small political unit, like a township or a ward, which included only Athenian male citizens age twenty years or older. They thus participated in the politics of the *polis,* or city-state. In a democracy, individuals can compete for political leadership and participate in a common cultural and political life. In true democracies the power of the government is derived from the consent of the governed, and citizens have a right to participate through voting for those who represent them in the government. Although the idea of democracy is old, in practice, democracy as a form of government has been rare—more of an ideal than a reality in many parts of the world. Many countries profess to be democratic but violate fundamental democratic principles, including freedom of speech, protection of human rights, freedom of assembly, and freedom of religion, to name a few.

Democracy as a political system includes three major dimensions. The first, universal suffrage, grants people the right to participate in a free and regular way, irrespective of race, gender, religion, class, national origins, or other social or cultural characteristics, to elect their representatives. Universal suffrage is a recent phenomenon, still not practiced in many countries of the world. Even in the United States women gained the vote only in the 1920s, and African Americans up until the 1960s could not vote in the South. The second dimension requires that the state apparatus be accountable to the elected parliament or congress, thereby to the people as well. Last is civil rights—freedom of expression and association, including political freedom. Civil rights in a democracy grant all citizens the same constitutional and political rights irrespective of race, gender, religion, or national origins. Even noncitizens must be treated with fairness and equality before the law. For a long time these rights have been denied in many countries of the world, including the United States. We will explore further the notion of democracy and democratization in Chapter 13.

There are three types of democracy: representative democracy, direct or participatory democracy, and liberal democracy. The most common is the representative form, in which citizens vote for politicians to represent them in a congress or parliament. Ideally, in a representative democracy the elected politicians promote policies that benefit the public interest. However, this is not always achieved in reality. Often government policies promote certain group interests at the expense of broader public or societal interests. An ideal in direct or participatory democracy allows all citizens to participate in making policies that affect their lives. In the United States this form of government was practiced in early New England town meetings. It also characterized ancient Greek city-states, though the government did not represent the entire adult population. No democracy has ever been universal; the Greek democracy excluded women, slaves, and foreign residents. The kind of democracy most developed in Western societies, including the United States, is liberal capitalist democracy. It defends the rights of private property; freedom of expression, assembly, and political participation; and equality under the law. Most liberal capitalist democracies tend to be representative democracies as well.

Although modern representative democracy encourages participation by its citizens, in reality only a few take an interest in politics, and many students of politics believe that U.S. democracy serves the interests of the privileged few. Political parties, elections, and the right to speak are not always effective vehicles of expression for the average citizen's interests. Michael Parenti (1995:2) argued that American democracy is for the few and not for the many, taking the view "that our government often represents the privileged few rather than the needy many, and the elections and the activities of political parties are insufficient measures against the influences of corporate wealth. The laws of our polity are written principally to advance the interests of the homs at the expense of the rest of us." In a similar vein, Alan Wolfe (1978:22) examined the "seamy side of democracy and repression in the American democracy," purporting that the capitalist state upholds the privileged few and that democracy constitutes the ideological manipulation of the many by the few. Modern American democracy is linked with a utilitarian philosophy of rationalism, hedonism, and individualism. *Rationalism* reverses the thinking processes and avoids emotions and sentiments, as in business, which thrives on calculation and profit. *Hedonism* promotes a consumerist psychology or way of life, stressing instant gratification and pleasure. *Individualism* holds the individual to be more important than the community, state, society, or nation, which represents the collectivity. One could argue that American capitalist democracy manifests all these elements—rationalism, hedonism, and individualism.

Nations, Nationality, and Nationalism

Like the concept of state, the interrelated terms *nation, nationality,* and *nationalism* are complex and cannot be treated in depth in a few pages. However, the idea of the state cannot be properly understood without a general knowledge of these concepts.

Usually when social scientists speak of states, they mean nation-states. How is the idea of nation related to the concepts of nationality and of nationalism? Even within a particular country the ideas of nation and nationality are broader than the concept of state. How did the ideas of nation and state emerge? The concept of nation is sociological as opposed to the idea of state which is more of a legal, territorial, and political entity. A nation can be defined as a group of people who share a common identity, traditions, history, aspirations, interests, language, religion and culture. Although the primary definition of a nation refers to a political body of citizens whose collective sovereignty (power) manifests itself in a state, not all national groups express their political will in the state. For example, the Palestineans in what is now Israel are a nation, but they don't have a state fully recognized by other nation-states. In most instances a nation or people is linked to a territory, because the structure and definition of a state is essentially territorial (Hobsbawm, 1991:19).

Related to the concept of nation is the term ethnic group or ethnicity. In Greek ethnic or ethnos means nation. Broadly speaking, ethnic groups are social groups defined by nationality, race, religion, or a combination of the three (Gordon, 1964). According to this definition African Americans, Jewish Americans, and Greek Americans are all ethnic groups. More narrowly, however, our ethnic group is defined by culture and nationality; for example, Poles, Nigerians, and Koreans in the United States are ethnic groups that trace their national origins (nationality) to the modern nation-states of Poland, Nigeria, and Korea.

Nationalism or ethnonationalism is the notion that the "political and national unit should be congruent," which led to the idea of nation-state (Hobsbawm, 1991:10). Modern ethnonationalism is not a new phenomenon. It existed in the form of tribalism among primitive peoples. Tribalism evolved into the city-state among the ancient Greeks, who called it *polis,* or city or political community. The ideas of politics, policies, and political have their origin in this concept.

During the Middle Ages in the West (circa A.D. 400–1400), elements of nationalism persisted among people with similar languages, customs, and traditions; although primary allegiance was accorded to civil authorities (kings, lords) and powerful church authorities (bishops, the pope). The Roman Catholic church was the most dominant religious institution. As the monolithic structure of the church eroded, Christianity was split into Eastern Orthodox (also known as Byzantine) and Western Christianity (twelfth century), and later the Protestant Reformation sundered Western Christianity into Roman Catholics and Protestants. The political power of the Roman Catholic Church and the pope declined. Allegiance was transferred to the group identity of the people who occupied a particular territory. Over the years they developed a sense of community closely related to the land they occupied. They shared similar customs, traditions, languages—in a word, a culture. Out of this shared identity and claim to the same land came the notion of the nation-state.

During the sixteenth century, the break of Henry VIII from Rome and the subsequent establishment of a national church of England helped shape English nationalism. The civil strife between the king and Parliament in England increased the sentiment of nationalism as personified in the king, a symbol of unity and strength. During the English Revolution of 1688, the law became the foundation for English nationalism. In 1690 John Locke (1632–1704), the British empiricist and rationalist philosopher whose ideas influenced the founders of the United States (especially Thomas Jefferson, who wrote most of the Declaration of Independence), wrote *Two Treatises of Government*, in which he defended the ultimate sovereignty of the British people. In the same year, he promoted religious liberty in his *Letters on Toleration*.

During the Enlightenment, also known as the Age of Reason (eighteenth century), French philosophers denounced medieval feudalism and called for a new social order. Three French philosophers advocated major reforms. Baron Montesquieu (1689–1755) wrote *The Spirit of Laws*, in which he discussed the relationship between political and social structures, religion and economics. He also advocated love of country and a republican form of government. "In republics," he wrote, "education ought to inspire a sentiment, which is noble but hard to maintain, that disregard for one's own interest whence arises the love of one's country" (1899:31–33). Similarly, Jean-Jacques Rousseau (1712–1778), a French social and political philosopher, helped inspire the French Revolution (1779) by rejecting government by the aristocracy and favoring democracy as the guiding principle of a nation. He urged citizens to love their country and become conscious of their national identity. Voltaire (1694–1778), a French writer, criticized the bigotry and superstition of the Roman Catholic Church. He did much to promote separation between church and state in France, and he championed French nationalism. The revolution inspired by the ideas of the French philosophers in turn catalyzed the growth of nationalism and the emergence of nation-states in mid-nineteenth-century Europe.

Nationalism as an ideology or movement contributed to the emergence of nation-states. We can identify different types of nationalism—political, economic, cultural, and so on. Ethnic nationalism has surfaced prominently both in the former Soviet Union and the former Yugoslavia and has become a formidable force throughout the world in establishing nation-states. Although nationalism is a powerful ideology that can effectively unite people in a collective whole, at the same time it can be a curse; it has given rise to much misery and bloodshed in the twentieth century. In many respects the strife we witness in the former Yugoslavia and the Soviet republics stems from the reemergence of ethnocracies (a particular ethnic group's dominion over a region's government) that predated the Communist regimes.

Louis L. Snyder (1990) stated that nationalism is a two-edged sword; it can be a force for unity as well as for disruption, for independence and for fraternity, for colonial expansion and aggression, as well as anticolonialism and economic development. A driving force in world history, nationalism has helped to unite and liberate nations and peoples, but has often left upheaval and destruction in its wake.

Nationalism is a form of consciousness, an emotional attachment and loyalty to a nation. By consciousness, we mean a strong identity and awareness of a particular national history and culture. Nationalists believe in the destiny of their nation as a distinct entity, believing a nation to possess a natural right to self-determination and independence. It is very difficult to view with objective detachment a nation that one loves and identifies with. The sight of a nation's flag or the playing of its national anthem may evoke deep emotions.

More specifically, nationalism includes four different shades of meaning: nationalism as a sentiment, nationalism as an actual historical process, nationalism as a theory, and nationalism as an ideology of political activities. As a sentiment, nationalism is fed by romanticism, the notion that each nation has its unique place in history. The romantic idea, which started in Germany in the eighteenth century and spread to other countries, idealized the human heart and spirit of the people against the rationalism of the Enlightenment. It glorified the idea of the nation-state and national culture as an expression of deep attachment to a nation and culture. As a historical process, nationalism nourished and promoted the liberation movements that sparked the creation of independent nation-states. For example, in the mid-nineteenth century, especially following the French Revolution, Europe saw the establishment of a number of new nation-states; for example, Greece in 1830 gained its independence from the Ottoman Empire. Similar nationalist movements occurred in other parts of Europe, in Germany, Italy, Serbia, and so on. Theories about nationalism attempt to explain why some people and nations develop a high sense of national or ethnic identity, whereas others do not. Nationalism as an ideology of political activities employs myths, ideas, propaganda, and courses of action (tactics, strategies, goals) to mobilize support for the creation of a nation-state, such as that of Israel in 1948.

Carlton J. H. Hayes, a pioneer scholar, stipulated that nationalism has a dual nature: it can be either a good or an evil, a blessing or a curse. As a blessing, nationalism promotes the notion of freedom and independence from oppression and external domination. For example, the United States as a new nation independent from the domination of England was founded on liberty and self-determination, providing a model of nationalism that has been followed by many other nations.

Nationalism can also be an evil, promoting an ideology of intolerance toward people of different cultures, races, religions, or nationalities. In this context Hayes (in Snyder, 1990:133) stipulates five major evils or abuses associated with nationalism: (1) The idea of *exclusivity* promoting the notion of a "chosen people" that prevents other groups from sharing the resources of society. Nationalism can emphasize uniformity at the expense of diversity. For example, previous U.S. immigration policies pressured all immigrants to assimilate to an Anglo-Saxon model of behavior and give up their own cultural values. (2) Nationalism can foster docility, obedience, and suppression of a critical attitude, beginning this indoctrination in the schools. The masses will seldom question the providential nature of their nationality, their state, their government. (3) Nationalism can exalt heroic, militaristic, and wartime values in society at the expense of the arts, sciences, and education. (4) Nationalism can encourage jingoism, an extreme form of chauvinism, by adopting an aggressive and warlike foreign policy. (5) Nationalism can also promote a policy of territorial expansionism involving acquisition of foreign land, out of intolerance for people having different beliefs and ideas, and a greed justified by exhancing the nation's glory.

The Modern Nation-State

The term *state* refers to the centralized form of civil rule that emerged in Europe beginning in the sixteenth century. This model has been imitated by most other peoples in the modern world. The modern European state system developed gradually. Niccolò Machiavelli's *The Prince* (1513), Jean Bodin's *Six Books on the Republic* (1606), Thomas Hobbes's *Leviathan* (1651), John Locke's *Two Treatises on Government* (published after the British revolution of 1688), Jean-Jacques Rousseau's *Social Contract* (1762), Baron Montesquieu's *The Spirit of Laws* (1748), and Georg Hegel's *Philosophy of Right* (1821) all dealt with the issues of state, order, law, civil authority, sovereignty, and the republic, and they influenced the development of nation-states such as the United States.

The origin of a specific state is defined both with respect to territory and the people (nation) who occupy it. A state originates through a process of institutional differentiation; it may evolve through an internal process along with the society's other social institutions, or through forces external to the society. In practice, these two patterns need not be mutually exclusive. Typically, a stateless society becomes a state in a process that begins in military conquest or external force (e.g., the creation of the United States through domination of the Native American population by European settlers). Initially, conquerors define the nascent state as a territory. Following conquest, the history of the new state begins, its territory identified with its corresponding society. The militarily and politically dominant group progressively extends its control and consolidation of people and resources, using symbols of nationalism such as flags, national anthems, ideologies, and myths to manipulate the populace. The civil administration and military arm of the state controls the territory and the people.

The process of democratization, which sometimes follows the consolidation of a state, involves three principles: sovereignty, bureaucratization, and rationalization. *Sovereignty* refers to the exercise of political and moral authority, of supreme power, by a people, a ruler, a class, a king, or even a deity. Throughout most of history, sovereignty has been vested in kings, gods, rulers, and aristocratic classes (Bendix, 1978); only recently did the notion of sovereignty emerge as embodied in the power of the people. *Bureaucratization* is a form of organization based on a hierarchy of offices and administrators guided by rules, regulations, and a system of reward and punishment. *Rationalization* in political structures refers to a system of consistent rules for arbitrary decisions of erratic rulers. Organizational structures means greater standardization, consistency, and coordination of a system of means and ends

(Theodorson and Theodorson, 1969:335–336). In modern times, most nation-states are based on these principles. Every nation-state is sovereign, which means it is independent and has control and authority over its own territory and the people residing within it.

To understand the nature of the modern nation-state, one has to examine the historical absolutist state, which was its antecedent. Absolutism means unlimited authority and control (or despotism). Absolutism informed the type of monarchy achieved under Louis XIV (1638–1715), king of France and the prototype of the absolute monarch, whose position entailed unlimited political authority. As a form of state power, absolutism is related to the concepts of *autocracy* (power in the hands of one person), *despotism* (ruler with unlimited power), and *totalitarianism.* Absolutism colored the monarchies of northern and western Europe in the seventeenth and eighteenth centuries.

In an effort to "bring the state back in" as the major focus in political sociology, a number of social scientists have focused on the nature of state formation and elite conflict among the nobility, the monarch, and the clergy as the major contenders for state authority in seventeenth-century England and France. Michael Kimmel (1986:54–74), for example, found that absolutism characterized a transitional state, or a state in crisis. The unlimited authority of kings and their officials, though the official stance of the state, was often severely challenged by local landlords and the clergy. Likewise, Richard Lachmann (1989:141) found that conflicts among three principal elites—the clergy, monarchs and their officials, and lay landlords—shaped the development of various absolutist states in Europe in the sixteenth and seventeenth centuries.

Those having a Marxist orientation view the absolutist state as a feudal state designed to perpetuate feudal class domination (Anderson, 1974:11). Feudalism was a system of landlord–serf relationships in which the landowner, known as the lord, gave his serfs (peasants) land to cultivate in return for the serfs' loyalty and their work on his land. Cösta-Esping Anderson emphasized class struggles between nobles and peasants and the aristocratic nature of the absolutist state. Lachmann (1989:143) contended that Marx and Engels viewed the absolutist state not as an instrument of noble class rule, as Anderson believed, but as an artifact of the nobility's loss of hegemony. In other words, the absolutist state was created by the noble class because it had lost the power and prestige it held in the past.

State theorists view the development of the absolutist state as essentially autonomous and independent of social class. According to this view, the absolutist state arose as the bourgeoisie (the middle class) arose. The state increased its power to prevent and neutralize class conflict. Michael Kimmel (1986:57), Michael Mann (1990), and C. Tilly (1981) viewed state formation as a process, and Richard Lachmann (1989:144) held that the bourgeoisie was a by-product of state formation. State formation as a process means here that the creation of the state as a political institution followed a series of steps and circumstances. Its final formation and legitimization was gradual. In this process of state formation the armed forces played a pivotal role in nation building. For example, the state of Israel without the contribution of its armed forces will be unthinkable. Still another group (Nicos Poulantzas, 1975;

Wallerstein, 1974) understood the absolutist state to be the first capitalist state. Immanuel Wallerstein, for example, argued that the capitalist world economy emerged in the mid-sixteenth century and consolidated itself during the seventeenth century through the absolute monarchy—in short, the Western absolutist state provided the legal and political framework for the development of both the modern nation-state and capitalism. In short, different theorists advance different perspectives concerning the emergence of the modern state. There are those who traced its emergence in the historical development of the absolutist state in the monarchies of northwestern Europe in the seventeenth and eighteenth centuries. There are those with Marxist orientation who viewed the absolutist state as a continuation of feudal class domination created by the noble class as an artifact due to the nobility's loss of hegemony. There are still others who viewed the development of the absolutist state as an autonomous process independent of class influence. Finally, there is another group who explain the absolutist state as the first capitalist state.

However, the various positions just outlined capture only part of the truth. Some find an identity of class and state interests. This means that the state serves the economic interests of capitalist class which is the Marxist position. Some link the state and international economy, and some deny the class character of the state altogether (Kimmel, 1986:58). Others view military and war as the primary causal factors in the emergence and expansion of nation-states, including the contemporary liberal constitutional states.

The Liberal Constitutional State

The liberal constitutional state resembles the present capitalist democratic state. It emerged out of the absolutist state, following the French Revolution. Two key elements characterize a liberal capitalist, constitutional state: (1) a centralized monopoly over its territory, which can be defended through the use of force, and (2) legitimation of authority over that territory based not on hereditary or traditional claims but on legal or bureaucratic authority, which embodies the accepted relationship between the rulers and the ruled. Consent of the governed is of paramount importance. Citizens are accorded civic, political, and social rights that give them a voice in the legitimation of the state; they form an important, broad part of the political community. We will discuss this more later.

The liberal constitutional state is characterized by a written constitution, which spells out principles that define the roles of both the rulers and the ruled, including obedience of the citizens to the rule of law and authorities of the state. In liberal states many organs of civil society have established authority, including self-rule. A liberal constitutional state has a unified sovereignty and control of its own territory, including single monetary currency, a unified legal system, a multiparty political system, a state educational system, and a single national language (though some states have more than one national language). Switzerland, in central Europe, is a confederation of three nationalities, each with its own language: French, German, and Italian; all three languages are equal and national in scope. Educational systems vary in the extent to which they are centralized. For example, the United States has a decentralized, locally oriented educational system, whereas most European countries have a more centralized, state-regulated educational system. The legal systems of liberal constitution states also vary in scope and complexity. The U.S. legal system is more diverse and complicated than those of most other countries; one state in the U.S. may permit capital punishment, whereas another may not. This is not the case in most European nation-states (Poggi, 1978:108–112).

Roger King (1986:53) outlined a number of distinctive attributes of a liberal constitutional state, the first of which is civility. First, a liberal constitutional state represses crimes committed internally and externally through a discursive, national, and peaceable (rather than brutal) means of punishment. For example, the military and police are subordinate to civil authority—this is not the case in an authoritarian dictatorial state. The second attribute is pluralism; there is no centralized absolute authority, even in a state. The liberal constitutional state consists of many different offices and agencies having distinct scopes and functions. Third, this type of state is open-ended. No single political party has a monopoly of state power. Politics is a continuous process, and the character of state power changes, depending on which political party holds sway. The fourth attribute, controversy, shows that in liberal democratic, constitutional states, people may freely express their opinions and disagreements on various issues and criticize the legislative, executive, and judiciary branches of government. Finally, the most salient feature of liberal constitutional states is the presence of representative institutions, such as parliamentary assemblies and congresses.

The Role Expansion and Functions of the State

Over time, the jurisdiction and functions of the states in the West have increased. More and more social domains, such as national health, social security, workers' compensation, and welfare benefits for the poor, have been assumed by the state. Most Western capitalist states are welfare states, in addition to fulfilling their more traditional roles and functions. Michael Mann (1993:320) distinguished four major state functions: (1) maintenance of internal order, (2) military defense and aggression (directed against foreign foes), (3) maintenance of communications infrastructures, and (4) economic redistribution of societal resources.

Maintenance of internal order means that modern nation-states are responsible for internal peace, protecting the state from individuals and groups that want to destroy it or overthrow the government. A large portion of the state budget is spent on military matériel and activities, including intelligence gathering and spying. One of the most important functions of the modern state is to defend its territory and to undertake aggressive military operations against any hostile nation-state. The armed forces are essential in this regard, and their role is pivotal in nation building, especially in newly emerging nations. Modern nation-states are also responsible for construction and maintenance of domestic infrastructure, such as roads, bridges, highways, communications, and transportation networks. A large amount of the tax revenues are spent on domestic projects. Finally, the state levies taxes to pay for its welfare role, redistributing economic and societal resources to various communities and groups. Many people view the state's welfare function as its moral responsibility to help the poor, the unemployed, and the underemployed. For example, in the United States, President Franklin D. Roosevelt's New Deal, President Harry S Truman's Fair Deal, President John F. Kennedy's New Frontier, and President Lyndon B. Johnson's Great Society included welfare programs to alleviate the social problems of American society and help the less fortunate classes. Many poor people in the United States depend on public assistance, state employment, and welfare. At present the welfare system has been attacked by many citizens and legislators who believe that it creates a counterproductive dependency for those it was originally designed to assist. Even the large military establishment is seen by some as a welfare institution, a vehicle of social mobility for racial minorities and the less fortunate. The extension of civil and political rights to all classes—including women, blue-collar workers, and African Americans—in the United States and elsewhere in the past two centuries was a state-directed activity. This means that the government through the legislative or executive process broadened the rights of its citizens. The welfare system that was introduced during the Great Depression and benefitted the weaker classes was a state-directed activity. In most countries in Europe, Latin America, and elsewhere, the government and state bureaucracies are the largest employers.

Interpretations and Theories of the Modern Nation-State

As we mentioned previously in this chapter, social scientists have viewed the emergence of states as the result of both internal and external forces. A number of explanations begin with the functionalist argument, which holds that states emerge from an internal evolution, or differentiation of societies. By differentiation of societies is meant that societies are internally undergoing a process of evolution or division of labor from a more amorphous and simple social structures to more differentiated and complex ones. States like societies are also products of the same evolutionary process. Talcott Parsons (1966) believed that states are products of the evolution of societal division of labor. The state as a more powerful political institution has the authority to maintain order in society, set the national goals, protect the citizens, and provide the leadership for the nation. The idea of the state as part of political institutions is a somewhat recent development. Historically, states emerged later than nations. For a long time there was no distinction between society and the state. It was only during the mid-nineteenth century that modern nations and states, or nation-states, emerged in western Europe. At present, the concept of independent nation, which, as of the end of the Cold War in 1989, has been adopted by most countries, is considered the only viable political entity by most of the world.

The present transition in political sociology from the society-centered to the state-centered approach has been a centerpiece debate. Those who take a state-centered approach to governmental policies and power view the state as an autonomous political institution (Block, 1993; Mann, 1993; Nordlinger, 1981; Skocpol, 1979, 1993) that can act independently of pressures and influences from various social groups—including social classes, ethnic and racial groups, and interest groups—in shaping social and economic policies. The study by Peter R. Evans et al. (1985), for example, points out that states are autonomous actors capable of making decisions independent of social classes.

Others contend that although the state-centered advocates have made important contributions, they have ignored the social nature of state institutions and policy makers (Gilbert and Howe, 1991:218). Those who take a society-centered approach view the state as shaped by various social forces including social classes, as well as ethnic, religious, and economic interest groups. Society-centered ways of explaining politics and governmental policies characterized the pluralist and structural-functionalist perspectives of the 1950s and 1960s. Robert Dahl (1961), for example, examined how pluralist democracy functions in New Haven, Connecticut, by looking at conflict and consent and the influence of the individual in a pluralist democracy in the United States. He found that the mayor was the key actor in New Haven.

One could argue that the state-centered versus society-centered debate has failed to capture the dynamic interplay between the state and societal forces in shaping public policies. The state is not a separate entity but a part of the larger society and social system. A number of political sociologists suggest that we must go beyond the dualism of the state versus society controversy and focus on the dynamics of the relationship. A similar approach has been taken by political sociologist William Domhoff (1990), who looks at the interplay between the state and the power elite, including the leadership segment of the governing class, in shaping public policies. Using an expanded version of C. Wright Mills's power elite thesis and drawing from Mann's (1988) four overlapping networks of ideological, economic, military, and political dimensions of public policies, Domhoff (in his book the *Power Elite and the State*, 1990) explained how and why coalitions within the power elite, along with the state, shape national policies. Domhoff (1990:38) strongly states that the upper class has a fundamental interest in maintaining state control and power. In his 1996 book Domhoff provides the most thorough critique to date of state autonomy theory by demonstrating its weaknesses in the case of the U.S. Utilizing new arguments and new archival material, he challenges every case study conducted by the advocates of state autonomy theory and reaffirms the political power exercised by ecomonic elites.

Domhoff offered an explanation of the way coalitions are formed within the power elite who supported state policies such as the Social Security Act of 1935, the National Labor Relations Act of 1935, and the Employment Act of 1946, which were passed even against the opposition of every major corporation. He explained how experts worked closely with the power elite in shaping economic policies. The Social Security Act was introduced by President Franklin Roosevelt and his labor secretary, Frances Perkins. It was one of the most important New Deal programs enacted during the Great Depression, eventually providing old age pensions. According to Domhoff, the formulation of the Social Security Act of 1935 was developed with the assistance of academic experts who worked as mediators between capital and labor. With the assistance of the academic experts, the moderate members of the power elite such as the American Association for Labor legislation, and Congress reached a compromise that became the Social Security Act (Domhoff, 1990:30–31). Similar acts were enacted about this time or later. The National Labor Relations Act of 1935 (also known as the Wagner Act, after its major sponsor, Senator Robert F. Wagner of New York [Domhoff, 1990:65]) dealt with legislation establishing collective bargaining over wages, hours, and working conditions for the American Federation of Labor. The basic idea of the Employment Act of 1946 was not to ensure full employment but to enable the federal government to create demand and make investments. The business community had to cooperate with the government to provide full employment.

To understand modern capitalist states, a number of social scientists and political sociologists have employed interpretations and political sociology models similar to those discussed in Chapter 2. Robert R. Alford (1993:258–67), for example, has articulated three major paradigms of the state–society relationship (pluralist, elite, and class) and their three corresponding and pathological images. Each paradigm offers both a utopian and a pathological image of the state–society nexus, and each has both empirical and normative, or ideological, aspects. According to Alford (1993:260), the utopian image of the pluralist paradigm is "pluralist democracy," and its pathological or degenerate form is "mass society," referring to the breakdown of the individual's identity and ability to communicate. Similarly, the elite model has its utopian and pathological images. In its utopian image, the state is viewed as a planned society; societal elites are not pressured to fulfill short-term demands but take time for long-term, rational planning and development of societal resources. The pathological image of the elite model is totalitarianism in which the elites become manipulators of public opinion to maintain control and use state organizations to secure personal advantages and power. According to Alford, the best way to guard against the rise of the totalitarian elite model is to encourage a system of elite competition. The absence of elite competition in Nazi Germany led to the rise of the totalitarian Nazi elite. The class paradigm also has a utopian and pathological image of the state–society relationship. The utopian image is anarchism, no rule at all, or a lack of strong government; its pathological image is fascism. In the latter case, the ruling class no longer submits to electoral politics and resorts to repression of dissent (Alford, 1993:262).

Neo-Marxist Theories of the Capitalist State

The most important interpretations of the capitalist state in the last twenty years have been those advanced by neo-Marxists.[3] The term *neo-Marxist* refers to the subschool within Marxism that is trying to rectify the failure of classical Marxism to explain the role of the state in modern capitalist society. Both the Marxists and neo-Marxists accept the fact that there is a ruling class, which serves the interests of the capitalist class. This view has been challenged by Fred Block (1993:295–305), who argued that the ruling class does not necessarily rule. Block maintained that state managers maintain the viability of the social order by fostering a balanced relationship among capitalists, workers, and themselves (Block, 1993:305). By contrast, almost all neo-Marxist interpretations have adopted a society-centered approach by looking at the relationship of modern states and the capitalist mode of production. They stress the role of the ruling capitalist class in using the machinery of the state to advance its own economic and class interests.

All neo-Marxists attempt to answer two complementary questions: (1) why does the state serve the interests of the capitalist class? and (2) how does the state operate to maintain and indeed expand the capitalist system? (Gold et al., 1975:31–32). Though a greater diversity of neo-Marxist perspectives exists, we will discuss the responses to these questions according to only two neo-Marxist models of the state: the structuralist and the instrumentalist.

The Structuralist View

The structuralist perspective is associated with the work of Nicos Poulantzas, a Greek-born neo-Marxist theorist of the 1970s who lived in France. His view of the state was based on the notion that the structures of society and the state are more important than the people who actually occupy the structural positions of society and the state. In other words, the structuralist argument purports that the ruling capitalist class does not have to rule directly as long as the state functions in a way that serves their interests. Here is how Poulantzas articulated that perspective:

> *The direct participation of members of the capitalist class in the state apparatus and in the government, even where it exists, is not the important side of the matter. The relation between the bourgeois class and the state is an objective relation. This means that if the function of the state in a determinate social formation and the interests of the dominant class in this formation coincide, it is by reason of the system itself: the direct participation of members of the ruling class in the state apparatus is not the cause but the effect, and moreover a chance and contingent one, of this objective coincidence. (Poulantzas, 1969:73–74)*

Because the functions of the capitalist state are broadly determined by the structures of the society rather than by the people who occupy positions of state power (Gold et al., 1993:271), the capitalist ruling class does not have to rule directly because the capitalist state from its inception serves the economic interests of the capitalist class. Three additional structuralist interpretations of the state were offered by David Knoke (1990), Göran Therborn (1978:34–35), and H. T. Wright (1977). Therborn showed how state policies produce and reproduce class interests and agreed with Poulantzas concerning the role of ideology in maintaining the hegemony, or the dominance and power, of the ruling class.

The Instrumentalist View

In contrast to the structuralist view, the instrumentalist interpretation of the state, associated with the work of Ralph Miliband (1969), views the state and the government as instruments manipulated by the capitalist ruling class. Miliband's instrumentalist position is based on the notion that a capitalist class occupies the interior positions of the state government, and personal ties bind members of the ruling class to those of the state apparatus. A similar position was advocated by C. Wright Mills (1956). Both Mills and Miliband drew heavily from Max Weber's views on the state. Miliband's first paragraph in his book *The State in Capitalist Society* (1969) echoes the general tenor of Weber's remarks.

> *More than ever before men now live in the shadow of the state, what they want to achieve, individually or in groups, now mainly depends on the state's sanction and support. But since that sanction and support are not bestowed indiscriminately, they must, ever more directly, seek to influence and shape the state's power and purpose, or try and appropriate it altogether. It is for the state's attention, or for its control, that men compete; and it is against the state that beat the waves of social conflict. It is to an ever greater degree the state which men encounter as they confront other men. (Miliband, 1969:1)*

In other words, Miliband viewed individuals, not positions or structures, as manipulating the state; these individuals, according to the instrumentalists, serve the interests of the capitalist class.

In general, the neo-Marxist instrumentalists believe that capitalists rule the state indirectly by manipulating or influencing political officials and dominant institutions, including the state itself. Instrumentalists think that the class interests of the capitalist class are maintained through the influence of political action committees (PACs) or lobbying, conspiracy, control and ownership of mass media, and the like. Although the instrumentalists stress the manipulation of the government by the capitalist ruling class, they seem, however, to lack in-depth analyses of the strategies and actions used by ruling class groups. Furthermore, despite their claim, not all government-initiated programs and policies—including, for example, cultural activities and social programs—are necessarily controlled by the capitalist class. To overcome some of the deficiencies of the structuralist and instrumentalist interpretations of the capitalist state, a number of Marxist political economists have suggested new approaches, which we cannot discuss here in detail.[4]

Summary and Conclusion

In this chapter the nature and importance of the concepts of nation and state and their relationship were discussed. (1) the nature and role of the modern nation state system including the different elements making up the state power system, forms, and varieties of government were defined. (2) An analysis of the concepts of nation, nationality, ethnicity, and nationalism and their relationship to each other and to the emergence of modern nation-state were also examined. (3) The development, expansion, and various types, and interpretations of modern nation-states were delineated.

More specifically an effort was made to give a comprehensive overview and development of the complex ideas of modern nation-states. It was argued that the concepts of nation, nationality, and nationalism are fairly new and are associated with the notion of state. While the concepts of nations and nationalities are sociological in nature, the concepts of states is political, legal, and territorial. Nationalism was considered as a sentiment, a theory, an ideology, and a history. It is nationalism that gave way to the notion of nation-state. Historically, city-states gave way to empires which in turn gave way to nation-states. Sovereignty, authority, central-tion, bureaucratization, and rationalization were essential processes in the emergence and development of modern nation-states.

Modern capitalist states were evolved from absolutist states of western Europe in the seventeenth and eighteenth centuries. The French Revolution, Enlightenment, and industrial revolutions of the nineteenth century contributed to the emergence and consolidation of modern nation-states. Two of the neo-Marxist theories of the capitalist state were discussed: the structuralist and instrumentalist. The former stresses the capitalist structures of the state as more important while the latter emphasizes the individuals who occupy these structures as more important in running the state.

Endnotes

1. The FBI is a government agency responsible for collecting information concerning domestic issues, groups, or individuals; the CIA deals with foreign intelligence, which the government collects to protect national interests; assemblies and parliaments are similar to the U.S. Congress. In a parliamentary system, voters elect the president and the representatives from different political parties directly, without primaries. A prime minister is the elected leader of the governing party.

2. Communism, Fascism, and Nazism are totalitarian systems of government. Communism is an applied form of Marxism that emerged in Russia after the Bolshevik Revolution in 1917. Communism was adopted in China in 1949, North Korea in 1953, and Cuba in 1959. The Soviet version of Communism collapsed in 1989, which led to the liberation of Eastern Europe from Soviet Communist domination and the end of the Cold War between the United States and the Soviet Union. Fascism emerged in Italy, Nazism in Germany, and in Japan during the 1930s and 1940s. In World War II, the combined Western powers fought against the Axis powers (Germany, Italy, and their allies) and defeated them. The Allies then imposed democracy on Italy, Germany, and Japan.

3. A sampling of the most important neo-Marxist works on the role of the capitalist state in modern societies includes those of Gösta-Esping Anderson et al. (1976), Ralph Miliband (1969), Claus Offe (1974), Nicos Poulantzas (1969), Göran Therborn (1978), and Immanual Wallerstein, (vols. 1 and 2; 1974, 1980). For non-Marxist interpretations and historical treatises of the state, see R. Bendix (1978), K. Dyson (1980), George A. Kourvetaris (1990), Giafranco Poggi (1991), and R. G. Wesson (1978).

Excellent overviews of the neo-Marxist debates include those of Martin Cannoy (1984), David A. Gold et al. (1975), Bob Jessop (1977; 1982), and Ralph Miliband (1977).

4. One such neo-Marxist approach is offered by James O'Connor, who distinguished three main categories of spending by the state: social expenses (e.g., welfare—see Jack Douglas [1989] on the role of the welfare state), social investment (e.g., land clearance and transport systems), and social consumption (e.g., social insurance). The first item serves to keep peace; that is, it is the cost of legitimation. The second is more profitable, and the third lowers the costs of labor. In this approach, where would public education or social welfare fit in? It is difficult to say.

References

Ard, Robert R. 1993. "Paradigms of Relations Between State and Society." In *Power in Societies*, ed. Marvin E. Olsen and Martin N. Marer. Boulder, CO: Westview Press.

Alford, Robert R., and Roger Friedland. 1985. *Powers of Theory: Capitalism, the State, and Democracy*. Cambridge: Cambridge Univ. Press.

Anderson, Cösta-Esping, Roger Friedland, and Erik Olin Wright. 1976. "Modes of Class Struggle and the Capitalist State." *Kapitalistate.* Nos. 4–5.

Anderson, P. 1974. *Lineages of the Absolutist State.* London: New Left Books.

Barker, Earnest. 1961. *The Politics of Aristotle.* Oxford: Clarendon.

Bendix, R. 1978. *Kings or People: Power and the Mandate to Rule.* Berkeley: Univ. of Calif. Press.

Block, Fred. 1993. "The Ruling Class Does Not Rule." In *Power in Modern Societies,* ed. Marvin E. Olsen and Martin N. Marger. Boulder, CO: Westview Press.

Cannoy, Martin. 1984. *The State and Political Theory.* Princeton: Princeton Univ. Press.

Dahl, Robert. 1961. *Who Governs?* New Haven: Yale University Press.

Domhoff, William. 1990. *The Power Elite and the State.* New York: Aldine DeGruyter.

———. 1996. *State Autonomy or Class Dominance?: Case Studies on Policy Making in America.* Hawthorne, N.Y.: Aldine de Gruyter.

Douglas, Jack D. 1989. *The Myth of the Welfare State Theory.* New Brunswick: Transaction.

Dyson, K. 1980. *The State Tradition in Western Europe.* New York: Oxford Univ. Press.

Evans, Peter R., Dietrich Rueschemeyer, and Theda Skocpol, eds. 1985. *Bringing the State Back In.* Cambridge: Cambridge Univ. Press.

Friedrich, Carl J., Michael Curtis, and Benjamin R. Barber. 1969. *Totalitarianism in Perspective: Three Views.* New York: Praeger.

Gerth, H. H., and C. W. Mills, eds. 1958. *From Max Weber: Essays in Sociology.* New York: Oxford Univ. Press.

Gilbert, Jess, and Carolyn Howe. 1991. "Beyond State vs. Society: Theories of the State and New Deal Agricultural Policies." *American Sociological Review.* Vol. 56 (April):205–20.

Gilbert, Neil, and Barbara Gilbert. 1989. *The Enabling State: Modern Welfare Capitalism in America.* New York: Oxford Univ. Press.

Gold, D. A., C. Lo, and E. O. Wright. 1975. "Recent Developments in Marxist Theories of the Capitalist State." *Monthly Review.* Vol. 27, no. 5:29–43.

Gordon, Milton. 1964. *Assimilation in American Life: The Role of Race, Religion and National Origin.* New York: Oxford Univ. Press.

Hobsbawm, E. J. 1991. *Nations and Nationalism Since 1780.* New York: Cambridge Univ. Press.

Huntington, Samuel P. 1991. *The Third Wave: Democratization in the Late Twentieth Century.* Norman and London: Univ. of Oklahoma Press.

Jessop, Bob. 1982. *The Capitalist State.* New York: New York Univ. Press.

———. 1977. "Recent Theories of the Capitalist State." *Cambridge Journal of Economics.* Vol. 1:353–73.

Kimmel, Michael. 1986. "The Ambivalence of Absolutism: State and Nobility in 17th-Century France and England." *Journal of Political and Military Sociology.* Vol. 14, no. 1 (summer):55–74.

King, Roger. 1986. *The State in Modern Society: New Directions in Political Sociology.* Old Greenwich, CT: Chatham House.

Knoke, David. 1990. *Political Networks: The Structural Perspective.* Cambridge: Cambridge Univ. Press.

Kourvetaris, George A. 1990. "On Power and the State." *Journal of Political and Military Sociology.* Vol. 18, no. 2 (winter):343–53.

Lachmann, Richard. 1989. "Elite Conflict and State Formation in the 16th and 17th Centuries." *American Sociology Review.* Vol. 54 (April): 141–62.

Mann, Michael. 1993. "The Autonomous Power of the State." In *Power in Modern Societies,* ed. Marvin E. Olsen and Martin N. Marger. Boulder, CO: Westview Press.

———, ed. 1990. *The Rise and Decline of the Nation State.* Cambridge, Mass: Basil Blackwell.

———. 1988. *States, War, and Capitalism: Studies in Political Sociology.* Oxford, England and New York: Basil Blackwell.

Miliband, Ralph. 1969. *The State in Capitalist Society.* New York: Basic Books.

———. 1993. "The State System and the State Elite." In *Power in Societies,* ed. Marvin E. Olsen and Martin N. Marger. Boulder, CO: Westview Press.

Mills, C. Wright. 1956. *The Power Elite.* New York: Oxford Univ. Press.

Montesquieu, De Baron. 1899. *The Spirit of Law* (published originally in 1748). New York: T' Colonial Press.

Nordlinger, Eric. 1981. *On the Autonomy of the Democratic State.* Cambridge, MA: Harvard Univ. Press.

O'Connor, James. 1973. *The Fiscal Crisis of the State.* New York: St. Martin's Press.

Offe, Claus. 1974. "Structural Problems of the Capitalist State." *German Political Studies.* Vol. 1:31–57.

Parenti, Michael. 1995. *Democracy for the Few,* 6th ed. New York: St. Martin's Press.

Parsons, Talcott. 1966. *Societies: Evolutionary and Comparative Perspectives.* Englewood Cliffs, NJ: Prentice Hall.

Poggi, Giafranco. 1978. *The Development of the Modern State.* London: Hutchinson.

———. 1991. *The State: Its Nature, Development and Prospects.* Stanford: Stanford Univ. Press.

Poulantzas, Nicos. 1975. *Classes in Contemporary Capitalism.* London: New Left Books.

———. 1969. "The Problem of the Capitalist State." *New Left Review.* No. 58:67–78.

Redner, Harry. 1990. "Beyond Marx-Weber: A Diversified and International Approach to the State." *Political Studies.* Vol. 308:638–53.

Skocpol, Theda. 1993. "The Potential Autonomy of the State." In *Power in Modern Societies,* ed.

Marvin E. Olsen and Martin N. Marger. Boulder, CO: Westview Press.

———. 1979. *States and Social Revolutions.* Cambridge: Cambridge Univ. Press.

Snyder, Louis L. 1990. *Encyclopedia of Nationalism.* New York: Paragon House.

Theodorson, George and Achilles G. Theodorson. 1969. *Modern Dictionary of Sociology.* New York: Thomas Y. Crowell Co.

Therborn, Göran. 1978. *What Does the Ruling Class Do When it Rules?* New York: Schocken.

Tilly, C., ed. 1981. *The Formation of National States in Western Europe.* Princeton: Princeton Univ. Press.

Wallerstein, Immanuel. 1974. *The Modern World System: Capitalist Agriculture and the Origins of the European World Economy in the Sixteenth Century.* New York: Academic.

Wesson, R. G. 1978. *State Systems: International Pluralism, Politics, and Culture.* New York: The Free Press.

Wolfe, Alan. 1978. *The Seamy Side of Democracy: Repression in America.* New York: Longman.

Wright, H. T. 1977. "Recent Research on the Origin of the State." *Annual Review of Anthropology.* Vol. 6:379–97.

Structure and Behavior of U.S. Elites

The study of elites and ruling classes has been of sustained interest to social scientists. Because of their strategic positions in the various social and political structures of U.S. society, elites usually exercise disproportionate power. This exercise of power has had far-reaching consequences in society and the polity. The study of elites and ruling classes has been rather controversial, especially since the power conflict perspective of the 1960s challenged the earlier dominant functionalist view. Political sociologists and social scientists have focused on power structure theories and to some extent, research in their approach to this topic.

Despite a high level of interest in empirical studies concerning elites, the amount of research undertaken has been slim. Perhaps this absence of sophisticated theoretical and empirical studies in elite power structures can be explained by these factors: First, power elite and ruling class subjects are generally inaccessible to social scientists. Second, elite and ruling class analyses are controversial in U.S. society because of its widespread emphasis on the ideology of egalitarianism; recognizing and focusing on the existence and influence of elites runs counter to the sense that we are all equals in U.S. society. Because these studies are not, to use a buzzword, "politically correct," many researchers shy away from them. Despite these constraints, empirical research continues, and the literature in this area has grown substantially in recent years.

Following in the footsteps of C. Wright Mills's power elite thesis and Robert Dahl's "pluralist school," a debate continues between those who take a critical view and those who take a functional view of U.S. society and politics. Those who subscribe to the former view are more likely to have a sociological orientation, whereas those who adhere to the latter view are more likely to have a political science background.

In general, there are three views of elites: the traditional view holds that elites meet a crucial need because of their special talents; a recent view sees them as influential figures in the institutional structure of society, fulfilling leadership and decision-making roles; and a third perspective calls them self-serving individuals, contemptuous of the masses and manipulators of public opinion. The functionalist perspective defines elites in terms of certain orientations and tasks. It classifies elites according to: (1) *Aims* or the objectives and goals elites pursue (oligarchic or modernizing elites). For example, during the 1960s military elites carried out numerous military coups and countercoups in Third World countries with the goal of modernizing their societies. The aims of elites are not always achieved: the majority of these military coups did not succeed. (2) *Style*. Elites may use innovative ideas and programs to bring about a change in society and politics. For example, President Bill Clinton in 1993 initiated a national service project, asking students to volunteer for a period of two years in domestic projects in return for federal student loans toward their college education. Style also refers to the way leaders convey messages to the people. Presidents, for example, usually use public relations experts and speech-writers to shape their images and messages. (3) *Institutional domain*. Elites located in institutions and various bureaucracies are called institutional elites. Suzanne Keller described them as "strategic elites"; because of the key positions they occupy, institutional elites usually make decisions that exert much influence on society and the polity. (4) *Resources*. Elites command tremendous resources, such as financial, media, people, knowledge, status, and other forms of social power. (5) *Decisional*. Elites plan and carry out projects and implement decisions (Kuper and Kuper, 1985). As they perform functions and decisions that are essential to society and polity, they also perpetuate and reflect their class's dominance in areas such as culture, religion, education, science, management, and so on.

Certain issues are common to all elites and ruling classes, both past and present. In this chapter, we will analyze a number of these issues by answering the following questions: (1) Is there an inevitability of elites? (2) How are elites recruited? (3) Is there a social cohesiveness of elites? (4) Is there a variability of elites? (5) What is the profile of elites in the United States? (6) What is the socialization and education of elites?

The Inevitability of Elites

Those who occupy top positions in a given society are always a minority that, as a rule, exercises more power than the majority. This minority is known by different names: elites, ruling classes, governing elites, upper classes, power elites, and so on. The rest of society has little power by comparison. Between the two extremes are the middle strata who maintain a balance between those on the top and those on the bottom. The middle class provides stability and the venue for social mobility (which many would state is an illusion).

Elites and ruling classes are constant phenomena in history and society. In his *Republic*, Plato called for "philosopher kings," an elite or ruling class that by birth and superior training would rule society wisely by stressing the "common good" of the city-state rather than the "private good of the ruling class." Likewise, Machiavelli argued for a strong ruler who must be feared, rather than loved, by his subjects. Machiavelli separated politics from ethics, maintaining that the "end justifies the means." He insisted that a ruler can use all means available in order to maintain power, including lies, murder, manipulation, cunning, fear, strength, or what he called the "lion and fox" ways. He also saw rulers as superior by nature and, therefore, entitled to rule. Pareto, Michels, and Mosca saw elites as inevitable and indispensable. Pareto spoke of history as the "graveyard of aristocracies." Mosca coined the term "the ruling class" and pointed out that those who rule are always the few, whereas those who are ruled are always the many. Michels introduced the "iron law of oligarchy," the tendency of any organization to be run by a small group, which by its very nature is undemocratic.

Functional elite analysts perceive elites and ruling classes as inevitable and superior by nature. They view them as inevitable because of their natural superiority and indispensable for any directed political and social change in society. Similarly, functionalists see social stratification or hierarchical ranking of positions as inevitable and necessary for social order in society and politics. They tend to be more pragmatic, likely to stress the power of the state, law, and order. The functionalists view the masses as untrustworthy and inconsistent, therefore incapable of initiating any substantive change in society and politics.

In contrast to the functionalist view, the power conflict and radical elite analysts tend to be more critical of elites. They point to the inherent undemocratic and oligarchic tendencies of elites by arguing that elites are more interested in power positions than in the common good. Those who espouse the conflict perspective do not believe in the inevitability of elites, nor do they perceive the masses as untrustworthy, incapable, and inconsistent. Furthermore, they view elites as self-serving power-seekers. In short, conflict theorists believe that this hierarchical ranking of positions is the cause of social conflict and reject the idea that elites are inevitable.

Elites and elitism are, of course, not unique to U.S. society (Bottomore, 1964). All societies, past and present, have been elitist. In most complex industrial societies, power is concentrated in few hands. Even democracies are elitist and competitive in nature. In any society, democratic or authoritarian, only a handful of individuals manages to climb to the top positions in the social and political structures of society. Elites certainly exist; to what extent is opportunity available to individuals, regardless of race, religion, sexual orientation, gender, or national origins, to move up to elite positions in society and politics? This issue will concern us in the next section.

Recruitment and Succession of Elites

An important issue in elite analysis is the recruitment process, succession, and circulation of elites, of major interest to social scientists and political sociologists alike (Lerner and Rothman, 1990; Nagle, 1977). The nature and character of a society and polity are directly related to the nature and processes of its elite recruitment. Through recruitment, vacant positions at different levels of society and the polity are filled; succession of elites refers to the replacement of those elites who retire or quit; through circulation, elites manage to climb the social ladder from generation to generation. The social background or origin of an elite helps in explaining its behavior and decisions.

An important issue in elite recruitment is *representativeness.* Because elites are always a small portion of the population, how are they to be selected to represent the interests of the majority? If elites are selected only from certain social groups or social classes, how can they represent the interests of the common people rather than serve the special interests of various groups? Social scientists and political sociologists do not agree on the issue of representativeness of elite recruitment. The pluralists argue that representativeness, especially of political elites, is unnecessary as long as the political elites represent the needs and interests of the people and the larger society. The Marxists and power elite theorists, on the other hand, find representativeness crucial: they believe that an elite drawn primarily from the upper strata of society cannot represent the interests of the lower classes.

Since the 1960s the question of representativeness of various social groups in elite and professional positions has become an important political issue. For example, affirmative action advocates argue that positions in a given organization should reflect the social composition of the community. Critics argue that recruitment must be open and equal to all qualified groups and individuals, regardless of religion, race, sexual orientation, national origins, and the issue of preferential group treatment. All these questions fall within the purview of elite studies in political sociology.

Radical power elite theorists and Marxists are even more critical of elites and the circulation of elites—the way elites manage to move from one top position to another, from one generation to the next, or from one society to another. Marxists and power elite advocates strongly argue that the social system in capitalist societies is essentially closed. They stress the idea of *birth elites,* those who are born to elite families and tend to perpetuate their elite positions and status from generation to generation. In other words, the radical elite theorists think that elites are self-recruiting and that they practice elite inheritance. For example, military elites promote their own children in military academies, just as doctors, lawyers, and politicians promote their children's careers. Pluralists counter this argument by stressing the possibility of elite competition and the notion of *mobile elites,* the view that individuals from different social class and ethnic backgrounds can rise to the top. They ask not what a person's background or social class might be, but rather what the person can do. Keller (1963) argued that there is a need to fill many elite positions in society with people who are technically qualified, regardless of their social origins.

But what happens when there are more qualified people to fill elite positions than openings? Many university graduates complain that they cannot find jobs, and for the first time children might be worse off than the generation that preceded them, something uncommon in the Unites States a generation ago. Earlier studies showed that younger generations expected to move up the social ladder, a phenomenon known as generational vertical social mobility. But in most societies, elite mobility is limited to a few highly qualified individuals rather than open to an entire social group or generation.

Thirty years ago, E. Digby Baltzell (1964) argued that upper-class institutions are essential for a leadership structure, but he saw a crisis in moral authority in the United States because the White Anglo-Saxon Protestant (WASP) establishment had failed to revitalize itself by recruiting talented minority group members. For instance, over 90 percent of the U.S. cabinet members from 1897 to 1972 have been recruited from members of social or business elites, and over half belonged to both. Over 90 percent had northern European backgrounds, and 80 percent were Protestant. Almost half were Episcopalian or Presbyterian, whereas only 6.2 percent of the general population belonged to those denominations (Kourvetaris and Dobratz, 1980:74). Similarly, Brownstein and Easton (1983) provided biographical data showing that people running the federal government during the Reagan administration were recruited from the business, industrial, and corporate world. (One can even make the argument that the Reagan administration was a government of the wealthy and the super-rich: President Ronald Reagan, Vice President George Bush, Secretary of Defense Caspar Weinberger, Secretary of State Alexander Haig, and Secretary of the Treasury Donald Regan were all multimillionaires.) Both the Reagan and Bush administrators appointed only a few minorities in cabinet positions. These were: Lauro F. Cavazus, a Hispanic American, was appointed Secretary of Education by Reagan in 1988 and continued by Bush. Louis W. Sullivan, an African American served as Secretary of Health and Human Services under the Bush administration. Clarence Thomas, an African American was nominated to the Supreme Court. He was confirmed after a televised testimony in which Judge Clarence Thomas was accused of sexual harassment by Professor Anita Hill, also an African American. However, the most important appointment and promotion during both to Republican administrations was Colin Powell. He became a four-star general and Chairman of the Joint Chief of Staff of the American Armed Forces. In contrast, President Clinton's cabinet has included more minorities, including African Americans and Hispanic Americans, and women than previous U.S. cabinets.

But Thomas R. Dye (1993:693–95) argued that, as in most previous administrations, the Clinton administration is also overwhelmingly drawn from among "the most-privileged, best-educated, well-connected, upper and upper-middle-class segments of America." Most cabinet members and 67 percent of all appointees in high positions in the Clinton administration are educated in the law. Table 4.1 shows a comparative profile of elite recruitment by Democratic and Republican administrations. Most cabinet and high-ranking officials in both Democratic and Republican administrations are recruited from a few professions, particularly law and business, preferring individuals with government experience and backgrounds in education and the military. Also most cabinet members are graduates of Ivy League schools and in both the Bush and Clinton administrations, most cabinet members held advanced degrees; at least one-quarter had earned the Ph.D. degree.

Both the executive and legislative branches of the U.S. government have a large number of millionaires. Richard Zweigenhaft (1975) found that the socioeconomic composition of Congress has barely changed in the past thirty years. The 1992 election seems to be an exception; six women senators were elected and more members of racial and ethnic minorities secured top positions in Congress than ever before. Overall, however, members of Congress are mostly from white upper-middle-class and upper-class backgrounds and employed in business and law. In a more recent study, Dye (1990), like Zweigenhaft, also documented the recruitment of elites having upper-class backgrounds. According to him, 30 percent of elites came from an

Table 4.1   Cabinet Recruitment of Republican and Democratic Administrations

	Truman, Eisenhower, Nixon, and Carter	Reagan	Bush	Clinton
Education				
Advanced degree	69%	68%	80%	89%
Law degree	40	26	40	67
Ivy League degree	48	58	50	50
Ph.D.	19	16	25	22
No college degree	0	0	0	0
Women	4%	5%	10%	17%
Blacks	4%	5%	5%	17%
Occupations				
Law	28%	11%	40%	5%
Business	28	32	55	5
Government	16	16	5	67
Education	19	16	25	11
Military	3	5	10	0

Source: Thomas Dye, "The Friends of Bill and Hillary" (1993:695); reprinted here by permission of the *American Political Science Association.*

upper-class background, compared to less than 1 percent of the general population. The remaining elites came from the upper middle class; only 3 percent came from lower-middle-class or lower socioeconomic backgrounds. Those at the top tend to be well-educated, urban, white Anglo-Saxon Protestant (WASP), and male. Dye pointed out that although the avenue of corporate recruitment is not the only path to top elite positions in political institutions, it does provide the majority of leaders in the corporate sector, civic and cultural organizations, foundations, and universities.

How do we interpret these findings? It goes without saying that elites do occupy top positions in U.S. society. Throughout history, regardless of the political system, the few have ruled the many. Power elite analysts argue that the overrepresentation of upper- and upper-middle-class strata elites is an indicator of power and provides evidence of ruling class hegemony in the United States. Pluralists counter by arguing that socioeconomic factors are not always a predictor of how one will use power. Marxists and neo-Marxists, especially structuralist Marxists, believe that no matter who is in control in a capitalist system, the structures and institutions of capitalist society favor the capitalist ruling class; the capitalists do not have to rule directly. To what extent are elites unified and cohesive? How unified or competitive are the elites in a democratic capitalist society?

The Social Cohesiveness of Elites

Social cohesiveness, or elite integration, refers to the extent to which elites develop strong social bonds that hold their members together over a period of time. Pluralists and power elite analysts disagree on this issue. Power elite analysts view elites and ruling classes as highly integrated, despite internal bickering. Following the tradition of C. Wright Mills, they find considerable elite integration and cohesiveness in the national power structure:

> *The conception of the power elite and of its unity rests upon the correspond-*
> *ing developments and the coincidence of interests among economic, politi-*
> *cal, and military organizations. It also rests upon the similarity of origins*
> *and outlook, and the social and personal intermingling of the top circles*
> *from each of these dominant hierarchies. (Mills, 1956:292)*

Pluralists, on the other hand, find little or no elite integration in U.S. social and political structures. In his study of power and the U.S. government, Grant McConnell (1966:339) stated:

> *The first conclusion that emerges from the present analysis and survey is that*
> *a substantial part of the government in the United States has come under the*
> *influence and control of narrowly based and largely autonomous elites.*
> *These elites do not act cohesively with each other on many issues. They do*
> *not "rule" in the sense of commanding the entire nation. Quite the contrary,*
> *they tend to pursue a policy of noninvolvement in the large issues of states-*
> *manship, save where such issues touch their own particular concerns.*

Along the same line, Moore (1993:184) indicated the following:

> *Pluralists argue that each elite group is distinct and narrowly based, with*
> *influence confined to the issues most relevant to its membership....Elites*
> *are seen as fragmented rather than integrated since each is involved prima-*
> *rily with its own relatively narrow concerns and constituencies.*

These opposing passages show that there is no single understanding of elite cohesiveness. It seems that elites in advanced industrial societies are sometimes united and sometimes disunited. The data are inconclusive, and the findings on the issue of elite cohesiveness are contradictory.

The concept of social cohesiveness has several dimensions. Robert Putnam (1976:107) distinguished five: *social homogeneity, recruitment patterns, personal interaction, value consensus,* and *solidarity.* Social homogeneity or cohesiveness is the extent to which elites share similar status, class origins, and common experiences, such as attendance at exclusive private schools. Value consensus refers to common values and beliefs that are essential to elite integration and political stability. According to Kenneth Prewitt and Alan Stone (1973), political elites in stable pluralist democracies in the West display high levels of consensus, similar codes of conduct, a commitment to the politics of bargaining and compromise, and tolerance of political opponents. Putnam 1976 proposed a typology of *consensual, competitive,* and *coalescent* elites. According to him, consensual elites must agree on both substantive and procedural matters (more about consensual elites later in this chapter). Competitive elites are free, in a democracy, to compete for positions of political or elite leadership. Competitive elitist democracy can tolerate differences of opinion among rival political elites. Coalescent elites are found in democracies wherein groups having religious, ethnic, and racial differences coexist despite their differences. *Solidarity,* a Durkheimian concept, refers to the creation of social bonds or a confraternity of power, a type of "class consciousness" among elites. On a different level of elite analysis, Anthony Giddens (1974) pointed out that the unity of elites can be based on both *moral integration,* sharing of common ideas or consciousness of kind (in this context, all social elites share some form of elite morality and purpose), and *social integration,* frequent and sustained social contacts and relationships. This means social elites, more than non-elites, develop social connections and networks over time.

Studies on Elite Integration

Two general hypotheses guide empirical research on the social integration of elites. The first is that the greater the similarity of elites in terms of social class background, recruitment patterns, personal interaction, value consensus, and solidarity, the greater the likelihood of elite integration. The second is the reverse: the greater the dissimilarity in these dimensions, the greater the fragmentation of elites. The first hypothesis is supported by power elite studies, which focus on elite integration, whereas the latter is supported by pluralists who emphasize the diversity of elites.

On the issue of unity of elites, John C. Donovan (1974) examined nine major decisions taken during the Cold War era, especially during the Vietnam War, and concluded that they were made by a single-minded elite force, based upon value consensus, common interests, and a deep respect for the capitalist system. This uniformity in values and attitudes was also discovered in the famous Pentagon papers, secret military documents describing the course of the Vietnam War. In these papers the Americans were discovering for the first time the the extent of misinformation and clandestine activities of the policy makers in the military establishment. The release of the Pentagon papers by Daniel Ellsberg, who had worked for the Pentagon, created a political crisis in the mid-1970s.

The most extensive work on the social cohesiveness of elites was undertaken by William Domhoff. On the basis of ingroup interaction—intermarriage, private schools, clubs, resorts, lifestyles, consciousness of kind, and great wealth—Domhoff (*The Higher Circles,* 1971) concluded that the upper class was cohesive. In *Bohemian Grove and Other Retreats* (1975), a study of three resort areas, Domhoff found that these retreats provided the environment and opportunity for interaction among members of the ruling class and business elites. Likewise, based on his analysis of four major processes—special interest process, policy formation process, candidate selection process, and ideology process—Domhoff concluded in *The Powers That Be* (1979) that the ruling class was a "clearly demarcated social class which has 'power' over the government and the underlying population within a given nation-state." He also found that the power elite was "the leadership group or operating arm of the ruling class." In *Who Really Rules?* (1978) and *Who Rules America Now* (1983), he argued that the upper class was less than 5 percent of the population and that the upper class, the corporate community, and the policy planning network were intersecting circles and that the corporate community was the major point of intersection.

Elite networks are a related issue. Both Gwen Moore (1979) and Michael Useem (1984) examined the cohesiveness of U.S. elite networks. Moore found that the structure of the major central circle is broad and inclusive and that issues are usually discussed in a collegial manner, which eases conflict resolution. In a survey of 545 top institutional positions in U.S. society conducted by the Bureau of Applied Social Research of Columbia University in 1971–72, Moore (1993) found a highly integrated structure of national elites among the major sectors of American society. Useem's inner group idea consisted of primary owners and top managers of major corporations, who can mobilize huge corporate resources and are involved in a common transcorporate social network. In his study of corporations and the corporate elite, Useem (1980:68) concluded that (1) the corporate elite is united by its primary commitment to capital accumulation; (2) it possesses a degree of internal integration, particularly within the dominant stratum; and (3) cohesion and intergenerational continuity give the corporate elite autonomy and power, which shape the corporate foundation and managerial interests and are indistinguishable from ownership interests. Still, although many observers find an internal cohesiveness among the corporate elite, other studies show heterogeneous interests; Useem (1980:58) himself stated that the U.S. corporate elite has never shown the same degree of cohesiveness as its European counterpart. Along the same line of argument of corporate *versus* managerial elite, Maurice Zeitlin's (1974) study also showed corporate ownership and control in the United States is in alliance with the managerial class.

The fact that individuals occupy elite positions on two or more boards of directors constitutes an important aspect of elite integration: the notion of interlocking directorates. The more interlocking, one finds the greater the cohesiveness of elites (Allen, 1974; Dye, 1990; Kolko, 1962; Mintz and Schwartz, 1985). In their study on interlocking directories of modern corporations, Beth Mintz and Michael Schwartz (1985) found a structure of intercorporate unity in U.S. business, a key device for concentrating corporate power. This integrated national network was dominated by New York banks and insurance companies.

Variability of Elites: The Consensual Unity of Elites

The issue of variability and consensus of elites follows the pluralistic model in political sociology. Scholars who focus on variability of elites generally distinguish between three basic types (Higley and Burton, 1989:18–19): (1) The *pluralistic,* or *consensually unified,* type is found in most Western societies at present. (2) The *totalitarian,* or *ideologically unified,* type exists in nation-states organized along Communist, fascist, or theocratic lines. The totalitarian type existed in Nazi Germany in the 1930s and 1940s, and in the Soviet Union prior to its demise in 1989. At present, it is found in the Communist regimes of Cuba, North Korea, and China. The totalitarian type of elites has declined in general, except for a few Communist regimes and some of the fundamentalist Islamic states in the Middle East. (3) The *divided* or *disunified* elite has been common in past and contemporary nation-states, including contemporary political regimes in Western polities.

In a number of studies (Burton and Higley, 1987a; Higley and Burton, 1989; Prewitt and Stone, 1973; and Putnam, 1976), the focus has shifted from fragmented or cohesive unity of elites to consensual unity of elites. A national elite[1] is *consensually unified* if its members (1) share a basic consensus on rules and codes of political conduct that amounts to restrained partisanship (DiPalma, 1970; Higley and Burton, 1989:19; Prewitt and Stone, 1973) and (2) participate in a comprehensively integrated structure of interaction that provides them with reliable and effective access to each other and to the most central decision makers (Higley and Moore, 1981; Kadushin, 1974). The key terms in a consensually unified elite are *tacit consensus* on rules of the game and *comprehensive integration.* In a consensual model, politics is viewed as a bargaining game rather than as a zero-sum or "politics as war" game (Sartori, 1987:224), meaning that politicians must reach a consensus or some form of compromise for policies to be made. Politics as a war game implies losers and victors as in a combat situation. For example, both the executive and the legislative branches of the U.S. government must cooperate and reach agreement on many issues (e.g., national health, welfare reform, etc.), rather than engage in partisan politics.

By contrast, according to Higley and Burton (1989:19), a national elite is disunified when its members: (1) share few or no common understandings of proper political conduct; and (2) engage in limited interactions and cooperation. The origin of elite disunity lies in the process of historical nation-state formation (Higley and Burton, 1989:20). An example of disunity was during the formation of most nation-states in Latin America during the Spanish rule in the early nineteenth century (Oszlak, 1981). We find similar elite disunity in postcolonial Africa during the 1960s (Johnson, 1983). In general, the historical record supports the proposition that the process of nation-state results, in most instances, in disunified national elites. The disunity of national elites leads to regime instability. This includes: (1) a high degree of political violence (strikes, riots, mass demonstrations, etc.); (2) frequent changes of the make-up of governing coalitions and cabinets; and (3) the occurrence of many coup d'etat or military take-overs of the civilian government (Sanders, 1981).

An important issue in comparative political sociology that has a bearing on the notion of consensual unity of elites is the relationship between stability and democracy. Under what conditions are democratic regimes stable? Under what conditions do democracies break down? A wave of transitions to democracy spurred by the disengagement of authoritarian military regimes in the mid-1970s (most notably in Latin America and southern Europe) have prompted a number of scholars to explore the idea of stability (more about this in Chapter 12, on civil–military relations).

The study of stability and democracy has a long history. Aristotle argued in his *Politics* that a large middle class promotes stability and democracy. He believed that in the best political community, the middle class makes up the majority of the people,

"For when there is no middle class and the poor greatly exceed in number, troubles arise and the state soon comes to an end" (Aristotle, 1971:336). Even in today's world, countries that lack a large middle class are more likely to be unstable and to be ruled by authoritarian military regimes. These countries usually occupy the periphery and semiperiphery in the world system.[2] A number of contemporary scholars (Cutright, 1967; Jackman, 1974; Lenski, 1966; Lipset, 1981; Rubinson and Quinlan, 1977) have found a relationship between economic inequality and instability in democratic regimes. Lipset (1981) and Dahl (1971) argued that extreme inequality reduces the legitimacy of regimes. A democratic regime depends a great deal on legitimacy for its survival (Bollen and Jackman, 1985:485). The centrality of class equality in democratization has also been confirmed in many other comparative studies. Dietrich Rueschemeyer et al. (1992:270–71), for example, has reported that the organized working class has been a key factor in the development of full democracy in many countries.

One study by Edward N. Muller (1988) found that democracy reduces inequality. Kenneth A. Bollen and Robert W. Jackman (1989), however, noted faulty indicators of measurement of democracy and political stability—democracy is a process, not something static and measurable. Other empirical studies have explained the relationship between stability and democracy in Western nation-states by using terms such as *legitimation crisis, crisis of confidence, government overload,* or *breakdown of governability* (exemplified by the protest movement of the 1960s). In a legitimation crisis, a society experiences a series of internal crises such as unemployment, underemployment, crime, violence, illegal drug use, and deterioration of the quality of life in general. These problems make the people skeptical about the ability of their government to solve problems and thus question its legitimacy to rule. The government, overburdened by problems it cannot solve, performs ever more poorly. Both new-left and new-conservative theorists argue that poor state performance can lead to a legitimation crisis (Weil, 1989:682–706). This feeling of cynicism about government has been prevalent in the United States for some time. Surveys in the U.S. show that voters have a very low opinion of American politicians (more about this in Chapter 7).

A number of researchers have argued that consensual unity of elites contributes to political stability. In their study of contemporary political regimes Higley and Burton (1989), for example, found that a transformation from elite fragmentation and disunity to consensual unity is an essential precondition for political stability and lasting democratic transitions. In their view, a political regime is unstable "whenever government executive power is subject to irregular seizures, attempted seizures, or widely attempted seizures by force" (Higley and Burton, 1989:20).

Paul Cammack (1990:415–20) criticized two dimensions of the consensual elite paradigm of Higley and Burton: (1) the relationship between consensual unity among elites and political stability, and (2) the role of elite settlement and consensual unity of elites. According to Burton and Higley (1987b:295) elite settlements are those previously warring elites who decide to comprise and negotiate their differences. They create some form of peaceful competition and stable regimes. Cammack argued that their dividing line between elites and non-elites was blurred and that the authors did not differentiate between elite sectors; also, he asserted that no clear distinction was made between stability and instability in democratic regimes. Higley and Burton (1990) defended their elite paradigm and found it to be almost axiomatic that consensus and accommodation among elites was a prerequisite for modern political democracies. Put simply, cooperation among various social elites is necessary for modern societies and politics to solve social problems that have paralyzed many governments.

Profile of the Elite Structure in the United States

Who's in charge of the United States? How do we identify elites in U.S. society? These questions have both empirical and methodological dimensions. In *The Power Elite and the State* (1990:1), Domhoff stated:

> *The debate on power in America triggered by Hunter and Mills has become depressingly predictable. There are said to be three general theories—plural-ist, institutional elitist, and* Marxist—*and three basic methods—decisional, positional, and* reputational.[3] *There are also three main indicators of power (according to him)—who decides, who sits, and* who benefits.

Domhoff identified three major components of elite analysis—a conceptual, a methodological, and an empirical one. The first deals with the pluralist, elitist, and Marxist models in political sociology, which were discussed in Chapter 2. The methodological component concerns the approach used to investigate various issues in politics and society. The empirical component attempts to determine who makes decisions, who occupies power positions, and who benefits from those decisions and power positions (this information would also tell us something about those who are excluded from power positions and benefits).

As pointed out previously, power is not an attribute of individuals but a relational and institutional characteristic. An institutional basis of elite power exists at all levels of community, national, and international structures of power. Ruesche-meyer and his colleagues (1992:269) identified three major clusters of power—class power, state power, and international structures of power. (Our emphasis in this chapter has been on national elite power and ruling classes.)[4]

C. Wright Mills (1956:9) aptly described the institutional nature of elite and ruling class power:

> *No one . . . can be truly powerful unless he has access to the command of major institutions, for it is over these institutional means of power that the truly powerful are, in the first instance, powerful. . . . If we took the one hundred most powerful men in America, the one hundred wealthiest, and the one hundred most celebrated away from the institutional positions they now occupy, away from their resources of men and women and money, away from the media of mass communication . . . then they would be powerless and poor and uncelebrated. For power is not of a man. Wealth does not cen-*

ter in the person of the wealthy. Celebrity is not inherent in any personality. To be celebrated, to be wealthy, to have power, requires access to major institutions, for the institutional positions men occupy determine in large part their chances to have and to hold these valued experiences.

Another social scientist, Adolph A. Berle (1967:92), studied private property and the American corporation; he was also equally emphatic about the institutional basis of power:

Power is invariably organized and transmitted through institutions. Top power holders must work through existing institutions, perhaps extending or modifying them, or must at once create new institutions. There is no other way of exercising power—unless it is limited to the range of the power holder's fist or his gun.

Here is how Dye (1990:1–2) described the institutional basis of elite power in the United States:

Great power in America is concentrated in a handful of people. A few thousand individuals out of 240 million Americans decide about war and peace, wages and prices, consumption and investment, employment and production, law and justice, taxes and benefits, education and learning, health and welfare, advertising and communication, life and leisure. In all societies—primitive and advanced, totalitarian and democratic, capitalist and socialist—only a few people exercise great power. This is true whether or not such power is exercised in the name of "the people."

Who's Running America? is about those at the top of the institutional structure in America—who they are, how much power they wield, how they came to power, and what they do with it. In a modern, complex industrial society, power is concentrated in large institutions: corporations, banks, utilities, insurance companies, broadcasting networks, the White House, Congress and the Washington bureaucracy, the military establishment, the prestigious law firms, the large investment houses, the foundations, the universities, and the private policy-planning organizations. The people at the top of these institutions—the presidents and principal officers and directors, the senior partners, the governing trustees, the congressional committee chairpersons, the Cabinet and senior presidential advisers, the Supreme Court justices, the four-star generals and admirals are the objects of our study in this book

On the basis of his institutional definition of American national elites, Dye identified a total of 7,314 leadership or elite positions in the corporate, public interest, and governmental sectors of American society and polity. (See Table 4.2.)

Dye (1990:12–13) concluded that these top positions

Table 4.2   Dimensions of America's Elite Structure

Corporate Sectors	Number of Leadership Positions
1. Industrial corporations (100)*	1,475
2. Utilities, communications, transportation (50)	668
3. Banks (50)	1,092
4. Insurance (50)	611
5. Investments (15)	479
Total	4,325

Public Interest Sectors	
6. Mass media (18)	220
7. Education (25)	892
8. Foundations (50)	402
9. Law (25)	758
10. Civic and cultural organizations (12)	433
Total	2,705

Governmental Sectors	
11. Legislative, executive, judicial	236
12. Military	48
Total	284
TOTAL	7,314

Source: Thomas R. Dye, *Who's Running America?* (1990:12); published by permission of Prentice-Hall.
*Numbers in parentheses indicate the number of the most important units in different sectors.

taken collectively control one half of the nation's industrial assets, one half of all assets in communication and utilities, over half of all U.S. banking assets, over three quarters of all insurance assets, and they direct Wall Street's largest investment firms. They control the television networks, the influential news agencies, and the major newspaper chains. They control nearly forty percent of all the assets of private foundations and two thirds of all private university endowments. They direct the nation's largest and best-known New York and Washington law firms as well as the nation's major civic and cultural organizations. They occupy key federal governmental positions in the executive, legislative, and judicial branches. And they occupy all the top command positions in the Army, Navy, Air Force, and Marines.

In short, the national elite power structure in the United States has the following features: (1) it is institutional in nature; (2) it is concentrated in a handful of people.

This elite power structure is universal and common in all societies, regardless of the level of complexity of that society or the type of political regime. Therefore, even in a democracy, we have elitism. The difference, however, between totalitarian and democratic regimes is that elites in democracies are competitive, pluralistic, and fragmented, whereas in totalitarian states and societies, they tend to be unified and ideological in nature. The totalitarian form of elitism has been rapidly declining in many parts of the world since the end of the Cold War in 1989.

The Socialization and Education of Elites

The nature and behavior of elites are much affected by their education, values, attitudes, and skills. How are U.S. elites socialized?—that is, how do elites learn their social roles, values, attitudes, and skills? The socialization and education of elites are related to the recruitment, cohesiveness, stratification, and institutionalization processes of elitism in U.S. society. Interest in the socialization and education of elites, at least in the West, goes back at least to Plato, who advocated a meritocracy and special education for the "philosopher king." An important component of socialization and education of elites addresses their politics and ideologies (Newstadt and Clawson, 1988). What are the political and ideological orientations of social elites in U.S. society? Are all social elites similar in their political behavior? In general, elites or professionals in the humanities and the arts tend to be more liberal, or left of the center, in their political orientation. Those in the hard sciences and business tend to be more conservative, or right of the center (Brint, 1985; Kornhauser, 1961; Lachman, 1990; Lipset, 1981).

What is the relationship of intellectual elites and power? When sociologists speak of intellectuals, they usually refer to all those elites who create and disseminate ideas, symbols, and knowledge. Intellectuals include academics, scientists, social scientists, research scholars, journalists, and writers. C. Wright Mills (1956:259) stressed the role of intellectuals as agents of radical change. Others view intellectuals as adversarial, fighting against the establishment. According to Eva Etzioni-Halevy (1986), there are two widely held views on the relationship between intellectuals and political power. Marxists view intellectuals as promoting ruling class interests. Marxists and neo-Marxists believe that intellectuals serve as functionaries of capitalism who facilitate the interests of the capitalist class. Even when intellectuals criticize the capitalist class, Marxists view them as contributing to the stability of the existing capitalist order. The second view looks at intellectuals as radicals, based on their economic insecurity. Karl Mannheim (1936:155, 1956:145) saw the intellectuals as a "classless" stratum and their ideologies as related not to their class position but to their mobility patterns. Intellectuals moving from lower to higher positions are more likely to endorse existent hierarchies and tend to identify with the class to which they have risen. On the contrary, intellectuals whose mobility is blocked tend to become radical (Etzioni-Halevy, 1986:32). The first group, becomes incorporated into the power structure and defends the existing capitalist system. The latter group plays an antiestablishment role (Lipset and Dobson, 1972:146). Empirical data from various

Western countries do not support Mannheim's thesis. A number of social scientists (Lazarsfeld and Thielens, 1958; Lipset, 1981; Noll and Rossi, 1966) argued that intellectuals, regardless of their economic success, tend to express more radical and left-of-center political views. Similarly, Etzioni-Halevy (1986) concluded that intellectuals tend to express more radical attitudes than the general population of their respective countries, whether or not they are upwardly mobile.

In his study of the political behavior and values of the top faculty elites, Lipset (1981:143–68) found that elite scholars and members of honorific academies such as the National Academy of Sciences, the American Philosophical Society, the American Academy of Arts and Sciences, the National Academy of Engineering, and the National Academy of Education are more liberal politically than those in professional schools. Professors in the social sciences and humanities tend most toward the Left, followed by those in the biological and physical sciences. Business, engineering, and agricultural school faculty tend to be the most conservative. Another group of social scientists (Kadushin, 1974; Ladd and Lipset, 1975; Rothman and Lichter, 1982) found that the new strategic elites, or symbol-producing groups such as intellectuals, journalists, writers for television and other media, elite intellectuals, and professors, are the leadership group most critical of U.S. institutions.

Summary and Conclusion

In this chapter the structure and behavior of United States elites were discussed. First, the concept and various views of elites were briefly described. Second, elites were examined in terms of six key issues that are found in most types of elites: inevitability of elites, recruitment, social cohesiveness, social variability, social profile of United States elite structure, and socialization/education of elites.

With respect to the issue of inevitability of elites, it was pointed out elites have been a recurrent phenomenon in history. There are those who perceive elites as indispensable for society and polity; while others look at elites as self-serving and undemocratic in nature.

Elites recruitment and succession of elites was also analyzed as an important issue of elite analysis and understanding. In general, elites are recruited from the upper middle class of society. As a rule, elites are more educated, they come from more privileged social backgrounds, manage to circulate from one top position to another, tend to be white, male, and well-connected.

The issues of social cohesiveness and social variability were also discussed. Although there is a variability and competition of social elites, it was pointed out that elites are socially cohesive. There is a basic value consensus among all social elites. Elites take care of their own kind. They are more organized, they know what they want, and they are status and class conscious. Three major types of elites were extensively discussed—consensual, ideological, and disunified. With the exception of the ideological, which were characteristic of former communist societies, both consensual and disunified elites are present in most societies.

The elite structure of United States elites or who's in charge of the top positions was examined. Drawing from a number of writers, the institutional elite structure and power elite thesis were widely used to characterize the present elite profile of the United States. There is an increasingly smaller and smaller group of individuals and corporations who run the most important institutions of the United States. Needless to say, elites receive the best education and are socialized to assume leadership roles in American society. In short, elites are those who make things happen and have been a constant phenomenon in history and society.

Endnotes

1. Burton and Higley (1987a) defined national elites as comprising all those individuals who occupy top positions of authority in power organizations and movements that affect political outcomes regularly and substantially. For cogent analyses of elites and classes see Dobratz and Burton (1986) and Etzioni–Halevy (1993).

2. According to world system theory, the capitalist system has a core, a periphery, and a semi-periphery. The core countries include Western European countries, Japan and the United States. The periphery includes those countries collectively known as the Third World, such as many nations in Asia, Africa, and Latin America. The semi-periphery contains those countries which are in between the two poles of development. The implication is that the core countries dominate those countries found in the periphery and semi-periphery not only in the economic sphere, but in the international sphere of politics as well.

3. The *decisional* method of identifying elites involves analyzing the extent to which possible elites contribute to major decisions or non-decisions in various institutions, including politics. The *posi-tional* method involves identifying the positions of authority individuals occupy. The *reputational* method involves identifying elites by analyzing their reputed importance in the community or the nation. In addition, we can use the so-called Who's Who method by looking at various biographical or professional directories of famous individuals in various institutional sectors of society.

4. Studies on community power structures are extensive and reflect theoretical and methodological orientations similar to those of studies on national power structures (Hunter, 1959; Polsby, 1963). Walton (1966) pointed out that studies of community power have used three basic approaches: *reputational, positional* and *decision-making*. Based on an examination of 33 studies of 55 communities, Walton concluded that pyramidal or monolithic power structures are most likely to be found when the researcher used the reputational approach by itself or in combination with other methods, while factional, coalitional, and amorphous (diffuse) types of power structures tend to be found when decision-making or other combined methods of investigation are used.

References

Allen, Michael P. 1974. "The Structure of Interorganizational Elite Cooperation: Interlocking Corporate Directories." *American Sociology Review* Vol. 39:393–406.

Aristotle. 1971. *Man in the Universe* (James E. C. Welldon, trans.). Roslyn, N.Y.: Walter J. Black, Inc.

Baltzell, E. Digby. 1958. *Philadelphia Gentlemen.* New York: The Free Press.

———. 1964. *The Protestant Establishment.* New York: Vintage Books.

Berle, Adolph A. 1967. *Power.* New York: Harcourt Jovanovich.

Bollen, Kenneth A., and Robert W. Jackman. 1989."Democracy, Stability, and Dichotomies." *American Sociological Review* Vol. 54:612–21.

———. 1985. "Political Democracy and the Size Distribution of Income." *American Sociological Review* Vol. 5:438–57.

Bottomore, T. B. 1964. *Elites and Society.* Harmondsworth: Penguin Books.

Brint, Steven. 1985. "The Political Attitudes of Professionals." *American Review Sociology* Vol. 11:389–414.

Brownstein, Ronald, and Nina Easton. 1983. *Reagan's Ruling Class.* New York: Pantheon.

Burton, Michael G., and John Higley. 1987b. "Elite Settlements." *American Sociological Review* Vol. 52:295–307.

———. 1987a. "Invitation to Elite Theory." In *Power Elites and Organizations*, ed. G. William Domhoff and Thomas R. Dye, 133–43. Newbury Park, CA: Sage.

Cammack, Paul. 1990. "A Critical Assessment of the New Elite Paradigm." *American Sociological Review* Vol. 55:415–20.

Cutright, Phillips. 1967. "Inequality: A Cross-National Analysis." *American Sociological Review* Vol. 32:562–78.

Dahl, Robert. 1971. *Polyarchy: Participation and Opposition.* New Haven: Yale University Press.

DiPalma, Giuseppe. 1970. *Apathy and Participation.* New York: The Free Press.

Dobratz, Betty, and Michael G. Burton, eds. 1986. *Elites and Ruling Classes. Journal of Political and Military Sociology* Vol. 14 (Spring). (special issue)

Domhoff, William G. 1975. *The Bohemian Grove and Other Retreats: A Study in Ruling Class Cohesiveness.* New York: Harper and Row.

———. 1971. *The Higher Circles: The Governing Class in America.* New York: Vintage.

———. 1990. *Power Elite and the State.* New York: Aldine de Gruyter.

———. 1979. *The Powers That Be.* New York: Random House.

———. 1978. *Who Really Rules? New Haven and Community Power Reexamined.* Santa Monica: Goodyear.

———. 1983. *Who Rules America Now?: A View for the '80s.* Englewood Cliffs: Prentice Hall.

Donovan, John C. 1974. *The Cold Warriors: A Policy-Making Elite.* Lexington, MA: Heath, D.C.

Dye, Thomas R. 1993. "The Friends of Bill and Hillary." *PS: Political Science and Politics.* Vol. 26 (December):693–95.

———. 1990. *Who's Running America? Institutional Leadership in the United States.* Englewood Cliffs: Prentice-Hall.

Edmond, Irwin. 1928. *The Works of Plato* (The Lowett Translation). New York: Random House.

Etzioni-Halevy, Eva. 1993. *The Elite Connection.* Cambridge, England: The Polity Press.

———. 1986. "Radicals in the Establishment: Towards an Exploration of the Political Role of Intellectuals in Western Societies." *Journal of Political and Military Sociology* Vol. 14 (Spring):29–40.

Field, G. Lowell, and John Higley. 1980. *Elitism.* London: Routledge and Kegan.

Giddens, Anthony. 1974. "Elites in the British Class Structure." In *Elites and Power in British Society,* ed. Phillip Stanworth and Anthony Giddens, 1–20. London: Cambridge University Press.

Higley, John, and Michael Burton. 1989. "The Elite Variable in Democratic Transitions and Breakdowns." *American Sociological Review* Vol. 54 (February):17–32.

Higley, John, Michael G. Burton, and G. Lowell Field. 1990. "In Defense of Elite Theory: A Reply to Cammack." *ASR.* Vol. 55, no. 3: 421–26.

Higley, John, and Gwen Moore. 1981. "Elite Integration in the Unites States and Australia." *American Political Science Rev.* Vol. 75:581–97.

Hunter, Floyd. 1953. *Community Power Structure, A Study in Decision Making.* Chapel Hill: University of North Carolina Press.

———. 1959. *Top Leadership U.S.A.* Chapel Hill: University of North Carolina Press.

Jackman, Robert W. 1974. "Political Democracy and Social Equality: A Comparative Analysis." *American Sociological Review* Vol. 39:29–45.

Johnson, Paul. 1983. *Modern Times: The World From the Twenties to the Eighties.* New York: Harper and Row.

Kadushin, Charles. 1974. *The American Intellectual Elite.* Boston: Little, Brown.

Keller, Suzanne. 1963. *Beyond the Ruling Class.* New York: Random House.

Kolko, Gabriel. 1962. *Wealth and Power in America: An Analysis of Social Class and Income Distribution.* New York: Praeger.

Kornhauser, William. 1961. "Power Elite or Veto Groups." In *Culture and Social Character*, ed. Seymour M. Lipset and Leo Lowenthal, New York: The Free Press.

Kourvetaris, George A., and Betty A. Dobratz. 1973. *Social Origins and Political Orientations of Officer Corps in a World Perspective.* Denver: University of Denver Press.

———. 1980. *Society and Politics: An Overview and Reappraisal of Political Sociology.* Dubuque: Kendal/Hunt.

Kuper, Adam, and Jessica Kuper. 1985. *The Social Science Encyclopedia.* London: Routledge and Kegan Paul.

Lachmann, Richard. 1990. "Class Formation without Class Struggle: An Elite Conflict Theory of the Transition to Capitalism." *ASR.* Vol. 55, no. 3:398–414.

Ladd, Everett, and Seymour Lipset. 1975. *The Divided Academy.* New York: McGraw-Hill.

Lazarsfeld, Paul F., and W. Thielens. 1958. *The Academic Mind.* Glencoe: Free Press.

Leggett, John. 1973. *Taking State Power.* New York: Harper and Row.

Lenski, Gerhard. 1966. *Power and Privilege.* New York: McGraw-Hill.

Lerner, Robert, Althea K. Nagar, and Stanley Rothman. 1990. "Elite Dissensus and its Origins." *Journal of Pol. and Mil. Soc.* Vol. 18 (Summer):25–39.

Lipset, Seymour M. 1981. *Political Man.* Baltimore: Johns Hopkins University Press.

Lipset, Seymour M., and R. B. Dobson. 1972. "The Intellectual as Critic and Rebel." *Daedalus.* Vol. 101 (Summer):137–98.

Lynd, Robert S., and Helen Merrell Lynd. 1927. *Mid-dletown.* New York: Harcourt, Brace and World.

Mannheim, Karl. 1936. *Ideology and Utopia.* New York: Harcourt, Brace and World.

McConnell, Grant. 1966. *Private Power and American Democracy.* New York: Knopf.

Mills, C. Wright. 1956. *The Power Elite.* New York: Oxford University Press.

Mintz, Beth. 1975. "The President's Cabinet, 1897–1972: A Contribution to the Power Structure Debate." *The Insurgent Sociologist.* Vol. 5 (Spring):131–48.

Mintz, Beth, and Michael Schwartz. 1985. *The Power Structure of American Business.* Chicago: University of Chicago Press.

Moore, Gwen. 1979. "The Structure of a National Elite Network." *American Sociological Review.* Vol. 44:673–92.

———. 1993. "The Structure of a National Elite Network." In *Power in Modern Societies,* ed.

Marvin E. Olsen and Martin N. Marger, Boulder: Westview Press.

Mosca, Gaetano. 1939. *The Ruling Class.* New York: McGraw-Hill.

Muller, Edward N. 1988. "Democracy, Economic Development, and Income Inequality." *American Sociological Review* Vol. 53:50–68.

Nagle, John D. 1977. *System and Succession: The Social Bases of Political Elite.* Austin: University of Texas Press.

Neustadt, Alan, and Dan Clawson. 1988. "Corporate Political Groupings: Does Ideology Unify Business Political Behavior?" *ASR.* Vol. 53 (April):172–90.

Noll, C. E., and P. H. Rossi. 1966. *General Social and Economic Attitudes of College and University Faculty Members.* Chicago: National Opinion Research, University of Chicago.

Olsen, Marvin E., and Martin N. Marger, eds. 1993. *Power in Societies.* Boulder: Westview.

Oszlak, Oscar. 1981. "The Historical Formation of the Nation-State in Latin America: Some Theoretical and Methodological Guidelines for its Study." *Latin American Research Review* 16:3–32.

Polsby, Nelson W. 1963. *Community Power and Political Theory.* New Haven: Yale University Press.

Poulantzas, Nicos. 1975. *Classes in Contemporary Capitalism.* London: Humanities Press.

———. 1973. *Political Power and Social Classes.* London: New Left Book.

Presthus, Robert. 1964. *Men at the Top.* New York: Oxford University Press.

Prewitt, Kenneth. 1970. *The Recruitment of Political Leaders: A Study of Citizen-Politicians.* Indianapolis: Bobbs-Merrill.

Prewitt, Kenneth, and Alan Stone. 1993. "The Ruling Elites." In *Power in Modern Societies.* Boulder: Westview. 125–136.

———. 1973. *The Ruling Elites: Elite Theory, Power, and American Democracy.* New York: Harper and Row.

Putnam, Robert. 1973. *The Beliefs of Politicians: Ideology, Conflict, and Democracy in Britain and Italy.* New Haven: Yale University Press.

———. 1976. *The Comparative Study of Political Elites.* Englewood Cliffs: Prentice-Hall.

Robins, Robert S. 1976. *Political Institutionalization and the Integration of Elites.* Beverly Hills: Sage.

Rothman, Stanley, and S. Robert Lichter. 1982. "Media and Business Elites: Two Classes in Contrast." *The Public Interest.* Vol. 69 (Fall): 117–25.

Rubinson, Richard, and Dan Quinlan. 1977. "Democracy and Social Inequality: A Reanalysis." *American Sociological Review* Vol. 42 (August):612–23.

Rueschemeyer, Dietrich, Evelyne Huber Stephens, and John D. Stephens, eds. 1992. *Capitalist Development and Democracy.* Chicago: University of Chicago Press.

Sanders, David. 1981. *Patterns of Political Instability.* London: Macmillan.

Sartori, G. 1987. *The Theory of Democracy Revisited: The Contemporary Debate.* Old Greenwich, CT: Chatham House.

Therborn, Goran. 1976. "What Does the Ruling Class Do When It Rules?: Some Reflections on Different Approaches to the Study of Power in Society." *The Insurgent Sociologist.* Vol. 6 (Spring):3–16.

Useem, Michael. 1980. "Corporations and the Corporate Elite." *American Review Sociology.* Vol. 6:41–77.

———. 1984. *The Inner Circle.* New York: Oxford University Press.

Walton, John. 1966. "Substance and Artifact: The Current Status of Research on Continuity Power Structure." *American Journal of Sociology* Vol. 71 (January):430–38.

Weil, Fred. 1989. "The Sources and Structure of Legitimation in Western Democracies: A Consolidated Model Tested with Time-Series Data in Six Countries since World War II." *American Sociological Review* Vol. 54 (October):682–706.

Wright, Erik O., and Luca Perrone. 1977. "Marxist Class Categories and Income Inequality." *American Sociological Review* Vol. 42 (February):32–55.

Zeitlin, Maurice. 1974. "Corporate Ownership and Control: The Large Corporation and the Capitalist Class." *American Journal of Sociology* Vol. 79:1073–1119.

Zweigenhaft, Richard. 1975. "Who Represents America?" *The Insurgent Sociologist.* Vol. 5 (Spring):119–48.

Chapter 5

Media Communication and Power

In the United States, as in many other countries, media communication plays a pivotal role in the initiation and continuation of various social processes that underlie the creation, transmission, and reception of information concerning critical issues.[1] Shanto Iyengar and Donald R. Kinder (1987:2,21) argued that television is the single most important shaper of "the American public's conception of political life." According to them, "television news is news that matters": those issues receiving most coverage by the national networks become most important to viewers; those receiving less coverage fade from viewers' consciousness.

The mass media have changed our lives profoundly. They have affected our way of life, tastes, and attitudes and transformed the world of politics. We are living through a mass media revolution: In the past it took months and even years to learn about events that occurred in our own country; today we learn instantly what happens in the most remote corners of the globe. Media communication has thus made us more aware of social problems not only in other countries, but at home as well— problems such as poverty, illegal drug use, crime, homelessness, pollution, and racism, to name only a few.

During the 1960s many Americans discovered the existence of another United States, a country plagued by unemployment, underemployment, poverty, and racism. Mass media coverage of the Civil Rights Movement awakened the consciences of many Americans by drawing attention to the plight of African Americans and other minority groups. Mass media exposure of the problems of the inner city and widespread poverty in the United States sent shock waves through the country, leading the way to the Great Society program and the massive civil rights legislative agenda of the 1960s and 1970s. The mass media are thus an important agent of socialization that can either contribute to the progressive democratization and modernization of society or lead to their reversal.

Although political parties and political bosses were once the most influential agents of political socialization, they have steadily declined in importance due to the spread of the mass media. National elections have become political spectacles conducted for the electronic media. The ascent of television to its present position as the primary news medium worldwide has yielded a more entertainment-oriented political process, regardless of the actual gravity of issues being discussed. Politicians have become celebrity elites; image has replaced substance in political discourse (Edelman, 1987). Coincidentally, political apathy in the United States has turned to cynicism and electorate anger has turned against elected officials, as demonstrated by the success of Ross Perot (who in 1992 captured twenty percent of the votes cast for presidential candidate, the highest captured by an independent candidate in U.S. history) and the crushing defeat of Democratic candidates for Congress in 1994. The mass media may simultaneously have a liberalizing and a conservative influence on both individuals and society, contributing to public (un)awareness, discourse, and (mis)understanding of social and political issues.

In this chapter the mass media will be discussed as a power structure and as an elite institution. What is the societal role of the mass media? Who controls access and who enjoys greater access to the media? Who determines the content of the media? What are the effects of the media on public opinion and social and political issues?

Mass Media and Society

The modern era of the mass media began in the 1920s and 1930s with radio broadcasts and talking films. Herbert Schiller (1989:136) identified three major periods in the changing view of media power: the post–World War II era (1945–1965); the upheaval decade of the mid-1960s to the mid-1970s; and the restoration era from the end of the 1970s to the present. Although during the 1930s and 1940s the media was seen as having limited effects, Paul Lazarsfeld and Frank Stanton organized the office of media research at Columbia University. They conducted a study of the 1940 presidential election, *The People's Choice* (Lazarsfeld et al., 1944).[2]

During the 1950s and 1960s the rise of electronic media, especially television, was an important development in presidential politics. Presidential candidates learned to use prime-time television to reach massive and diverse audiences. In 1952 Dwight Eisenhower became the first candidate to use television advertising (Jamieson, 1984). But 1960 was the first time American voters were exposed to a televised debate between presidential candidates—Richard M. Nixon and John F. Kennedy.

Kennedy won the election by a margin of only 100,000 votes, and many political pundits believed that his poise in the televised debate clinched his victory. In the next three decades entirely new types of public opinion pollsters, political analysts, campaign managers, political spokespersons, speech writers, and image makers—all oriented toward making the best use of television—emerged and were in demand (McQuail, 1975; Wright, 1985).

The mass media also played an increased role in influencing public opinion on other issues. Television coverage of the Civil Rights Movement brought the extent of poverty and racism in the United States home to many Americans and in large part led to legislative passage of the Great Society and War on Poverty programs of the 1960s and 1970s. Televised reports from the battlefields of the Vietnam War and of student anti-war protests swayed public opinion away from the government's Vietnam policy. This had a direct impact on President Lyndon Johnson's decision not to seek reelection in 1968. Television broadcast of the Watergate hearings led to President Richard Nixon's resignation. And daily television reports on the American hostage crisis in Iran caused many people to question President Jimmy Carter's executive ability and played a major role in his defeat in the 1980 election by Ronald Reagan.

In industrial societies, the mass media have become an important social institution. Indeed, the media now compose one of the largest industries in the world. They create and recreate our social world by focusing and refocusing on local, state, national, regional, and international issues.The two major types of mass media are print media and electronic media. Print media include books, newspapers, and magazines. Electronic media include television, radio, films, audio recording, and computer media. The electronic media have undermined the position of the print media; more and more people rely on electronic media rather than on print media for political news and information concerning social and political issues.

Like social scientists, specialists in the study of the mass media and communications use a wide variety of concepts and models to investigate many empirical issues. Many of these concepts and models are borrowed from sociology, political science, and psychology. *Political culture* (the learning of political attitudes and behaviors), *political socialization* (the way we acquire our political attitudes and values), *political communication* (public discussion about the distribution of resources, public policies, and public sanctions), *public opinion* (opinions and beliefs that are openly communicated), and *propaganda* (a systematic attempt to influence the attitudes and behavior of people through the manipulation of symbols) are part of the vocabulary used in media studies.

Functionalists believe that the mass media serve vital functions for society and the polity. They believe that, along with other social institutions and organizations, such as schools, families, religions, and politics, the mass media are an agent of socialization, including political socialization, that transmits and inculcates social norms and values. Functionalists believe that the mass media also contribute to national integration, social cohesiveness, and societal consensus by stressing shared social, political, and cultural values such as equality, democracy, citizenship, freedom, individualism, and education, as well as shared aesthetic, economic, and material values.

From the conflict perspective, the mass media are seen as a means of social control used by social elites (especially government, corporate, intellectual, political, cultural, and military elites), who manage the flow of information and decide what is to be printed or aired in the electronic media in order to maintain the legitimacy of the prevailing social and political system. Similarly Marxists and neo-Marxists see the mass media as serving the interests of capitalists and the ruling classes. A version of the neo-Marxist perspective is what Antonio Gramsci (1891–1937) referred to as "hegemony." According to this model, the mass media transmit the dominant elite's values and interests and the lower classes come to accept them as being in their own best interest. Richard Dawson et al. (1977:26) explained that

> *Hegemonic theory starts with the assumption that government would not be possible unless the strains and tensions associated with the unequal alloca-tion of values in society were somehow noted.... Unless the losers come to see that the way things are is 'natural' or 'appropriate' or 'legitimate,' social disruptions are likely. Socialization is viewed as the learning that leads the losers to accept the way things are, even to think that the way things are is in their best interests.*

The basic idea of the hegemonic model is that those elites who control the political, cultural, and economic structures of society are more likely to control the message and the social construction of reality (Bennett, 1983:133). Karl Marx believed that the dominant ideas in a capitalist society were those of the capitalist class. Both the structuralist and instrumentalist neo-Marxists view the mass media as favored by the structures of capitalist society which serve the interests of the ruling class. Those who occupy elite positions in the mass media, according to neo-Marxists, serve the inter-ests of the ruling class because they can manipulate public opinion and are reluctant to be critical of the very ruling class which they serve. In constrast, conservatives accuse the media elites of promoting liberal views.

Ideally, the mass media in democratic societies play a vital role in providing cit-izens with information. It can be argued that a democracy is only as good as the extent to which its citizens are well informed, and so able to make intelligent deci-sions in the political process. In reality, however, it is possible to manipulate the news and consensus even in democracies. In mass societies, psychological manipulation is a form of power and control.

Power Control of and Access to Media

Control of and access to the mass media in the United States, and in most advanced industrial societies, is directly related to economic and political power. In the United States almost all the mass media are privately owned, profit-making corporations. In most other industrial societies, the print media are privately owned and the electronic media are a mixture of both private commercial and public enterprises. Prior to the 1980s, commercial television did not exist in Europe, with the exception of Britain. In Europe and in most Third World countries, most television networks are state monopolies that justify political control of programming. Since the 1980s, however, there has been a rise in the number of commercially and privately owned electronic media. It must be stressed, though, that in more authoritarian and autocratic nation-states such as China, Cuba, and North Korea, in those countries having military or quasi-military dictatorships, and in Islamic fundamentalist states, the mass media are subject to strict control and censorship. In such regimes public opinion has little or no influence on public policies.

Antonio Pilati (1991:53–68) found five major factors underlying both the quan-titative and qualitative expansion of media communications and its impact on the social fabric of society and politics: (1) the increasing importance of media communications in business strategy (especially in the promotion and advertising of products); (2) the decline of public television; (3) the increased functional integration of various media components—creating a homogeneous system of various media components mutually reinforcing one another; (4) an increased consumption of media communications, which is linked to the global increase in opportunity for leisure and levels of literacy; and (5) technological innovation that makes production and distribution of media products more effective and so makes such products more available to people throughout the world.

The questions of who controls the media and how accessible the media are to the average American are legitimate questions of power structures. Ideally, every American has the constitutional rights of freedom of speech and freedom of expression. In reality, however, those who have the most opportunity to exercise these rights are those who control the media—the corporate managerial, political, cultural, governmental, celebrity, and media elites. Parenti (1995:27) argued that "freedom of the press belongs to the man who owns one." The majority of Americans have no access to or control of any form of mass media. Who are the owners of the mass media in the United States? Who are the media elites who control the flow of information to the masses? And how does control of and access to the media by the elite get translated into meaningful social and political outcomes?

Ownership of the Media

Many mass media outlets are huge commercial profit-making enterprises. In an oligopoly market a few firms dominate the market; in a monopoly market a single company dominates. Not all media markets in the United States can be called monopolies or oligopolies (Gomery, 1993: 48). This is especially true for radio and magazines. But there are oligopolies that either directly or indirectly own and operate newspaper chains; broadcast radio and television stations; recording, motion-picture, and book publishing units; and/or cable television systems (Marger, 1993:239; Parenti, 1995:165). And the ownership interests of some of these oligopolies extend into ventures that have symbiotic relationships with the mass media. For example, the Tribune Company, one of the largest media conglomerates in the United States, owns the Chicago Cubs. Here is how Parenti (1986:27; 1993:165–66) described the oligopolistic ownership of mass media in the United States a decade ago:

> *Ten business and financial corporations control the three major television and radio networks (NBC, CBS, ABC), 34 subsidiary television stations, 201 cable TV systems, 62 radio stations, 20 record companies, 59 magazines including* Time *and* Newsweek, *58 newspapers including the* New York Times, *the* Washington Post, *the* Wall Street Journal, *and the* Los Angeles Times, *41 book publishers, and various motion picture companies like Columbia Pictures and Twentieth-Century Fox. Three-quarters of the major stockholders of ABC, CBS, and NBC are banks, such as Chase Manhattan, Morgan Guaranty Trust, Citibank, and Bank of America.*

Consolidation of the media industry has continued over the past decade. According to Parenti (1993:165–66),

> *As of 1989 twenty-three corporations controlled most of the national media—down from fifty in 1982. About 80 percent of the daily-newspaper circulation in the U.S.A. belongs to chains like Gannett and Knight-Ridder. For example, from 1966 to 1990, Gannett grew from 26 dailies to 88 dailies, 23 weeklies, 13 radio stations, 17 TV stations, and numerous cable and satellite operations. "A handful of publishers dominate the magazine business, and six major companies distribute virtually all the magazines sold on newsstands. Eleven publishers control most of the book-sales revenues, and a few bookstore chains enjoy the lion's share of the distribution. A handful of companies and banks control the movie industry. Three giant networks, ABC, CBS, and NBC, still dominate the television industry, and ten corporations command most of the nation's radio audience. The major stockholders of ABC and CBS are banks such as Chase Manhattan, Morgan Guaranty Trust, CityBank, and Bank of America. Representatives of the more powerful banks and corporations—including IBM, Ford Motor Corporation, American Express, General Motors, Mobil Oil, Xerox, and many others— sit on the boards of all the major networks and publications (Parenti, 1993:165–166).*

The overall pattern of media ownership is one of increasing concentration of economic power and control, as demonstrated by recent high-profile media mergers and acquisitions. (For further discussion see Alexander et al, 1993; Dye, 1995:108–126; Marger, 1993:238–49; Paletz and Entman, 1981.)

To communicate one's views in modern societies, one must have access to both print and electronic media. Who owns the media is not as important as who has access to or can use the media. In modern industrial societies, only the government, including the military, and big business have the resources, money, authority, and influence needed to make use of the media regularly and effectively (Marger, 1993:240–41; Parenti, 1995). Access even to public television is limited to a few groups. Although many ethnic, religious, and racial groups in the United States have their own television programs, most ethnic media are cultural or religious in focus and have very little influence on public policy.

The Nature of Media Control

Ownership and control of the media in the United States is of three kinds: public, semipublic, and private.

Public Control

Public control means that public ownership, such as ownership by the armed forces or other federal agencies, controls media. For instance, the federal government owns various broadcast programs, including the Voice of America,[3] which presents the

United States in the best possible manner by broadcasting only the positive aspects of its actions to other countries and to uniformed personnel. The content of these broadcasts is determined by government officials, communication departments of the CIA, and its intelligence community.

Public control may also be exerted over privately controlled media. For example, in 1991 during the Gulf War, the military had absolute control of most information presented to the private media. The same was true during the invasion of Grenada during the Reagan administration and the invasion of Panama during the Bush administration. In war, media control by the government and the military is common. The blackout of news confuses the enemy. It makes military objectives easier to achieve and helps to conceal failures from the public. However, control of the news by the government and its agencies is close to censorship of the news and censorship violates the right of people in a democracy to know what the government is doing.

Semipublic Control

Some media have a mixture of public and private financing and control. For instance, public broadcasting in the United States was created by the Public Broadcasting Act of 1967 to support educational or public service programs. One fourth of all U.S. broadcast television stations are public. In addition, in 1983 286 noncommercial television stations and 280 noncommercial FM radio stations linked together as National Public Radio. Corporations and business enterprises finance almost half of public television and radio programs (the rest are financed by private foundations, government grants, private groups, and individuals). This financial sponsorship allows corporations, private foundations, and institutions to influence programming and, in turn, public opinion. Thus, even public electronic media are not totally independent in the selection and the content of their programs.

Private Control

Most media operations in the United States are privately owned by individuals or corporations. Many of these individuals and corporations own a combination of several media outlets, such as one or more newspapers, television stations, and radio stations. And many of these corporations are conglomerates—large corporations consisting of companies operating in a variety of businesses. The three major television networks: (1) American Broadcasting Corporation (ABC) was a subsidiary of Capital Cities, Inc. before it was bought by Disney Company for $19 billion in December 1995. (2) Columbia Broadcasting System (CBS) is a subsidiary of Westinghouse Electric Corporation. (3) The National Broadcasting Corporation (NBC) is a subsidiary of General Electric Company. All three major broadcasting corporations dominate the viewing patterns of about half of all households in the United States that own televisions. The major radio stations in major cities are also owned by ABC, CBS, and NBC. Moreover, these conglomerates are owned by larger conglomerates. Because of the high cost of producing news and entertainment programs, most of the one thousand local commercial television stations are forced to affiliate with these networks (Dye, 1995: 112–113).

Such concentration of ownership also occurs in the print media. The traditional dominance of the three major television networks, ABC, CBS, and NBC has been eroded over time. Cable and satellite technology have challenged the media giants. More and more homes in the United States are cable subscribers, about 60 percent in 1992 (Dye, 1995:112). Turner's Cable Network (CNN) along with a host of other Turner's networks have challenged the older media giants. In December of 1995 both ABC and NBC officially announced plans to start competing 24-hour cable news service sometime in the near future (Bill Carter, *The New York Times,* Wed., Dec. 6, 1995:C5).

The newspaper industry is the most profitable of all media industries and is in fact one of the most profitable of all manufacturing industries in the United States (Picard, 1993:181). According to Robert Picard it collects $40 billion in advertising and circulation sales annually. There are approximately sixteen hundred daily newspapers in the United States, 90 percent of which exist as the only papers in their markets (Picard, 1993:182). The major newspaper companies are among the largest corporations in the nation. The Chicago Tribune Company and Knight-Ridder both have assets of more than $2 billion, the Gannet Company of more than $3 billion, and the Times Mirror Company of more than $4 billion (Picard, 1993:186). During the early 1990s, the Thomson Newspapers owned 125 U.S. dailies, Gannet owned 82 and Donrey Media owned 56. Five other firms owned 24 or more daily papers and 23 companies owned more than 12 (Picard, 1993:187). Moreover, the nation's daily newspapers get most of their national news from the Associated Press (AP) wire service. (Radio stations also rely heavily on AP.) This series of facts shows the tremendous concentration of power and the frequent monopoly power of the newspaper industry in the United States.

Although about eleven thousand individual magazine titles are published in the United States, a small number of corporations own most of them. Time-Warner alone controls more than 40 percent of the magazine business (Marger, 1993:240). The same concentration of ownership exists in book publishing; about six corporations dominate most book sales. Three major studios control most of the movie business, and three corporations draw most of the audience and revenue in the television industry (Bagdikian, 1989:32–34).

Cable television became a big business in the 1980s. By the early 1990s more than half of all U.S. households had cable television installed (Gomery, 1993:49). As in other media industries the top ten firms control more than half of all business (Owen and Wildman, 1992: 49).

Access to the Media

Access to the mass media is correlated with power, status, and class. The higher the socioeconomic status and power of a person, group, or institution, the greater its access to the media: government, economic, military, cultural, political, religious, educational, and celebrity elites have greater access than do non-elites.

The government and government elites have a symbiotic relationship with the media and government access to the media is founded not on financial power but rather on this relationship. The media rely on the government elites because the government is a primary source of political news. At the same time, government elites depend on the mass media to deliver their messages to the masses.

Terence Qualter (1985:198–200) summarized the major characteristics and role of mass media communication: (1) The originators of messages are usually structured collectives, such as parties and governments, communicating to an amorphous mass public. (2) The originators are elitist and stratified in nature. The higher their social status or the greater their social and economic power, the greater their control of and access to the processes of communication. The masses have access to the media as receivers, seldom as contributors. (3) The flow of communication moves downward, from the more powerful to the less powerful. (4) Access to the media is a resource of the elites that is zealously guarded and protected. (5) The major defense of the masses in the communication process lies in the voluntary nature of reception. The public can resist media manipulation by simply not listening or by critically analyzing messages. (6) The mass media are usually system supportive—they support the existing system rather than challenge it. This means that those in the media are usually supportive of the values of society and the social system and are rarely critical of the sponsors and owners of the media for fear of losing their jobs. (7) The media promulgate and reinforce conservative values, which seldom challenge the existing power arrangements and class structures.

Mass Media Content and Agenda Setting

Just as important as control of and access to the media are the media's agenda and content. Agenda setting is the process by which certain news issues are identified as more important or worthy than others. Conceptually, media agenda usually refers to all those issues that the media people present as most important in terms of the amount and the quality of coverage. Some analysts believe that the direction of influence on the agenda-setting process is from the media to the public. Others believe that the opposite may occur, that public concerns about certain issues may influence the media agenda. Still others believe that the agenda simply reflects events in the environment (Roberts and Maccoby, 1985:564).

According to Robert E. Denton Jr. and Gary C. Woodward (1992:146–50), agenda setting is one of the three basic effects of mass communication (the other two are gatekeeping, or the construction of political realities, and the personalization of ideas), and it determines what has news value. Herbert J. Gans (1980:146–52) emphasized that the mass media set their agenda by choosing news items that deal with public officials or national issues, affect lots of people, or tell something about where the country is heading. For Ed Epstein (1974:37–43), agenda setting was greatly affected by the organizational and business concerns of the mass media. And for Kurt Lang, "agenda setting is simple correlations between content emphasis and attention shifts" (written communication, March 1994).[4] This means that agenda setting and media content are related and vary from time to time depending on the perceived importance of the issues.

News is socially created and recreated by those who want to shape and influence public opinion. Those who set the agenda tell us "what to talk about, how to think about it, and even what to think." Theodore White (1972:327), a political journalist, wrote:

> *The power of the press in America is a primordial one. It sets the agenda of public discussion; and this sweeping political power is unrestrained by any law. It determines what people will talk about and think about—an authority that in other nations is reserved for tyrants, priests, parties, and mandarins.*

The world is made up of different realities. What is reality for one person may not be reality for another. Reality is comprehended in individual and personalized terms, not in institutional terms. It is the individual who selects and internalizes the values, including the political values of society as they are presented to him or her by various agents of socialization, including authority figures—parents, teachers, presidents—and various social elites, including media elites (reporters and commentators). The internalization of values and attitudes takes place in the context of specific social and political events in U.S. history. In other words, we become conscious of the social world as we live through different social realities. We cannot exist in the world without continually interacting with others. In short, the reality of everyday life is a social reality.

Media communication plays an important role in creating the social reality of everyday life. Media personnel structure the social and political world schematically—they select a few categories of events and ignore others. By doing so, they give us a narrow picture of social reality. In addition, people tend to pay more attention to the vivid representation of an event on television than to colorless, abstract information in books. As the media elite cater to this predisposition, simplicity overtakes complexity in presentation of the news. Public preference for visual representation of events, preoccupation with "event" coverage rather than "issue" coverage and the resulting lack of context, and the general lack of interest in and understanding of foreign issues on the part of the public leads to what Paraschos (1988:203) referred to as "parachutist" reporting.

In addition, studies have shown that the simpler the presentation of news items and the fewer the categories of events presented, the greater television viewers' retention of what they have seen. The average viewer has neither the patience nor the time to listen to in-depth analyses of issues. Simple presentations also cost news programmers less and so are attractive in business terms. Understanding these realities, politicians make use of photo-ops, or rituals such as inaugural balls, parades, ceremonies, speeches, shaking hands, and baby kissing, as well as slogans and negative advertising as effective means of political communication. Such rituals and slogans structure our perceptions and discourage critical thinking.

The source of media content is of crucial importance. It is axiomatic that different content results in different effects on power and on society in general. The mass media, as Marger (1993:242) argued, have become our "window on the world." Because the public relies on the mass media for information and analysis, whoever controls the content of the media has a powerful influence on the public's concerns and the way it perceives issues. Even if the media do not determine public attitudes on social and political questions, they can determine the issues with which the public will be most deeply involved. If our perceptions are limited, then our power or ability to choose from a variety of sources is limited. Who are the people behind the news? Who are the people who decide what is to be selected and communicated to the public?

The news media elites are composed of media owners, media executives, and members of the celebrity elites—producers, anchors, editors, and reporters. In the early 1990s, Dye (1995:108–126) listed six people who, at the time, essentially governed the flow of information to U.S. society: William S. Paley, the founder of CBS; Arthur Ochs Sulzberger, publisher and president of the *New York Times;* Lawrence A. Tisch, chairman of the board of CBS; Thomas S. Murphy, chairman of the board of Capital Cities–ABC; Ted Turner, owner and chairman of Cable News Network (CNN); Thorton Bradshaw, associated with RCA and NBC; and Katharine Graham, owner and publisher of the *Washington Post* and *Newsweek.* Although a number of these people are no longer active and a number of these organizations have since been taken over by larger conglomerates, the successors of these six members of the media elite continue to control much of the public's perception of events.

The Power Elite and the Media

Despite the fact that, independently of the business and government elites, the media elites exercise considerable power, especially as gatekeepers of information or news, the mass media elites must be understood within a sociopolitical and economic context. In socialist and authoritarian political systems, governments control the media. But in democratic capitalist societies such as the United States, mass media outlets are business enterprises. In these business enterprises, when the media elite make content decisions, they take into consideration the interests of the business elites who supply much of their revenue and the government elites who supply much of their program content. Because the media elite cannot ignore the wishes and interests of these suppliers, they are reluctant to be critical of the capitalist economic system or of the two-party political system. Reporters treat new ideas or movements outside the existing political system as aberrations or curiosities. This is particularly true during national elections. Political debate and discussion of issues is largely limited to the two major political parties unless a third party can buy its own television time, as occurred with the Ross Perot campaign.

Doris A. Graber (1984:22) wrote that the media usually support the political system and rarely question its fundamental tenets. They limit their criticism to what they perceive as perversions of fundamental social and political values or noteworthy examples of corruption and waste. Their links to the existing power structures are strong because they depend heavily on the high and mighty as sources of news. They operate within a framework of common understandings and discourse, and they are not willing to deviate from this framework (Kurt Lang, written communication, March 1994).

Carl J. Friedrich (1972:193) expressed much stronger feelings toward the mass media: "The mass communication media have produced one of the most dangerous tensions in modern constitutional democracies. At the same time, they have become a prime instrumentality of the dictatorships." Friedrich believed that media elites have played an important role in "whipping up mass hysteria in critical situations" and have "magnified the hate reactions after the wars and contributed to the difficulties of organizing peace." However, in general, Friedrich referred primarily to media use by totalitarian regimes who use hysteria to eradicate all discourse (Kurt Lang, written communication, March 1994).

For a number of reasons, mass media elites distort or practice a kind of censorship that impacts on the content of what is reported to the public. Some of these reasons are:

(1) *Time and space constraints.* The deadlines the media must meet do not allow time to cover all aspects of issues thoroughly. Also, especially in television, it costs more to analyze an issue in depth. The result is often an unbalanced treatment of issues.

(2) *Self-censorship and co-optation.* Despite the efforts of media personnel to report all sides of issues objectively, there is an implicit understanding that they should uphold the status quo and not be critical of the capitalist system. The privileges and income that media elites enjoy often lead to their co-optation by the power elite; they therefore often serve the power elite's interest rather than the public interest. Media elite self-censorship, often unconscious, means that there is usually little need for corporate sponsors and government officials to apply pressure. The salaries that media personnel are offered makes it easier for them to be co-opted.

(3) *Audience passivity.* Viewers of electronic media are passive spectators. The media usually control what is presented to their consumers and there is little or no feedback. A study by Allan McBride and Sylvia Thompson (1986) that compared television owners and non-owners found that owners were less involved in serious social and political activities. The authors argued that "television functions like a 'narcotic drug.'" There is also little audience feedback in the print media. Most letters to editors are never published because little space is allotted to them. Usually, in order for one to publish one's opinions in one of the major newspapers or magazines, one must be a member of the elites. This is also true about securing an appearance on television or radio.

(4) *Politicians' use of symbols as diversionary tactics.* The use of symbols such as flags, crosses, photographs, and pictures greatly sways us and influences our perceptions. Symbols simplify reality and structure our perceptions. Politicians often try to divert attention from major issues by stressing insignificant or irrelevant issues that work to their advantage. They often accomplish this by using the media to associate themselves with certain symbols. During the 1988 presidential campaign, for example, George Bush implied that he was more patriotic than his opponent, Michael Dukakis, by visiting a flag factory. Due to their own tendency to follow politicians' leads, the media often show such orchestrated photo-ops without questioning them.

Media Effects

One of the most important issues concerning the mass media is their impact on public opinion. We may know who controls the media, who has more access to them, and what their content is, but unless we understand the effects that the media have on public opinion, we cannot be sure that they produce the results desired by those in control.

Mass communication research in the United States tries to answer the question of how mass communication influences human behavior and shapes our social and political attitudes (Defleur & Ball-Rokeach, 1982; Gans, 1980). Early thinking on media effects was represented by Walter Lippman (1922) and Harold Lasswell (1927), two pioneers in the analysis of political communication and public opinion. Both stressed that the mass media had major effects on society (Kazan, 1993:1). Lippman (1922), for example, believed that the mass media, by selectively reporting and interpreting events and personalities, contribute to the formation of stereotypes, or the way that we simplify social reality by stressing certain aspects of a phenomenon and disregarding others.

Most early research on the effects of mass communication asked one of two types of questions. One type deals with the intent of the source of the message, asking questions about how mass media can be used to influence people intentionally. For example, how do we convince people not to smoke? The other has to do with the audience and the unintended effects of media content, asking questions about the consequences that may follow from media exposure regardless of the source's intent. For example, can violent movies increase violence among children? Do pornographic movies increase aggression toward women? Both types of questions follow a simple stimulus model known as the direct-effects model. It is assumed that direct immediate effects will follow from exposure to a message. This simple direct-effects model had many drawbacks and tended to exaggerate media effects. It also ignored the sociopolitical context of the message and the sociodemographic attributes of the viewers, including social class, ethnicity, and religion. Although communication experts and social scientists doubt the extent to which media effects shape our attitudes and our social and political world, public opinion continues to hold that the media exert tremendous power by molding and shaping social attitudes and public opinion.

It is clear, however, that the media have several interwoven, usually unintentional, effects on power and politics. These effects are general and cover the entire spectrum of the relationship between media, power, and politics. Paletz and Entman (1981:6) outlined six major interwoven effects, which are not always comprehended by elites, the public, or even media personnel themselves. (1) The media influence the decisions and actions of politicians and officials, change their priorities, and can reduce their ability to control events. (2) The media's openness to manipulation by the powerful contributes to the insulation of some power holders from accountability to the public. (3) The media reallocate power among the already powerful. (4) The media decrease, to a marked extent, both the ability of ordinary citizens to judge and their power to respond quickly in their own self-interests to political events and power holders. (5) The media foment discontent among the public. (6) The media help to preserve the legitimacy of the U.S. political, economic, and social system. Paletz and Entman argue that media effects are not always understood even by the very people who profess to be specialists in the study of communication.

On a more specific level, Paletz and Entman argue that the media have five specific effects on public opinion: (1) *Stabilization* (the media stabilize prevailing opinions or dominant ideology). (2) *Priority setting* (the media tend to provide or set the issues that most people come to think of as important). (3) *Elevation* (closely related to agenda setting, or the elevation of events and issues to the position of news). The status of gays in the military, for example, has been an issue for a long time, yet in the first month of Bill Clinton's presidency, it received massive media attention. Such elevation of an issue can be used by politicians and institutions to divert attention from other more pressing issues. The military budget, for example, can be viewed as just as important an issue as gays in the military, yet by emphasizing the latter issue, politicians and the media steered the public's attention away from the military budget. (4) *Changing opinions* (the media can change and influence people's opinions by the way they report events and issues and the way they use symbols). (5) *Limiting our options* (people respond to the stories or issues presented by the media, which tend to exclude stories or issues that are embarrassing to or critical of government elites, corporate elites, and elites in general).

The mass media, particularly television, operate as important agents of socialization, the process by which people learn the values and norms of their culture and come to develop an understanding of the nature of society. Mass media influence our ethnic, racial, and sex-role attitudes and stereotypes. There are those who believe that media messages distort reality in ways that perpetuate the interest of the existing power structure. The proponents of this view contend that the mass media creates routine news practices that perpetuate existing social and political norms and legitimize power relationships and established norms and conventions (Roberts and Maccoby, 1985:580).

Summary and Conclusion

In this chapter, the role of media communication was discussed as a power structure and as an elite institution. More specifically, five questions were examined: (1) What is the societal role of the mass media? (2) Who controls access and who enjoys greater access to the media? (3) Who owns the media? (4) Who determines the content of the media? (5) What are the effects of the media on public opinion?

Although the modern era of the mass media began in the 1920s and 1930s, for all practical purposes the explosion of mass media is a post-World War II phenomenon. The mass media—both print and electronic—have become an important social institution. The functionalists believe the mass media serve vital functions for society and the polity and along with a host of other social institutions and organizations, are an important agent of socialization. From the conflict perspective the mass media are seen as a means of social control used by social elites to manage the flow of information.

The power control and accessibility to media were also discussed. The majority of Americans are consumers of mass media. Those who control and manage the flow of information are a small minority of corporate managers, political, cultural, governmental, celebrity, and media elites. Accessibility and control of the mass media are also related to the ownership of the media. Many mass media outlets are huge commercial profit-making enterprises. More and more the mass media are owned and dominated by a few giant corporations and conglomerates.

Three basic forms of ownership and control of mass media were examined—public, semi-public, and private. Public control refers to the ownership such as the armed forces or other federal agencies, controls media. Semi-public refers to a mixture of public and private financing and control. Private control is the most common operation of media ownership in the United States.

Mass media content and agenda setting are also linked to those who have control and access to the media. What news or what people talk about are socially created and recreated by all those who shape and influence public opinion. In short, those who set the agenda tell us "what to talk about, how to think about, it, and even what to think." Whoever controls the agenda and the content of the media exerts a powerful influence on society. The power elite and the media are the gatekeepers of information and do have a tremendous impact on public opinion and society in general.

Endnotes

1. See Kraus and Davis (1976), Lang and Lang (1975), and McQuail (1975).

2. Some of the findings of *The People's Choice* were that: (1) media strengthen voters' existing predispositions and attitudes; (2) voters exposed to propaganda favoring their own candidate were more likely to select those communications supporting those predispositions and attitudes; (3) mass media communications either reinforced prior preferences or activated latent ones.

3. The Voice of America was a powerful propaganda medium used extensively against the former Soviet Union and other Communist regimes during the Cold War. It is not known what happened to the fate of the Voice of America following the end of the Cold War in 1989.

4. To point out the shallowness of agenda setting formulation Lang, in the same letter and in comments on an early version of this chapter, referred to his book *The Battle for Public Opinion* (especially chapters 3 and 4) (Lang, 1983), which deals with the role of the media during Watergate.

References

Alexander, Alison, James Owers, and Rod Carveth (eds). 1993. *Media Economics: Theory and Practice*. Hillsdale, NJ: Lawrence Erlbaum Associates.

Bagdikian, Ben. 1989. "Missing from the News." *The Progressive*. Vol. 53 (August):32–34.

Bennett, W. Lance. 1983. *News: The Politics of Illusion*. New York: Longman.

Dawson, Richard, Kenneth Prewett, and Karen Dawson. 1977. *Political Socialization*, 2nd ed. Boston: Little, Brown.

Defleur, Melvin, and Sondra Ball-Rokeach. 1982. *Theories of Mass Communication*. New York: David McKay.

Denton, Robert E. and Gary C. Woodward 1992. *Political Communication* Wesport, Connecticut: Praeger

Dye, Thomas. 1995. *Who's Running America?*, 6th ed. Englewood Cliffs: Prentice Hall.

Edelman, Murray. 1987. *Constructing the Political Spectacle*. Chicago: University of Chicago Press.

Epstein, Ed. 1974. *News from Nowhere: Television and the News.* New York: Vintage.

Friedrich, Carl J. 1972. *The Pathology of Politics.* New York: Harper and Row.

Gans, Herbert J. 1980. "Deciding What's News: A Study of CBS Evening News, NBC Nightly News." In *Newsweek and Time.* New York: Pantheon.

Gomery, Douglas. 1993. "Who Owns the Media?" In *Media Economics: Theory and Practice.*

Graber, Doris A. 1984. *Mass Media and American Politics.* Washington: Congressional Quarterly Press.

Iyengar, Shanto, and Donald R. Kinder. 1987. *News That Matters.* Chicago: University of Chicago Press.

Kazan, Fayad E. 1993. *Mass Media, Modernity, and Development: Arab States of the Gulf.* Westport: Praeger.

Kraus, Sidney, and Dennis Davis. 1976. *The Effects of Mass Communication on Political Behavior.* University Park: Pennsylvania State University Press.

Lang, Gladys E., and Kurt Lang. 1975. "Critical Event Analysis." In *Political Communication: Issues and Strategies for Research,* ed. S. H. Chaffee. Beverly Hills: Sage.

Lang, Kurt. 1983. *The Battle for Public Opinion.* New York: Columbia University Press.

Lasswell, Harold. 1927. *Propaganda Technique in World War I.* Cambridge: MIT Press.

Lazarsfeld, Paul F., Bernard Berelson, and Hazel Gaudet. 1944. *The People's Choice: How the Voter Makes Up His Mind in a Presidential Campaign.* New York: Duell, Sloan and Pearce.

Lippman, Walter. 1922. *Public Opinion.* London: Allen and Unwin.

Marger, Martin N. 1993. "The Mass Media as a Power Institution." In *Power in Modern Societies,* ed. Marvin E. Olsen and Martin N. Marger. Boulder: Westview.

McBride, Allan, and Sylvia Thompson, 1986. "Does Television Breed Political Passivity?" Presented at Midwest Political Science Association Meeting, Chicago.

McQuail, Denis. 1975. *Towards a Sociology of Mass Communication,* 2nd. ed. London: Collier-Macmillan.

Owen, B. M., and Wildman, S. S. 1992. *Video Economics.* Cambridge: Harvard University Press.

Paletz, David L., and Robert M. Entman. 1981. *Media Power and Politics.* New York: The Free Press.

Paraschos, Manny. 1988. "News Coverage: A Case Study in Press Treatment of Foreign Policy Issues." *Journal of Pol. and Mil. Soc.* Vol. 16, no. 2:201–13.

Parenti, Michael. 1986 and 1993 (2nd edition). *Inventing Reality: The Politics of the Mass Media.* New York: St. Martin's.

———. 1995 *Democracy for the Few* (6th edition) New York: St. Martin's Press

Picard, Robert G. 1993. "Economics of the Daily Newspaper Industry." In *Media Economics: Theory and Practice.*

Pilati, Antonio. 1991. "The Mass Media and 1992." *The International Spectator.* Vol. 26, no. 2:53–68.

Qualter, Terence. 1985. *Opinion Control in the Democracies.* New York: St. Martin's Press.

Roberts, Donald F., and Nathan Maccoby. 1985. "Effects of Mass Communication." In *Handbook of Social Psychology,* ed. Garner Lindzey and Elliot Aronson. Vol. 2, 3rd. ed. New York: Random House.

Schiller, Herbert. 1989. *Culture, Inc.: The Corporate Takeover of Public Expression.* New York: Oxford University Press.

White, Theodore. 1972. *The Making of the President.* New York: Bantam.

Wright, Charles R. 1985. *Mass Communication: A Sociological Perspective,* 2nd. ed. New York: Random House.

Civil–Military Relations

The rise of the nation-state in the eighteenth and nineteenth centuries was concomitant with the rise of the power of the military in the Western world. Indeed, the military played a pivotal role in nation building. Its immense political power has continued into the present, reaching its zenith in this century between the two world wars. Charles Moskos Jr. (1973) believed that two conditions contributed to the growth of the military as a political power: a sharp distinction between military and civilian structures, and universal male conscription. Despite the end of the arms race between the United States and the Soviet Union, the end of the draft in the United States in 1973, the conversion of military into civilian industries in both the United States and the former Soviet Union (Cross and Oborotova, 1994; Melman, 1988; Sorokin, 1993; Sorokin and Danopoulos, 1994), and the transitions to democracy of at least 30 countries between 1974–1990 (Huntington, 1991), the military remains one of the most powerful institutions in most countries. Accompanying this continuation of military power, however, is the perception that the military is being marginalized, which may result in new strains in civil-military relations.[1]

It can be argued that the end of the Cold War has diminished the threat of a nuclear holocaust. However, it may be premature to argue that, with the end of the arms race, conflicts in other areas of the world will cease. Although the early 1990s have witnessed the demise of the former Soviet Union and lessening tension between East and West, they have also seen a resurgence of neonationalism in many parts of the world. A new role for the military must therefore be forged. As yet, however, no clear vision of its shape exists. What are the possible roles of the military in a changing political landscape?

In the United States, those who have a more conservative orientation view the world as unstable and unpredictable, and tend to support the presence of a strong U.S. military. Those who have a more liberal orientation tend to be critical of the large military budget, and to prefer a smaller military force. They urge the government to start a process of conversion from defense to civilian industries. Konstantin Sorokin (1993) saw a need for such conversion and a balanced civilian-military strategy for Russia if that country was to stay competitive in the twenty-first century. Similarly, Sorokin and Danopoulos (1994:1) argued for "military-civilian conversion" in both the United States and Russia involving three distinct yet interdependent processes: "First, utilization of existing but no longer needed weapons; second, demilitarization of all spheres of social life and public mentality; and third, switching research and development efforts of the military-industrial complex to peaceful use, rather than purely military technologies."

Another recent example of the search for a new military identity involves the North Atlantic Treaty Organization (NATO). Formed after World War II, NATO had as its *raison d'être* the threat of Soviet aggression in Europe. Such a threat, however, no longer exists. Critics wonder, then, why the United States and the other NATO countries maintain NATO military forces. What is the role of NATO in a post–Cold War era?

In this chapter we will examine a number of issues and perspectives concerning civil-military relations. There are those who see the military as a client of the state and want to extend civil authority over the military. Others view the military as part of the power elite and as an essentially independent institution; they believe that its power and influence cannot be taken for granted or subsumed under the political authority of the government. This latter view can be seen most clearly in countries ruled by praetorian regimes—regimes headed by the military or by some form of civil-military coalition. Our analysis will focus on the military in general and the U.S. military in particular as part of the power elite. What is the role of the military in society and in the state? Is there a military-industrial establishment, and what is its relationship with the power elite? What is the role of the military in politics? And what is the future role of the U.S. military?

Analysts have approached these questions from a number of directions. Political scientists have been concerned primarily with the relationship between the military and the state. Military sociologists, however, are concerned with the interactions between the military and other social institutions. Military sociology is a quite new discipline,[2] commencing only during World War II (Kourvetaris and Dobratz, 1977). Quite obviously, the military cannot be ignored in studies of the political processes of a country, especially in studies of foreign policy issues. Yet the systematic study of the sociopolitics and the political economy of the military is a recent phenomenon.

One can distinguish between two broad methods of analyzing military institutions. The first is a universalistic or structural approach, in which common structural uniformities and patterns are stressed. The second is a more idiographic or particularistic approach, in which military organizations are analyzed as distinct units reflecting political, cultural, and historical influences. Morris Janowitz (1971b) referred to these as "organizational analysis" and "armed forces and society," respectively (Kourvetaris/Dobratz, 1977:5). Building on Harold D. Lasswell's (1962) definition of the military institution as the management of the organized means of violence and warfare, Kurt Lang (1972) placed the sociological study of the military within the more inclusive framework of the sociology of conflict. Lang (1972:10–12) identified five major areas of military sociology: study of the profession of arms, of military organizations, of military systems, of civil-military relations, and of war and warfare.

Before we consider civil-military relations, we will discuss briefly some professional aspects of the U.S. military. This will help us to understand better the nature and character of the military as an institution and its officer corps as a professional elite.

Professional Considerations

The study of the military profession, as embodied most fully by its officer corps, is a study of an idealized managerial/organizational profession (Kourvetaris, 1971b: 1043). Despite the fact that changing staffing and recruitment policies in the U.S. military—the end of the draft in 1973 turned the military from a conscriptive force to an all-volunteer force—have led to some convergence of professional attributes between military and civilian occupational structures, their differences are salient (Feld, 1975; Harries-Jenkins, 1990; Huntington, 1957; Janowitz, 1960; Kourvetaris, 1971a, 1971b; Margiotta, 1978; Moskos & Wood, 1988; Van Doorn, 1965, 1975). Four major characteristics differentiate the military from the civilian professional: (1) The military is by nature a conservative institution and a client of the nation state that it pledges to defend. (2) The military profession is an *ascribed* profession and a fusion of profession and organization. (Here, *ascribed* means that the officer, after he/she receives his/her commission, automatically becomes an officer and does not have to compete for a job in civilian society.) The military profession combines elements of both profession and organization and cannot operate as a free profession in the civilian sense of the term. In a democratic society, civilian authorities and the constitution define the goals and objectives of the armed forces. (3) Although only a small portion of the U.S. military can be defined as "experts in the organized means of violence," the military is characterized as the management of the institutionalized means of violence when national objectives, as defined by the civilian political leadership, call for such action. The wider society, however, does not approve of these objectives, as was the case in the latter phase of the Vietnam War. In fact, most United States wars have been undeclared wars. (4) "Ethics" and "character" are important characteristics in most professions, but they are especially important in military officers' career advancement. A constellation of attributes, including willingness to sacrifice personal objectives, honor, duty to one's country, all serve to differentiate markedly the military profession from nearly all civilian professions (Kourvetaris, 1971b).

In his sociological analysis of the military, Moskos (1988) suggested that the military was moving away from a traditional view of the military as a profession or institution and toward an occupational model. In his view, such issues as norms, values, roles, recruitment, and compensation demonstrated differences between the institutional and occupational models. According to Moskos, an institution is legitimized by norms, values, and societal goals that transcend self-interest, while an occupation is legitimated by marketplace norms such as supply and demand and self-interest (Moskos & Wood, 1988:16–17). Moskos's model is not universally accepted. Many students of military institutions think that a combination of the occupational and the institutional model is a more accurate description of the U.S. military.

Conceptual Frameworks

Military sociologists and other analysts have developed a number of conceptual frameworks to be used when studying civil–military relations. These frameworks have in turn been used by civilian authorities and military leaders as blueprints for various internal and external reform efforts. Most analyses of civil–military relations have taken the structural-functionalist, or consensus, approach (Jenkins & Moskos, 1981; Kourvetaris & Dobratz, 1977). Very few have applied the conflict and Marxist approaches (Jenkins and Moskos, 1981). Three major models have predominated: (1) The military is an independent, self-contained entity displaying sharp differences from civilian institutions and holding values different from civilian values. (2) The military is a reflection of societal bureaucratization and increasingly overlaps with civilian structures. (3) The military is a coercive force and acts as a peculiar form of social organization and power structure.

A number of political and military sociologists (Abrahamson, 1972; Albright, 1980; Huntington, 1957, 1968; Janowitz, 1971b; Larson, 1974; Luckham, 1971; Moskos, 1973; Moskow & Wood, 1988) proposed a broad range of conceptual frameworks of civil-military relations. Using western European political and military history as their material for analysis, these authors emphasized "structural" and "symmetrical" dimensions in military and civilian institutions, which tend to have limited application in attempts to explain the complexity of modern civil-military relations.

Janowitz (1971b) proposed four major historical models of civil-military relations: Based on U.S. and European experience, the *aristocratic/feudal,* the *democratic,* the *totalitarian,* and the *garrison* models. In the aristocratic/feudal model, a convergence of the interests and values of the civilian and military elites is present. These elites are linked by shared social status, kinship relations, and political beliefs. With the decline of the aristocracy and feudalism, this model gave way to the democratic, totalitarian, and garrison models of civil-military relations.

The most prominent feature of the democratic, or competitive professional model, is the divergence of the civilian and military professional elites. According to this model, education and professional expertise take precedence over ascriptive and feudal kinship-like characteristics. In addition, the military officer corps is no longer recruited from a narrow, aristocratic social base but rather from a more democratic, middle-class social base. The increasing democratization of recruitment, however, does not always make the military more democratic politically. In a comparative study of fourteen officer corps, George A. Kourvetaris and Betty A. Dobratz (1973) found that broadening recruitment did not deter officers from staging coups against civilian governments and imposing military dictatorships. Also, in the democratic model, the military is governed by the civilian political elite, which imposes a set of formal rules and regulations specifying the military's functions. As professionals in the service of the state, the officer corps has no social and political role but to provide military strategy and expertise and management of the military.

Janowitz argued that, in the absence of a democratic tradition, some industrial societies (e.g., Germany) saw the totalitarian model replace the aristocratic/feudal model. In the totalitarian model, a new revolutionary political elite, usually a lower-middle-class group that has infiltrated the military, emerges and becomes highly politicized. It allies temporarily with the traditional military elite. Its ultimate goal is to infiltrate and politicize the officer corps and thus destroy the professionalism of the military.

Finally, Lasswell introduced the garrison model during World War II. This model arises during conditions of prolonged international tension, during which a decline of civil supremacy over the military occurs. The garrison model can arise even in societies having effective democratic politics.

Two major interpretations of civil-military relations, advanced by Samuel Huntington and Janowitz, have guided our understanding of civil-military relations for a half a century. Huntington defined the military profession as a special type of profession characterized by expertise, social responsibility, and corporateness, or a sense of collective consciousness (Huntington, 1957:8–10). He identified three strands of U.S. military tradition that predated the Civil War: technicism, or the principle of specialization; popularism, or the "great principle of amalgamating all orders of society"; and military professionalism and expertise (Huntington, 1957:195–211). Huntington's description of civil-military relations was known as "objective civilian control" of the military; in other words, the military should be politically neutral and detached from social and political issues. Under objective civilian control, the power of the officer corps is minimized by fully professionalizing the corps, making it an efficient and politically neutral instrument of state policy (Larson, 1974:50–51). In short, the military services are "controlled and directed" by the government (Huntington, 1957:261). More specifically, Huntington's view of civil-military relations involved four major elements: (1) Military officers and civilians constituted two distinct groups. (2) Relations between these two groups were basically conflictual. (3) The subordination of the officer corps, except in matters requiring military expertise, kept the conflict in check. (4) Shifts in civil-military relations were, over time, perceived as a function of the degree of effectiveness of civilian control (Albright, 1980:555; Kemp and Hudlin, 1992).

Bengt Abrahamsson (1972) questioned Huntington's linkage of military professionalism and political neutrality. He rejected Huntington's proposition that military professionalism was the best guarantee of civilian supremacy over the military. Also, Abrahamsson argued that Huntington's concept of objective civilian control did not explain praetorian regimes. A number of writers (Nordlinger, 1977; Perlmutter, 1981; Welch, 1976) described praetorianism as the antithesis of civilian control; they saw praetorianism as likely to arise from conflict between soldiers and civilians that leads to a breakdown of civilian supremacy. Again, military professionalism does not always deter officers from taking over a civilian government (Kourvetaris, 1971b; Kourvetaris and Dobratz, 1977).

Like Huntington, Janowitz accepted officership as a profession. He stressed as its defining characteristics expertise, a lengthy education process, group identity, ethics, and standards of performance. But he saw the military as a dynamic, bureaucratic organization that responded to changing conditions and technologies. Janowitz argued that, as a result of broad social changes, the professional role of the officer has changed from the traditional warrior, or heroic role, to a managerial-technical role. He referred to this transformed role as one that had been civilianized, a term that indicated symmetrical development of the civilian and military occupational and organizational structures. At the same time, Janowitz employed the concept of "constabulary force": modern military professionals must be politically sensitive and prudent in the use of force, he believed. "Constabulary force" also suggests that the military should simultaneously be able to keep the peace and be prepared to make war (Larson, 1974:51). In addition, Janowitz suggested that the traditional officer, the warrior who uses maximum force to achieve military objectives, must be replaced by the thoughtful professional who takes into account political, economic, cultural, and other nonmilitary factors when formulating policy. In other words, Janowitz advocated a military broadly educated in both military and civilian matters that has developed political, sociological, managerial, historical, and technological skills. Only in such a military, he believed, would the civilianized (or citizen-soldier-type) officer be responsive to civil control of the military, or to what he referred to as "subjective control" (i.e., law, tradition, and professionalism integrated into civilian values and institutions).

In his critical analysis of officer corps, Arthur Larson (1974:53) argued that the different interpretations proposed by Huntington and Janowitz resulted in two different forms of U.S. military professionalism. One is known as pragmatic professionalism, a reconciliation of military professionalism with civil supremacy which leads to the civilianized model advanced by Janowitz. The other is radical professionalism, a more traditional warrior-type military which is distinct from civilian type institutions; this was the model proposed by Huntington. Huntington's position was that civil supremacy and control can be strengthened only by the abandonment of pragmatic professionalism and the embracing of radical professionalism, which would make objective control possible. Janowitz, on the other hand, proposed that pragmatic professionalism should not be abandoned but instead adapted to the new conditions of national security and civil control; the result would be a constabulary force.

To reconcile these divergent views, a number of military sociologists and professional officers (Deagle, 1973; Hauser & Bradford, 1971; Jordan, 1971; Moskos, 1971a, 1973; Taylor & Bletz, 1974) suggested a "military pluralistic" model. Moskos (1973), for example, proposed that the process of institutional transformation of the military be understood as a dialectical one in which "institutional persistencies" of the military react against the pressures toward "civilianization." He argued that, historically, the military has undergone several successive phases of "convergence" and "divergence," resulting in a "pluralistic" military in which some parts are convergent and others divergent with the civilian society. According to Moskos, the pluralistic model is more applicable to a U.S.-American or Western-type military.

Briefly stated, Moskos's framework contained three components: the convergent, which sought to bring military institutional structures closer to civilian structures; the divergent, or traditional, which sought to increase differentiation between military and civilian social structures and to achieve greater autonomy for the former; and "the segmented," which sought both to bring together and to compartmentalize civilianized and traditional trends, sometimes favoring convergent and sometimes favoring divergent features. Moskos also identified four major levels of variation on civil-military issues: (1) social recruitment/social composition (a measurement of whether armed forces are representative of the broader society); (2) institutional parallels (or discontinuities) between military and civilian structures;

(3) occupational/professional differentiation; and (4) ideological contrasts between civilian and military men.

These three models have become the brunt of much criticism. Larson (1974) called Moskos's pluralistic model untenable; he believed it would destroy the cohesiveness and discipline of the officer corps. Today, more military sociologists favor Janowitz's interpretation over Huntington's because they believe that it reflects contemporary trends and the forces at work in an all-volunteer force.

There is still a fourth view of military professionalism and civil-military relations. A number of scholars (Abrahamsson, 1972; Feld, 1975; Van Doorn, 1965, 1975) proposed the model of a politically independent and powerful military that acts and functions for its own corporate interests. According to these scholars, if these interests are under scrutiny and attack by civilian elites, the military mobilizes a lobby apparatus to counter its negative image. In this instance the military acts like an interest group. In this post–Cold War era, the military has increasingly adopted this strategy.

The Concept of the Military-Industrial Complex

In his farewell address to the nation in 1961, President Dwight D. Eisenhower, a professional soldier, warned "against the acquisition of unwarranted influence, whether sought or unsought, by the military-industrial complex." Moskos (1974) argued that the concept of the military-industrial complex was a logical development of U.S. political and sociological theory. Its conceptual and empirical underpinnings can be traced to C. Wright Mills. Mills's (1956) power elite thesis[3] provided the intellectual catalyst for the analysis of a tripartite national elite structure made up of the military, the corporate rich, and political leaders. During the 1960s and early 1970s the concept of the power elite and the military-industrial complex dominated much of the critical discussion about the U.S. military institution. Many critics argued that the military establishment was a grossly swollen, global institution. For example, it was argued that both the domestic and the international economies of the United States are intertwined with military spending.

The debate about the actual power of the military-industrial complex intensified during the 1970s with an outpouring of articles and books presenting different points of view. Carroll W. Pursell Jr. (1972) saw a strong link between the military and industrial complexes, while Sam C. Sarkesian (1972) argued for a more pluralist and promilitary view. Using the idea of "compensating strategies," Stanley Lieberson (1971) argued that the U.S. economy did not require extensive military outlays to sustain itself because diverse interest groups used various strategies to maximize their net gains in order to compensate for their long-range investments in the defense industry. Paul Stevenson (1971, 1973), on the other hand, criticized Lieberson for not taking into consideration the maximization of profits by those involved in the defense industry.

Those on the left of the political spectrum, especially Marxists and neo-Marxists, generally believe that the capitalist economy could not survive without huge military spending. According to them, military budgets favor the capitalist class and take away from spending on education, the poor, infrastructure improvements, and other public programs. In general, those critical of military spending are more likely to be well-educated, politically liberal, nonsouthern, younger, nonwhite, and atheistic. Conversely, those who are older, less educated, southern, and politically conservative tend to support military spending (Goertzel, 1987:61). The latter group associates the U.S. military with traditional U.S. values of patriotism and national strength and with traditional mores. They also view the military as a vehicle for mobility for minority groups and as one of the nation's largest employers.

Now that the Cold War is over, what is the rationale for the continuation of large military budgets? Despite some reductions in military expenditures, the military-industrial complex is still the most powerful and highly technological institution in the world. Critics argue that the military-industrial complex has been a self-serving symbiosis involving the corporate elites, government bureaucrats, and the military hierarchy. In addition, some critics believe that the military-industrial complex is a repressive force both at home and abroad (Moskos, 1974:499).

Indicators of the Military Industrial Complex

We have already seen that one of the most important manifestations of the military-industrial complex is military expenditures. Many people oppose military spending not only on moral grounds, but also for economic reasons. For example, Stanislaw Andreski (1968) argued that high military participation should increase economic growth rates and egalitarianism in society. But Erich Weede (1994) found no support for Andreski's contention that military participation promotes egalitarianism. Indeed, Albert Szymanski (1973) found a relationship between military spending and economic stagnation. And although Stevenson's (1973) findings indicated that U.S. corporations, especially those associated with defense industries, profit from huge military spending and that military spending stimulates the economy and provides jobs to millions of Americans, Y. H. Clarence Lo (1982), in his survey of national security expenditures between 1948 and 1953, found that top corporate leaders opposed higher military spending because they felt it did not contribute to significant increases in employment.

In the post-World War II years, the United States has led the world in introducing new weapons systems, especially in the strategic, or nuclear category, and we are the largest exporter of weapons and armaments in the world. The U.S. arms industry is enveloped by a culture of weapons procurement. Gordon Adams (1982:441–44) called that culture the "Iron Triangle," saying that it was created by three mutually supportive groups: defense contractors, congressional committees, and Defense Department personnel. Sam Marullo (1993:145) proposed that it should in fact by called the Iron Pentagon because it included two more groups, weapons laboratories and defense industry labor. The weapons laboratories designation includes some of the nation's best engineers and defense researchers who are located at various universities, defense institutes, and think tanks. The link between defense contractors and Defense Department personnel is especially strong: Adams (1982) found that a large number of retired U.S. military officers became leaders in major U.S. arms manufacturing firms.

Jerome Slater and Terry Nardin (1973) pointed to three primary characteristics of this mammoth military-industrial complex. First, it involves both formal and informal contact and mutual interest in a large-scale negotiation-producing-purchasing process. In this process, the federal government encourages the concentration of economic power within a relatively small number of military contractors. Second, there is a symbiotic relationship between the military and industry. Many defense industries have become dependent upon a single customer (the federal government) and their fates are determined by the political decisions and policies of the federal government. The military-industrial complex operates almost entirely with public funds channeled through government agencies. Third, both private and governmental agencies justify and maintain their positions by tying military-industrial contracts to the cause of national security; many now believe that this is no longer a credible rationale.

An often-cited critic of the military-industrial complex is Richard Barnet. Barnet (1991:152–55) argued that the unprecedented rate of technical progress in military technology and the spread of nuclear weapons was a new development in human history. He described the world in which we live as a "Balkanized world," that is, "a world of small, poor, and over-militarized states struggling for power." For some time, the United States had a monopoly in the nuclear weapons market, but this is no longer the case. As more countries supply nuclear arms, and they therefore become more easily available, the cost of maintaining military competitiveness has become astronomical, and this has depleted the national economies of many countries.

Given the nature of modern warfare, nuclear weapons, beyond their deterrent function, are relatively useless as instruments of foreign policy. Despite this fact, the United States still seems to operate on the old assumptions that military power has a significant political utility as an instrument of policy in the international system. In his earlier, more comprehensive work, *The Roots of War* (1972), Barnet argued persuasively that the roots of war must be found in the social institutions of U.S. society. War itself is also a social institution. More specifically, Barnet analyzed and explained three main roots of war: the concentration of power in the national security bureaucracy, the capitalist economy and business creed, and the vulnerability of the public to manipulation on national security issues (Barnet, 1972:339–41). He believed that the only way to end the United States wars and militarism was to steer its economic and political structures away from a policy of expansionism and imperial democracy to one built upon the interdependence of nations and peace.

A number of social scientists proposed different strategies, which emphasize the politics of peace and security rather than the military industrial complex. Johansen (1982:83, 293–349) suggested that peace and security required progress towards four major goals—"demilitarization," "depolarization," "denationalization," and "transnationalization"—to be pursued as national and/or international policies. Demilitarization is the de-emphasis of military power as a coercive instrument of the state. Demilitarization, in turn, leads to depolarization, or the lessening of tensions between nations. For example, the end of the Cold War between the United States and the former Soviet Union has contributed to both of these processes. However, the end of the Cold War did not result in denationalization but in its resurgence instead. Transnationalization means the de-emphasis of the nation state as a political unit and the emphasis on interdependence and cooperation among nations. In practice, however, opposite strategies to these goals are currently pursued by many nation states, especially by the military.

The late Boulding (1989:151–52) argued that the military diverts important resources which could be used for integrative development, or the development of respect, love, and a sense of community. He examined the destructive capacity of weapon systems, threat power, the power to conquer, defensive power, and consequences of military threat, and argued that this "hegemony" was the justification for military power of such powerful nations and empires as France, Britain, Spain, Belgium, the Netherlands, and the United States.

Similarly, Barnet (1972:48–75) found that the roots of war were initiated in the national security managers themselves, including the foreign policy makers and intelligence community, and the defense and military establishment. The abortive coup in the Soviet Union in 1991 was a case in point; a number of officers in the Russian military attempted to stage a dictatorship and take over the country. Along with "managers of war," a number of observers argue that in capitalist countries there exists a holy alliance of militarism, foreign policy, and multinational corporations. Barnet, for example, argued that most of the national security, foreign, and defense elites in the U.S. have been successful corporate men lawyers and bankers. Men such as Lovett, McCloy, Acheson, Dulles, Forrestall, Rusk, McNamara, Maxwell Taylor, Rostow, Bundy, Nitze, Harriman, Kissinger, and Brzesinski are some of the most visible members of an in-group fraternity with a high degree of group consciousness; in short, a governing class par excellence. It is an elite group of men by breeding and training. With a few exceptions, most of them have never held an elective office, and according to Barnet, advise the presidents of the United States by helping to initiate national security and defense establishments.

Another crucial political dimension of the military industrial complex (MIC) is arms sales and spending. On the subject of arms sales, Pierre (1982) envisioned a global politics of arms. For example, arms production and arms sales are major contributing factors in the emergence of regional powers with ambition to become hegemonic, such as Israel, Brazil, South Africa, and Turkey. The transfer of military technology from the more advanced to the less advanced countries contributes to the diffusion of militarism both in conventional and nuclear weapons. Politically and psychologically, arms sales to less advanced countries, and thus the procurement of sophisticated military technology, create a tremendous sense of legitimacy and advantage for one nation over another. As a rule, armaments, in and of themselves, do not lead to war. The underlying roots of war are usually found in political, economic, territorial, ethnic nationalist or ideological competition among nation states. For according to Clausewitz (1780–1831), a Prussian general and writer, if politics and diplomacy fail, war becomes a continuation of politics by other means. And as amassing of armaments is a prelude to war, arms sent into a region may exacerbate tensions while, at the same time, may deter aggression, restore a local imbalance, or enhance stability (Pierre, 1982:5).

With the end of the Cold War and the demise of state socialism in Eastern Europe and the former Soviet Union, what is the future of the arms industry and the military-industrial complex? For example, the Stockholm International Peace Research Institute (SIPRI) reported that because it would have resulted in mass unemployment, Russia's attempt to convert traditional military industries into civilian-type industries failed; thus the military-industrial complex there remains intact (Stockholm International Peace Research Institute Yearbook, 1993). Likewise, restructuring of NATO forces has not proceeded as fast as one would expect, partly because of recession and unemployment in NATO countries.

Although many argue that military spending stimulates the U.S. economy, others argue that it drains the economy by significantly fattening the already bloated federal budget deficit. The most comprehensive analysis of the overall impact of the military-industrial complex and "state capitalism" on the economy was undertaken by Seymour Melman. In his books *Pentagon Capitalism* (1970) and *The Permanent War Economy* (1985), Melman revealed how war-based state capitalism (by which he meant the federal government's control of investment, production, and labor) has harmed the overall economy (Marullo, 1993:154–55). According to Melman, "the most prominent indicator of this harm is the size of the Pentagon's administrative office, which had grown to a staff of 55,000 by the late 1960s, and was the largest industrial central administrative office in the United States—perhaps the world" (quoted in Marullo, 1993:155). By 1985 this number had increased to 120,000 men and women employed in material acquisition alone—"a central management definitely unmatched throughout the world" (Marullo, 1993:155). Because of its control over personnel, capital, and decision making, "the federal government does not 'serve' business or 'regulate' business," Melman concluded. "Government is business" (quoted in Marullo, 1993:155).

In 1993, the Clinton administration proposed military expenditures of $270.6 billion for 1994, $271.3 for 1995, and $266.2 for 1996 (SIPRI Yearbook, 1993:351). Active-duty military strength will shrink from 2.1 million persons in 1989 to 1.4 million or lower by the end of the 1990s (written communication, Moskos, 1994; see also Wong and McNally, 1994). However, because Republican majorities took over both the Senate and the House in 1994, it is questionable whether military spending can be expected to decrease. Republicans are traditionally in favor of a larger defense budget.

Military Interventionism and Praetorianism

An important issue in civil-military relations is what is known in the literature as military interventionism, that is, the intervention of a country's military officer corps (or a segment of it) directly in that country's national politics. While military interventionism also refers to military intervention of one country in another (e.g., the United States invasions of Panama and Grenada in the 1980s or the negotiated military intervention of the United States in Haiti in 1994), in this section we will primarily deal with internal military intervention. Internal military intervention refers to a country's use of extraparliamentary or dictatorial means to impose military rule on its people without regard to the civilian elected authority. The armed forces assume both a political and a military role and suspend any political authority except its own by abolishing political parties and parliament. Military intervention is a recurring and persistent phenomenon, especially in the countries of the Third World.

Military interventionism is also known as praetorianism.[4] In this section both terms will be used interchangeably. More specifically, praetorianism is a form of military authoritarianism in which no political institutions or political leaders are accepted as legitimate. A praetorian society, often beginning with a military coup d'etat, is usually preceded by a period of intense politicization and social fragmentation. For this reason, praetorianism may bring temporary relief from the social and political tensions existing in a country but does not solve the chronic problems of the society and polity.

There exist two primary schools of thought in regard to military intervention. One sees military institutions as energizing and modernizing forces and views the military as a champion of middle class aspirations, social change, and development. The other school sees military elites as ineffective agents of social change and development; thus intervention is seen to operate as a divisive force in society, especially between the "old" and the "new" emerging political and military elites.

While a substantial number of countries in the Third World are ruled by military elites, a number of students of civil-military relations have underscored an ongoing process of military disengagement from politics. Huntington (1991) referred to this process as the third wave, or the process of democratization that started first in southern Europe in the mid 1970s, when Portugal, Greece, and Spain moved from authoritarian regimes to democracy (Kourvetaris, 1987; O'Donnell et al., 1986). Terry Lynn Karl and Phillipe C. Schmitter (1994:43) have termed this the fourth wave of democratization.[5] This process of military disengagement from civilian politics has now also occurred in a number of countries in the Third World (Danopoulos, 1988; 1992). Most of these transitions to democracy can be found in Latin America, Asia, Africa, and eastern and southern Europe. We must be cautious, however, about concluding that all these countries have adopted the U.S., or Western model of democratization. For example, Turkey has moved to a democratic-type government, but its armed forces continue to have an enormous influence on domestic and regional politics. There is no democratization of social structure in Turkey. The largest ethnic minority, the Kurds, have been denied their civil and political rights of self-determination for many years.

Praetorianism is so common in Third World political systems that it is often impossible to distinguish between civilian and military regimes. In most of these countries, the military is part of the elite structure, and its corporate interests are interwoven with the very raison d'être of the nation-state. Andrew Ross (1987) believed that while overt forms of praetorianism are declining, covert forms are ascending and stated that the number of military-dominated regimes in the Third World has increased rather than decreased. According to Ross, 33 of the 110 developing countries in 1973 had military-dominated governments, compared to 55 of 107 developing countries in 1985.

During the l960s and 1970s, social scientists advanced theories to explain military intervention in the internal political processes of Third World countries. Some argued that military interventionism must be explained in terms of external or ecological causes. Huntington stated (1968) that the most salient factor underlying military intervention in domestic politics was not military professionalism but rather political decay, corruption, and the general politicization of society in general. Others (Bienen, 1971; Johnson, 1962; Needler, 1966; Pye, 1962; Tannahill, 1976) advanced modernization and development theories by looking at middle-class values and national development factors (i.e., strategic considerations, superpower rivalry, balance of power, and geopolitics). Still others, especially Janowitz, sought to explain military interventionism in terms of the internal or organizational aspects of military institutions themselves.

Yet another theory explained interventionism in terms of size of the military and propinquity. Edward Feit (1975) argued that, in the Third World, the smaller the military, the more likely it was to intervene in the domestic political order. The propinquity theory holds that if one country in a region is ruled by a military dictatorship, other countries in the region are more likely to follow the same pattern. Lee Sigelman (1975) challenged this domino-effect thesis and also found no supporting evidence of Feit's size-intervention hypothesis. William R. Thompson (1978) challenged both Feit and Sigelman, saying that they failed to clarify the empirical relationship between relative military size as measured by military participation ratios (MPR) and the likelihood of a military coup; Thompson found weak negative correlations between MPR and coup likelihood at the world level. He also found that the propinquity thesis is not supported by empirical evidence.

S. E. Finer (1967) suggested that the principle of civil supremacy and the level of political culture were the most important inhibitors of military intervention. In his survey of military interventions he found an inverse relationship between the propensity of militaries to intervene and nations' levels of political culture. Thus, in countries having high levels of political culture (e.g., the United States, England, and Canada), the armed forces engaged only in prescribed modes of political influence, whereas in countries having low levels of political culture, military intervention was more overt, frequent, and enduring. In other words, weak governments, not strong armies, account for the prevalence of military coups.

Some theorists believe that military interventions are characteristic of societies having low levels of economic productivity and high degrees of social cleavage. When a political process has been disrupted, a vacuum is created into which the military steps and assumes control. In this instance, the military becomes politicized by conditions of civilian political failure. If a civilian political leadership's corruption, factionalism, illegitimacy, and inefficiency endanger national cohesiveness and security, the military justifies intervention by adopting the pretext of preserving stability, law, and order. Also, if the civilian populace demonstrates strong discontent with existing economic inequities, this creates an opportunity for ambitious officers to assume administrative control of the national government.

Some agreement exists among students of civil-military relations regarding the beliefs that the armed forces in Third World nation-states follow a developmental orientation and that economic development and modernization are consequences of military rule. However, no consensus exists regarding the political orientations of military officers. One group of researchers sees the military in Third World countries as progressive; another, as defenders of the status quo. A third group views the military as varying with societal development. Civil-military relations scholars seem no longer to be interested in the causes of military intervention but rather in the processes of military disengagement and democratization. The demise of military regimes in Greece, Spain, and Portugal in the 1970s, in Argentina and the Philippines in the 1980s, and in Haiti in 1994 raises the following questions: What motivates the military to withdraw from civilian politics? Is military disengagement based on a genuine interest on the part of the military in advancing the processes of democratization, or do military leaders simply use disengagement as a tactical move?

The main argument that praetorians make when rationalizing intervention is that their patriotism and dedication allow them to be more effective governors than corrupt and unprincipled civilian rulers. Neal R. Tannahill (1976), however, in a comparative study of military and civilian governments in South America from 1948 to 1967, did not find any significant differences between civilian and military rulers. The chief difference was the military's tendency to be more repressive and conservative than civilian governments. Due to its conservative nature, the military is often incapable of understanding the forces that drive social change. In their study of the political orientations of fourteen officers corps, Kourvetaris and Dobratz (1977) found that broadening the social base of recruitment has not been accompanied by political democratization in officers' political attitudes and/or political behavior. They argued that broadening the base of officer recruitment has in fact encouraged officers to intervene in the processes of domestic politics. The authors of eight different case studies (Danopoulos, 1988) of countries that had experienced praetorianism made an effort to shed light on the nature of praetorianism, military disengagement, and the future of civilian rule in these societies and polities. In reviewing these case studies Kourvetaris (1988:278) concluded:

> *While we are seeing more military disengagement from civilian politics, it is not clear that such a trend will continue in the future. As long as the military does not respect the principle of civilian authority, military praetorianism will continue. Moreover, if the corporate interests of the military are in any way undermined under civilian political elites, the propensity to disengage from politics will all but disappear. Along the same issue Karl and Schmitter (1994:60–61), reviewing the prospects for democratization around the world, concluded that "the contemporary international system will be deeply affected by this fourth wave of democratization, but not in a single or predictable way...long established democracies like the United States will be pushed to decide whether or not to make the promotion and sustenance of democracy a central foreign policy goal...." The same authors also*

conclude, "Sanctions may be frequently applied to those who dramatically and systematically violate widespread norms of human rights....What ultimately will determine the efficacy of these external incentives depends as much upon the sensitive recognition by 'conditioners' that democracies come in diverse types, by various routes, from different points of departure, and under different constraints, as it does upon the actions taken by authoritarians reluctant to reform." By the early 1990s one can argue that most countries irrespective of political regimes (capitalist, socialist, or mixed economies) are more interested in international trade and business rather than issues of human and democratic rights, e.g., China, Asian conference on trade in Indonesia in Nov. 1994, Middle East peace accords, etc. Most of these foreign policy initiatives are motivated more by economic and trade considerations than human and democratic rights for the people of these nations.

Summary and Conclusion

The growth of the military as a political power structure and civil-military relations were discussed. The end of the Cold War in 1989 has brought to focus the role of the American military establishment in a post-Cold War era. Those who have a conservative orientation view the world as unstable and unpredictable and tend to support a strong United States' military. Those who have a liberal orientation tend to be critical of the large military budget.

From a different perspective there are those who perceive the military as a client of the state, and subordinate to civilian authority. Others view it as a power elite and as an essentially independent institution. Military sociologists are more interested in the relationship between the military and other social institutions. Kurt Lang places the sociological study of the military within the more inclusive framework of the sociology of conflict.

The study of the military combines elements of both profession and organization. Moskos argues that the military is moving away from a traditional view as a profession or institution toward an occupational model. The most prominent feature in a democratic or competitive professional model is the divergence of the civilian and military professional elites. According to this model, education and professional expertise take precedence over ascriptive and feudal kinship-like characteristics.

Two major interpretations of civil-military relations were advanced by Morris Janowitz and Samuel Huntington. Huntington defined the military profession as a special type of profession characterized by expertise, social responsibility, and corporateness. Huntington's description of civil-military relations is viewed as politically neutral and detached from social and political issues. Like Huntington, Janowitz accepted officer corps as a profession but he saw the military as a dynamic, bureaucratic organization that responds to changing conditions and technologies. Janowitz advocated a military broadly educated in both military and civilian matters.

Arthur Larson argued that the different interpretations proposed by Huntington and Janowitz resulted in two different forms of United States military professionalism. One is known as pragmatic professionalism or close to a civilianized model and the other is radical professionalism or close to a traditional warrior-type military.

The concept of military-industrial complex was also analyzed. The debate about the actual power of the military-industrial complex intensified during the 1970s. There were those who were critical of the strong link between the military and industrial complexes while others took a more promilitary view. Indicators of the military-industrial complex were also discussed by looking at military expenditures, military spending, arms sales, and transfers.

Finally, the issue of military interventionism and praetorianism was seen as a recurrent and persistent phenomenon. Two schools of thought in regard to military intervention were examined. One sees military as modernizing forces and a champion of middle class aspirations. The other sees military elites as ineffective agents of social change and development.

Endnotes

1. See also Kaplan (1994), Kohn (1994), Melman (1988), and Van Creveld (1991). These works argue that war between nation-states will no longer be the dominant mode of conflict.

2. One can make a distinction between the sociology of the military and military sociology. The former is more conceptual, placing emphasis on the study of organizational, professional, and institutional aspects of the military, while the latter is more applied, placing emphasis on studying ways to make the military more efficient. Most research on and teaching about the military takes place outside departments of sociology. In the American Sociological Association directories and in graduates departments of sociology, only a handful of sociologists list sociology of the military or military sociology as their specialty. In reality, however, the categories of sociologists of the military and military sociologists are not necessarily mutually exclusive.

3. Following the traditiion of Mills "power elite" concept (1956) are such studies as Lasswell's (1945) concept of the "garrison state," Mosca's "ruling class" thesis, Michels's notion of the "iron law of oligarchy," (1959) Burnham's (1941) "managerial revolution," Melman's (1970) *Pentagon Capitalism* (1970), Cook's (1962) *Warfare State* Wolpin's (1981) *Militarism and Social Revolution in the Third World*.

4. Praetorianism originated with the Roman Praetorian Guard, the prototype of historical military interventionism. A small military contingent in Rome preserved the legitimacy of the empire by defending the Senate against rebellious military garrisons (see Perlmutter (1981)). The term *praetorianism* is used extensively by political scientists and signifies the active intervention of the military in national politics, especially in countries of the Third World.

5. Huntington (1991) identifies three major historical waves of democratization: The first wave had its roots in the American and French revolutions, the second short wave occurred during World War II, and the third wave began in the mid-1970s in southern Europe with military disengagement from politics. Karl and Schmitter (1994) identify four somewhat different historical waves of democratization: The first began in the 1820s with a limited male suffrage in the United States but receded quickly; the second corresponded with World War I but failed; the third took place during World War II and its aftermath but many countries in the Third World degenerated into authoritarian regimes during the 1960s; and the fourth wave is Huntington's third wave.

References

Abrahamsson, Bengt. 1972. *Military Professionalization and Political Power.* Beverly Hills: Sage.

Adams, Gordon. 1981. "Inside the Weapons Elite— The Iron Triangle." *The Nation.* October 31.

Albright, David E. 1980. "A Comparative Conceptualization of Civil-Military Relations." *World Politics.* Vol. 32, no. 4:553–76.

Andreski, Stanislaw. 1968. *Military Organization and Society,* 2nd ed. Stanford: Stanford University Press.

Barnet, Richard. 1972. *The Roots of War.* Baltimore: Penguin.

———. 1991. "The Search for National Security." In *Crisis in American Institutions,* 8th ed. ed. Jerome H. Skolnick and Elliot Currie, Pp. 529– 535. New York: Harper Collins.

Bienen, Henry. 1971. *The Military and Intervention.* Chicago: Aldine.

Boulding, Kenneth E. 1989. *Three Faces of Power.* London and New Delhi: Sage.

Burnham, T. B. 1941. *The Managerial Revolution.* New York: John Day.

Cook, Fred J. 1962. *The Warfare State.* New York: Mcmillan.

Cross, Sharly, and Marina A. Oborotova, eds. 1994. *The New Chapter in United States-Russian Relations.* Westport, Conn.: Greenwood.

Danopoulos, C., ed. 1992. *Civilian Rule in the Developing World.* Boulder: Westview.

———, ed. 1988. *Military Disengagement from Politics.* London: Routledge.

Deagle, Edwin A., Jr. 1973. "Contemporary Professionalism and Future Military Leadership." *Annals.* Vol. 406 (March):162–70.

Feit, Edward. 1973. *The Armed Bureaucrats.* Boston: Houghton Mifflin.

———. 1975. "A Comment on Sigelman's Military Size and Political Intervention." *Journal of Political and Military Sociology.* Vol. 3 (Spring):101–02.

Feld, M. D. 1975. "Military Professionalism and the Mass Army." *Armed Forces and Society.* Vol. 1 (Winter):191–214.

———. 1968. "Professionalism, Nationalism, and the Alienation of the Military." In *Armed Forces and Society,* ed. Jacques Van Doorn, ed. 55–70. The Hague: Mouton.

Finer, S. E. 1967. *The Man on Horseback: The Role of the Military in Politics.* New York: Praeger.

Goertzel, Ted. 1987. "Public Opinion Concerning Military Spending in the United States: 1937– 1985." *Journal of Political and Military Sociology* Vol. 15 (Spring):61–72.

Harries-Jenkins, Gwynn. 1990. "The Concept of Military Professionalism." *Defense Analysis.* Vol. 6, no. 2:117–30.

Hauser, William M., and Zeb B. Bradford, Jr. 1971. "Modernizing the Military Profession." Inter-University Seminar on Armed Forces and Society. Chicago, IL.

Huntington, Samuel. 1968. *Political Order in Changing Societies.* New Haven: Yale University Press.

———. 1957. *The Soldier and the State: The Theory and Practice of Civil-Military Relations.* Cambridge: Harvard University Press.

———. 1991. *The Third Wave: Democratization in the Late Twentieth Century.* Norman: University of Oklahoma Press.

Janowitz, Morris. 1971b. "Military Organization." In *Handbook of Military Institutions,* ed. Roger W. Little, Pp. 13–51. Beverly Hills: Sage.

———. 1960. *The Professional Soldier: A Social and Political Portrait.* New York: Sage Foundation.

Jenkins, Harries Gwyn, and Charles C. Moskos. 1981. "Armed Forces and Society." *Current Sociology.* Vol. 29, no. 3:1–170.

Johansen, Robert C. 1982. Toward an Alternative Security System: Moving Beyond the Balance of Power in the Search for World Security. In *Alternatives.*

Johnson, John, ed. 1962. *The Role of the Military in Underdeveloped Countries.* Princeton: Princeton University Press.

Jordan, Amos A. 1971. "Officer Education," ed. Roger W. Little. *Handbook of Military Institutions.* Beverly Hills: Sage.

Kaplan, Robert. 1994. "The Coming Anarchy." *Atlantic Monthly.* February:44–81.

Karl, Terry Lynn, and Phillipe C. Schmitter. 1994. "Democratization around the Globe: Opportunities and Risks." In *World Security Challenges for a New Century,* 2nd ed., ed. Michael T. Klare and Daniel C. Thomas. New York: St. Martin's Press.

Kemp, Kenneth W., and Charles Hudlin. 1992. "Civil Supremacy over the Military." *Armed Forces and Society.* Fall.

Kirby, Andrew, ed. 1992. *The Pentagon and The Cities.* Newberry Park, CA: Sage.

Kohn, Richard H. 1994. "The Crisis in Military-Civilian Relations." *The National Interest.* No. 35, (Spring):1–17.

Kourvetaris, George A. 1988. "Civil-Military Relations and Military Disengagement." In *Military Disengagement from Politics,* ed. C. Danopoulos, Pp. 269–279. London: Routledge.

———. 1987. "Elites, Electoral Politics, and Democratization of Post-Dictatorial Regimes of Greece, Spain, and Portugal." Comparative Studies of Elites section of the American Sociological Association Meetings. August, Chicago.

———. 1971a. "Professional Self-Images and Political Perspectives in the Greek Military." *American Sociological Review.* Vol. 36 (December): 1043–57.

———. 1971b. "The Role of the Military in Greek Politics." *International Review of History and Political Science* August:91–114.

———. with Betty A. Dobratz 1973. "Social Recruitment and Political Orientation of the Officer Corps in a Comparative Perspective." *Pacific Sociological Review* Vol. 16, no. 2:228–54.

Kourvetaris, George A., and Betty A. Dobratz, eds. 1977. *World Perspectives in the Sociology of the Military.* New Brunswick: Transaction Books.

Lang, Kurt. 1972. *Military Institutions and the Sociology of War.* Beverly Hills, CA: Sage.

Larson, Arthur. 1974. "Military Professionalism and Civil Control: A Comparative Analysis of Two Interpretations." *Journal of Political and Military Sociology.* Vol. 2 (Spring):57–72.

Lasswell, Harold D. 1962. "The Garrison-State Hypothesis Today." Pp. 51–70 in Samuel P. Huntington (ed.) *Changing Patterns of Military Politics.* New York: Free Press.

Lieberson, Stanley. 1971. "An Empirical Study of Military-Industrial Linkages." *American Journal of Sociology* January:563–84.

Lo, Y. H. Clarence. 1982. *Pentagon Capitalism.* New York: McGraw-Hill.

Luckham, A. R. 1971. "Comparative Typology of Civil-Military Relations." *Government and Opposition.* Vol. 6 (Winter):5–35.

Margiotta, Franklin, ed. 1978. *The Changing World of the American Military.* Boulder: Westview.

Martin, Creveld Van. 1991. *The Transformation of War.* New York: Maxwell Macmillan International.

Marullo, Sam. 1993. *Ending the Cold War at Home.* New York: Lexington.

Melman, Seymour. 1988. *The Demilitarized Society.* Montreal: Harvest House.

———. 1970. *Pentagon Capitalism.* New York: McGraw-Hill.

———. 1985. *The Permanent War Economy: American Capitalism in Decline,* rev. ed. New York: Simon and Schuster.

Mills, C. W. 1956. *The Power Elite.* New York: Oxford University Press.

Moskos, Charles Jr. 1988. "Institutional and Occupational Trends in Armed Forces." In *The Military: More Than a Job?,* ed. Charles Moskos and Frank R. Wood, Pp. 15–26. New York: Pergamon-Brassey's, International Defense Publishers, Inc.

———. 1974. "The Concept of the Military-Industrial Complex: Radical Critique or Liberal Bogey?" *Social Problems.* Vol. 21, no. 4:487–512.

———. 1973. "The Emergent Military: Civil, Traditional, or Plural?" *Pacific Sociological Review* vol. 16, no. 2:255–80.

———, ed. 1971a. *Public Opinion and the Military Establishment.* Beverly Hills: Sage.

Moskos, Charles Jr., and Frank R. Wood, eds. 1988. *The Military: More than a Job?* New York: Pergamon-Brassey's.

Needler, Martin C. 1966. "Political Development and Military Intervention in Latin America." *American Political Science Review,* Vol. 60 (September):616–26.

Nordlinger, Eric. 1977. *Soldiers in Politics: Military Coups and Governments.* Englewood Cliffs: Prentice-Hall.

O'Donnell, Guillermo, Philippe C. Schmitter, and Laurence Whitehead. 1986. *Transitions from Authoritarian Rule: Southern Europe.* Baltimore: Johns Hopkins University Press.

Perlmutter, Amos. 1981. *Political Roles and Military Rules.* London: Frank Cass.

Pierre, Andrew J. 1982. *The Global Politics of Arms Sales.* Princeton: Princeton University Press.

Pursell, Carroll W., Jr., ed. 1972. *The Military-Industrial Complex.* New York: Harper and Row.

Pye, Lucien. 1962. "Armies in the Process of Political Modernization." In ed. John J. Johnson, 69–90. *The Role of the Military in Underdeveloped Countries.* Princeton, N.J.: Princeton University Press.

Ross, Andrew L. 1987. "Dimensions of Militarization in the Third World." *Armed Forces and Society.* Vol. 13, no. 4:561–78.

Sarkesian, Sam C., ed. 1972. *The Military-Industrial Complex: A Reassessment.* Beverly Hills: Sage.

Sigelman, Lee. 1975. "Research Note: Military Size and Political Intervention." *Journal of Political and Military Sociology.* Vol. 3 (Spring):95–100.

Slater, Jerome, and Terry Nardin. 1973. "The Concept of a Military-Industrial Complex." In *Testing the Theory of the Military-Industrial Complex,* ed. Steven Rosen, 27–60. Lexington, Mass.: D.C. Heath.

Sorokin, Konstantin. 1993. "Conversion in Russia: The Need for a Balanced Strategy." *The Journal of Political and Military Sociology* Vol. 21 (Winter):163.

———, and C. P. Danopoulos. 1994. "Challenges of Military-Civilian Conversion: U.S. and Russian Experiences." In *The New Chapter in United States-Russian Relations: Opportunities and Challenges,* ed. Sharly Cross and Marina A. Oborotova, Westport, Conn.: Greenwood.

Stevenson, Paul. 1971. "American Capitalism and Militarism: A Critique of Lieberson." *American Journal of Sociology.* Vol. 77 (July):134–38.

———. 1973. "The Military-Industrial Complex: An Examination of the Nature of Corporate Capitalism in America." *Journal of Political and Military Sociology.* Vol. 1 (Fall):247–59.

Stockholm International Peace Research Institute (SIPRI) Yearbook. 1993. New York: Oxford University Press.

Szymanski, Albert. 1973. "Military Spending and Economic Stagnation." *American Journal of Sociology.* Vol. 79 (July):1–14.

Tannahill, Neal R. 1976. "The Performance of Military and Civilian Governments in South America, 1948–1967." *Journal of Political and Military Sociology.* Vol 4 (Fall):233–44.

Taylor, William J., and Donald F. Bletz. 1974. "A Case for Officer Graduate Education." *Journal of Political and Military Sociology.* Vol. 2 (Fall):251–67.

Thompson, William R. 1978. "Another Look at the Feit-Sigelman Dispute over the Relative Military Size-Coup Propensity Hypothesis." *Journal of Political and Military Sociology.* Vol. 6 (Spring):93–99.

Van Doorn, Jacques. 1975. "The Decline of the Mass Army in the West; General Reflections." *Armed Forces and Society.* Vol. 2 (Winter):147–57.

———. 1965. "The Officer Corps: A Fusion of Profession and Organization." *European Journal of Sociology.* Vol. 6 (August):262–82.

Weede, Erich. 1994. "The Impact of Military Participation on Economic Growth and Income Inequality: Some New Evidence." *Journal of Political and Military Sociology.* Vol. 21, no. 2: (Winter) 241–258.

Welch, Claude, Jr., ed. 1976. *Civilian Control of the Military.* New York: State University of New York Press.

Wolpin, Miles D. 1981. *Militarism and Social Revolution in the Third World.* Ottowa: Allanheld, Osmun and Company.

Wong, Leonard, and Jeffrey McNally. 1994. "Downsizing the Army: Some Policy Implications Facing Survivors." *Armed Forces and Society.* Winter:199–216.

C h a p t e r 7

Political Participation and Voting

The democratic ideal demands citizen participation. Ironically, although Americans are considered a rather "high participation" society, or a society of joiners (even Tocqueville made that observation long ago), we are a "low turnout" society when it comes to voting. Moreover, the majority of Americans participate in the political process only by voting, and fewer citizens are voting than ever before. Political organizations at all levels of the electoral process find themselves struggling, not only because voters refuse to participate, but also because voters are unreliable in their voting habits (Gans, 1988:67). In addition, most citizens dislike professional politicians, tend to be critical of them, and entertain unrealistic expectations of them. Accompanying decreasing voter participation and increasing criticism of professional politicians is the decline of party loyalty. The meteoric rise in the polls of Ross Perot during the 1992 presidential election was in part an indication of popular revolt against professional politicians. William Schneider (1992) argued that dislike of political professionalism and politics in general in the United States is usually reinforced by political complexity, political apathy, and the cynicism of the middle class. Jeffrey C. Goldfarb (1991) showed how cynicism has undermined the culture of politics and perverted U.S. social and political institutions. Voting participation and political involvement have been a lasting preoccupation of many political sociologists. *Psephology* (the study of voting) was one of the earliest focuses of political sociology. It continues to draw interest today: A survey of five recent years' worth of sociological and political science abstracts on twenty different topics in political sociology found that voting was mentioned 8,383 times—more than any other topic.

The United States has one of the lowest voting records among the industrialized nations of the world. Sidney Verba and Norman H. Nie (1972) summarized citizen participation twenty years ago:

Only about 4 to 5% are active in a party, campaign, and attend meetings. About 10% make monetary contributions, about 13% contact public offi-

cials, and about 15% display a button or sticker. Around 25 or 30% try to proselytize others to vote a certain way, and from 40 to 70% vote in any given election. . . . [T]here seems to be a hierarchy of political involvement, in that persons at a given level of involvement tend to perform many of the same acts, including those performed by persons at lower levels of involvement. . . .

About one-third of the American adult population can be characterized as politically apathetic or passive; in most cases they are unaware, literally, of the political part of the world around them. Another 60% play largely spectator roles; they watch, they cheer, they vote, but they do not battle. . . . [T]he percentage of gladiators does not exceed 5 to 7%.

R. R. Alford and R. Friedland (1975) noted that participation without power is more characteristic of the poor and the working classes, while power with or without participation is more characteristic of the rich and the upper classes. This means that voting is the only form of power exercised by the poor, while the rich can influence politics in different ways. Those in higher socioeconomic classes tend to participate more than those on the bottom of the social class structure (Harrigan, 1993:122). Voting is therefore not equally representative of all the classes in the U.S. political system.

Reviewing the empirical evidence of the social roots of political participation and voting in western democracies, Seymour M. Lipset (1981:229) concluded that neither high nor low rates of participation and/or voting are in themselves good or bad for democracy. Lipset (1981:226–27) pointed out that there are those who believe that democracy is best served by high voter turnout because it contributes to a healthy citizenry and consensus on various social and political issues, while others believe that a lack of participation and representation may indicate a less effective citizenship and an absence of loyalty to the political system as a whole.

Classical theorists of democracy believe that active citizen participation in the political process can prevent the power elites from gaining undue power. However, active citizen involvement in politics also creates problems because (1) not every citizen is equally informed about politics, politicians, and issues; (2) voting is not always a result of a rational decision on the part of voters; and (3) increased citizen participation may lead to greater demands for social services, benefits, and programs from the government, which is already over-extended and in debt. On balance, the downward trend of voter participation in the last thirty years pleases realists and upsets some advocates for the poor and the classical proponents of democracy.

In this chapter, three basic questions will preoccupy us: (1) What is the nature of political participation? (2) Why do people vote or not vote? (3) What are some sociodemographic, organizational, stratification, and sociopsychological correlates of political participation? The emphasis in this chapter will be on conventional or institutionalized forms of political participation, for example, voting. The more unconventional forms of political participation, for example, political protest, will be discussed in Chapter 10.

The Nature and Concept of Political Participation

Widespread political participation and universal suffrage are rather recent phenomena. In the United States, women gained the right to vote only in the 1920s. In certain areas of the country African Americans could not exercise their right to vote until the 1960s. In South Africa, the African Black majority was only recently granted political and civil rights such as voting. Throughout much of political history, voting was limited to certain privileged classes and property owners. Even today, the right to vote is still denied to certain populations in many countries of the Third World. Also, Western-type political participation and electoral politics are generally denied the citizens of countries under military rule or dictatorship. For example, until 1989, there were no competitive elections in Eastern European communist regimes or in what are now the former Soviet republics. In the remaining communist countries, including the People's Republic of China, North Korea, Vietnam, and Cuba, there is still no open political participation. This, however, does not mean that people in those countries are not interested in politics or political issues. Instead, their politics is usually controlled or manipulated by the ruling party which controls the government and does not allow criticism. In general, widespread political participation and electoral politics are most characteristic of capitalist liberal democracies.

Defining Political Participation

Most definitions of political participation emphasize the influence of the citizen on the decision-making process at various levels of local, state, and national government. People may vote regularly but have very little direct influence on government policies. Thus, policy decisions are not always democratically arrived at even in nations that purport to be democracies.

Aristotle explained the idea of citizen participation in terms of linking the community and citizen in a sharing relationship between polity, constitution, and citizenship. Lester Milbrath and M. L. Goel (1977:2) defined political participation "as those actions of private citizens by which they seek to influence or to support government and politics." Similarly, Verba and Nie (1972:2) defined it in terms of the influence citizens have in the selection of government personnel. For our purposes, political participation includes all the activities of individuals or groups that seek to influence government policies.

Political participation can take two basic forms—"conventional" and "unconventional." Conventional forms include activities such as voting, campaigning, and contacting elected officials. They involve all those activities that take place within a relatively prescribed, structured, and institutional environment. Conventional activities aim primarily at legitimation of the political system. Unconventional, or less conventional, forms of participation include all those activities by citizens, groups, and organizations that do not follow the routinized institutional forms of politics, such as social protest, demonstrations, picketing, political violence, radicalism, and revolution. Activities of this nature aim at partial or total change of the political system.

Participation, Conceptualization, Sophistication

The impact of political participation on the individual in a democracy has been recognized not only by contemporary political sociologists, but also by classical political theorists: Jean-Jacques Rousseau (1712–1778) and John Stuart Mill (1806–1873) recognized the necessity of citizen participation beyond voting. Jan Leighley (1991) viewed participation as a stimulus to political conceptualization and enhanced knowledge and sophistication about politics. Patrick Pierce (1993) found that political sophistication and perception of a candidate's personality were helpful in candidate evaluation. But Stephen L. Bennett and William R. Klecka (1970) believed that participation enhances conceptualization and knowledge about politics only when it meets three criteria: (1) when it places the participant in direct conflict with others' beliefs, (2) when tangible benefits are at stake, and (3) when both individual initiative and input are necessary for political participation. Bennet and Klecka's theory has been supported by empirical findings reported by Leighley (1991:207). Also, six variables are crucial in determining our understanding of politics, according to Leighley (1991:204). These are education, media use, age, influence of friends, political interest, and complexity of issues. For instance, the more educated an individual, the greater his/her political interest is likely to be. The extent to which political issues are easily understood determines the probability of voters' political participation. And studies show that younger and elderly adults do not have high participation rates in electoral politics. Participation is also influenced by such demographic characteristics as race, sex, family income; sense of civic duty; strength of partisanship; and the presence or absence of other ways to influence government. Interestingly, in a study on voting, Robert B. Smith (1993) argued that the U.S. voter is no more sophisticated in the 1990s than he/she was in the 1950s.

Marvin Olsen (1982:22) believed that citizen participation allows individuals "to be informed, interested and involved citizens who have a sense of control over their own lives." Similarly, Kenneth Thomson (1971a) noted that political participation increases individuals' political knowledge, enhances their subjective sense of governmental legitimacy, and hastens individual self-realization. In short, those who are involved in political participation tend to be more politically sophisticated, to have a greater understanding and knowledge of politics, and to have an enhanced sense of political efficacy. The more efficacious a person feels, the greater is his/her tendency to participate in conventional politics (Kourvetaris/Dobratz, 1980:51).

K. Knight (1985) found that political sophistication has an effect on the extent to which voters rely on issues and ideology when evaluating candidates but has no effect on how individuals will be influenced by a candidate's traits.

Herbert J. Gans (1988:71–75) discussed a number of direct and indirect forms of political participation and middle class individualism. His direct methods of political participation include voting, a sudden spurt of citizen letter writing or cable activity, and vigorous support of single-issue interests. This participation may take place individually or through organizations or interest groups. Those who have an overwhelming commitment to an issue are more likely to be active in politics. However, as the issue dies out or is resolved, there is usually a decline in their political interest. There are three indirect forms of political involvement, according to Gans: political surveillance, griping, and holding an important position. Political surveillance, a concept originally introduced by Harold D. Lasswell (1951:37–51), is monitoring of the environment and learning about potential dangers that political issues pose to one's life and interests. Most people perceive politics as something remote, and they do not see it as a potential source of danger. According to one study of television news, only 7 percent of viewers are really interested in political surveillance (Gans, 1988:71). An example of griping is when citizens complain about politicians or political situations in reaction to a particular event or issue, such as Watergate, the Iranian hostage crisis, or the Iran-Contra arms deal. Griping is aggravated by our basic mistrust of professional politicians. Furthermore, because people fail to understand the complexity of political issues, they expect instant solutions to societal problems. Finally, holding an important and influential position in industry, a union, a church, or the armed forces is also an indirect form of political involvement. Such positions enable us to exercise indirect influence on the political process.

Why People Participate in Politics

Although political participation is the right and civic duty of every citizen in a democratic society, the proportion of people participating varies from one polity to another. Why people participate or not has continually interested political sociologists.

People participate in politics for many reasons. These reasons usually involve various rewards, interests, or beliefs. John Wilson (1973) identified three major rewards sought by those who participate in politics: material benefits (tangible rewards such as government jobs), nonmaterial benefits (intangible rewards such as friendship), and purposive benefits (intrinsic rewards such as a sense of satisfaction). These benefits can be divided into collective and selective rewards. The former benefit the entire community or group, while the latter benefit only those who participate in politics (Rosenstone & Hansen, 1993:16–18). Steven J. Rosentstone and John M. Hansen (1993:18–19) believed that, in general, those people who have an immediate interest in political outcomes are more likely to participate in politics than are those who do not. Such people strongly prefer one political outcome over another, are closely identified with the political contenders, and hold strong beliefs and preferences. In general, those voters who identify closely with the political beliefs and political attitudes of politicians tend to support those politicians and actively participate in electoral politics. Lasswell (1951:6) suggested that a number of social and social-psychological factors are associated with political participation, including needs for power, wealth, a sense of well-being, development of a skill (communication), enlightenment (sophistication, knowledge), rectitude (having good judgment or moral integrity), and respect. In a similar vein, Robert E. Lane (1959:102) examined a number of conscious and unconscious motives for participating in politics, including the need for friendship and affection, a desire for relief from psychological tensions, a need to understand the world, a desire to influence others and to enhance one's self-esteem, and a desire for political efficacy.

People may enter politics because of family tradition, idealism, the influence of friends and relatives, or a strong feeling about political issues. Ross Perot entered politics in 1992 because he said he wanted to give something back to the country. Carol Mosley-Braun, the first African American woman to be elected senator from Illinois, said she was motivated to enter the race by the way white male senators interrogated Anita Hill during the Clarence Thomas Supreme Court confirmation hearings.

Models of Political Participation

There are a number of models and typologies of conventional political participation. In his early formulation, Milbrath (1965) described a three-tiered hierarchy of political participation: (1) The *apathetics:* those persons who do not participate or who have withdrawn from the political process; they make up about 33 percent of the eligible voting population. (2) The *spectators:* those persons who are minimally involved; they make up about 60 percent of the eligible voting population. (3) The *gladiators:* those persons who are active in politics; they make up only 5 to 7 percent of the eligible voting population. In their later work, Milbrath and Goel (1977) extended Milbrath's typology by dividing the gladiator group into four conventional subtypes (contact specialists, communicators, party and campaign workers, and community activists) and one unconventional subtype (protesters).

Somewhat similar models have been suggested by Verba and Nie (1972) and by Olsen (1973). Drawing on national survey data, Verba and Nie described various types of voters or political actors: the *totally inactive* (apathetics, about 22 percent of eligible voters), *voting specialists* (about 21 percent), *parochial activists* (citizens engaging in political activity for a personal reason; about 4 percent), *communalists* (those having a high level of communal activity but low level of campaign activity; 20 percent), *campaigners* (those active in political campaigns but not communally active; about 15 percent), and the *totally active* (active in all types of affairs; about 11 percent), and *unclassifiable* (7 percent). The inactives rank consistently low on measures of psychological involvement, feelings of efficacy, possession of information, partisanship, and civic-mindedness. They also tend to have low levels of education and income, and to be female, African American, residents of small towns, Protestant, and either young or over 65. The totally actives are the opposite of the inactives except that they also tend to be from small towns and to be Protestant.

Unlike Verba and Nie, Olsen (1973) conceptualized political participation as a major dimension of social stratification. Social stratification is a ranking system of various social strata, or categories of people distinguished from one another by such criteria as income, education, and occupation. The six strata of his model of political participation were: *political leaders, political activists* (roughly equivalent to Verba and Nie's communalists and campaigners), *communicators* (persons who receive and transmit political ideas and attitudes to others), *citizens, marginals* (persons who have very limited contacts with the political system), and *isolates* (persons who participate very rarely). The last two strata are roughly similar to Verba and Nie's inactives. Typologies of this nature abound in sociology and can be used for purposes of classification and generalization, but in reality not every individual voter fits neatly into one of these categories.

Scholars have also suggested explanations for nonvoting along demographic, sociopsychological, contextual, and rational dimensions. (1) Demographic dimension: Those who have fewer personal resources such as income, education, and other socioeconomic advantages are less likely to participate. (2) Sociopsychological dimension: Those who have problems such as political alienation, political dissatisfaction, and feelings of low political efficacy tend to participate less. (3) Contextual dimension: Factors such as successful campaign mobilization, competitiveness of the political process, and registration laws tend to influence voter turnout. (4) Rational dimension: Some researchers look at the decision not to vote as a rational decision in which persons weigh the cost of voting against the benefits (Downs, 1957:266).

As they compare and evaluate candidates, voters can either become indifferent when they see little difference between candidates or alienated when they dislike all candidates. Samuel J. Eldersveld (1982) thought that nonvoting was explained by such factors as election laws, the extent to which people are exposed to political parties, and media communication during campaigns.

These explanations give some understanding of nonvoting, but they are not specific enough. They do not describe the perceptions and understanding that nonvoters have of candidates or campaign issues. One can suggest additional factors that provide the conditions for nonvoting. A number of voters are ignorant of politics and are willing to become familiar with political issues. Others perceive or generalize about politicians as dishonest and double talkers which turns them away from professional politicians and voting.

Who Are the Participants?

For the majority of citizens, political participation consists of voting in local, state, and national elections. Voting is the most common and important indicator of political participation, or the way citizens express their political preferences and their attitudes toward politicians and political parties. Citizens in a civil democracy have three options: vote for one candidate, vote for the other, or abstain from voting altogether. Who votes and who does not can tell us something about the nature of and the interface between the political and the social worlds. Lipset (1981:191), one of the pioneers in this area, advanced four general explanations of higher voter turnout. He wrote that a group is more likely to have a higher rate of voting if: (1) Its interests are strongly influenced by the policies of the government. (2) It has access to information about the relevance of political decisions to its interests. (3) It is exposed to various social pressures demanding voting. (4) It is not forced to vote for different political parties (however, although some people vote independently, many individuals have developed a differential group consciousness and vote along ethnic, racial, religious, regional, gender, or class lines).

Roughly 90 million Americans of voting age do not participate in any national election. Many people believe that the extent of nonvoting contributes to biased election outcomes and unrepresentative policy choices. John Kenneth Galbraith's (1992) *The Culture of Contentment* elaborated on this thesis. Galbraith believed that government policies represent the preferences of those who vote, and that those who vote are more likely to be the more socioeconomically comfortable. The nation's attention is therefore directed away from pressing social needs. He stated,

> *In past times, the economically and socially fortunate were a small minority—characteristically a dominant and ruling handful. They are now a majority, although as it has been observed, a majority not of all citizens, but of those who actually vote... They rule under the rich cloak of democracy, a democracy in which the less fortunate do not participate. (Galbraith, 1992:15)*

"Weapons expenditures," according to Galbraith, "unlike spending for the urban poor, reward a very comfortable constituency" (Galbraith, 1992:23). Although political participation, whether conventional or unconventional, seldom brings immediate results from the government, John J. Harrigan (1993:121) made the following conclusion as a general principle of politics: "Although political participation will not bring a category of people everything they want, the lack of participation will almost certainly ensure that they will get very little of what they want." For example, the Civil Rights Act of 1964 would not have been passed without the mass Civil Rights Movement of the 1960s.

Sociodemographic Correlates

To explain voting patterns, we must examine various sociodemographic characteristics. The sociodemographic basis of voting patterns is the most researched area of political sociology.

Age/Generation

Age and generation are two important variables in voter turnout and preferences. A number of empirical studies have shown that people between twenty-five and fifty-five years of age tend to participate in politics more than do those who are younger or older (Asher 1976; Campbell et al., 1964; Ladd & Hadley 1975; Lane, 1959; Lipset, 1981; Lipset & Bendix, 1959; Milbrath & Goel, 1977; Verba & Nie, 1972). Surveys also show that those who came of age politically during Ronald Reagan's and George Bush's presidencies are more likely to vote Republican than Democrat. Young Americans who vote Republican tend to vote less often than older Americans.

As regards political generation,[1] those who were of voting age during the Great Depression of the 1930s are more likely to vote Democrat. As a result, contrary to historical trends, the elderly, normally the most Republican group in the population, are now the most Democratic because those who came of age during the Great

Depression are now in their seventies or eighties. Everett Carl Ladd (1993:9) found that in the 1972 and 1976 elections, the Democrats' most loyal age group was the youngest cohort while the oldest cohort favored the Republicans. In 1988 and 1992, the situation was almost the opposite. In general, however, aging produces a net shift away from the Democratic Party. Although in the 1980 election the young split evenly between Ronald Reagan and Jimmy Carter, overall their political identification shifted toward the Republicans (Clymer & Frankovic, 1981:44).

Gender

Although in the past women's political participation rates were lower than men's, especially in the Deep South, they now have participation rates similar to and often higher than those of men (Braungart, 1978; Ladd, 1993; Pomper 1975). In every election, women voters are more likely to give their votes to female than to male candidates. Various research surveys have found no gender gap in party identification among voters having high school degrees or less education. However, among those who have at least an undergraduate degree, women were much more likely to be Democrats: the gender gap was 18 percentage points (Ladd, 1993:6).

Carol A. Christy (1987) examined three major models of women's increasing political participation: (1) the *development model,* which backs urbanization, industrialization, increased affluence, and education as factors in the reduction of gender differences in political participation; (2) the *generational model,* which is predicated on the notion that political participation rates of older and younger cohorts are more likely to differ due to the historical context of the enfranchisement of women; and (3) the *diffusion* model, which attributes the reduction of gender differences to the dissemination of egalitarian values and ideology. She tested these models in fourteen nations including the United States, operationalizing political participation by both conventional and unconventional activities. Christy found that all three models offer inadequate explanations for gender differences in political participation because: (1) the impact of culture supersedes the impact of economic development on women's political activities; (2) a generational model adds little to our understanding of gender differences in voting; and (3) "general cultural changes set off waves of diffusion, which may be in the direction of less egalitarian gender attitudes" (Christy, 1987:115).

Surveys show that employed women have political views and rates of participation more similar to those of men than to those of full-time housewives. Employed women are also more concerned with feminist issues. The data on congressional elections show consistent Democratic leanings among women. Internationally, women are generally underrepresented in elected offices and in senior civil service positions in most countries and typically vote farther to the left than men.

Ethnicity/Race

For a long time ethno-religious and racial demographic characteristics have been considered meaningful predictors of voting patterns in the United States. Jews, for example, are slightly more active in politics than are Roman Catholics, who in turn are slightly more active than are Protestants (Braungart 1981; Knoke, 1976). As groups, Protestants are more Republican than they used to be and Roman Catholics less Democratic (Clymer & Frankovic, 1981). Frequent church attendance increases the propensity of Protestants to support Republicans, and Roman Catholics to support Democrats (Knoke 1976). According to many surveys, about 40 percent of Roman Catholics identify themselves as Democrat and 30 percent as Republicans, while 30 percent of Protestants identify themselves as Democrats and 40 percent as Republicans. N. Nie et al. (1979) found that upper-class Roman Catholics have become more independent and less likely to vote for the Democratic Party. Irish and Polish Roman Catholics are more Democratic than are German and Italian Roman Catholics. David Knoke (1976) found that religion tends to have a stronger effect than socioeconomic status on party identification. Knoke and Richard B. Felson (1974) found that ethnicity continues to have an influence on politics mainly because of the impact of persons' religious backgrounds and because of intergenerational socialization concerning traditional ethnic group loyalties. But as one becomes less associated with the traditions of the older generation, the relationship between ethnicity and politics weakens.

Hispanic Americans, the fastest-growing ethnic collectivity in the United States, vote Democratic in most elections, with the exception of Cubans, who overwhelmingly vote Republican. Although Latinos are underrepresented in politics, they are rapidly becoming an important voting group. Asian Americans, a small but fast-growing group, by and large voted Republican in 1992. This was primarily due to the fact that Asian Americans, as a collectivity, have incomes higher than the national average. Also, as a group, they tend to be more culturally and economically conservative than are other racial and ethnic groups.

Socioeconomic Class

Income is the most important indicator of socioeconomic class. Many surveys of political participation show that more affluent Americans are more likely to vote than are less affluent ones. Three major generalizations about class and socioeconomic status (as measured by income, education, and occupation), race, and voting emerge from Bureau of the Census data and the University of Michigan's American National Election Studies. (1) There is a general decline in voter turnout, but the decline is sharpest among those in the lowest socioeconomic classes. Between 1972 and 1988, for example, voter turnout among those in the lowest census bureau income category ($7,500 or less) dropped 7.4 points (from 47.2 to 39.8 percent); for those in the highest category ($60,000 or more), it dropped 3.7 points (from 79.1 to 75.4 percent). (2) There is a class gap in voting in the United States. In 1988, there was a 36-point gap in voter turnout between those in the lowest and highest income groups and a high-point gap in terms of education between those having low levels (zero to eight years) and those having high levels of education. (3) A gap exists between African Americans and non-Hispanic white voters, but it has been narrowing over time (Teixeira, 1992:53).

For a long time, scholars have debated whether there is a socioeconomic class basis to American politics. There are two views of the relationship between class and voting. The predominant view, called the "declining significance" hypothesis, is that there has been a steady decline in class politics in the United States (Huckfeldt and

Kohfeld, 1989; Ladd & Hadley 1975; Lipset 1981). Those who subscribe to this hypothesis believe that class no longer plays an important role in predicting voting behavior. However, more recent advances in statistical analysis as well as the refinement of conceptualization and measurement of social class have led to the "trendless fluctuation" hypothesis (Hout et al., 1993a, 1993b:1–2). Those who espouse the trendless fluctuation hypothesis argue that the class factor does not really decline in importance but instead fluctuates. According to researchers, two other positions— "increasing significance of class" and "class realignment"—are possible alternatives to these hypotheses but as yet have not appeared in the literature.

Class Voting: The Declining Significance Hypothesis

The declining significance hypothesis as regards the importance of class as a basis of politics in Western democracies, including the United States, is mostly associated with Lipset. In his updated edition of *Political Man*, Lipset stated:

> In every modern democracy conflict among different groups is expressed through political parties which basically represent a "democratic translation of the class struggle." Even though many parties renounce the principle of class conflict or loyalty, an analysis of their appeals and their support suggests that they do represent the interests of different classes. On a world scale, the principal generalization which can be made is that parties are primarily based on either the lower classes or the middle and upper classes. This generalization even holds true for the American parties, which have traditionally been considered an exception to the class-cleavage pattern of Europe. The Democrats from the beginning of their history have drawn more support from the lower strata of the society, while the Federalist, Whig, and Republican parties have held the loyalties of the more privileged groups. (Lipset, 1981:230)

However, Lipset (1981:504) believed that "class cleavages" and "class consciousness" in "postindustrial" capitalist democracies have declined and that there is a discernible decline in class voting in many advanced industrial countries as well. A cleavage is a form of division on the basis of some criterion. Cleavages may lead to conflict, but the two concepts are not synonymous. We can identify different types of cleavages in a community based on such criteria as religion, ethnicity, class, region, language, and so on. Class-based cleavage is most conspicuous in Southern Europe and in France, whereas it is less conspicuous in Northern Europe.

Class consciousness is a dimension of class-based cleavages. Two indicators can be used to describe class consciousness—(1) the Alford Index of class voting as an expression of class identification and (2) trade union membership. The more even the income distribution among various social strata, the higher the class consciousness and the degree of unionization. Class consciousness as measured by class identification and unionization is not always higher in nations having unequal distribution of income. Class consciousness may operate against economic inequalities. In his more recent writings, Lipset and his colleagues elaborated on the declining political significance of social class. They argued that:

> *Social classes have not died, but their political significance has declined substantially; this justifies a shift from class-centered analysis towards multicausal explanations of political behavior and related social phenomena.... [One must take into account] the impact of organizations like parties and unions, independent of classes, in affecting political processes.... [One must also look] to the rise of the welfare state as generally weakening class conflict by providing a safety net and benefits. The diversification of the occupational structure toward small firms, high tech and services weakens class organizational potentials. Political parties have correspondingly shifted from class conflict to non-economic issues like the environment. The socialist and communist parties have drastically altered their programs in dozens of countries, away from traditional class politics toward new social issues.... New nationalist parties have arisen stressing national identity and limiting immigration. These developments cumulatively weaken class politics. (Clark et al., 1993:293–316)*

In many ways race has replaced class as the most significant factor in electoral politics. The most sophisticated analysis of the effects of race on class voting, which defends a declining significance of class, was undertaken by Robert Huckfeldt and Carol W. Kohfeld who argued that

> *the decline of class as an organizing principle in contemporary American electoral politics is directly related to the concurrent ascent of race.... The prominence of race in American politics is not so much the consequence of virulent racism on the part of individuals, even though such racism often exists. Rather it is a frequent result of the electoral competition that is structured in terms of both race and class. In that competition, race is likely to drive out class and emerge as the most significant factor in electoral politics. (Huckfeldt & Kohfeld, 1989)*

Indeed, in the 1980s the Republicans captured the anti-black, white working-class vote and made it increasingly difficult for the Democrats to hold the allegiance of both African American and white voters. This was most evident in the 1988 Bush-Dukakis campaign, in which George Bush used ethnic and racial fear tactics to capture the White House. The Willie Horton case and the "L word" slogan (which castigated the liberalism of Michael Dukakis) were used successfully to attract working-class white voters, who, especially in the South, had traditionally favored the Democratic Party. Learning from this experience, in the 1992 elections, Bill Clinton played down race and ethnic issues and concentrated on broader domestic issues, for example the economy.

Some researchers argue that, even in societies having an absence of racial cleavages, there is a decline of class politics due primarily to welfare policies that have alienated working-class voters who object to being taxed to support marginal groups, immigrants, and poorly paid part-time workers. Proposition 187, which was directed against illegal immigrants and passed by California voters in 1994, is an illustration of the political importance of anti-foreign and anti-welfare sentiments.

Another aspect of the declining significance hypothesis is the dealignment hypothesis. This hypothesis holds that we are seeing not so much a shift of working-class or poor voters from the Democrats to the Republicans but rather a decline of party identification and loyalty and an increase in voter independence.

Further evidence of the declining significance of class as a basis of politics is the thesis of "two lefts" having distinct social bases. Lipset (1981:511) argued that "both lefts are in the same party..., but they have different views and interests." The postmaterialist thesis advanced by Ronald Inglehart and Jacques-Rene Rabier (Inglehart 1977, 1990; Inglehart & Rabier 1986) argued that while traditional class-based political cleavages are declining, they tend to be replaced by conflict over "postmaterialist" issues such as the environment, crime, quality of life, education, and values. These changes, according to Inglehart, promote "two lefts"—one rooted in the working class and concerned mainly with material issues and the other largely middle class and primarily interested in social issues (Hout et al., 1995:806).

Along the same line, Jan Pakulski (1993:279–92), who supported the conclusions of Lipset and his colleagues, argued that what is "dying" are the old industrial classes: the "old socio-economic divisions" along with the "old institutional actors" representing these divisions no longer hold much power. But Pakulski believed that the demise of the old industrial classes and the Marxian divisions do not necessarily signal the abandoning of class as a dynamic analytical category in social stratification.

Class Voting: The Trendless Fluctuation Hypothesis

An alternative to the declining significance hypothesis is the trendless fluctuation hypothesis. Most researchers acknowledge a fluctuation in class-based voting patterns from election to election. However, according to Adam Przeworski and John Sprague (1986), comparative studies of European voting patterns and election returns show that while class-based voting patterns have fluctuated over the years the importance of class has not declined. They suggest that party strategy, rather than shifts in the social bases of party support, is the major source of variation in class voting. In the United States, the success of cross-class appeals advocated by Kevin Phillips (1969) and of racial appeals by candidates can be thought of as the results of party strategy rather than of shifting social bases of class politics. Anthony Heath et al. (1985) have reported similar findings concerning British class-voting patterns.

Using sophisticated statistical measures of class voting in the United States from 1956 to 1992, Michael Hout et al. (1995 and 1993) reached the following conclusions: (1) Class continues to play an important role in American politics. (2) There has been no significant decline in class voting since the 1950s. (3) The Democratic Party is not a labor or working class party and the Republican Party has always made appeals to the working class. (4) In every election blue-collar workers by and large vote Democratic, and managers and the self-employed tend to vote Republican.

(5) Professionals appear to have moved closer to the Democratic Party, especially since the 1960s—about one-half of all professionals voted for Bill Clinton in 1992. At the same time skilled workers have shown more volatility in their voting patterns in recent elections.

Also, the findings of David Halle and Frank Romo (1991) on blue-collar politics suggest two major trends in U.S. working-class politics: (1) Working people are deeply interested in politics but tend to focus on political scandal rather than on public policy. The key to "working person" political philosophy is a basic antipathy to bigness and the cynical belief that bigness invites corruption. (2) As long as the Democratic party represents "big government" and the Republican party represents "big business," workers will withhold loyalty from both parties and will tend to support that candidate who convinces them that he or she represents neither of the two. The strong support of skilled workers for Ross Perot validates this interpretation of working people and politics.

Class Mobility and Status Inconsistency

Two more sociodemographic factors affecting voting are class mobility and status inconsistency. Class mobility, in this context, refers to movement from one class position to another either horizontally (i.e., change of status positions without any substantial change in status occurring) or vertically (i.e., either upward or downward change of status positions).

Three explanations of the relationship between class mobility and political attitudes have been offered: the additive interactive model, the overconformity model, and the status rejection model (Kourvetaris & Dobratz, 1980:48). The additive interactive model states that mobile individuals do not essentially differ from nonmobiles in their politics (Barber, 1970; Blau, 1956; Jackman, 1972). But both the overconformity and the status rejection models hold that an individual's mobility (upward or downward) affects his/her political orientations and likelihood of political involvement. In their early work on mobility and politics, Lipset and Reinhard Bendix (1959) and Lipset and Hans L. Zetterberg (1964) argued that upwardly mobiles, in both the United States and Europe, are likely to be more conservative than are nonmobiles because overconformity, or overidentification, leads them to aspire to identify with the class of destination (or the class to which they aspire). So, for example, those who have moved from the working class to the middle class would likely be more conservative than those already having middle-class status and middle-class voters from ethnic, working-class backgrounds would likely change their allegiance from the Democratic Party supported by their immigrant parents, to the Republican Party.

This tendency to become more conservative as one becomes upwardly mobile has been seen as an expression of gratitude for the sociopolitical system which has given one the opportunity to move up (Jackman, 1972; Lopreato et al., 1976). But the relationship between mobility and politics remains controversial. Many researchers find no mobility effects on political choice and support the additive interactive model (Jackman 1972; Knoke, 1976; Segal & Knoke, 1968, 1973; Thomson, 1971a, 1971b).

Status inconsistency refers to a discrepancy between two or more dimensions of social stratification in a single individual. For instance, a person may rank high on income but low on education or occupation. Early studies (Goffman, 1957; Lenski, 1954, 1967) supported the view that status inconsistents were likely to be either more liberal or more conservative in their politics than consistents. The reasoning behind this view was that those experiencing status inconsistency, such as African American professionals and women professionals, are more likely to feel certain pressures and demands due to their conflicting status levels. While some findings support this hypothesis, other studies do not find these status inconsistency effects on politics. Before we accept or reject the value of these concepts we need more specificity in research methodology and theory.

Thomas Edsall and Mary Edsall (1991) argued that of the four factors of race, rights, reform, and taxes, race has become the most critical force shaping U.S. politics. They found that by adopting the "politics of inclusion" the Democratic Party had identified itself with minority groups while the Republican Party became the "party of resentment." Many whites, Edsall and Edsall argued, switched from the Democrats to the Republicans because of their perception of the Democratic Party as the party of welfare and big taxes. African Americans are now overwhelmingly Democratic, and they represent an essential voting bloc to the party. Bill Clinton's victories in Arkansas, Georgia, Louisiana, and Tennessee were due largely to African American support (Ladd 1993:3). Contrary to past trends, racial differences in political and social attitudes are greatest in the working class and are based primarily on consideration of such issues as equal employment opportunity, school integration, housing, and public accommodations. African American working-class support for the Democratic Party has increased since 1960 while white working-class support has declined sharply (Abramson 1977).

N. Danigelis (1978) suggested that different regions and historical periods in U.S. history can be characterized by different political climates that are either intolerant, unsupportive, indifferent, or supportive to African American political participation. He found that a strongly intolerant political climate suppresses African American registration and voting but has little effect on more harmless methods of political participation such as family political discussion and monetary contributions to causes. A supportive political climate encourages highly visible forms of political participation, particularly registration and voting.

Sociopsychological Correlates

A number of sociopsychological factors affect rates of voting and other political participation. One of these is political alienation, part of the more inclusive sociopsychological and structural concept of alienation, which includes feelings of estrangement from the political system. According to Melvin Seeman (1959), an alienated individual finds the political system irrelevant to everyday life. Issueless campaigns, "diversionary tactics of politics," ideological confusion, and image making rather than discussion of political issues of substance can promote this sense of social and psychological isolation. In such a political climate voters become cynical, feel frustrated because they cannot change things, and, therefore, become indifferent to politics and feel alienated. Low voter turnout is an indication of such alienation. Political alienation is also reflected in the decline of party identification and the emergence of strong independent candidates.

Marxists see alienation as a result of the economic relationships of individuals to the means of production, which lead to the alienation of workers from their employers. In a similar fashion, voters become alienated from the political process because of the low opinion they have of professional politicians. According to James S. House and William M. Mason (1975:145), various sociodemographic characteristics such as income, education, occupation, age, race, and religion help to determine a person's views on political issues which, in turn, determine the person's level of alienation.

Explanations of political alienation abound. There are those who see political alienation as a function of "cohort variability" in economic well-being. Richard Easterlin (1978, 1980) argued that a number of large cohorts suffer economically, and this alienates them from social and political affairs. Robert M. Obrien and Patricia A. Gwartney-Gibbs (1989) supported Easterlin's hypothesis. But others saw the rise of political alienation in the 1960s as a response to political and social issues, not economic issues (Kahn & Mason, 1987:155). House and Mason (1975) explained political alienation in terms of "actual historical events," such as the Vietnam War and Watergate, that influence all cohorts. Lipset and William Schneider (1983) suggested that political alienation, especially during the 1960s, reflected "feelings of dissatisfaction" with leaders who were unable to solve major problems; they found that Americans have lost confidence in political institutions and in the efficacy of their leaders. More recently, Lipset (1994) has argued that nonvoting should be looked upon as a form of deviancy. But at the same time, he argued that political alienation is part of our national character: Americans, Lipset stated have always been less inclined to conform, more individualistic, less "communal," more anti-statist, more distrustful, and more suspicious of government than people in other countries.

The term *political efficacy* refers to a sense of individual empowerment and a perception that one's involvement in politics matters. The more efficacious a person feels, the greater his/her tendency to participate in conventional politics and the smaller his/her tendency to feel politically alienated. This relationship is more evident among the educated and the higher socioeconomic strata of society. The politically alienated tend to have little feeling of political efficacy. In a comparative study of political efficacy among students in the United States, the United Kingdom, and India, Rashmi Shrivastava (1989) found a relationship between political efficacy and a number of sociodemographic characteristics, including sex, area of study, age, religion, language, residence, economic status, choice of career, extracurricular activities, union, and association membership. In India law students had the highest sense of political efficacy, while in the United States and England there was no correlation with area of study. In all three countries, men tended to feel more efficacious than did women, and religion played an important role. In England and the United States more Christians than minority groups had high senses of political efficacy. Language was also correlated with political efficacy: English-speaking students were found to have higher senses of efficacy than were those who spoke other languages. High economic status and party or union association were found to contribute to higher perceptions of political efficacy.

(Dis)trust is also related to political alienation. Those who distrust the government and politicians are more likely to abstain from participation. As a rule, blacks tend to be more distrustful and cynical than are whites (Pomper, 1975:140). During the 1960s youth were overwhelmingly politically alienated and distrustful of politicians and older generations. Significantly, more affluent students, especially those from the upper-middle class, were in the forefront of the student movement against the Vietnam War. House and Mason (1975:123–47) found that increased political alienation during the 1960s and 1970s was primarily due to growing discontent with government policies concerning the Vietnam War and to the popular success of mass civil rights movements. The 1980s saw a conservative reaction to civil rights and social programs, which made liberals and middle-class white Americans more alienated from and cynical about politicians.

Another issue related to alienation is the notion of civic duty and citizenship, the responsibilities of citizens in a polity and society. Citizenship gives the citizens of a nation state a collective identity and national consciousness. It is intertwined with democracy and equality. As a citizen of a democracy an individual ideally has certain rights, including the right to vote, the right to criticize the government, the right to free speech, and the right to assemble. Most of these rights are denied in countries under authoritarian rule. Citizenship also entails certain obligations and responsibilities of the citizen to the nation state, such as the payment of taxes and the obeying of laws. In many countries serving in the armed forces is a duty of every citizen. In the United States, the United Kingdom, Canada, and Australia service in the armed forces is voluntary. Ideally, all citizens of a given nation state must be treated equally by the state irrespective of race, gender, religion, national origin, and sexual orientation. In reality, however, discrimination and unequal treatment are common phenomena.

Current approaches to the notion of modern citizenship began with the publication of T. H. Marshall's (1965) book *Class, Citizenship and Social Development.* Marshall defined citizenship in rather general terms as "a status bestowed on those who are full members of a community." All citizens, under this definition, must enjoy equal rights and duties, including equal treatment under the law. He identified three elements of citizenship: *civil, political,* and *social* rights. The civil rights of citizenship spell out the rights of individuals. The political rights of citizenship consist of the right of every citizen to participate in politics. The social rights of citizenship entail rights or entitlements such as rights to public education, welfare provisions, and the sharing of the resources and social heritage of society in general. Marshall (1965) explained the relationship between citizenship and social class by making three basic assumptions: (1) Citizenship must be defined as a status, (2) capitalist development and citizenship must occur simultaneously, and (3) explanations of citizenship must be based on the relationship between the state and capitalism.

Margaret R. Somers (1993:587–620) challenged these assumptions by showing the existence of different elements of citizenship in eighteenth century England by linking various patterns of institutional relationships among law, communities, and political cultures. Focusing on these variations in citizenship practices, Somers suggested that: (1) Citizenship should be defined as an "instituted process" rather than as a status. This means that to understand citizenship rights we must explain the institutional nexus of communities, law, and politics. According to her, citizenship is a process, a more dynamic concept, rather than a status or a structural or honorific position bestowed on individuals. (2) Citizenship rights in eighteenth-century England depended on the relationship between England's national legal system and community participation. (3) Future research on citizenship and democracy must go beyond the nexus of capitalism and states to include a sociology of relationships including public life, community associations, and political culture (Somers, 1993:587).

The struggle of the disadvantaged and the disenfranchised for civil, political, and social rights runs through most of the history of the West, including the Unites States. The Civil Rights Movement and the Women's Movement during the 1960s were calls for the expansion of civil, political, and social rights of citizenship. At present, citizenship means a universal and more inclusive ideology of social and economic well-being of citizens, including equality before the law and rights to participate politically (Barbarlet, 1988). Advancement of citizenship rights to previously excluded groups are often opposed by more privileged groups. In his book *Citizenship and Capitalism* (1986), Bryan S. Turner argued that citizenship enhances universalism and justice, while it reduces particularism.

A more pragmatic view of citizenship stresses a balance between the rights and responsibilities of citizens. For instance, the Clinton administration has adopted the idea of national service by the young as domestic Peace Corps volunteers. Clinton's national service/college tuition idea was suggested by Charles Moskos, Jr., the leading military sociologist in the world.[2] The relationship between the expanded nature of citizenship and political participation is a central idea in political sociology. Those who have a stake in the system and enjoy full civil, political, and social rights are more likely to participate and to be part of the political process (Korpi, 1989).

Morris Janowitz (1983) made an effort to reconstruct the ideas of patriotism, citizenship, and civic consciousness. He believed that the notion of citizenship was influenced by western nationalist revolutions. The nation-state was the organizing unit for political, social, and economic reform. For Janowitz (1983:8) citizenship involves some form of nationalism and patriotism but does not encompass xenophobia or militarism. Patriotism is a form of primordial attachment to a territory and society—a sense of identification and belonging similar to religious, racial, or ethnic identifications.

Political Socialization

The concept of political socialization as a framework for political analysis in general and political participation in particular is central to political sociology (Niemi & Sobiesyek, 1977). Political socialization is an aspect of the more inclusive concept of socialization, which is the learning of the values, attitudes, and behaviors of the group (Gould & Kolb, 1964:672). Political socialization is, then, the process by which an individual learns, through various agencies and institutions such as schools, families, peer groups, the mass media, political parties, and political culture in general, the attitudes, beliefs, values, and behaviors related to the political system of which the individual is a member. William C. Mitchell (1970) defined political socialization as who learns what from whom under what circumstances with what effects. The literature on political socialization has been extensive; the seminal work on the subject is Herbert Hyman's (1959) *Political Socialization* (Greenberg, 1970; Langton, 1969).

In authoritarian and totalitarian regimes political socialization takes the form of party guidelines and political guidance from above. Only those political attitudes, values, and behaviors that are consistent with the formal political ideology of the authoritarian regime are taught and approved. In every political system, including democracies, the political regime or government seeks to instill in its young people values, beliefs, and behaviors consistent with the prevailing political order or the political world view so that they will become attached and loyal to that political system as adults. U.S. students are usually taught about the workings of the nation's government and the nature of its political system. In the Soviet Union and communist Eastern Europe, there was a systematic political socialization that was largely indoctrination in Marxist ideology and the political culture of communism.

Related to political socialization is what is known as "life-course politics and generational politics" (Braungart & Braungart, 1983:205–31, 1990). There is a dynamic relationship between age, generation, historical events, and personal politics. People who grew up during the Great Depression, for example, were inculcated with the democratic ideology of the New Deal, which stressed the importance of societal protection of the poor and the elderly and the rights of the working class (Domhoff, 1990). The 1960s were a watershed for political socialization of the young to favor the left, but by the 1980s, with the Republican ascent to political power, the young were socialized in a more conservative political culture.

Early studies of political socialization stressed the role of the family, especially of the father (Campbell et al., 1964; Davies, 1965; Hyman, 1959), and of early school experiences (Easton & Dennis, 1969; Hess & Torney, 1967; Greenstein, 1965). These studies found that children were socialized to respect authority and regarded presidents and policemen as benevolent and as idealized extensions of father figures, although middle- and upper-class children were more realistic than were working-class children (Kourvetaris and Dobratz, 1980:49; Orum, 1988:411). Other researchers stressed schools, especially colleges, as agents of political socialization. More recent studies view political socialization as a life-long process and stress people's tendency to change political attitudes and values over time (Glenn & Hefner, 1972; Jennings & Niemi, 1974; Miller, 1974). Researchers have also discovered that party identification is learned early in life while more abstract concepts of politics are developed later (Orum, 1988:411).

Social class, ethnicity, race, gender, and region are also important factors in political socialization. Researchers have found that both children and adults hold different views about politics depending on their sociodemographic and social class origins. These differences hold fast as individuals become voters and participants in the political process.

Summary and Conclusion

For most people voting is the only form of participation in the political process. Voting and political participation have been a persistent and sustaining interest to many political sociologists. However, despite the fact that voting is the most important expression of political participation, we find the United States has one of the lowest rates of voter turnout. Reviewing the empirical evidence of political participation, Lipset has concluded that neither high nor low rates of participation are in themselves good or bad for democracy.

Political participation and electoral politics are rather recent phenomena and are more characteristic of capitalist liberal democracies. Aristotle explained the idea of citizen participation in terms of linking the community and citizen in a sharing relationship between polity, constitution, and citizenship. Most contemporary definitions of political participation involve some form of action or activity of citizens seeking to influence the political process either directly or indirectly. It can take two basic forms: conventional or unconventional. Conventional forms include activities such as voting or contacting elected officials. Unconventional include all those non-routinized or non-institutionalized activities such as social protest, demonstrations, or violence.

Most classical and contemporary political theorists have recognized the necessity of citizen participation in a democracy. It enhances our understanding, sophistication, and knowledge of politics. Why people participate in politics or not has continually interested political sociologists. There are those who participate for material or non-material benefits. For others, participation serves some social and social-psychological need including power, a sense of well-being, development of a skill, knowledge, rectitude, friendship and the like. There are certain typologies explaining various ways of voter participation. Close to one-third of the American voters are apathetic or totally inactive, about two-thirds are minimally involved. This group can be characterized as spectators or voting specialists, and the rest are actively involved in campaign activity.

Sociodemographic characteristics of participants are also discussed. In general, those individuals are more likely to vote whose interests are strongly influenced by the policies of the government, have access to information dealing with these interests, are exposed to various social pressures for voting, and are not forced to vote for different political parties. The higher socioeconomic strata are more likely to participate more than those in lower socioeconomic strata. People between the ages of twenty-five and fifty-five tend to participate more than those who are younger or older.

The issue of class voting is extensively discussed. There are those who believe that there is a decline in class voting in post-industrial societies. Race has replaced class as an organizing principle in American politics. Others suggest an endless fluctuation of class. The latter believe that there is no decline in class voting, but a fluctuation in class trends. According to this view, voters have become more sophisticated in their voting patterns. In their contention political parties use different strategies to appeal to cross sections of the United States electorate.

The impact of class mobility and status inconsistency on voting behavior were also explored. Three explanations of the relationship between class mobility and political attitudes were discussed: the additive interactive model, the overconformity model, and the status rejection model. In these models, the interactive model states that mobile individuals do not differ substantially from non-mobiles; both the over-conformity and the status rejection models hold that an individual's mobility affects his/her political orientations. The tendency to become more conservative as one becomes upwardly mobile has been seen as an expression of gratitude for the socio-political system.

Ethno-religious and racial demographic characteristics as predictors of voting patterns in the United States are examined. Jews are slightly more active in politics than are Roman Catholics who in turn are slightly more active than are Protestants. Hispanic Americans, the fastest growing ethnic collectivity in the United States, with possible exception of Cuban Americans who vote overwhelmingly Republican, vote Democratic in most elections.

A number of sociopsychological factors affect rates of voting and other political participation including factors such as political alienation, cynicism, political effi-cacy, distrust, citizenship, political socialization, and generation. In short, political participation and voting are essential in understanding electoral politics in the United States.

Endnotes

1. The idea of political generations can be traced back to Plato and Aristotle. In modern times the concept was popularized by Karl Mannheim (1936) in his book *Ideology and Utopia,* in which he argued that individuals usually learn their politi-cal attitudes and values as members of particular cohorts or generations. The prevailing political cli-mate of the period during which a generation comes of age affects the political views and orientations of that generation. A similar concept involves the notion of life-cycle and generational politics. See also Braungart and Braungart (1990).

2. See Moskos (1988), which argued that U.S. society and the political system have become weak due to individualism, cynicism, hedonism, consum-erism, and the end of the draft. He calls for national service by the young to restore a sense of commu-nity. His model is based on military service, which he sees as a civic duty and one of the obligations of citizenship. However, who is going to volunteer for national service in return for tuition aid? Those in the higher socioeconomic strata do not need to.

References

Abramson, P. 1977. *The Political Socialization of Black Americans.* New York: Free Press.

Alford, R. R., and Friedland, R. 1975. "Political Participation and Public Policy." In *Annual Review of Sociology,* Inkeles, Alex Coleman James and Neil Smelser pp. 429–479 Palo Alto: Annual Reviews.

Asher, H. 1976. *Presidential Elections and Ameri-can Politics.* Homewood: Dorsey.

Barbarlet, J. M. 1988. *Citizenship: Rights, Struggle and Class Inequality.* Minneapolis: University of Minnesota Press.

Barber, James. 1970. *Social Mobility and Voting Behavior.* Chicago: Rand McNally.

Bennett, Stephen L., and William R. Klecka. 1970. "Social Status and Political Participation: A Multivariate Analysis of Predictive Power." *Midwest Journal of Political Science.* Vol. 14:355–82.

Blau, Peter. 1956. Social Mobility and Interpersonal Relations. *American Sociological Review.* Vol. 21 (June):290–95.

Braungart, Richard. 1978. "Changing Electoral Politics in America." *Journal of Political and Military Sociology.* Vol. 6:261–69.

———. 1981. "Political Sociology: History and Scope." In *Handbook of Political Behavior,* ed. S. Long, 1–80. New York: Plenum.

Braungart, Richard G., and Margaret M. Braungart. 1983. "Life-Course and Generational Politics." In *Annual Review of Sociology,* 12:205–31. Palo Alto: Annual Reviews.

———. 1990. "Political Generational Themes in the American Student Movements of the 1930s and 1960s." *Journal of Political and Military Sociology.* Vol. 18, no. 2:177–230.

Campbell, Angus P., Converse W. Miller, and D. Stokes. 1964. *The American Voter.* New York: John Wiley and Sons.

Christy, Carol A. 1987. *Sex Differences in Political Participation: Processes of Change in Fourteen Nations.* New York: Praeger.

Clark, Terry N., Seymour Lipset, and Michael Rempel. 1993. "The Declining Political Significance of Social Class." *International Sociology.* Vol. 8, no. 3:293–316.

Clymer, A., and K. Frankovic. 1981. "The Realities of Realignment." *Public Opinion.* Vol. 4:42–47.

Danigelis, N. 1978. "Black Political Participation." *American Sociological Review.* Vol. 33:756–71.

Davies, James C. 1965. "The Family's Role in Political Socialization." *The Annals.* Vol. 361:10–19.

Domhoff, William G. 1990. *The Power Elite and the State.* New York: Walter de Gruyter.

Downs, Anthony. 1957. *An Economic Theory of Democracy.* New York: Harper and Row.

Easterlin, Richard. 1980. *Birth and Fortune: The Impact of Numbers on Personal Welfare.* New York: Basic.

———. 1978. "What Will 1984 Be Like? Socioeconomic Implications of Recent Trists in the Age Structure." *Demography.* Vol. 15:397–432.

Easton, D., and J. Dennis. 1969. *Children in the Political System: Origins of Political Legitimacy.* New York: McGraw-Hill.

Edsall, Thomas, and Mary Edsall. 1991. *Chain Reaction.* New York: Norton.

Eldersveld, Samuel J. 1982. *Political Parties in American Society.* New York: Basic.

Galbraith, John Kenneth. 1992. *The Culture of Contentment.* Boston: Houghton Mifflin.

Gans, Herbert J. 1988. *Middle American Individualism: Political Participation and Liberal Democracy.* New York: Oxford University Press.

Glenn, N. D., and T. Hefner. 1972. "Further Evidence on Aging and Party Identification." *Public Opinion Quarterly.* Vol. 36:31–47.

Goffman, Richard. 1957. "Status Consistency and Preference for Change in Power Distribution." *American Sociological Review.* Vol. 22 (June): 275–81.

Goldfarb, Jeffrey C. 1991. *The Cynical Society.* Chicago: University of Chicago.

Gould, Julius, and William L. Kolb. 1964. *A Dictionary of the Social Sciences.* New York: Free Press.

Greenberg, Edward S., ed. 1970. *Political Socialization.* New York: Atherton.

Greenstein, F. I. 1965. *Children and Politics.* New Haven: Yale University Press.

Halle, David, and Frank Romo. 1991. "Blue Collar Working Class." In *America at Century's End,* ed. Alan Wolfe, 152–84. Berkeley: University California Press.

Harrigan, John J. 1993. *Empty Dreams, Empty Pockets: Class and Bias in American Politics.* New York: Macmillan.

Heath, Anthony, Roger Jowell, and John Curtice. 1985. *How Britain Votes.* Oxford: Pergamon.

Hess, R. D., and J. V. Torney. 1967. *The Development of Political Attitudes in Children.* Chicago: Aldine.

House, James S., and William M. Mason. 1975. "Political Alienation in America, 1952–1968." *American Sociological Review.* Vol. 40 (April): 123–47.

Hout, Michael, Clem Brooks, and Jeff Manza. 1995. "The Democratic Class Struggle in the United States, 1948–1992." *American Sociological Review.* Vol. 60 (December):805–828.

———. 1993. "The Persistence of Classes in Post-Industrial Societies." *International Sociology.* Vol. 8, no. 3:259–77.

Huckfeldt, Robert, and Carol W. Kohfeld. 1989. *Race and the Decline of Class in American Politics.* Champaign: University of Illinois Press.

Hyman, H. H. 1959. *Political Socialization.* New York: Free Press.

Inglehart, Ronald. 1990. *Culture Shift in Advanced Industrial Society.* Princeton, N.J.: Princeton University Press.

———. 1977. *The Silent Revolution: Changing Values and Political Styles among Western Publics.* Princeton, N.J.: Princeton University Press.

Inglehart, Ronald, and Jacques-Rene Rabier. 1986. "Political Realignment in Advanced Industrial Society: From Class-Based Politics to Quality of Life Politics." *Government and Opposition.* Vol. 21:456–79.

Jackman, Mary R. 1972. "Social Mobility and Attitude toward the Political System. *Social Forces.* Vol. 50 (June):462–72.

Janowitz, Morris. 1983. *The Reconstruction of Patriotism: Education for Civic Consciousness.* Chicago: University of Chicago Press.

Jennings, M. K., and R. G. Niemi. 1974. *The Political Character of Adolescence.* Princeton: Princeton University Press.

Kahn, Joan R., and William M. Mason. 1987. "Political Alienation, Cohort Size, and Easterlin Hypothesis." *American Sociological Review.* Vol. 52 (April):155–69.

Kleiman, M. B. 1977. Trends in Racial Differences in Political Efficacy: 1952–1972. *Soc. Abstracts.* Vol. 25:2.

Knight, K. 1985. "Ideology in the 1980 Election: Ideological Sophistication Does Matter." *Journal of Politics.* Vol. 47:828–53.

Knoke, David. 1976. *Change and Continuity in American Politics.* Baltimore: Johns Hopkins University Press.

Knoke, David, and Richard B. Felson. 1974. "Ethnic Stratification and Political Cleavage in the U.S., 1952–1968." *American Journal of Sociology.* Vol. 80 (November):630–42.

Korpi, Walter. 1989. "Power, Politics, and State Autonomy in the Development of Social Citizenship." *American Sociological Review.* Vol. 54 (June):309–28.

Kourvetaris, George A. and Betty A. Dobratz. 1980. *Society and Politics: An Overview and Reappraisal of Political Sociology.* Dubuque: Kendall/Hunt.

Ladd, Everett Carl. 1993. "The 1992 Vote for President Clinton: Another Brittle Mandate?" *Political Science Quarterly.* Vol. 108, no. 23:1–28.

Ladd, Everett Carl, and Charles D. Hadley. 1975. *Transformations of the American Party System: Political Coalitions from the New Deal to the 1970s.* New York: W. W. Norton.

Lane, Robert E. 1959. *Political Man.* London: Collier-Mcmillan.

Langton, Kenneth P. 1969. *Political Socialization.* New York: Oxford University Press.

Lasswell, Harold D. 1951. "Psychopathology and Politics," in Harold D. Lasswell. *The Political Writings of Harold D. Lasswell* pp. 1–282 (passim) Glencoe: The Free Press.

Leighley, Jan. 1991. "Participation as a Stimulus of Political Conceptualization." *Journal of Politics.* Vol. 53, no. 1:198–211.

Lenski, Gerhard. 1954. "Status Crystallization: A Non-Vertical Dimension of Social Status." *American Sociological Review.* Vol. 19 (August): 405–13.

———. 1967. "Status Inconsistency and the Vote: A Four Nation Test." *American Sociological Review.* Vol. 32(April):298–301.

Lipset, Seymour M. 1981. *Political Man: The Social Bases of Politics,* updated ed. Baltimore: Johns Hopkins University Press.

———. 1994. "Why Americans Refuse to Vote" in *Insight* (February):24–26.

Lipset, Seymour, M. and Reinhard Bendix. 1959. *Social Mobility in Industrial Society.* Berkeley: University of California.

Lipset, Seymour, M. and William Schneider. 1983. *The Confidence Gap: Business, Labor, and Government in Public Mind.* New York: Free Press.

Lipset, Seymour, M. and Hans L. Zetterberg. 1964. "A Theory of Social Mobility." In *Sociological Theory,* ed. L. Coser and B. Rosenberg, 437–62. New York: Macmillan.

Lopreato, Joseph, Frank D. Bean, and Sally Cook Lopreato. 1976. "Occupational Mobility and Political Behavior, Some Unresolved Issues." *Journal of Political and Military Sociology.* Vol. 4 (Spring):1–15.

Mannheim, Karl. 1936. *Ideology and Utopia.* New York: Harcourt, Brace.

Marshall, T. H. 1965. *Class, Citizenship and Social Development.* New York: Anchor Books.

Milbrath, Lester W. 1965. *Political Participation.* Chicago: Rand McNally.

Milbrath, Lester, and M. L. Goel. 1977. *Political Participation.* Chicago: Rand McNally College.

Miller, Arthur H. 1974. "Political Issues and Trust in Government: 1964–1970." *American Political Science Review* 68:951–972.

Mitchell, William C. 1970. *The American Polity: A Social and Cultural Interpretation.* New York: Free Press.

Moskos, Charles Jr. 1988. *A Call to Civic Service: National Service for Country and Community.* New York: Free Press.

Niemi, Richard G., and B. I. Sobiesyek. 1977. "Political Socialization." *Annual Review of Sociology.* Vol. 3:209–33.

Obrien, Robert M., and Patricia A. Gwartney-Gibbs. 1989. "Relative Cohort Size and Political Alienation: Three Methodological Issues and A Replication Supporting the Easterlin Hypothesis." *American Sociological Review.* Vol. 54 (June):476–84.

Olsen, Marvin. 1973. "A Model of Political Participation Stratification." *Journal of Political and Military Sociology.* Vol. 1 (Fall):183–200.

———. 1982. *Participatory Pluralism.* Chicago: Nelson-Hall.

Orum, Anthony. 1988. "Political Sociology." In *Handbook of Sociology,* ed. Neil J. Smelser, pp. 393–422. Newbury Park, CA: Sage.

Pakulski, Jan. 1993. "The Dying of Class or Marxist Class Theory?" *International Sociology.* Vol. 8, no. 3:279–92.

Phillips, Kevin. 1969. *The Emerging Republican Majority.* New York: Anchor.

Pierce, Patrick. 1993. "Political Sophistication and the Use of Candidate Traits in Candidate Evaluation." *Political Psychology.* Vol. 14, no. 1:21–35.

Pomper, G. 1975. *Voters' Choice: Varieties of American Electoral Behavior.* New York: Dodd, Mead.

Przeworski, Adam, and John Sprague. 1986. *Paper Stones: A History of Electoral Socialism.* Chicago: University of Chicago Press.

Rosenstone, Steven J., and John M. Hansen. 1993. *Mobilization, Participation, and Democracy in America.* New York: Macmillan.

Schneider, William. 1992. "Public Resentment of Professionalism in Politics: Its Cause and its Consequences." *The American Enterprise.* (July/August):30–37.

Seeman, Melvin. 1959. "On the Meaning of Alienation." *American Sociological Review.* Vol. 24: 783–91.

Segal, David R. 1989. *Recruiting for Uncle Sam: Citizenship and Military Manpower Policy.* Lawrence: University of Kansas Press.

Segal, David R., and David Knoke. 1973. "The Impact of Social Stratification, Social Mobility, and Status Inconsistency on the German Political Party Infrastructure." *Journal of Political and Military Sociology.* Vol. 1 (Spring):19–37.

———. 1968. "Social Mobility, Status Inconsistency, and Partisan Realignment in the United States." *Social Forces.* Vol. 47 (December): 154–57.

Shrivastava, Rashmi. 1989. "Political Efficacy: A Comparative Study of the United States, the United Kingdom, and India." *Youth and Society.* Vol. 21, no. 2:170–95.

Smith, Robert B. 1993. "Social Structure and Voting Choice: Hypotheses, Findings, and Interpretations." *Social Science Research Inc,* presented at American Sociological Association. Miami (August).

Somers, Margaret R. 1993. "Citizenship and the Place of the Public Sphere: Law, Community, and Political Culture in the Transition to Democracy" *American Sociological Review.* Vol. 58 (October):587–620.

Teixeira, Ruy A. 1992. "What If We Held an Election and Everybody Came?" *American Enterprise.* (July/August):52–59.

Thomson, Kenneth. 1971a. "A Cross-National Analysis of Intergenerational Social Mobility and Political Orientation." *Comparative Political Studies.* Vol. 4 (April):3–20.

———. 1971b. "Upward Social Mobility and Political Orientation: A Reevaluation of the Evidence." *American Sociological Review.* Vol. 36 (April):223–35.

Turner, Bryan S. 1986. *Citizenship and Capitalism: The Debate over Reformism.* London: Allen and Unwin.

Verba, Sidney, and Norman H. Nie. 1972. *Participation in America: Political Democracy and Social Equality.* New York: Harper and Row.

Wilson, John. 1973. *Introduction to Social Movements.* New York: Basic Books.

Chapter 8
Political Parties

Political parties are of great interest to political sociologists because they serve as the link between social and political structures. Political parties provide the organizational base through which party regulars and activists organize the electorate, set the issue agenda, and articulate these issues to voters. Party leadership is responsible for selecting party candidates from a pool of party notables and political eligibles who can appeal to voters and who seem electable to political offices. Ideally, in a democracy political parties are enduring and stabilizing structures that perform an intermediary role between citizens and the government. In reality, however, in some political systems—especially in those polities having many political parties and weak political institutions—parties can function as polarizing and destabilizing forces. For example, in the United States the two major political parties have been contesting elections for a long time. In fact, the two-party system in the United States is the most enduring political institution in the world. In a multiparty system governing is more difficult unless political parties have learned to cooperate and to form coalitions and alliances.

The emergence and power of political parties is a rather recent phenomenon. Maurice Duverger (1959) believed that up until as recently as 1850 no country except the United States knew about political parties. Other countries had various parliamentary groups and electoral committees but no real political parties. Political activity took place through extraparliamentary groups such as philosophical societies, working men's clubs, newspapers, trade unions, industrial and commercial groups, and employees' federations and these gave way to the genesis of political parties. The extension of suffrage along with the creation of local electoral committees brought about the expansion of socialist parties in most European countries at the turn of the twentieth century. Indeed, the power of political parties grew with the expansion of universal suffrage, political participation, and democracy. Both political participation and political parties are central to democratic politics.

Although political parties were once little more than electoral committees composed of local elite individuals having high status and wealth, the gradual extension of the franchise and the increased power of elected assemblies brought political parties more permanent national recognition (Bottomore, 1993:34). With the advent of labor and socialist parties toward the end of the nineteenth century, first in Germany and Austria, the permanent mass party became the prevailing factor in western capitalist societies and polities. During the twentieth century political parties and mass parties have spread throughout the world. The dissemination of equalitarian ideology and universal education in industrial and postindustrial societies have somewhat undermined the power of the elites and ruling classes of the past. The rise of the masses further eroded the power of elites and contributed to the emergence of diversity of a political parties in the western capitalist societies. Following the American, French, and Russian Revolutions three major political ideologies led to the creation of socialist, liberal, and conservative political parties. Socialist parties espoused a working-class ideology and were critical of the capitalist class and the institution of property. Communist parties emerged in many western European countries following World War I. Extending this critique, and following the lead of the ruling Communist party in the Soviet Union, the fascist parties emerged in Italy and Germany as a reaction against the socialist and Communist parties. Soviet-controlled Communist parties ruled Eastern Europe following World War II. Since the end of the Cold War in 1989 only a few Communist parties are still in power, although voters in the new democracies are beginning to elect members of the "reformed" Communist parties back into office. Between the two political extremes of Communism and fascism are the liberal and conservative parties that emerged following the French Revolution. Both conservative and liberal parties represent class interests and function within a capitalist social and political order.

Following the collapse of the imperial powers after World War II the nationalist movements in the emerging nation-states in Asia and Africa developed into political parties. During the 1960s many students of Western politics believed that these political parties would follow the Western models of competitive, multiparty systems. However, in most emerging-nation states one-party systems or military dictatorships rather than the expected multiparty systems emerged (Randall, 1988). It is only in the last few years that we have seen a trend away from military or authoritarian one-party states to multiparty politics in many countries in the Third World.

Despite the essential role of political parties in representative democracy, there has been a decline in the power of political parties and in political partisanship in most countries of the world, including the United States (Reiter, 1993:35; Silbey, 1990:3–17). More and more citizens are less tied to political parties when deciding how to vote. As we saw in Chapter 7, there is widespread political apathy and political alienation. Many believe that the political parties have been undermined by the rise of mass communication and the proliferation of interest groups.

In this chapter we will examine a number of questions: What is the nature and scope of political parties? What is the structure and function of political parties? What is the nature of partisanship and its sociodemographic correlates? And what is the future of political parties?

Defining Political Parties

Definitions of political parties abound in the literature. Most students of political parties define a party as an organization of like-minded people whose major role is to elect the government through the electoral process by nominating candidates for political office and seeking to ensure their election. Samuel J. Eldersveld (1964:1–2, 524, 525) conceptualized a political party as a dynamic, complex, and intermediate organization having distinctive and meaningful patterns of activities which penetrates deeply into the U.S. society, a critical institution characterized by a system of interdependent activities and a "meaningful organizational system of interpersonal relationships." Further, it is a decision-making system that performs critical functions for the political system, including a representative process, an electoral process, and subprocesses for recruiting leaders, defining goals, and resolving internal system conflicts (Eldersveld, 1964:1). Seymour M. Lipset and Stein Rokkan (1967:3) viewed political parties as both agents of "conflict" and instruments of "integration." Historically, a "party" in the West meant "division, conflict, and opposition" within a body politic. Etymologically, *party* means a "part" that is in competition with another "part" within a political system. Lipset and Rokkan (1967:4) believed that regardless of the structure of the polity, parties serve as agents of "mobilization." As agents of mobilization political parties help to organize and integrate local communities into the nation or federation. At the same time political parties function as channels for expression of manifest and latent conflicts among various ethnic, religious, regional, gender, generational, and class groups. This conflict-integration dialectic is of central importance to the study of political parties by political sociologists not only within, but also across political systems.

Arend Lijphart (1985:574; Sorauf & Beck, 1988:8) cited three principal dimensions according to which political parties are classified: ideological, hierarchical, and functional. The first dimension, the ideological, can be explained in terms of its form of organization, which subdivides into "mass" and "cadre" parties. The former tend to be more centralized, disciplined, and oligarchical in nature, while the latter tend to be less formal, less centralized, less disciplined, and less oligarchical. In other words, as Robert Michels argued, large political organizations tend to be oligarchical, prone by their very nature to the rule by the few. Parties' programs may be ideological or pragmatic or may reflect a leftist, centrist, or rightist orientation. This means that most political parties espouse some political ideology or political view which may reflect a more pragmatic, conservative, or progressive political orientation toward various political, economic, and social issues in general. By ideological we mean that political parties are distinguished from each other in terms of commonly held beliefs, values, and/or political stands they take toward certain issues. For example, the more conservative political parties are supportive of a strong military and defense establishment as compared to more liberal political parties, who are more inclined to support social programs for the less fortunate segments of society. The second dimension, the hierarchical, is observable in the system of political parties which, like most large organizations, operate on a ranking system of higher and lower positions within the political organization. There are leaders and followers; most of us are followers. The final dimension, the functional, is revealed by the fact that all political parties perform some function or task as intermediaries or brokers between the state or government and the voters. They strive to gain political power and they believe that they can bring about changes and reforms to improve society.

Factions, Movements, and Interest Groups

Related to political parties are factions, movements, and interest groups. The term *faction* is derived from the Latin *factio,* meaning faction, group, or party. The Romans used the term *factio* for the teams of charioteers who competed at the circus. The supporters of these factions of charioteers bet heavily, and their partisanship often led to bloodshed (Lipson, 1964:255–56). Out of factions emerged the political parties. Indeed, in many countries *party* is another name for any faction, clique, coalition, or individual, that is organized around a political leader and that competes for political power against another faction. Because they are usually formed around the charismatic personalities of their leaders they may be referred to as personality-oriented political parties, and they are likely to be conflict-oriented rather than consensual political parties. Political conflict takes place not only between political parties and factions, but also within parties. For example, multiparty European political systems are more prone to internal party conflict and factionalism due to the large number of contenders for political power. Other kinds of political parties, for example the major U.S. and United Kingdom political parties, are based not on personalities but on principles or political platforms.

For a long time the terms *party* and *faction* were used interchangeably even in the United States. In the Federalist Papers James Madison argued in 1787 that

> [a]mong the numerous advantages promised by a well-constructed union, none deserves to be more accurately developed than its tendency to break and control the violence of faction....By a faction, I understand a number of citizens, whether amounting to a majority or minority of the whole, who are united and actuated by some common impulse of passion or of interest, adverse to the rights of other citizens, or to the permanent and exaggerate interests of the community. (Beloff, 1948:41–2)

Even Washington (1796) in his farewell address cautioned against the dangers of faction, and he too made no distinction between party and faction. In more modern times the terms *factions* and *factionalism* are used by political scientists and political sociologists interchangeably to mean political units or coalitions competing for political power and control of resources.

Social or political movements have some resemblance to political parties. Social movements are collectivities aiming at or opposing some change in societal institutions. A social or political movement is less structured and permanent than a political party. Social movements (e.g., women's movements, civil right movements, student movements) use different tactics and strategies from parties and rely mostly on nonconventional or noninstitutionalized means of political participation, including social protest, demonstrations, riots, boycotts, and violent and nonviolent forms of behavior. In some instances, political or social movements can lead to the formation of political parties. For example, most Communist, socialist, or social democratic parties in Europe and the Soviet Union started as mass movements.

A number of scholars (Gusfield, 1963; Laslett and Lipset, 1974; McNall, 1988; Redding, 1992) have argued that although a number of social movements in search of political power have transformed themselves into political parties others have failed. For example, Scott McNall (1988) examined the failures of populist and agrarian movements in Kansas at the turn of the century, while Kent Redding (1992) described the failure of the populist movement in North Carolina at about the same time. John M. Laslett and Seymore M. Lipset (1974) have documented extensively the failure of the socialist movement in the United States to transform itself into a mass political party and to develop a socialist power base. This was not the case in Europe, where socialist parties have long existed.

Interest groups are engaged in various types of activities and are related to political parties insofar as they influence government policies and the legislative process through lobbying. In the United States, lobbying is a process usually run by professionals who directly communicate with legislators and political elites at all levels of the government and civil bureaucracy and who mobilize people at the grass roots level through print or electronic media. Most lobbying is financially supported by political action committees (PACs). According to Kenneth Godwin (1988), although citizen action groups have a long and distinguished history in U.S. politics, PACs are a relatively new phenomenon. The first PACs were established by labor unions, but by the early 1990s the business community was dominant in the field.

Theodore J. Elsmeer and Philip H. Pollack III (1988) found that once the corporate world began to create PACs, these committees grew in size and assumed a greater variety of activities. Their behavior can be categorized as accommodationist,

Table 8.1   Number of Political Action Committees, by Type, 1974–1987

Year	Total	Corporate	Labor	Other
1974	608	89	201	318
1975	722	139	226	357
1976	1,146	433	224	489
1977	1,360	550	234	576
1978	1,653	785	217	651
1979	2,000	950	240	810
1980	2,551	1,206	297	1,048
1981	2,901	1,329	318	1,254
1982	3,371	1,469	380	1,522
1983	3,525	1,538	378	1,609
1984	4,009	1,682	394	1,933
1985	3,992	1,710	388	1,894
1986	4,157	1,744	384	2,029
1987	4,165	1,775	364	2,026

Source: U.S. Bureau of the Census, *Statistical Abstract of the United States* (1989:262).

partisan, or adversarial. By *accommodationist* we mean that PACs follow a process of peaceful coexistence and pursue a policy of compromise and arbitration while trying to influence legislators or the political party in power. Other PACs follow a more partisan path—that is to say, they stick to a party line or support political candidates who represent their views in Congress. In their partisanship they sometimes become adversarial or antagonistic toward those who hold views opposing their own. For example, the issue of abortion has led to the formation of adversarial "pro-life" and "pro-choice" PACs.

The tremendous increase in the number of PACs has become a controversial issue. In fact, under pressure from voters, Congress has passed legislation limiting the contributions PACs can make to legislators. There are those who argue against the ever-growing power of PACs and see them as subverting the democratic process of U.S. politics in several ways. A major concern is that they undercut the importance of political parties and make politicians less responsive to their constituents.[1] Because money becomes more important than the size of an interest group or the merits of its positions, PAC influence takes place at the expense of the people or of those average citizens who are not organized in PACs to influence the government. For example, two of the most powerful PACs, representing the American Medical Association and the National Rifle Association, have in the past several years defeated efforts both to reform the health-care system and to pass strict gun control laws.

Jack L. Walker (1991:187–88) underscored the importance of the rise and mobilization of interest groups in the United States. He found three basic types of interest groups. First are those representing economic-interest or profit-oriented groups, such as the National Association of Automobile Manufacturers. Second are those non-profit groups having strong appeals to professionals, such as the National Association of Drug Abuse. Third are those citizen-oriented groups or movements representing collective interests in civil rights, occupational health and safety, environmental protection, or consumer affairs. Although Walker found that the interest-group system was still dominated by occupational and commercial groups, he discovered that one fifth of respondents to a survey supported citizen-oriented interest groups. Interest groups organized around an idea or a cause and open to all regardless of occupational or commercial interest, such as Common Cause or Citizens for Clean Air, have emerged as participants in the policy-making process. This is an important development because citizen groups transcend occupational based self-interest and reflect more broadly defined societal or public interests. Citizen-interest groups are characterized by distinctive objectives and strategies which go beyond the narrow interests of most occupational and profit-oriented interest groups. Citizen-oriented interest groups also have implications concerning the civic responsibility, political participation, and social consciousness of the citizens in a political and civic culture.

Party Structure

Political parties are essentially forms of *social organization,* a term that sociologists often use synonymously with *social structure.* George Theodorson and Achilles G.

Theodorson (1969:287) define social organization as a "relatively stable pattern of social relationships of individuals and subgroups within a society or group, based upon systems of social roles, norms, and shared meanings that provide regularity and predictability in social interaction." Somewhat similarly, Robert E. L. Faris (1964:661) defines social organization as both a structure and a process. "As *structure,* an organization is any stable pattern of interrelations among component parts which form a whole having characteristics not manifest in the separate parts....As *process* organization is used to refer to the manner in which these entities are formed." Political parties are not only enduring forms of social organization, but also processes marked by change and diversity. Some political parties endure longer than others. For example, the two major political parties in the United States are the oldest parties in the modern western world. In other countries political parties have much shorter life spans. They emerge with their founders and disappear or change names when their founders die out. This is more common in political systems that are unstable and personalistic.

David R. Mayhew (1986;19–20) identifies five major attributes of a political party. (1) A party has a substantial autonomy and its own dynamic. This means that a party has its own independence and can function independently of the influence of external groups and organizations. (2) It lasts a long time and outlives its leadership. (3) It has hierarchy in its internal structure, including leaders and followers or rank and file members. (4) Its main purpose is to nominate candidates for a wide range of public offices at all political levels. (5) It relies mostly on "material," or more tangible, incentives to motivate people to get involved in the goals of the political organization. This means that those who are active and support political parties are more likely to receive political offices or appointments as rewards of client-patron relationships rather than to be offered only appeals to lofty ideals and goals of the organization.[2]

In a landmark work Michels (1962) offered an organizational analysis of political parties and his famous "iron law of oligarchy," which influenced generations of scholars. In addition, Michels examined a number of technical/administrative, psychological, intellectual, and social aspects of leadership of political parties. He believed, for example, that the masses had a psychological need for leadership and venerated leaders and that "he who says organization says oligarchy." The source of oligarchy, indeed the culprit, Michels found in large-scale organizations and bureaucracies. The apathy and incompetence of the masses, he believed, led to the inevitability of the iron law of oligarchy in all forms of social organization including socialist and democratic political parties. Michels's study of the socialist and democratic parties in Europe influenced the work of Max Weber and a number of other European and U.S. scholars of politics and society, including Duverger (1959).

Michels's empirical conclusion that in every party organization, regardless of its ideological basis, there is a tendency to oligarchy has been challenged by a number of writers. Commenting on Michels's thesis of the iron law of oligarchy, Seymour Lipset (1968: 412–435) argued that many of Michels's critics, including Maurice Duverger, Sigmund Newman, and Robert McKenzie, have shown that Michels was over-deterministic in his organizational analysis of European political parties. However, most elite theorists of democracy still accept Michels's iron law.

An alternative hypothesis concerns what Harold Lasswell and Abraham Kaplan (1950) called "stratarchy." According to this hypothesis, instead of a centralized unity of command or more diffused power throughout the structure of political parties there are "strata commands" or layers of echelons of authority operating with a substantial degree of autonomy throughout the party structure. Eldersveld (1964:5–14) identified three more structural elements of political parties: parties are clientele-oriented structures, they seek to convert winning elections into political power, and their leaderships tend to be open, tenuous, and unstable. According to Eldersveld (1964:12–13), all three structural properties of political parties operate within three clusters of factors: the sociopolitical environment, the internal dynamics of the party and the political culture, and time. In other words, a political party depends a great deal on its grass roots or its base for its survival and its elite structure is contingent upon its ability to deliver its promises within a reasonable amount of time.

Duverger's (1959) work became another landmark in the organizational analysis of political parties. It dealt with such issues as the origin of parties, party organization, party membership, party leadership, and the political system in general. Writing within the European tradition of organizational analysis and following Michels's ideas, Duverger did a comparative study of various political parties in Europe. In his comparative analysis of party organization, he identified four basic structural elements of political parties: the caucus, the branch, the cell, and the militia. A caucus, according to Duverger, is a limited, closed, and semipermanent group. As primary groups, caucuses gather around election time to nominate candidates for the elections. With the rise of the electronic media and the decline of partisanship, the caucus has lost its original importance. Now the nominating process of candidates is carried out more by pollsters and media people and those who have the greatest appeal to voters usually receive their parties nominations. While the caucus is a group of experts or notables chosen because of their influence, the branch appeals to the masses. A branch, according to Duverger, is more extensive than a caucus and its membership is wide open. Both branch and caucus are local in nature but the branch is narrower and less decentralized than the caucus. The cell consists of all party members who work at the same place. There are factory workers' cells, office workers' cells, sailors' cells, and so on. The cell as party structure was widely used by Communist parties in the Soviet Union. The purpose of both branches and cells is to encourage citizens to participate more in local politics and to familiarize themselves with political ideology. The word *militia* as used by Duverger, means a paramilitary group whose members are subjected to the same discipline as regular soldiers. The idea of a militia has been important to different political factions and political leaders in many countries. In Lebanon, for example, each ethnoreligious political faction has its own militia and in many Latin American countries militia known as *caudilos* were extensively used.[3]

In discussing party membership, Duverger (1959) also distinguished between cadre and mass parties. The difference between the two was structure, not size. The cadre parties were small groups of people who prepared for elections, conducted campaigns, and maintained contacts with candidates or directed the activities of the parties. Cadre parties were analogous to caucuses, but they were decentralized and weakly knit. Mass parties are more centralized, are based on branches that seek to engage large numbers of people in political movements, and are more characteristic of European parties.[4]

Two major issues related to political leadership and party are the notions of "elite recruitment" and "elite integration." Elite recruitment or the replenishment of party leadership is essential in the viability of political parties. Elite integration refers to the unity and consensus of political elites. Both recruitment and integration are important in the ability of political parties to compete for political leadership and power in electoral politics. The study of recruitment and integration is important not only for political elites but for other societal elites in general. Both phenomena have an impact on specific and important issues such as stability, democracy, oligarchy, system effectiveness, political conflict, social, and political change. For some, elite integration may be undesirable in a democracy for it fosters conformity and discourages diversity, innovation, and renewal. The same argument is made by elite recruitment. In political parties it is very difficult for new members to be elected in political offices.

Party Functions

Political parties' major function is to link the people and other societal institutions with the government and its various political institutions by contesting elections, mobilizing social interests, and advocating ideological positions. Parties recruit political elites and decision makers whose decisions have a great impact on the entire society. Legislative and policy-making processes and the implementation by government bureaucracy of such decisions and policies are carried out by political parties in power. As the society becomes more complex, so do its social and political institutions. The interdependence of political institutions and other social institutions—religious, economic, educational, cultural, kinship, scientific, and military—is the major focus of political sociology.

Eldersveld (1982:4) cites three basic linkage functions of political parties. According to him, political parties provide some cooperation and linkage between national, state, and local institutions and leadership. They also serve as forums and vehicles for interest groups to present their views on behalf of their constituents and coalition members. Finally, they can form a channel for communication between citizens, organizational leaders, and government officials. Political parties are the principal means for citizens' and groups' participation in the political process. This means that political parties set the agenda for the public discourse of major issues. For the linkage functions of political parties in the United States see Figure 8.1.

Jan-Erik Lane and Svante O. Ersson (1991:102–03) stressed the roles of political parties as intermediaries between social cleavages and political decision-making organizations in governmental structures. In those political systems having representative forms of government, political parties serve as the major vehicles for political action or inaction. It is through political parties that citizens organize, support, and express political demands vis-à-vis various social cleavages. By *social cleavages* we

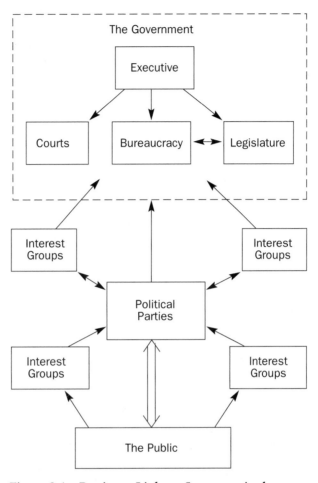

**Figure 8.1   Parties as Linkage Structures in the
Political System**

Source: Samuel J. Eldersveld, *Political Parties in American Society*
(1982:5); reprinted here by permission from the author.

mean the division of society into various social groups or collectivities in terms of
various characteristics such as race, class, ideology, religion, region, and status. Political parties organize themselves on the basis of various social, political, economic,
and cultural cleavages. Cleavages are potential sources of latent and manifest patterns of conflict (Rae & Taylor, 1970; Zuckerman, 1975:231–48).

Lipset and Rokkan (1967:5) saw political parties as playing expressive and
instrumental/representative roles. By *expressive* the authors meant that political parties develop a rhetoric by which contrasts in the social and cultural structure become
demands for action or inaction. This function is more characteristic of small parties

because as parties become larger they must form broader alliances and represent more citizens and groups.

Sartori, (1976:575) believed that, to be counted as parties, parties should have either "coalition potential" or "blackmail potential." A party having coalition potential can participate in cabinet coalitions to form a government. This is especially characteristic of European political parties. A party not having coalition potential may have blackmail potential: it may be ideologically unacceptable as a coalition partner but large enough to exert considerable influence, as are, for example, the Communist parties in some European countries, such as Italy.

Western European and U.S. Party Systems

A party system consists of interdependent parts of a number of political parties operating within a political system. Three issues will be our focus in this section: (1) partisanship, (2) the social and sociopsychological bases of partisanship, and (3) trends and changes in electoral politics in general.

Partisanship

One of the most widely discussed and debated issues in electoral politics in western industrial nations is the notion of partisanship and its alleged recent decline. In its simplest form partisanship can be defined as party identification and party preference or the extent to which a voter is committed to the ideology of a particular political party. Morris Janowitz and Dwaine Marvick (1964:11) argued that the arena of political competition varies according to the partisanship of the electorate and the intensity of the campaign.

Surveys show that the Republican Party made striking gains in party identification during the 1980s. For example, in 1978 Democrats had a 25 percentage point lead over the Republicans, but in the period 1989 to 1991, the parties stood at parity. Support among the Democratic Party's traditional constituencies—women, members of minority groups, southern whites, and ethnics—has somewhat declined. After tilting toward the Democrats in the late 1970s, college graduates ages eighteen to forty-four became one of the strongest Republican constituencies during the 1980s. But Ross Perot's candidacy and his capture of 20 percent of the popular vote in the 1992 national elections is an indication of voters' rejection of both major parties. Despite the decline of partisanship, partisanship and ideology affected the outcome of the 1992 elections: Bill Clinton captured most Democrats and liberals and George Bush captured most Republicans and conservatives (Pomper, 1993:140).

Although partisanship is widely reported to be declining in the United States, a major study of partisanship carried out in the 1960s (Campbell et al., 1964) suggests that it may never have been a strong force. While Angus Campbell and his colleagues found that most voters identified with either of the two major political parties, their commitment to the parties was shallow: only 10 percent of the U.S. public could be classified as truly committed to either political party (Orum, 1988). Only a small percentage of people was found to think of political issues and principles. Most U.S. citizens think of a party identification as a label to be used occasionally in the voter's booth (Orum, 1988). Philip E. Converse (1964) found that most U.S. citizens do not think of politics in conceptual or ideological terms. The supposed decline in partisanship has been associated with the increasing involvement of mass media in electoral politics (Converse and Dupeux, 1976; Knoke, 1976; Ladd, 1978, 1980; Nie et al., 1979). Others associate the decline in partisanship with the emergence and proliferation of interest groups, political action committees (PACs), and, more recently, citizens' groups. Howard L. Reiter (1993:89–104), after analyzing 229 public opinion surveys mostly based on Eurobarometer data from 17 nations, concluded that those who held "postmaterialist" values, such as ecological, civil rights, and health concerns and those who preferred new politics were more likely to be strong partisans than were those who held "materialist" values. The "new politics" is identified with the post-materialist values. The post-materialist parties and movements reject: (1) the traditional goals of economic growth and technocracy; (2) they pursue decentralization and local power; (3) their demands tend to be non-negotiable and unconditional; (4) they reject oligarchical and hierarchical structures of traditional parties; (5) they focus on a few issues; (6) they aim at cultural transformation rather than state action; (7) they espouse a communitarian, gemeinschaft style and rhetoric; (8) they are open to illegal or violent methods; and (9) they renounce state and party (quoted in Reiter, 1993:90). This "new politics" includes those groups that support environmental issues, various positions on abortion, rights of women, ethnic minorities and all those who participated in various anti-war movements (especially against the war in Vietnam), against nuclear energy, and the arms race (Reiter, 1993: 89–90). He found that the distinction between parties and social movements had been exaggerated and that the mass public did not differentiate between the two.

Alignment, Realignment, Dealignment

Central to the concept of partisanship are the issues of alignment, realignment, and dealignment. William Schneider (1980:95–9) defines alignment as "the process by which partisanship emerges through association of parties with position issues." One of the dominant themes in political sociology is the cleavage basis of party and voter alignments. Lipset and Rokkan (1967:3) saw class, religion, region, and political tradition as influencing voter alignments. Other cleavage bases of party and voter alignment and political party support include generation, ethnicity, gender, and race. Structural factors contributing to alignment are all those enduring social classifications that differentiate people into various social collectivities, such as socioeconomic, religious, ethnic, racial, regional, or gender social collectivities. Structural factors interact with more transitory nonstructural domestic factors, such as candidates and issues. Political parties vary in their stands on various ecological, economic, domestic, and international issues, which impact alignment.

Realignment refers to a major shift in party preference or party identification. Knoke (1976) lists three factors responsible for realignment—the growth of independents, an increase in split-ticket voting, and the weaker impact of party identification on congressional elections (Kourvetaris & Dobratz, 1982:311). The realignment process was first suggested by political scientist V. O. Key Jr. (1955). Key's realignment theory was basically a cyclical theory of electoral politics. For instance, in the United States the two dominant political parties tend to alternate in winning national elections. The realignment argument was revived in the early 1970s by Walter Dean Burnham, who thought that the U.S. party system was in a period of realignment due to the changing social and economic topography (Orum 1988:410). Scholarship on the realignment perspective has proliferated both in the United States and elsewhere (Bass, 1991:141–78). However, a substantial number of scholars have criticized the realignment theory, arguing that declining partisanship undermines the notion of realignment. Joel H. Silbey describes the end of realignment:

> *There has been increasing electoral fragmentation since the 1960s, due to the decline of party loyalty among voters; the voters' commitment to either the Democrats or the Republicans no longer exists at levels that once defined the norms of the American political world; the number of independent voters has grown to levels previously unrecorded, as has the constant uncertainty of the people's choices on any election day. Certainly, much evidence has accumulated suggesting that the New Deal party system did not realign into a successor one; that the electoral universe dealigned instead; and, most critically, that our political system seems unable to have a realignment under present electoral conditions. All these are new conditions, and together they add up to a major deviation from the cyclical norms that have heretofore characterized our political history. Vernon Bogdanor suggests, "the case for realignment sits uneasily with the 'decline of party' thesis." (Silbey, 1991:4)*

A number of scholars (Beck, 1977; Carmines, 1987; Crewe et al., 1977; Ladd, 1978; Niemi & Weisberg 1976) suggest that a process of dealignment, rather than realignment, is taking place in U.S. electoral politics. Schneider (1980:96) defined dealignment "as defection from traditional partisanship in the direction of no-party preference, or anti-party preference, as an expression of no confidence in the conventional alternatives." Ross Perot's relative success in the 1992 presidential elections can be seen as a symptom of dealignment. In the early 1970s dealignment in the United Kingdom took the form of an upsurge of voting for liberals and for nationalist candidates (Crewe et al., 1977).

In summarizing U.S. politics between 1789 and 1989, Silbey (1991:17) described four eras, each defined by a different characterization of partisanship (see Table 8.2).

In short, most scholars of electoral politics agree that there has been a decline in partisanship but disagree about the causes of such a decline. Some see the decline in terms of "antipartyism" and electoral fragmentation that can be traced back to the 1896 elections (Burham, 1974). Others trace the decline in partisanship to more modern times. We can clearly see the influence of the 1968 Democratic convention in Chicago and the Civil Rights and anti–Vietnam War movements during the 1960s and 1970s on partisanship. The decline of the political parties has produced an electorate whose main concerns lie with issues rather than with partisanship, further polarizing U.S. politics and making the executive branch of government more powerful.

Table 8.2   American Political Eras, 1789–1989

Era	Description	Years
1	Prealignment	1789–1838
2	Alignment/Realignment	1838–1893
3	Realignment/Dealignment	1893–1948/52
4	Postalignment	1948/52–present

Source: Joel H. Silbey, in Byron E. Shafer, *The End of Realignment?* (1991:17);
reprinted by permission from the publisher.

The Social Bases of Partisanship and the 1992 Presidential Election

Is there a class basis for partisanship? How do demographic characteristics such as gender, religion, education, income, region, and age, correlate with one's political party identification and political preference?

Since the New Deal of the 1930s the bulk of Democratic supporters has included those who are of lower socioeconomic status, less educated, urban, black, members of ethnic minority groups, white southerners, and lower-middle-class. However, in more recent elections this Democratic coalition has somewhat dissolved. The issue of race has proven most diverse. As Thomas Edsall and Mary Edsall (1992:5) argued, "Race has crystallized and provided a focus for value conflicts over subjects as diverse as social welfare spending, neighborhood schooling, the distribution of tax burdens, criminal violence, sexual conduct, family structure, political competition, and union membership." By focusing on some of these issues, the Republicans succeeded in winning all but one of the presidential elections in the last quarter of a century. The party made inroads especially in the traditionally Democratic constituencies of Roman Catholics and southern whites. Pomper (1993:135–36) argues Clinton "won three of every five votes from those below the poverty level, with decreasing proportions up through the income ladder, and only about one of three votes from the wealthy. Jews, as in the past, were an exception; although relatively high in social status, they gave Clinton a higher proportion of their vote than any other white ethnic or religious group." As in the 1988 presidential election the "gender gap" persisted in the 1992 national election. Women gave five percent more support for Clinton than did men. However, in the 1992 election men showed greater support for Perot than the women. According to Pomper (1993:138) women's support for the Democrats was due to economics rather than gender. For example, among disadvantaged minority women, Latino, and African American women voted overwhelmingly for Clinton as opposed to housewives or homemakers who supported George Bush.

In the 1992 presidential election the "Democratic Core" was revived and its social cleavages patched up. Bill Clinton's support came from the bulwarks of the Democratic Party, including African Americans, Latinos, the poor, the unemployed, those having only high school educations and those espousing postmaterialist values (e.g., gays, environmentalists, and abortion-rights advocates). In general, those who voted for Clinton in greater percentages were more likely to be Democratic, independent (liberal or moderate), unmarried, elderly, Jewish or Catholic, or to have a postgraduate degree or to lack a high school diploma; or to make less than $30,000 a year; or to live in a large city (Pomper, 1993:138–39).

Table 8.3 shows that an equal percentage of Democrats and Republicans switched parties. However, 4 percent more Republicans than Democrats voted for Ross Perot.

In general, the 1992 election demonstrated alignment. For example, African Americans were again the Democrats' most loyal group, as they have been since 1964. White southerners, who have increasingly aligned with the Republicans for the last thirty years, were that party's strongest supporters. As usual, Asians tended to vote Republican, while the majority of Hispanics voted Democrat. Again, as in the past, born-again Christians and those who regularly attend religious services voted for the Republicans (see Table 8.4).

By comparing voting patterns in the 1984 and 1992 national elections, Robert B. Smith (1993) analyzed the effects of occupational class, socioeconomic status, and ethnicity on alignment. He found that ethnic groups, especially African Americans, Jews, white Catholics, and white Protestants, had different interests concerning economic and social justice issues and that these differences explained their different voting patterns. He found that ethnicity had a stronger effect on voting alignments than did socioeconomic status. More specifically, Smith found that (1) African Americans and Jews favored government interventions to bring about social equality and reduce prejudice; (2) cross-pressure between Catholic affluence and concern for the poor had resulted in weaker ties between white Catholics and the Democratic Party, and affluent white Catholics voted for their economic interests more strongly than for their ethnic interests; (3) white Protestants aligned with the Republican Party because they opposed government intervention to bring about social equality

Table 8.3   1992 Presidential Vote, by Party Identification

Percentage of voters identifying themselves as:

Democrats	Republicans	Independents/Others
10% for Bush	10% for Clinton	32% for Bush
13% Ind/Others	17% Ind/Others	38% for Clinton
77% Clinton	73% Bush	30% Perot

Source: Voter research survey data by the Roper Center for Public Opinion Research, University of Connecticut. Reprinted here by permission from *The Christian Science Monitor* (Dec. 11, 1992:19).

Table 8.4   Ethnic and Religious Voting Patterns, including Southern Whites
in the 1992 Election

	Presidential Vote			House Vote	
	Clinton	Bush	Perot	Democrats	Republicans
Asians	30%	55%	15%	49%	51%
Blacks	83	10	7	89	11
Hispanics	61	25	14	72	28
Jews	80	11	9	79	21
White Catholics	42	36	22	54	46
White Northern Protestants	36	44	20	45	55
White Southern Protestants	30	53	17	42	58
Born-Again/Fundamentalists	30	56	14	41	59
Attend Religious Services at Least Once a Week	36	48	16	47	53

Source: Voter research surveys data by the Roper Center for Public Opinion Research, University of Connecticut. Reprinted here by permission from *The Christian Science Monitor* (Dec. 11, 1992:19).

for disadvantaged groups; (4) qualitatively, the alignments of white Protestants, white Catholics, Jews, and African Americans were roughly similar to alignments during the Roosevelt and Truman eras, though the loyalty of Catholics to the Democratic Party is no longer taken for granted. Of course, the voting patterns of the electorate can be explained in a number of other ways. The nature of current political issues, candidates' personal qualities, the role of the mass media, voters' perception of the economy, and women's changed circumstances all contribute to voting patterns (Lipset, 1981; Nie et al., 1979:47–73).

Table 8.5 shows a number of factors other than sociodemographic variables that accounted for voting patterns in the 1992 presidential election. In addition to sociodemographic variables two questions were asked in the 1992 exit polls: (1) What were the most important issues? and (2) What were the most important personal qualities of the candidates?

The Future of Political Parties: Continuity and Change

Even as people in the former Soviet Union, the former Yugoslavia, Eastern Europe, and other parts of the world yearn for self-determination and democracy, Americans are losing patience with political parties and electoral politics. More and more, Americans dislike politics and professional politicians and view the electoral process as a spectacle rather than as a genuine democratic process. Voter turnout in the United States tagged far behind turnout in the other industrialized nations. While we

Table 8.5   Sources of the Presidential Vote

	Total Mentions	Percent Voting for			Contribution to Vote for		
		Clinton	Bush	Perot	Clinton	Bush	Perot
Issue priorities							
Health care	19	67	19	13	8.4	2.4	1.6
U.S. deficit	21	36	27	38	5.0	3.8	5.3
Abortion	12	36	56	8	2.9	4.5	0.6
Education	13	60	25	15	5.2	2.2	1.3
Economy/jobs	43	52	25	24	14.8	7.1	6.8
Environment	6	72	15	13	2.9	0.6	0.5
Taxes	14	26	57	17	2.4	5.3	1.6
Foreign policy	8	8	87	5	0.4	4.6	0.3
Family values	15	23	66	11	2.3	6.6	1.1
Totals	151				44.3	36.9	19.1
Personal qualities							
Experience	18	22	65	13	2.6	7.7	1.5
Bring change	37	58	20	23	14.2	4.9	5.6
My party	5	45	42	13	1.5	1.4	0.4
Cares about people	14	55	25	20	5.1	2.3	1.9
Honest	14	30	50	20	2.8	4.6	1.9
Best plan	25	51	27	22	8.4	4.5	3.6
Crisis judgment	16	25	64	11	2.6	6.8	1.2
Vice-president	8	64	24	11	3.4	1.3	0.6
Strong convictions	14	32	44	24	3.0	4.1	2.2
Totals	151				43.7	37.6	18.9

Source: Gerald Pompers, *The Election of 1992* (1992:146); reprinted here by permission from the publisher.

praise the virtues of democracy and encourage pluralistic and electoral politics abroad, we do little or nothing to encourage the politics of discourse and public involvement at home. Many believe that we have become a society of individuals lacking a sense of community, citizenship, and common purpose. E. J. Dionne Jr. (1991) argued that most of the problems of political life in the United States can be explained in terms of the failure of the two prevailing ideologies of the U.S. political system: liberalism and conservatism. According to Dionne, both political ideologies have failed to address the major issues that have polarized U.S. society and politics for a long time; issues such as race, social inequality, the national debt, civil rights, crime, illegal drug use, the environment and health care. Both political parties reflect the cleavages of the larger society and have failed to work together to resolve these issues. Surveys show that the public in general is not satisfied with the way political parties, Congress, and the president conduct the business of politics and government.

Examples of public discontent abound. The Democrats have been accused of escalating the Vietnam War and of failing to create the Great Society. The New Left movement of the 1960s was primarily critical of liberalism and the Democratic Party and tried to expose the hypocrisy of the liberal capitalist establishment. The split of the Democratic Party between "conservatives" and "progressives" gave the Republicans the opportunity to exploit cultural and social divisions and issues such as race, family, and crime, and they succeeded in breaking up the New Deal coalition that had enabled the Democratic Party to win elections and carry out a social agenda for the benefit of disadvantaged minority groups. The 1960s and 1970s brought about the conservative reaction and the Ronald Reagan and George Bush victories during the 1980s.

According to Sandy Pope and Joe Rogers (1992), the structure of U.S. political parties is outmoded. Public opinion polls show that the majority of Americans are disgusted with both parties on several counts. The parties are business-dominated organizations having weak linkages between leaders, voters, and a small and vanishing membership. Both parties are too weak and disjointed to articulate a coherent policy and programs for general benefits. They are not interested in creating an informed citizenry and are unwilling to discuss the issues. Pope and Rogers believed that there is a need for renewal and reorganization to reflect the changing social and economic realities of the United States and the world.

Pope and Rogers and a number of others have proposed a new party movement as an alternative to the two-party system. According to them, the new party should ideologically be a social democratic party resembling the European social democratic parties. Among other things, the authors believe that the new party movement should: (1) reexamine the electoral system, (2) organize locally but think in long terms, (3) run progressive candidates for offices, (4) espouse a democratic ideology, (5) forge a coalition of ticket-splitter women's groups and ecology, peace, and justice advocates, (6) include Latinos, African Americans, Asians, gays, and other minority group members.[6]

Despite the problems and deficiencies of the two major political parties in the United States, the fact that the two-party system has endured for over a century is in itself a great achievement. The American political parties are the most enduring political institutions in the world. But stability does not always mean the best choice for all social groups and constituencies alike. The political parties, like the political system as a whole, must be reformed to reflect a rapidly changing world. L. Sandy Maisel (1990:307–23) argued that as we move toward the twenty-first century the picture of political parties in the United States is a blurred one. Parties must be able to adapt to changing circumstances and chart a new course for the next century.

Summary and Conclusion

In this chapter the structures and functions of political parties were examined. Political parties provide the organizational base for linking the electorate to the political process by setting the political agenda, nominating candidates, and articulating the issues to the voters. Political parties grew with expansion of suffrage, democracy, and equality. With the exception of the United States, the emergence of political parties is a rather recent phenomenon.

Some scholars define political parties as dynamic organizations of like-minded people whose major role is to control the government through the electoral process by nominating candidates for political office and seeking to ensure their election. Others look at political parties both as agents of "conflict" and instruments of "integration." They also serve as "agents of mobilization" to organize and integrate local communities into the nation or federation.

Related to politics are the concepts of factions, movements, and interest groups. In most instances, political parties emerged out of factions, cliques, or coalitions organized around a political leader. Political movements are collectivities aiming at some change or opposing change. Political movements are less structured and permanent than political parties. In some instances political or social movements can result in the formation of political parties. Interest groups are citizen groups organized around an issue and engaged in political action by influencing legislators and political elites. The number of interest groups commonly known as PACs or political action committees has increased and has become a controversial issue in American politics. The political power and influence of PACs have undermined the political process and undercut the effectiveness of political parties.

The decline of party identification and partisanship were also noted. The concepts of alignment, realignment, and dealignment were briefly discussed. The growth of independent voters and split ticket voting gave way to realignment. The defection of traditional partisanship, or no-party preference led to dealignment of the electorate. Some ideas of "new politics" and third party movements were also discussed along with a brief analysis of the 1992 national election.

Endnotes

1. The decline of party influence is not due only to the rise of interest groups and PACs. Two more factors have contributed to that decline: (1) the increased number of primaries and (2) the Federal Election Campaign Act of 1971. In the past delegates to the national conventions were picked by party bosses; now most delegates are chosen in state primaries by voters. The result is that by the time they reach the national conventions, delegates, like candidates, have less commitment to party bosses and to party positions. The FECA of 1972 (with amendments in 1974) supplies eligible candidates with almost half their campaign funds in the primaries and the major-party candidates with all their campaign funds (subject to a $21.8 million ceiling for each candidate). (See Sherrill, 1972.)

2. In client-patron relationships those active in electoral politics (the clients) support particular political candidates (patrons) who in turn reward them by giving them positions in the government. For a conceptual and empirical analysis of "political clientelism" see Kourvetaris and Dobratz (1984:35–59).

3. *Caudilos* refer to the private militia or paramilitary force common in many countries in Latin America in the past.

4. In addition to the two major political parties in the United States, we find a number of small parties, such as the Socialist and Communist parties, and new political movements, such as the ecology movement in the 1970s.

5. According to Pomper, each item was calculated by multiplying the proportion who mentioned

the item by the proportion of that group voting for Clinton, Bush, or Perot. Because more than one response was permitted, the figures presented were calculated on a base of 100. An illustration of this is as follows: 19 percent mentioned "health care," 67 percent of that 19 percent voted for Clinton, and total responses were 151% of all issue priorities of all individuals. The contribution of health care to Clinton's 44 percent of the vote was then calculated as: .19×.67 + 1.51 = 8.4 percent (Pomper, 1992: 155).

6. A number of people in the past have attempted to start a third party movement but they had limited success. In more recent times Governor Wallace started a reactionary racist type of political movement that failed during the 1970s. John Anderson, a liberal Republican, ran as an independent during the 1980 national election but failed to gain enough support. In 1992, Perot as a Third Party candidate succeeded in capturing twenty percent of the vote. In the Fall of 1995, Perot and his followers registered officially as a Third Party candidate. About the same time, Colin Powell, a former United States General and chairman of Joint Chief of Staff raised the issue of the Third party movement. However, later he decided not to be a candidate for any elected office. For a movement for the establishment of a populist Third Party, see Scott McNall, 1988, *The Road to Rebellion* at the turn of the century.

References

Bass, Harold F. Jr. 1991. "Background and Debate: A Reader's Guide and Bibliography." In *The End of Realignment? Interpreting American Electoral Eras,* ed. Nyron E. Shafer, Pp. 141–178 Madison: University of Wisconsin Press.

Belloff, M. 1948. *The Federalist* (editor) Oxford: Blackwell

Beck, Paul Allen. 1977. Partisan Dealignment in the Postwar South. *American Political Science Review* Vol. 77 (June):477–96.

Bottomore, Tom. 1993. *Political Sociology,* 2nd ed. Minneapolis: University of Minnesota Press.

Burham, Walter Dean. 1974. "Theory and Voting Research: Some Reflections on Converse's Change in the American Electorate." *American Political Science Review* Vol. 68:1002–27. No. 3.

Campbell, Angus, P. Converse, W. Miller, and D. Stokes. 1964. *The American Voter,* abridged. New York: John Wiley & Sons.

Carmines, Edward G. 1987. "Unrealized Partisanship: A Theory of Dealignment." *Journal of Politics* Vol. 49 No 2 (May):376–400.

Converse, Philip E. 1964. The Nature of Belief Systems in the Mass Public. In *Ideology and Discontent,* ed. D. E. Apter, Pp. 206–261 Glencoe, Illinois: Free Press.

Converse, P., and George Dupeux. 1976. *The Dynamics of Party Support.* Beverly Hills: Sage.

Crewe, Ivor, Bo Sarlvic, and James Alt. 1977. "Partisan Dealignment in Britain." *British Journal of Political Science.* Vol. 7 (April):129–90.

Dionne, E. J. Jr. 1991. *Why Americans Hate Politics.* New York: Simon and Schuster.

Duverger, Maurice. 1959. *Political Parties.* Barbara and Robert North, (trans). London: Lowe and Brydone.

Edsall, Thomas, and Mary Edsall. 1992. *Chain Reaction: The Impact of Race, Rights, and Taxes in American Politics.* New York: Norton.

Eldersveld, Samuel. J. 1982. *Political Parties in American Society.* New York: Basic Books.

———. 1964. *Political Parties: A Behavioral Analysis.* Chicago: Rand McNally.

Elsmeier, Theodore J., and Philip H. Pollock III. 1988. *Business, Money, and the Rise of Corporate PACs in American Elections.* Westport, Conn.: Quorum Books.

Faris, Robert E. L. 1964. "Social Organization." In *The Dictionary of the Social Sciences,* ed. Julius Gould and William L. Kolb, 661–62. New York: Free Press.

Godwin, Kenneth. 1988. *One Billion Dollars of Influence: The Direct Marketing of Politics.* Chatham, N.J.: Chatham House.

Gusfield, Joseph R. 1963. *Symbolic Crusade: Status Politics and the American Temperance Movement.* Urbana: University of Illinois Press.

Janowitz, Morris, and Dwaine Marvick. 1964. *Competitive Pressure and Democratic Consent.* Chicago: Quadrangle.

Key, V. O. Jr. 1955. "A Theory of Critical Elections." *Journal of Politics.* Vol. 17 (February):3–18.

Knoke, David. 1976. *Change and Continuity in American Politics.* Baltimore: Johns Hopkins University Press.

Kourvetaris, George A., and Betty A. Dobratz. 1984. "Political Clientelism in Athens, Greece: A Three Paradigm Approach to Political Clientelism." *East European Quarterly.* Vol. 18, no. 1:35–59.

———. 1982. "Political Power and Conventional Political Participation." *Annual Review of Sociology* Vol. 8: 289–317. Palo Alto: annual Reviews, Inc.

Ladd, Everett Carl Jr. 1978. "The Shifting Party Coalitions 1932–1976." In *Emerging Coalitions in American Politics,* ed. Seymour Martin Lipset, Pp. 81–102, San Francisco: Institute for Contemporary Studies.

———. 1980. "A Rebuttal: Realignment? No. Dealignment? Yes." *Public Opinion.* no. 5 3:13–20.

Lane, Jan-Erik, and Svante O. Ersson. 1991. *Politics and Society in Western Europe,* 2nd ed. Newbury Park, CA: Sage.

Laslett, John M., and Seymour M. Lipset, eds. 1974. *Essays in the History of American Socialism.* New York: Anchor.

Lasswell, Harold, and Abraham Kaplan. 1950. *Power and Society.* New Haven: Yale University Press.

Lijphart, Arend. 1985. "Political Parties." In *Social Science Encyclopedia,* ed. Adam Kuper and Jessica Kuper, p. 574. London: Routledge and Kegan Paul.

Lipset, Seymour. 1981. *Political Man: The Social Bases of Politics.* Baltimore: Johns Hopkins University Press.

———, ed. 1978. *Emerging Coalitions in American Politics.* San Francisco: Institute for Contemporary Studies.

——— (Lipset) 1968 *Revolution and Counterrevolution: Change and Persistence in Social Structures* New York: Basic Books.

Lipset, Seymour M., and Stein Rokkan, eds. 1967. *Party Systems and Voter Alignments.* New York: Free Press.

Lipson, Leslie. 1964. "Faction." In *Dictionary of the Social Sciences,* ed. Julius Gould and William L. Kolb, 255–56. New York: Free Press.

Maisel, L. Sandy, ed. 1990. The Parties Respond: Changes in the American Party System. Boulder: Westview

Mayhew, David R. 1986. *Placing Parties in American Politics.* Princeton: Princeton University Press.

McNall, Scott. 1988. *The Road to Rebellion: Class Formation and Kansas Populism 1865–1990.* Chicago: University of Chicago Press.

Michels, Robert. 1962. *Political Parties.* New York: Free Press.

Nie, Norman H., Sidney Verba, and John R. Petrocik, eds. 1979. *The Changing American Voter.* Cambridge: Harvard University Press.

———. 1976. *The Changing American Voter.* Cambridge: Harvard University Press.

Niemi, R., and H. Weisberg. 1976. *Controversies in American Voting Behavior.* San Francisco: W. H. Freeman.

Orum, Anthony. 1988. "Political Sociology." In *Handbook of Sociology,* ed. Neil J. Smelser, Pp. 393–422 Newbury Park, CA: Sage.

Pomper, Gerald M. 1993. "The Presidential Election." In *The Election of 1992,* ed. Gerald M. Pomper, Pp. 132–156.

———. ed. 1992. *The Election of 1993.* Chatham, N.J.: Chatham House.

———. 1977. The Decline of the Party in American Elections. In *The Impact of the Electoral Process,* ed. Luis Maisel and Joseph Cooper, 13–38. Beverly Hills: Sage.

Pope, Sandy, and Joe Rogers. 1992. "Out with Old Parties, in with the New Party." *Nation,* July 20/27:102.

Rae, D. W., and M. Taylor. 1970. *The Analysis of Political Cleavages.* New Haven: Yale University Press.

Randall, Vicky, ed. 1988. *Political Parties In the Third World.* Newbury Park, CA: Sage.

Redding, Kent. 1992. "Failed Populism: Movement-Party Disjuncture in North Carolina, 1890 to 1900." *American Sociological Review* Vol. 57 (June):3400–52.

Reiter, Howard L. 1993. "The Rise of the New Agenda and the Decline of Partisanship." *West European Politics.* Vol. 16 (April):89–104.

———. 1993. *Parties and Elections in Corporate America,* 2nd ed. New York: Longman.

Sartori, G. 1976. *Parties and Party Systems: A Framework for Analysis,* vol. I. Cambridge: Cambridge University Press.

Schneider, William. 1980. "Styles of Electoral Competition." In *Electoral Participation: A Comparative Analysis,* ed. Richard Rose, Pp. 75–100, Beverly Hills: Sage.

Shafer, Byron E. 1991. *The End of Realignment? Interpreting American Eras.* Madison: University of Wisconsin.

Sherrill, Robert. 1972. *They Call It Politics: Guide to America's Government.* New York: Harcourt Brace.

Silbey, Joel H. 1991. "Beyond Realignment and Realignment Theory American Political Eras, 1789–1988." In *The End of Realignment: Interpreting American Electoral Eras,* ed. Byron E. Shafer, Pp. 3–23 Madison: The University of Wisconsin Press.

———. 1990. "The Rise and Fall of American Political Parties 1790–1990." In *The Parties Respond: Changes in the American Party System,* ed. L. Sandy Maisel, Pp. 3–17 Boulder: Westview.

Smith, Robert B. 1993. "Social Structure and Voting Choice: Hypotheses, Findings, and Interpretations." Paper presented at the American Sociological Association meeting Miami (August).

Sorauf, Frank J., and Paul Allen Beck. 1988. *Party Politics in America.* Glenview, IL: Scott, Foresman/Little Brown.

Theodorson, George A. and Achilles G. Theodorson 1969. *Modern Dictionary of Sociology.* New York: Thomas Y. Crowell Co.

Walker, Jack L. 1991. *Mobilizing Interest Groups in America.* Ann Arbor: University of Michigan Press.

Washington 1796 "Farewell Address" in M. Beloff (ed.), 1948. *The Federalist.* Oxford: Blackwell.

Zuckerman, A. 1975. "Political Cleavage: A Conceptual and Theoretical Analysis." *British Journal of Political Science* Vol. 5:231–48.

$$
C \; h \; a \; p \; t \; e \; r \quad 9
$$

Political Ideology

Ideology is the most elusive concept in the social sciences, but we can deal with it more simply if we recognize that it has been used mainly in two ways. Most commonly, ideology refers to the combination of ideas that represents the platform of a political, economic, or social group. Secondly, when it is used by Marxists, *ideology* is a pejorative term used to represent what Marxists believe to be the distortions of history and the rationalizations that capitalism uses to continue to repress the working class. We will be concerned with three questions in this chapter: (1) What is the nature of political change and political attitudes and their relationships to political ideology? (2) What are the major varieties of political ideologies, and how do they manifest themselves in society and politics? (3) Is there an end of ideology?

The Beginnings of Ideology

The concept of ideology can be traced back to the eighteenth century, when the French scholar Antoine Destutt de Tracy (1754–1836) first used the term in his systematic study of the Enlightenment. To him, ideology was a process of forming ideas, or the study of ideas which he believed the emergence of ideology was stimulated by the rise of physical, or empirical, sciences. Originally, *ideology* had a progressive and positive connotation, for such study aimed at the material improvement of social and political life.

While Destutt de Tracy and his followers were credited with first using *ideology* in a social context, the direct precursors of the concept of ideology were British social and political thinkers such as Francis Bacon (1561–1626), Thomas Hobbes (1588–1679), and John Locke (1632–1704). In his *Novum Organum* (1620), Bacon attempted to outline a new approach to the study of society based on observation and analysis. He believed that human understanding was hindered by what he called false idols, or mental falsifications which clutter our minds and must be eradicated before we apply the new methods of science.[1] The Baconian theory of idols influenced both the English empirical tradition of Hobbes and Locke and the French Enlightenment, which eventually produced the concept of ideology (McLellan,

1986:4). The Enlightenment thinkers were the intellectual precursors of the French Revolution of 1789.

Later however, ideology became a nineteenth-century phenomenon that marked the beginning of a new era. Crane Brinton (1963) believed that the nineteenth century was characterized by a belief in the perfectibility of the individual and by the idea of progress. Indeed, the mood of the nineteenth century was exemplified by two distinct yet interdependent historical events, the French Revolution and the Industrial Revolution. In response to these revolutions and to the Enlightenment, a host of new movements, doctrines, and ideologies emerged in Europe. Later, we will discuss three of the most important ideologies—liberalism, socialism, and conservatism—in more detail.

Attitudes Concerning Political Change

Before discussing ideology in depth, we must briefly examine a number of political terms describing attitudes concerning political change. One way to examine the terms *radical, liberal, moderate, conservative,* and *reactionary* is to place them from left to right[2] along a continuum.

Radicals are defined as those who are dissatisfied with the way things operate in society and the polity. Because of their profound dissatisfaction, they tend to support extreme methods for bringing about change. In general, radicalism refers to a nonconformist approach to social and political change and behavior that challenges the established order. The 1960s, for example, saw the emergence of many radical groups and movements, such as Students for a Democratic Society (SDS) and the more extreme faction of the SDS, the Weathermen. Liberals are those who favor progressive change in society. Liberals tend to be less impatient than radicals with the deficiencies of society, and thus, unlike radicals, they tend to show a greater respect for the law and to be willing to work within the existing political framework to change society. However, just as there are many different types of radicalism there are many different types of liberalism. Economic liberalism refers to advocacy of big government and state intervention in the economy. Social and political liberalism refer to advocacy of equal civil rights, equal pay for equal work, and other such causes. Liberals tend to stress freedom, equality, and rationality and to support civil rights for all groups. They are also more optimistic about society and human nature, believing in the ability of individuals to change for the better. Moderates are those who reject any drastic political or social changes because they are basically satisfied with the way things are in society. They believe that political change should be gradual. Conservatives, as a rule, are content with the general status quo and usually oppose any fundamental change in society. Conservatives are supportive of the social and political system and tend to favor the community and its institutions, including the state, over the individual. In comparison to liberals, they are more pessimistic about human nature, skeptical about human reason, and doubtful about the perfectibility of individuals and society. Furthermore, while the political Left is more prone toward internationalism, the political Right is more rooted in nationalism. Those who advocate a return to a previous condition are called reactionary. For example, the Ku Klux Klan (KKK) is a reactionary group that advocates the social and political supremacy of white Anglo-Saxon Protestants.

Models of Ideology

Mansoor Moaddel (1992:353–79) writes that sociological research on ideology has been guided by three major models: the subjectivist, the organizational, and the Marxian. The subjectivist model stresses the link between the individual and the social structure—in other words, the attitudes of individuals toward certain aspects of society such as authority, modernization, and power. In the subjectivist models the connecting link between ideology and human action is psychological. This psychological link is also cited by Charles Tilly (1978: 487), who believed that revolutions and rebellions are individual acts by those who rebel against some authority. These acts of defiance and rebellion are the result of unresolved tensions in society that produce disorder if societal controls are weak. Tensions may take different forms: (1) an unbalanced social system may produce disoriented individuals (Johnson, 1964, 1966); (2) "intermediate social and political organizations," which generate a mass society, may break down (Arendt, 1958; Kornhauser, 1959); (3) a gap may exist between rising expectations on the one hand and needs gratification on the other (Davies, 1962; Gurr, 1970); and (4) a rapid political and economic modernization in society may outpace established norms, or what Samuel Huntington (1968) referred to as institutionalization. In the subjectivist model, ideology is perceived as a hierarchy of values and beliefs. The extent to which these values and beliefs are internalized by individuals determines whether they are propelled to human action (Moaddel, 1992:354). Some subjectivist models have been applied to religious fundamentalist and charismatic movements, such as the Iranian Revolution of 1979, but they are difficult to operationalize.

The organizational model is based on the notion that dissatisfied individuals who accept a revolutionary ideology go about organizing collectively against the state. The most important variable in this model is the organization or the collectivity. Ideology must be presented to interested audiences and organized groups to obtain political action. According to Tilly (1978:200), political ideology manifests itself when organized power contenders justify their "exclusive claims to the control over the government." In addition, Theda Skocpol (1979) perceived revolutionary ideologies as "self-conscious political arguments by identifiable political actors." On the issue of ideological change David Zaret (1989:163–179) argues that "Order and change in ideological systems cannot be explained directly by social structural or cultural factors. These factors are important, but their influence is mediated by the specific contexts for the specialized tasks of cultural production. It is these contexts that ideological producers respond to the problem of authority." Zaret believes that "ideology and social structure can be framed not only by an *organizational* context but also by an *episodic* context—by historical events" (1989:164). Both organizational and episodic contexts are important because they deal with problems of authority for the ideological producers. In his words: "The issue of contested authority cannot be reduced either to ideological or social structural factors" (Zaret, 1989:164). In other words, for any ideological change to emerge historical events, contextual pressures, and intellectual precedents interact to form the structure of authority.

It was the Marxian model that provided the first comprehensive theory of ideology. In his *German Ideology*, Karl Marx dealt extensively with the concept of ideology. According to David McLellan (1986:3), three basic ideas were stressed in later Marxist conceptions of ideology: (1) the general doctrine of economic determinism, which viewed ideology and false consciousness as synonymous; (2) the emergence of socialist or Marxist ideology along with Lenin's negative view of ideology; and (3) ideology as an independent force in society and history.

Initially, Marxists thought ideologies to be false ideas used by one group of people to dominate another group of people. Marx considered ideology a fabrication by the ruling class to justify its rule and control of society. Most Marxists therefore tend to associate the concept of ideology with the class struggle between those who control the forces and means of production (e.g., natural resources, technology, and capital) and the proletarians, who own nothing but their labor. For Marxists, the forces of production and the social relations of production make up the mode of production, or the nature of the economic system upon which society is based. This economic foundation, Marxists believe, represents the material base, or infrastructure, of society which in turn determines the social superstructure, or all forms of social consciousness, including ideologies and societal institutions (e.g., political, military, religious, educational, kinship, and cultural values).

For Marxists, the social superstructure represents the nonmaterial aspects of society, including all forms of social consciousness. The various forms of social consciousness are conditioned by social relations of production (Larrain, 1979:39). In Marx's words, "the mode of production of material life conditions the social, political, and intellectual life process in general. It is not the consciousness of men that determines their being, but, on the contrary, their social being that determines their consciousness" (Marx and Engels, 1970:181). Fig. 9.1 is a schematic representation of the Marxian view of social structure.

In the Marxian model, the material foundation of society is also known as economic determinism, or the materialist interpretation of history. Marx's linkage of the mode of production with social consciousness or ideology was explained within his theory of action (*praxis*). The individual human being, Marx argued, is a creature of needs (biological, social, political). According to Marx, as analyzed by John Houghton (1977:161), the individual participates in a dialectical process of need-work-enjoyment which is expressed in three basic forms of activity: (1) the *productive activity*, which satisfies the individual's basic needs of food, water, clothing, and shelter; (2) the *reproductive activity* (sexual need and procreation); and (3) the *social activity* (interests and social relationships). Marx thought that every period of history was characterized by those who control the major sources of production, including needs, interests, ideas, and ideologies, versus those who do not. The former are the "haves," or exploiting classes, and the latter are the "have-nots," or those who are exploited by the ruling classes.

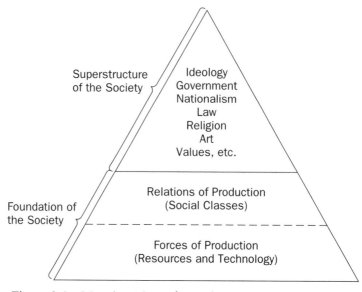

Figure 9.1   Marxian View of Social Structure

Source: Leon Baradat, *Political Ideologies* (1979:155); reprinted here by permission of the publisher.

Marx saw a historical dichotomy between two antagonistic classes—the free versus the slaves (antiquity), the feudal lords versus the serfs (feudalism), and the bourgeoisie versus the proletariat (capitalism). According to Marx (1988:15), "The ideas of the ruling class are in every epoch the ruling ideas." In the Marxist view, each class embraces an ideology that serves its own class interests. In sum, ideology for Marx was a form of social consciousness peculiar to an historical period and expressed both in ideas and actions by individual human beings.

In the Marxian model of ideology we must include the views advanced by Vladimir Ilyich Lenin (1870–1924), Georg Lukács (1885–1971), Antonio Gramsci (1891–1937), and Louis Althusser (1918–1990). According to Raymond Boudon (1986:18), Lenin viewed ideologies as "systems of ideas or theories" used by the protagonists of the class struggle. Somewhat similarly, Althusser perceived ideology as a system of representation of images, myths, ideas, or concepts endowed with an historical existence and role within a given society. "In every society," Althusser wrote, "we can posit...the existence of a basic economic activity, a political organization, and 'ideological forms' (religion, ethics, philosophy). Ideology is therefore an organic part of every totality...human societies secrete ideology as their very element and atmosphere indispensable to their historical respiration and life" (Althusser, in Boudon, 1986:18). For Lukács, ideology was close to what Marx referred to as "class consciousness." Gramsci believed that ideologies are of two types: historically organic ideologies and arbitrary or "willed" ideologies. He favored the former concept, which gave rise to the conception of ideology as a weltanschauung, or worldview (Larrain, 1979:77–81). Gramsci (1971) emphasized the concept of hegemony, or moral/spiritual supremacy, according to which a class or group rests on its ability to translate its own worldview into dominance. According to Gramsci, Marxists should adopt a non-Bolshevik strategy based on persuasion, culture, and mass participation. His ideas have influenced the "Eurocommunists," or those European Communist parties which distanced themselves from the Soviet style of Communism. Gramsci believed leftist ideas must gain ideological hegemony over the masses as the preparatory stage for radical social transformation. He wanted workers to embrace leftist ideas the same way as the philosophies of the Enlightenment influenced the bourgeoisie. In this process the role of the Marxist intellectuals was very important.

The Non-Marxian View of Ideology

With the exception of Vilfredo Pareto (1843–1923), most classical sociologists did not consider the concept of ideology in their writings because they associated it with the Marxist tradition. While Marx was considered the champion of working class ideology, Pareto and the entire conservative elite school of political sociology can be considered the champions of the bourgeoisie. While Marx represented the underprivileged, Pareto's followers are likely to represent the privileged economic and elite classes. Marx believed that social change would come through the class struggle of the working class against its oppressors, the capitalists. In contrast, Pareto believed that any social change comes from the top, through the actions of the elites (Kourvetaris and Dobratz, 1980:93). Both Marx and Pareto perceived society as a social system, but their respective class analyses represent two divergent interpretations of society and human action. Pareto did not use the concept of ideology. Instead he used such concepts as "residues" and "derivations," which are similar to the concept of ideology. Pareto defined residues as manifestations of sentiment and feelings expressed in such ideals as honor, virtue, and country that propel individuals to action. He thought of residues as basically psychic states that have no objective reality. Pareto argued that residues gave rise to derivations, which are used by elites to rule societies. Derivations were seen by Pareto as rationalizations, or psychological explanations of human action. He stressed the symbolic and qualitative aspects of sentiments that play a masking, distorting, legitimating, and even revolutionary role in societies and polities (Houghton, 1977:163). It is from these nonlogical psychic forces that he believed ideologies originate. Pareto's ideas of residues and derivations were very similar to Sigmund Freud's (1856–1939) beliefs about the subconscious as the major source of human behavior.

Pareto's contribution to the theory of ideology was enhanced by his analyses of speeches, myths, sorcery, poetry, political theory, ethics, religion, and philosophy. Like Freud later, Pareto thought men's actions originate in psychic states (sentiments) or nonrational forces that shape society and history. Pareto urged us to look into the underlying thoughts of people, for it is rationalizations rather than rational thinking that may determine human behavior.

Writing within the German historicist tradition, Karl Mannheim (1936:55–59) produced the last comprehensive theory of ideology. Mannheim distinguished between two distinct types of ideology: a "particular" and a "total." To him, the particular referred to specific assertions or points of view, including falsification, distortions, and lies, that operate entirely on the psychological level. In this case, the frame of reference is always the individual. The total, he believed, is inclusive and refers either to the collective life of the individual in a social group or system or to the spirit of an era as found in a social class, an ethnic group, capitalism, and communism. While for Mannheim ideology was thought to be a class-based distortion that preserves social order, utopias for him are systems of ideas which, if implemented, would transform it (Mannheim, 1936).

Contemporary Conceptions and Typologies of Political Ideology

Reflecting the more positivist and empirical orientation of U.S. social science, political sociologists have not paid much attention to the concept of political ideology. Most works on political ideology stress conceptual rather than empirical aspects. Martin Seliger (1976) sought to codify the literature on ideology since Mannheim. He suggested an all-inclusive, value-neutral definition by arguing that all "ideas are weapons" and that one man's distortion is another man's truth. Seliger's aim was to construct a theory of ideology by identifying the political parameters of ideas. In surveying the various conceptions of ideology, one can identify three major contemporary conceptions of political ideology: (1) attitudinal-behavioral, (2) structural-functional, and (3) psychocultural.

Attitudinal and Behavioral Conceptions

The attitudinal-behavioral conception views ideology in terms of an attitude-behavior nexus (Ashford, 1972; Drucker, 1974; Rejai, 1971; Sartori, 1969a). There is an interdependence between attitudes (values, ideas, beliefs) and behaviors (mobilization, actions, movements). Giovanni Sartori (1969b), for example, defined political ideology as a forceful belief system used by elites to obtain political mobilization and mass manipulation. He considers ideology a dimension of politics and power, the knowledge of which is crucial in understanding the varieties of ideological politics. Based on his analysis of belief-elements (cognitive-closed versus open and affective, emotive-strong versus weak), Sartori constructed a typology of political ideology. He then applied these elements to concrete social groups or publics. He thought that the rich elites operate within a more closed and strong political ideology, compared to those who find themselves on the lower levels of society, who operate on a more open and simple belief system. Elites tend to be more conservative or traditional, more intolerant, and more pragmatic and ideological than do the mass publics.

Using a similar attitudinal-behavioral framework, Mostafa Rejai (1971) identified five dimensions for the analysis of political ideology: (1) cognitive (knowledge and beliefs), (2) affective (emotional and feelings), (3) evaluative (norms and values), (4) programmatic (plans and goals), and (5) a social base (groups and collectivities). Using the programmatic and affective dimensions, Rejai constructed a typology of belief systems. A belief system that is high on emotions and goals is termed a consummatory type of ideology (e.g., fascism, nazism, and communism), while a belief system that is low on emotive intensity but high on ultimate goals is termed transcendent (e.g., old fashioned elitism, social Darwinism, and utilitarianism). An expressive belief system is concerned with intermediate goals and is high on emotive intensity (e.g., varieties of romanticism and new-Left ideology). Finally, an instrumental belief system is characterized by intermediate programmatic goals and low emotive intensity.

Structural-Functional Conceptions

The structural-functional conception of ideology maintains that ideology cannot be understood outside the structures of society and the functions they perform. We must understand the various tasks ideology performs in the social institutions and organizations of society, including politics. A group of social scientists (Aron, 1957; Bell, 1976; Feuer, 1975; Lipset, 1981; Mannheim, 1936; Seliger, 1976; Shils, 1968) views ideology in structural-functional terms.

Lewis S. Feuer (1975), for example, singled out three functional ingredients of ideology—the mythological, the philosophical, and the empirical. The mythological dimension of ideology helps us identify with something bigger and more powerful than ourselves. It enables the individual to connect and feel part of the whole. In fact, in every religious ideology, we can find a mythological component that explains the origin of the universe and gives order and meaning to our social existence (Kourvetaris, 1994: 53). Ideologies are also based on some philosophical justification—that is to say they try to answer ultimate questions concerning life itself, such as: What is the meaning of life? What is social existence? In this instance, ideologies try to explain questions of reality in rational and intellectual terms. Ideologies also rely on experience and observation, or what we refer to as the empirical world of reality. In other words an ideology is very much a reality. Something that we can experience and observe or what is known as an empirical dimension. Ideology can be studied empirically by using the various methods of social research and analysis. There is very little of this kind of empirical research however. In addition, according to Feuer, ideologies include the dramatic, ritualistic, and new images of the social world. *Dramatic* means that ideologies are not only ideas but actions, like a drama. Rituals are those forms of behavior that we perform over and over again. Rituals, like myths, serve as links between past, present, and future. Ideologies give us new ways of making sense of the world. They are vantage points from which we view the world. New images or ideologies challenge old ones. For Feuer, utopias (or imaginary or ideal places) can be viewed as pre-ideologies organized along the interests of intellectuals and elites; therefore, all intellectuals are bearers of ideology. Along these lines, Edward Shils (1968) defined ideology as a comprehensive and explicit cognitive or moral belief system dealing with the nature of the individual in society and in the universe. In Shils's view, ideology as a cognitive and moral belief system should include elements such as authority and core cultural and moral values, including ideal visions of the world.

A number of other social scientists (Apter, 1964; Converse, 1964; Geertz, 1964; Linz, 1972) also promote the structural-functional conception of ideology. Juan J. Linz (1972) developed a typology of political systems by distinguishing three dimensions of political systems—monism, limited pluralism, and pluralism. He then identified certain types of political systems that fit these dimensions. Sultanism (a form of authoritarianism practiced by Ottoman Turks in the eastern Mediterranean region and the Middle East during the Ottoman Empire) and other forms of totalitarianism (such as fascism and Communism) are monistic political systems. According to Linz, these types of political systems are highly ideological in that they can mobilize large numbers of people. Examples of limited pluralism include bureaucratic/military, oligarchic, and authoritarian regimes characterized by a certain mentality (nationalist, populist, traditional, religious, and conservative)—for example, Spain under Francisco Franco, Egypt under Gamal Abdel Nasser, Argentina under Juan Domingo Peron, and Turkey under Mustafa Ataturk (1920s). Finally, according to Linz, pluralism includes different types of democracies characterized by a certain mentality, ideology, and mobilization participation or apathy. Linz's typologies are useful in analyzing historical and contemporary political systems as political ideologies. The difficulty with structuralist-functionalist conceptions of ideology, however, is that they cannot deal with social and political change. They tend to see ideology as static and distorted forms of reality. In doing so, they dismiss the explanatory-theoretical capacity of ideology in contemporary social and political systems.

David E. Apter (1964:15–46), a structuralist-functionalist political scientist, linked ideology with some form of discontent. In his view, ideology is a link between action and belief. As such, ideology helps to make explicit the moral basis of action (Apter, 1964:17). For him, ideology performs two basic functions: a community or binding function and an individual commitment function. According to Apter (1964:18), both of these functions help legitimate authority. Socialism, nationalism, and fascism are examples of political ideology, and those who embrace them serve the functions of both binding and individual commitment.

Psychocultural Conceptions

Still a third group of writers (Adorno et al., 1950; Converse, 1964; Geertz, 1964; Goertzel, 1992; Gouldner, 1976; Reich, 1970) perceive ideologies as forms of psychological rationalizations; images; perceptions; and spiritual, cultural, and emotional ideas. They see ideologies as forms of self-fulfilling prophecies that reassure people that what they want to believe is true. Alvin W. Gouldner (1976) defined ideology as a special kind of consciousness and unconsciousness—an effort to bridge the real and the ideal by transforming ideology into some conformity with the good. Ideologies, he believed, are ways of organizing and reconstructing a defective thought and value system. Gouldner was critical of academics, who tend to treat ideology in historical and negative terms. Along the same lines, Wilhelm Reich (1970) explained the rise of fascist ideology as an expression of the common man's primary biological and sexual needs, which had been repressed by the family and the church.

Clifford Geertz (1964:47–76) conceptualized ideology as a cultural system of norms, beliefs, meanings, and values. Geertz argued that "the problem of ideology arises where there is a discrepancy between what is believed and what can be [established as] scientifically correct" (Geertz, 1964:50). Geertz identified two main approaches to the study of the social determinants of ideology: an interest theory and a strain theory (Geertz, 1964:52). In interest theory, ideology is used as a mask and weapon in the social struggle for advantages, while in strain theory ideology is looked upon as a symptom of and a remedy used to correct sociopsychological imbalance. According to interest theory, individuals and groups pursue power; according to strain theory, individuals or groups use ideology to relieve anxiety. Geertz (1964:52) believed that social science has been influenced by the major intellectual and ideological movements, including Marxism, Darwinism, utilitarianism, Freudianism, behaviorism, and positivism.

Philip E. Converse (1964:206–61) saw ideology as a belief system that is not easily empirically quantified. By "belief system," Converse meant "a configuration of ideas and attitudes in which elements are bound together by some form of constraint or functional interdependence" (Converse; 1964:207). According to Converse, ideologies as belief systems encompass logical, psychological, and social constraints. Such constraints have consequences for our belief systems in society and politics. Using ideology as a belief system, we can understand political, religious, psychological, social, economic, and other ideas at the level of belief or idea but not at the level of empirical or scientific fact. For example, our perceptions and beliefs concerning the United States as a society of egalitarianism and equal opportunity reflect both a myth and a reality. The discrepancy between the myth and the reality is known as ideology.

Another theorist who perceived ideology as self-fulfilling prophecies is Ted Goertzel (1992:39–40), whose innovative study of ideology examined ideologies as life scripts in the life cycles of true believers. Using a biographical and life-cycle approach, and including his own family background and life experiences as a pacifist and Leftist during the 1960s, Goertzel identified nine major ideological scripts: the *utopian-dystopian* (one who seeks to transform the world into an idyllic place); the *survivor* (one who moves with the flow and tries to survive); the *committed* (one who is committed to a cause); the *hawk* (one who seeks power and strength), the *dove* (one who seeks peace, cooperation, and love); the *authoritarian* (one who seeks to conform to established doctrines and powerful authority figures); the *protestor* (one who defends the oppressed from exploitation by elites); the *skeptic* (one who doubts and seeks objective truth by examining scientific evidence); and the *pragmatist* (one who is practical and realistic). According to Goertzel, each of these ideological scripts defines the beliefs and behaviors occurring in the life cycle of true believers. A person can use more than one script over the course of his or her life. Goertzel's typology shows the dynamics of political beliefs and disillusionment. In other words, he examines ideology as something dynamic which changes in the life cycle of individual believers.

According to him, the left-right dichotomy is not sufficient explanation of one's ideological orientations and political beliefs. While this is an innovative way of understanding ideology, it is too descriptive, which is the problem with most typologies.

Historical Political Ideologies and Contemporary Political Systems

One way to understand the importance and application of political ideologies in contemporary political systems is to briefly discuss these ideologies and their evolutions throughout modern history.

Liberalism, Conservatism, and Socialism

The ideologies of liberalism, conservatism, and socialism all grew out of the French and Industrial Revolutions, but their origins can be traced even further back in western political thought. All three political ideologies, however, are associated primarily with the nineteenth century, which was known as the century of ideology. Each of the three ideologies has a distinct worldview and all have played a pivotal role in shaping modern political systems: Most modern political systems exhibit an interplay between the three. In general, conservatism favors the institutions of property and church, social inequality, and the established capitalist social order; socialism minimizes the importance of property; and liberalism falls between the other two (Nisbet, 1986:22).

John Gray (1986:x) singled out four major elements of liberalism: (1) *individualism* (the primacy of the individual over the collectivity), (2) *egalitarianism* (all individuals are entitled to equal opportunity), (3) *universalism* (all humankind is one), and (4) *meliorism* (things can be improved). It must be stressed, however, that while liberalism embraced an egalitarian ethos, in reality it practiced social, economic, and political inequality. While liberalism professes to adopt the notion of liberty in both economic and political areas, it often sacrifices political liberty at the altar of economic liberty in the capitalist world system. As a result, some groups are still treated differently on the basis of race, religion, gender, and national origins.

Historically and in more contemporary times, opposition to liberalism came from both the conservatives and the socialists. Conservative thinkers shared a reaction against liberalism and modernity, especially as they were articulated by the tenets of the Enlightenment and the French Revolution. Conservatives were critical of individualism: They believed that individuals are shaped by the values and institutions of community, history, and country (Gray, 1986: 83). Socialists were also opposed to individualism.

A politically and ideologically conservative individual is more likely to express allegiance to an existing authority and social order and to support tradition and the existing social institutions, especially the institutions of the state, the family, the church, and the notion of patriotism (Kourvetaris, 1994). While a conservative perceives the ideas of state and society as two sides of the same coin and views them as inseparable, a liberal sees them as two distinct entities.

While both liberalism and conservatism accept the capitalist mode of production, socialism rejects the basic principles of capitalism and espouses a new social order based on collective ownership of the means of production. Socialism emerged in western Europe during the Industrial Revolution as an antithesis to both liberalism and conservatism. Those who espoused a socialist ideology believed that the working class would develop a class consciousness that would eventually lead to a revolutionary role in transforming the capitalist society into a socialist one. This, of course, did not happen, and with the demise of state Communism in the Soviet Union and Eastern Europe, it appears highly unlikely that it will occur in the future.

In many respects, the recent decline of socialist ideologies that has triggered the reemergence of nationalism and ethnocracies in the former Soviet Union and the former Yugoslavia is a consequence of the failure of socialism as an economic system. However, the failure of state socialism does not automatically mean that capitalism is the best socioeconomic system. Most capitalist societies undergo internal political and economic crises, including widespread unemployment, underemployment, poverty, and crime. The resurgence of regional, ethnic, religious, and racial tensions, including the resurgence of militant nationalism and fascism, indicate deepseated problems associated with the persistence of inequality, racism, militarism, poverty, and exploitation.

Capitalism, Political Power, and Ideology

Although there are important philosophical and ideological differences between liberalism, socialism, and conservatism, the demise of the Soviet Union, the end of the Cold War between the two super-powers, and the disintegration of Yugoslavia have brought all three ideologies closer together. At present, the only viable sociopolitical and economic system is the capitalist world system, which includes elements of liberal, conservative, and socialist ideology. However, although socialism as a state collective economic system has failed, capitalism is plagued with all kinds of domestic and international crises and contradictions.

James O'Connor (1973) viewed the capitalist crisis in economic and fiscal terms and argued that when spending in a capitalist state exceeds revenues a perpetual fiscal crisis occurs. O'Connor's recommendation to offset such fiscal crisis was a form of socialism. Others have tried to explain the capitalist crisis in "cultural" and "technostructural" terms. For example, Daniel Bell (1976) was critical of the efficient capitalist system and the hedonistic U.S. culture. Bell's political ideal was some form of "cultural elitism" along with an ideology of the common good of the community, a notion stressed by many early classical political and social philosophers (Kourvetaris, 1994). Jürgen Habermas (1975) found the cause for the crisis of human dignity, ideals, morality, reason, and truth in the technostructure and efficiency of the capitalist system. He drew many of his ideas from the Enlightenment and believed that these ideas can help us find a remedy for the current crisis of capitalism. Habermas's view resonates with John Kenneth Galbraith's (1971) *The New Industrial State* and Herbert Marcuse's (1971) *One Dimensional Man*. There are also those who see the current crisis of capitalism expressed in the pervasiveness of the welfare state, which has drained most of the Western capitalist economies. Morris Janowitz (1976), for example, lamented the growing size of the welfare state, which he thought has contributed to the present crisis in political legitimacy. Richard Hamilton (1972, 1975) challenged the prevailing centrist, mass society, and pluralist theories of contemporary capitalist class politics. After reviewing the empirical evidence, Hamilton (1972, 1975:270) cast doubt on the authoritarianism of the working and lower-middle classes, advanced by Seymour Martin Lipset (1981), and argued that the lower-middle class is at least as democratic as the upper-middle class.

In his study of ideology and power, Göran Therborn (1980) defined ideology as a "social process" and a "discourse." As a social process, ideologies are not "states of mind" but ways of perceiving and interpreting the social world. As a discourse, ideology is organized through some form of symbolism or ritual. For example, a presidential political election can be seen as a form of symbolism or legitimation in a capitalist system. In any political system, including bourgeois liberalism, there are restrictions on who is allowed to speak, when one is allowed to speak, and the length of time of discourse. There is also a "shielding of discourse," which means that there are procedures designed to protect a given discourse from other discourses. This structuring of discourse, according to Therborn, is ideological in nature. In addition, there are ideological apparatuses of discourse. "Apparatuses are settings of clustered discourse and related non-discursive practices, and settings or sites of ideological conflict" (Therborn, 1980:85–86). In a capitalist society and polity, these apparatuses are linked to power structures and ruling classes, which means that those in power positions regulate and control the terms of the discourse. Only a handful of functional elites, especially those who are supportive and uncritical of the capitalist system, are slated to engage in a public discourse or to become communicators in the large mass media profit enterprises and power communication networks.

There is a link between ideology and political power whereby ideology becomes a powerful mechanism in the hands of the powerful. The elites use ideology as a form of domination and control in modern societies. Therborn identified six such mechanisms or effects of ideological domination in contemporary bourgeois-democratic and capitalist societies (Therborn, 1980:94–5). These are accommodation, inevitability, representation, deference, fear, and resignation. By *accommodation*, Therborn meant that the ruling class and the existing regime succeed in eliciting the support and cooperation of the masses by using work-related issues such as hiring, firing, and benefits to make employees and workers obey employers. *Inevitability* refers to the obedience of the masses due to ignorance of any other political or ideological alternative or to a process of political marginalization in which half of the eligible voters in a presidential election abstain from voting. Both ignorance and marginalization lead to the cynical feeling on the part of the electorate that nothing changes. When rulers are seen as good, Therborn believed that people develop a sense of obedience resulting from a misleading sense of *representation*. This sense of representation is a result of ideological domination or manipulation because no alternative ideologies contest capitalism. *Deference* is another form of subservience to the capitalist rulers. Elites are conceived as possessing superior qualities derived both from descent and special training, a view that is stronger in some countries, such as England. *Fear* is another form of ideological domination that brings about compliance. Force and violence operate as forms of rule and control through the ideological mechanism of fear. Fear plays an important role not only in Third World praetorian military regimes, but also in bourgeois capitalist societies. For example, people are reluctant to be critical of the capitalist system for fear of losing their jobs (this is especially true of those occupying elite positions in society). *Resignation* is a process of giving up on any alternative to the present situation. People simply resign any further hope of change of the present capitalist rule. As a result, they passively obey.

According to Therborn, related to the concepts of political ideology and political power are the concepts of legitimacy, consensus, and class consciousness, which are used extensively in liberal and political democratic theory. Here, *legitimacy* means the belief that the government and the political system, in general, are legitimate. Viewed through the lens of ideological legitimacy and consensus, elections are seen as a form of legitimation or approval of the political system. According to liberal democratic ideology, legitimacy results from the voluntary acquiescence of a majority of the voters to the existing form of government. This consensus is renewed in the United States every four years in the presidential elections. The fact that half of the voters in any U.S. national election do not bother to vote or that important issues of social inequality—including unequal distribution of societal resources such as quality education, high-pay jobs, and key positions in government—are avoided, usually never reaches discussion. Legitimacy can also be manipulated; in other words, consensus can be manipulated by the mass media and political elites. This means that the mass media create the impression that voters express their views through public opinion polls and thus influence public policies. However, public policies do not always benefit the common good of society but rather serve special interest groups.

William G. Domhoff (1979) provided additional empirical support to the power of ideology in the United States by considering four specific processes through which he believed the ruling class in the United States dominates the government. According to him, these processes include the *special-interest process* (the various means utilized by wealthy individuals and corporations to advance their own economic interests), *the policy formation process* (all those policies beneficial to the ruling class), *the candidate-selection process* (the ruling class supports only those political candidates for political office who are sympathetic to them so they can have access to them), and finally *the ideology process* (which involves the beliefs and attitudes of those politicians who are supportive of the policies and privileges of the ruling class). Domhoff argued that the ruling class is a small wealthy class (less than 1 percent of the population) that dominates over 25 percent of the nation's privately held wealth and yearly income.

The End of Ideology Debate

During the 1950s and 1960s, a number of political sociologists of the pluralist and functionalist persuasions advanced the proposition that came to be known as the "end of ideology" thesis.[3] The most prominent of the end of ideology proponents were Raymond Aron (1957), Bell (1960), Lipset (1981), and Shils (1955). Simply stated, they observed that (1) politics in the West no longer follows ideological lines, (2) ideological issues traditionally dividing along the left and right political spectrum have been transformed and replaced by issues of the welfare state which are accepted by Democrats and Republicans alike, and (3) there is universal political suffrage in the West along with a mixed economy and cultural and political pluralism.

These end of ideology advocates believed that ideology, especially of the Marxian version, was irrelevant in contemporary Western politics. They believed that people were interested not in revolutionary or ideological movements but rather in the good life. On the other side of the debate stood a less well-known and more heterogeneous group of Leftist and conflict-oriented social scientists including Gouldner (1976), Kenneth Keniston (1970), Joseph La Palombara (1966), C. Wright Mills (1956), Stephen Rousseas and James Farganis (1963), and others who sharply criticized the end of ideology advocates. Despite the challenge of the end of ideology thesis by the Left, Lipset (1981:524–65), in a comprehensive and perceptive survey of the concept and history of the end of ideology controversy, found ample evidence in the writings of many scholars of the decline of political ideology in Western capitalist democracies. Reiterating the argument advanced by H. Stuart Hughes in the conclusion to "The End of Political Ideology," Lipset (1980:303) stated that

> ...the decline of such total ideologies does not mean the end of ideology. Clearly, commitment to the politics of pragmatism, to the rules of the game of collective bargaining, to gradual change whether in the direction favoured by the left or the right, to opposition both to an all-powerful central state and to laissez-faire constitutes the component parts of an ideology. The "agreement on fundamentals," the political consensus of Western society, now increasingly has come to include a position on matters which once sharply separated the Left from the Right. And this ideological agreement, which might best be described as "conservative socialism," has become the ideology of the major parties in the developed states of Europe and America.

It seems that the end of ideology controversy has run its full course. Political scientists such as Beller (1971), Mason, Mostafa Rejai *et al.*, (1971), and John Clayton Thomas (1974), have found empirical support for the validity of the end of ideology thesis. In a comprehensive and comparative survey of social democratic and leftist parties, Lipset (1991) noted an ideological road back to capitalism or to the Right. In addition to the startling shifts in the Communist world's attitudes toward free-market economics and competitive politics, there is an equally important shift in the non-communist parties of the Left, Lipset (1991:106) argued:

> The struggle between the left, the advocates of change, and the right, perceived as defenders of the status quo, is not over. In the once communist-dominated countries, the terms left and liberal are now used to describe free market and democratic tendencies which seek to reduce the power of the state bureaucracies, the words right and conservative refer to groups which

defend state controls. Ironically, this is the way these ideological concepts were first used in much of the nineteenth century. In the west, following the rise of socialist movements, left came to mean greater emphasis on communitarianism and equality, and the state as an instrument of reform. The right, linked to defensive establishments, has, particularly since World War II, been identified with opposition to governmental intervention.

Even if socialism is now a dirty word, the contest between the Left and the Right has not ended. One can argue that the end of ideology debate has not disappeared; rather, its focus has shifted. As we pointed out, we can identify two types of the Left: a materialist Left and a postmaterialist Left. The end of ideology thesis ignores a substantial portion of the world that has not yet reached industrialization, much less postindustrialism and postmaterialist levels of development. In a post–Cold War era, we are faced with new challenges and new ideologies, including the reemergence of ethnic nationalism, which we will examine more extensively later.

Summary and Conclusion

In this chapter a number of issues dealing with the nature, history, conceptualization, major typologies, and models of ideology in general and political ideology in particular were discussed. The contours of political ideology were explored and discussed. Historically, the concept of ideology was traced to the British social philosophers, French Enlightenment thinkers, and nineteenth century theories of progress and revolutions. Over the centuries, the meaning and nature of ideology has changed. Originally, it meant the process of forming ideas or the study of ideas. At present, ideologies in general and political ideologies in particular refer to various world views of systems of beliefs and actions that aim at some political change or unresting that change.

The use of terms such as radical, liberal, moderate, conservative, and reactionary in our everyday political discourse has a direct bearing on the understanding of the nature of politics and political ideology. A radical is someone who is dissatisfied with the way things are in society and politics. Similarly, a liberal is that individual who favors progressive change and is willing to work within existing political frameworks to change society. A moderate is that person who rejects any drastic political and social change and favors gradual change. A conservative is that person who usually opposes any fundamental change in society. A reactionary is that person who advocates a white Anglo-Saxon supremacy and cannot handle any change in society. We can speak of radical, moderate, conservative, and reactionary political ideologies depending on one's politics and views toward change.

Three major models have guided the sociological research on ideology: the subjectivist, the organizational, and the Marxian. The subjectivist refers to the link between the individual and society or the attitudes of individuals toward such ideas as authority, power, modernity, etc. The organizational model involves groups of individuals or organizations who are dissatisfied with the existing structures of society and form revolutionary ideologies and organize collectively against the state. Finally, the Marxian model was the first comprehensive view of ideology both as a theory and praxis. To the Marxists ideology is a fabrication by the ruling class to justify its hegemony and control of society. For the Marxists ideology is the social superstructure and various forms of social consciousness reflecting the social relations of production.

The non-Marxist view of ideology along with the contemporary conceptions and typologies of political ideology were also examined. With the exception of Pareto, most classical sociologists did not deal in any profound way with the concept of ideology. Pareto, an Italian social theorist, used the concepts of "residues" and "derivations" as manifestations of sentiments and feelings which give rise to various rationalizations. The underlying sentiments and feelings are closest to what is meant by ideologies *or* rationalizations.

Most contemporary works on political ideology emphasize the conceptual rather than empirical aspects of ideology. Three major contemporary conceptions of political ideology were identified: (1) attitudinal-behavioral (2) structural-functional and (3) psychocultural. The attitudinal-behavioral conception views ideology in terms of an attitude-behavior nexus. There is an interdependence between attitudes (values, ideas, beliefs) and behaviors (mobilizations, actions, movements). Mostafa Rejai identified five dimensions of political ideology (1) cognitive (knowledge and beliefs) (2) affective (emotional and feelings) (3) evaluative (norms and values) (4) programmatic (plans and goals) and (5) social base (groups and collectivities).

The structural-functional conception explains ideology in terms of structures and functions they perform in society and polity. A number of social scientists including Aron, Bell, Feuer, Lipset, Mannheim, Seliger, Shils, Linz, view ideology in structural-functional terms. Lewis Feuer singles out three functional dimensions of ideology: the mythological, the philosophical, and the empirical. David Apter links ideology with some form of discontent. For him, ideology performs a community or binding function and an individual commitment function. Both of these functions help legitimate authority.

The psychocultural conceptions perceive ideologies as forms of psychological rationalizations, images, perceptions, spiritual, cultural, and emotional ideas. Those who define ideologies in psychocultural terms see them as forms of self-fulfilling prophesies or systems of beliefs, values, and meanings. Wilhelm Reich explains the rise of fascist ideology as an expression of the common man's biological and sexual needs which had been repressed by the family and the church. Clifford Geertz sees ideology as a cultural system of norms, beliefs, meanings, and values. He identifies two main approaches to the study of ideology: an interest theory and a strain theory. According to the interest theory, individuals and groups pursue power. According to strain theory, individuals and groups use ideology to relieve anxiety. Ted Goertzel examines ideologies as life scripts of true believers. Using a biographical and life cycle approach and including his own family background and life experiences he identifies a typology of nine major ideological scripts: the utopian-dystopian, the survivor, the committed, the hawk, the authoritarian, the protestor, the skeptic, and the pragmatist.

A brief analysis of the historical development of political ideologies of liberalism, conservatism, and socialism as an outgrowth of the French and Industrial Revolutions were discussed. These nineteenth century ideologies were then linked to the contemporary political systems of liberal democracy, capitalism, and collapse of socialism in the former Soviet Union. In this last section, the issue of the end of ideology was also raised both by political sociologists and political scientists alike.

In short, without understanding the nature of political ideology and its various conceptualizations and dimensions, it would be difficult to understand the workings of modern societies and polities.

Endnotes

1. Bacon recognized four classes of idols: idols of the tribe, idols of the cave, idols of the market place, and idols of the theatre. According to him, the idols of the tribe are innate tendencies that interfere with the acquisition of rational knowledge. The idols of the cave are those preconceptions and individual biases that preclude a more general perspective. The term *idols of the marketplace* refers to semantic and linguistic confusion which mislead and obstruct our rational understanding of phenomena. Finally, the idols of the theatre are all those dramatic fictions which lack any empirical foundation.

2. The terms *political left* and *political right* have their origins in the French Revolution. Those who supported the revolution were seated on the left side of the National Assembly, those who were against it were seated on the right, and those who were neutral or moderate were seated in the middle.

3. The origin of the phrase *end of ideology* has been attributed to Friedrich Engels. In his essay "Ludwig Feuerbach and the End of Classical Philosophy" (Mark & Engels, 1886), Engels argued that "there would be an end to all ideology" unless the material interests of all ideologies remained unknown (Lipset, 1981:528).

References

Adorno, T. W. E., E. Frenkel-Brunswick, D. Levinson, and R. Sanford. 1950. *The Authoritarian Personality.* New York: Harper and Row.

Andreski, S. 1964. Totalitarianism. In *Dictionary of the Social Sciences,* ed. Julius Gould and William L. Kolb, 720. New York: Free Press.

Apter, David E., ed. 1964. *Ideology and Discontent.* New York: Free Press.

Arendt, Hannah. 1958. *The Origin of Totalitarianism.* Cleveland: Meridian.

Aron, Raymond. 1957. *The Industrial Society.* New York: Praeger.

Ashford, Douglas E. 1972. *Ideology and Participation.* Beverly Hills: Sage.

Baradat, Leon 1979. *Political Ideologies.* Englewood Cliffs, N.J. Prentice-Hall, Inc.

Bell, Daniel. 1976. *The Cultural Contradictions of Capitalism.* New York: Basic Books.

———. 1960. *The End of Ideology.* New York: Free Press.

Boudon, Raymond. 1989. *The Analysis of Ideology.* Chicago: University of Chicago Press.

Brinton, Crane. 1963. *Ideas and Men.* Englewood Cliffs, NJ: Prentice Hall.

Converse, Philip E. 1964. "The Nature of Belief Systems in Mass Publics." Pp. 206–261 in *Ideology and Discontent,* edited by D. Aptez. New York: Free Press.

Davies, James C. 1962. "Toward a Theory of Revolution. *American Sociological Review.* Vol. 27 No. 1:5–18.

Domhoff, William G. 1979. *The Powers That Be: Processes of Ruling Class Domination in America.* New York: Vintage.

Drucker, H. M. 1974. *The Political Uses of Ideology.* London: Macmillian.

Feuer, Lewis S. 1975. *The Conflict of Generations: The Character and Significance of Student Movements.* New York: Basic Books.

Galbraith, John Kenneth. 1971. *The New Industrial State.* Boston: Houghton Mifflin.

Geertz, Clifford. 1964. "Ideology as a Cultural System." In *Ideology and Discontent,* edited by David E. Aptez. Pp. 47–76. Collier-Macmillan, London: The Free Press of Glencoe.

Goertzel, Ted. 1992. *Turncoats and True Believers.* Buffalo: Prometheus.

Gouldner, Alvin W. 1976. *The Dialectic of Ideology and Technology: The Origins, Grammar, and Future of Ideology.* New York: Seabury.

Gramsci, Antonio 1971. *Selections From the Prison Notebooks* New York: International Publishers.

Gray, John. 1986. *Liberalism: Concepts in Social Thought.* Minneapolis: University of Minnesota Press.

Gurr, Tedd R. 1970. *Why Men Rebel.* Princeton: Princeton University Press.

Habermas, Jürgen. 1975. *Legitimation Crisis,* trans. Thomas McCarthy. Boston: Beacon.

Hamilton, Richard. 1972. *Class and Politics in the United States.* New York: John Wiley & Sons.

———. 1975. *Restraining Myths: Critical Studies of U.S. Social Structures and Politics.* New York: Halsted.

Houghton, John. 1977. "Ideology: A Marxian-Paretian Critique of the Weberian Orientation." *Journal of Political and Military Sociology.* Vol. 5 (Fall):155–68.

Huntington, Samuel. 1968. *Political Order in Changing Societies.* New Haven: Yale University Press.

Janowitz, Morris. 1976. *Social Control of the Welfare State.* New York: Elsevier.

Johnson, Chalmers. 1964. *Revolution and the Social System.* Stanford University: Hoover Institution.

———. 1966. *Revolutionary Change.* Boston: Little, Brown and Co.

Keniston, Kenneth. 1970. *Young Radicals: Notes on Committed Youth.* New York: Harcourt Brace Jovanovich.

Kornhauser, William. 1959. *The Politics of Mass Society.* Glencoe, Illinois: Free Press.

Kourvetaris, George A. 1994. *Social Thought.* Lanham, MD: University Press of America.

Kourvetaris, George A., and Betty A. Dobratz. 1980. *Society and Politics: An Overview and Reappraisal of Political Sociology.* Dubuque: Kendall/Hunt.

La Palombara, Joseph. 1966. "Decline of Ideology: A Dissent and Interpretation." *American Political Science.* Vol. 6 (March):5–16.

Larrain, Jorge. 1979. *The Concept of Ideology.* London: Hutchinson and Co.

Linz, Juan J. 1972. "Notes Toward a Typology of Authoritarian Regimes," presented at American Political Science Association (September 5–9), Washington, DC.

Lipset, Seymour Martin. 1991. "No Third Way: A Comparative Perspective on the Left." In Daniel Chirot (editor), *The Crisis of Leninism and the Decline of the Left* Seattle: University of Washington Press.

———. 1981. *Political Man: The Social Bases of Politics.* Baltimore: Johns Hopkins University Press.

———. 1980. *Revolution and Counterrevolution: Change and Persistence in Social Structures.* New Brunswick, N.J.: Transaction Books.

Mannheim, Karl. 1936. *Ideology and Utopia: An Introduction to the Sociology of Knowledge.* New York: Harcourt, Brace and World.

Marcuse, Herbert. 1971. *One Dimensional Man.* Boston: Beacon.

Marx, K. *Preface to a Contribution to the Critique of Political Economy* in K. Marx and F. Engels, *Selected Works in One Volume,* Lawrence and Wishart, 1970, p. 181 quoted in Jorge Larrain, *The Concept of Ideology,* 1979. London: Hutchinson and Co. p. 39.

McLellan, David. 1986. *Ideology.* Minneapolis: University of Minnesota Press.

Mills, C. Wright. 1956. *The Power Elite.* New York: Oxford University Press.

Moaddel, Mansoor. 1992. "Ideology as Episodic Discourse: The Case of the Iranian Revolution." *American Sociological Review*. Vol. 57 (June):353–379.

Nisbet, Robert. 1986. *Conservatism*. Minneapolis: University of Minnesota Press.

O'Connor, James. 1973. *The Fiscal Crisis of the State*. New York: St. Martin's.

Rejai Mostafa, L. Mason, and D. C. Beller, "Empirical Relevance of the Hypothesis of Decline." In M. Rejai, ed., *Decline of Ideology?* Chicago & New York: Aldine-Atherton, 1971, pp. 268–85.

Reich, Wilhelm. 1970. *The Mass Psychology of Fascism*. New York: Farrar, Straus, Giroux.

Rousseas, Stephen, and James Farganis. 1963. "American Politics and the End of Ideology." *British Journal of Sociology*. Vol. 14, no. 4:347–362.

Sartori, Giovanni. 1969a. "From the Sociology of Politics to Political Sociology." In *Politics and the Social Sciences*, ed. Seymour M. Lipset, 65–100. New York: Oxford University Press.

———. 1969b. "Politics, Ideology and Belief System." *American Political Science Review*. Vol. 63 (June):398–411.

Seliger, Martin. 1976. *Ideology and Politics*. London: George Allen and Unwin.

Shils, Edward. 1968. "The Concept and Function of Ideology." In *International Encyclopedia of the Social Sciences*, David L. Sills Vol. 7:74–78.

———. 1955. "The End of Ideology." *Encounter*. Vol. 5 (November):52–58.

Skocpol, Theda. 1979. *States and Social Revolution*. New York: Cambridge University Press

Therborn, Göran. 1980. *The Ideology of Power and the Power of Ideology*. London: Redwood Burn Ltd., Trowbridge and Esher.

Thomas, John Clayton. 1974. *The Decline of Ideology in Western Political Parties: A Study of Changing Policy Orientations*. Beverly Hills: Sage.

Tilly, Charles. 1978. *From Mobilization to Revolution*. Reading, MA: Addison-Wesley.

Zaret, David. 1989. "Religion and the Rise of Liberal-Democratic Ideology in 17th Century England." *American Sociological Review*. Vol. 54, No. 2:163–79.

Chapter 10

Social and Political Movements

The turmoil of the 1960s and early 1970s in the United States and in other parts of the world spurred research concerning social and political movements to advance to a level of grand theory, contributing to a process of transformation of social and political systems (Bottomore, 1993:29; Foss & Larkin, 1986:111). The topic of social and political movements became a field of study in itself. Broadly conceived, this topic includes nonconventional forms of social and political participation such as worldwide student revolts, guerrilla and counterinsurgency movements, and military coups and countercoups in most countries of the Third World, as well as nationalist movements in most of Africa and Southeast Asia.[1] Daniel A. Foss and Ralph Larkin (1986:7) argued that most social movements in the United States of the 1960s arose among two groups—minority groups, especially blacks, Chicanos, and native Americans; and youth, student, women's, and counterculture groups, who were mostly from the bourgeois class. In general, the adherents of these movements were defined in terms of race, age, gender, and sexual preference. The proliferation of research and theory concerning social and political movements has led the American Sociological Association to establish a separate section in the *Journal of Contemporary Sociology Reviews*. Many sociology, political science, and even history departments offer courses in social and political movements, including such topics as revolution; social and political change; peasant, nationalist, military, and guerrilla movements; and feminist, ethnic, and religious fundamentalist movements.

In this chapter we will discuss a number of questions. What is the nature of social and political movements? What are some of the major models of explanation of these nonconventional forms of political participation? Why do people participate in social and political movements? Who are the actors in social and political movements, and how do they differ from those who participate in conventional politics? What are some typologies of social and political movements? How can we understand and analyze a social movement?

Defining Social and Political Movements

A group of anti-abortion activists firebombs an abortion clinic, forcing it to shut down permanently. A group of U.S. citizens demonstrate near a nuclear power facility, eventually causing the shutdown of the plant. Both of these protest activities are examples of social movements occurring outside the conventional channels of political participation and aiming at some change in present policy.

There are hundreds of such social movements. People join social movements to express their dissatisfaction with the way things are, while other people join counter-movements to maintain the status quo. Typically, those most likely to participate in social movements believe that their own values, needs, goals, beliefs, and interests are threatened. According to Erich Goode (1992:408), for people to participate in social movements, three basic conditions must be met: (1) there must be some real, potential, or imaginary condition that some people oppose; (2) there must be a subjective feeling or perception that this condition is unsatisfactory or undesirable and has to be changed; and (3) there must be an organized means or collective activity to spearhead the movement or the social movement organization.

Friedhelp Neidhardt and Dieter Rucht (1991:450) defined a social movement "as an organized and sustained effort of a collectivity of interrelated individuals, groups, and organizations to promote or to resist social change with the use of public protest activities." They distinguished between two types of social movements: those that focus on the realm of politics, aiming to influence the distribution of political power; and those that focus on the realm of culture, aiming to influence belief systems, ideologies, values, social roles, and cultural norms. The politically oriented social movements are also known as sociopolitical movements. The culturally oriented social movements are also known as sociocultural movements. In reality, most movements combine elements of both these types. While sociopolitical movements tend to be more outwardly oriented, focusing on quantitative mobilization and the formation of broad alliances, sociocultural movements tend to be more inwardly-oriented, focusing on qualitative mobilization (Neidhardt and Rucht, 1991:450–51).

Other typologies distinguish between these movements aiming at the restructuring of society and those aiming at the restructuring of individuals (Zald et al. 1966). According to Craig J. Jenkins (1981:83), "political movements make changes in power arrangements, especially as these are structured through the state, a central part of their program." In this chapter our emphasis will be on sociopolitical movements.

One way to understand the nature of sociopolitical movements is to distinguish between social movements and more institutionalized forms of politics, such as political parties and interest groups. While more institutionalized entities rely on more conventional means of political participation (e.g., voting) to achieve their goals, social movements rely on protest—such tactics as demonstrations, sit-ins, blockades, and strikes—to compensate for their lack of the kind of power that political parties and interest groups have at their disposal. Such protest generates conflict and provoke reaction(s) from organs of the state such as the police, the courts, or the military. A. Morris and C. Herring (1987:145) argued that "what distinguishes social movements from their institutional counterparts is their political situation, that is, their relative lack of direct power in the government which causes them to rely heavily on a repertoire of disorderly tactics such as strikes, demonstrations, violence, and protest activities to accomplish political ends."

Despite the fact that social movements mobilize many groups and individuals, their structures and decision-making processes are not formalized, hierarchical, or highly specialized, which contrasts sharply with parties, unions, firms, and interest groups. Social movements are thus more fluid than are political parties. A social movement's forms of action, social composition, and degree of radicalism vary according to the phases through which the movement passes (Neidhardt & Rucht, 1991:451; Tarrow, 1988). Furthermore, people involved in social movements play various roles. One can identify various functional subgroups within any social movement. Neidhardt and Rucht (1991:451) differentiated two major categories: (1) Core activists represent the backbone of the movement. They include leaders, spokespersons of the movement, staff members, organizers, recruiters, and transitory teams. (2) Participants, contributors, and sympathizers are also important subgroups of social movements. Contributors are those who donate money, time, and energy to the movement, while sympathizers are those who are not active in the movement but identify with the goals and objectives of the movement. Both contributors and sympathizers can be part of supportive groups that are necessary for the success of the movement.

While political parties engage in the struggle for power either to retain or to capture the government, social movements act in a more diffuse manner in order to establish the preconditions for changes by challenging the legitimacy of the existing political systems. Howard L. Reiter (1993:89–104) linked the emergence of new social movements to the decline of political parties. In his view, social movements differed from traditional political parties in this way: (1) they reject traditional social goals such as economic growth and technocracy; (2) they seek decentralized and local power; (3) they deliver demands that tend to be non-negotiable and unconditional; (4) they reject the oligarchical and hierarchical structure of the traditional parties; (5) they focus on a few issues, thereby renouncing vote-maximizing strategies; (6) they aim at general cultural transformation rather than merely state action; (7) they have a communitarian, *gemeinschaft* style and rhetoric; (8) they are open to more extreme, illegal, or violent methods; and (9) they often explicitly renounce state and party. Goode (written communication, May 16, 1994) saw these as matters of degree rather than as absolute qualities that social movements possess. We will see that more similarities than differences exist between political parties and movements. Indeed, any social movement presupposes some form of organization and structure aimed at effective collective action, as Mayer Zald and colleagues (1966) argued.

Another way to understand the nature of social movements is to compare them with other forms of collective behavior such as riots, crowds, mobs, panics, and publics.[2] Social movements may initiate or generate these other forms of collective behavior. Compared to collective behavior, social movements display the following features: (1) They tend to be more organized, (2) the participants tend to be more goal-oriented and intentional, (3) social movements last longer, and (4) they seek or oppose substantial social change (Goode, 1992:408).

Typology of Social Movements

William Bruse Cameron (1966:22–24) and Naomi Rosenthal and Michael Schwartz (1989:44–46) classified social movements and social movement organizations in terms of their direction and degree of change and in terms of their geographical scope (e.g., local, regional, national, or international). Concerning direction and degree of change, social movements can be classified as reactionary, conservative, reformist, revolutionary, escapist, or expressive (Goode, 1992:410).

Reactionary social movements seek to restore society or some part of it to a previous condition. An example of this is the Ku Klux Klan in the United States, which started in the South after the Civil War, flourished in the 1920s, and still exists in many states. It advocates white, Anglo-Saxon supremacy and the use of violence when necessary to accomplish its goals.

Conservative movements seek to retain the status quo; they therefore usually oppose change in society. In the United States, Republicans and southern Democrats tend to support more conservative causes. The movement against allowing homosexual couples to marry or to adopt children is an example of a conservative movement. In Europe, the Christian democratic parties are more likely to support conservative causes than are the social democratic and socialist parties, which are more change oriented.

Reformist or revisionist movements pursue partial or moderate changes. Such movements focus on limited or specific issues. For example, ecological movements deal with issues concerning the environment; antinuclear movements try to block the establishment of new nuclear plants or to shut down existing ones; feminist or women's liberation movements seek equal occupational rights such as "equal pay for equal work" or the restructuring of gender roles and sexual relations between men and women; the Civil Rights Movement sought to bring about racial equality and racial justice between black and white Americans.

Revolutionary movements seek large-scale change. They can be political revolutionary movements seeking the overthrow of the present political system, such as the American Revolution, or they can be social revolutionary movements seeking the social transformation of an entire society, such as the Russian Revolution of 1917 or the Chinese Revolution of 1949. A social revolution aims at total social and political change. The distinction between revolutionary and reformist movements lies in the degree of change sought.

Escapist social movements withdraw, in substance or in thought, from active participation in the social and political activities of their society and culture. These social movements do not aim at change but instead encourage people to drop out of society, usually because they believe that salvation lies in withdrawal from things secular. Monastic communities, religious messianic movements such as Jim Jones's People's Temple (whose members withdrew into the jungles of South America and committed mass suicide in the 1970s), and Marcus Garvey's Back to Africa movement in the 1920s are just a few examples of escapist movements.

Finally, expressive movements seek to change individual attitudes about a specific problem, such as crime, racism, or poverty, rather than the conditions which cause the problem. Because these movements take no concrete actions, many researchers doubt they should be called social movements.

Goode (1992:412) classified social movement organizations according to their geographical scope. A federal social movement organization is multigeographical in scope and may include city, state, national, and even international organizations. It has a central headquarters through which it coordinates all the activities of various movement organizations. Most of these subordinate regional organizations have a certain autonomy, but their goals and objectives are similar. Examples of federal social movement organizations include labor unions, national organizations of women, and the Women's Christian Temperance Union. Local movement organizations are local in scope, less bureaucratic, more autonomous, and more informal. They deal with small face-to-face groups, promote personal interaction, are situational specific, and are transitory in nature.

Other writers classify social movements according to criteria such as size (number of participants), duration (how long a movement lasts), strategy (goals and objectives), and tactics (methods used—peaceful or violent) (Bottomore, 1993; Kourvetaris & Dobratz, 1980).

Perspectives on Social and Political Movements

Political sociologists have advanced a variety of perspectives to explain why individuals and groups join social and political movements. Some attempt to explain protest or antiestablishment activities using collective behavior and breakdown models. Until the early 1970s most social and political movements were studied as if they were simply collective behavior phenomena. Most such phenomena were viewed as symptoms of psychological aberration, social disorganization, and social pathology (an organic disease). Social and political movements were thus explained in psychological and social psychological terms and researchers emphasized such ideas as irrationality, discontent, deprivation, marginality, and mass society. Those who joined protest movements were branded as abnormal because they deviated from the norms or conventions of accepted social and political behavior. The breakdown, or discontent, model is analytically distinct from the collective behavior model, although some overlap exists. The breakdown model states that collective protest automatically and almost spontaneously occurs when "things go wrong."

Morris and Herring (1987:137) identified five classic perspectives on social and political movements: Karl Marx's view, Max Weber's view,[3] the collective behavior view (subdivided into the Chicago school and the structure school of collective behavior), the mass society view, and the relative deprivation view. They contrasted these perspectives with the more recent resource mobilization perspective, which they subdivided into three subcategories: rational action, organizational/entrepreneurial, and political process. Morris and Herring (1987:728–29) pointed out three important information gaps: (1) a lack of knowledge about the dynamics of collective action beyond the initial aspects of movements, (2) a lack of analysis of the effects of movements or of individuals' activism, and (3) a lack of systematic, qualitative fieldwork into the dynamics of social movements. Interestingly, P. B. Klandermans and S. Tarrow (1988) found that European scholars focus more on larger structural issues, the structural causes of movements, and ideologies and their relationship to the cultures of advanced capitalist societies. U.S. researchers, on the other hand, tend to depict social movements as organized group protests or forms of mass action.

The basic idea behind the relative deprivation view of social and political movements (Davis, 1962; Gurr, 1970) is that discontent and rebellion are more likely to occur if individuals subjectively compare their social statuses to those of others and find themselves to be worse off. This perceived deprivation is believed to motivate individuals to join protest movements. Cumulative deprivation theory states that deprivation multiplies itself over time: Economic deprivations create frustrations and, in turn, encourage people to participate in protest movements. The rising expectations theory is related to these two deprivation theories. It states that if there is a discrepancy between rising individual expectations and actual individual achievements, individuals are more likely to participate in protest movements. Crane Brinton (1956) and James C. Davies (1962) used this framework to explain revolutions. Despite the persistence of these perspectives, the empirical evidence does not support them. Although one would expect the poor and deprived to be in the forefront of protest movements, the fact is that these populations are less likely to participate in protest movements. With a few exceptions, John Leggett's (1964) study on Detroit workers and Maurice Zeitlin's (1966) study on Cuban workers found that those who were economically insecure and had developed a class or economic consciousness supported protest movements. But studies by Richard Braungart and Margaret Braungart (1990), Gary T. Marx (1967), Anthony M. Orum and Amy Orum (1968), James Petras and Zeitlin (1968), Maurice Pinard (1968), and Alejandro Portes (1970) on various civil rights movements do not support the relative deprivation, cumulative deprivation and rising expectations theses.

Status inconsistency is another social psychological theory used to explain participation in protest movements. According to this view, those individuals who occupy incongruent status positions are more likely to participate in protest movements. For example, if an individual is high on the occupational scale but low on the income scale, there is a status inconsistency and such individuals tend to hold extreme political attitudes (Lenski, 1954). According to Seymour Lipset and Earl Raab (1970), those individuals who experience a loss of status in the community are more likely to join right-wing movements. Along the same line, Richard Hofstadter (1963) believed that status politics, a concept introduced by Lipset, were more likely to occur during prosperous times while class or interest politics were more prevalent during hard times. Status politics generally emerge when people feel that they are not accorded the status they deserve. For instance, the emergence of minority groups in the political arena has fanned right-wing political activity among certain white groups, especially in the South, because some whites feel that they have lost power to minority groups. One reason why many southern whites have shifted their loyalties from the Democrats to the Republicans is precisely because of their perception of the rise of African American political power. In many Third World countries, the decline of the traditional status accorded the officer corps has produced anxiety and frustration among this group. This has propelled some leading officers to stage coups or to go outside the normal channel of politics to address certain grievances or resolve certain political conflicts.

The isolation, mass society, and marginality theories attempt to explain that participation in protest movements is a result of social isolation, which includes the isolation affecting the uprooted or the marginal in society (Arendt, 1963; Feuer, 1969; Hoffer, 1951; Kornhauser, 1959; Lipset, 1981). The main idea here is that those who are socially isolated are less likely to participate in either conventional or unconventional politics. However, these types of explanations are those least supported by empirical findings.

During the 1960s two new models emerged to explain social movements: the new social movement (NSM) model in Europe and the resource mobilization (RM) model in the United States. In Europe the emphasis of new social movements was on larger structural and cultural issues; in the United States, most researchers noted the organizational and individual levels of protest and the forms of action these mass protests followed (Tarrow, 1988). In the following section our emphasis will be on U.S. research models.

Resource Mobilization and Organizational Models

Most recent work on social protest movements has shifted from the social psychological and collective behavior levels of explanation to organizational or resource mobilization levels. The development of organizational and resource mobilization perspectives was triggered by the mass protest movements of the 1960s. Thus the bulk of the literature deals with civil rights, women's, student, anti-war, and peace movements. In the organizational/mobilization models, the concepts of organization and mobilization are crucial to understanding and explaining protest movements in general. Overall, resource mobilization and organizational theories stress the similarities between conventional and unconventional political behavior.

A cornerstone of resource mobilization theory is Mancur Olson's (1965) theory of collective action. According to this theory, rational individuals are more likely to join protest movements if the cost of participation does not outweigh the benefits. The main critique of this theory states that people do not always participate in protest movements for economic benefit. Resource mobilization theories stress calculated interest, minimize impulsive passion, and hold that social structure generates collective interests and conflicts. Resource mobilization theorists try to determine specific situations in which grievances can be translated into collective action.

William Gamson (1990), John D. McCarthy and Mayer N. Zald (1977), Anthony Oberschall (1973), and Charles Tilly (1978), emphasize that "social movements are organized activities that form a normal part of the processes of social and political life rather than being an aberration and symptom of disorganization" (Ferree & Miller, 1985:38). Oberschall, Gamson, and Tilly are considered the most important advocates of this approach. It was Oberschall (1973), however, who made the most comprehensive effort to provide an alternative to the collective behavior approach. Drawing from Olson (1965), who stressed economic interests, goals, and incentives for collective action, Oberschall used a resource mobilization and group conflict perspective to posit individuals who make rational decisions based on rewards and sanctions, costs, and benefits to mobilize their resources for group action. According to Oberschall (1973:28),

> *in ordinary everyday activity, at work, in family life, and in politics, people manage their resources in complex ways: they exchange some resources for other resources; they make up resource deficits by borrowing resources; they recall their earlier investments. Resources are constantly being created, consumed, transferred, assembled and reallocated, exchanged, and even lost. At any given time, some resources are earmarked for group ends and group use, not just individual use. All of these processes can be referred to as "resource management."*
>
> *Group conflict in its dynamic aspects can be conceptualized from the point of view of resource management. Mobilization refers to the processes by which a discontented group assembles and invests resources for the pursuit of group goals. Social control refers to the same processes, but from the point of view of the incumbents or the group that is being challenged. Groups locked in conflict are in competition for some of the same resources as each seeks to squeeze more resources from initially uncommitted third parties.*
>
> *The individuals who are faced with resource management decisions make rational choices based on the pursuit of their selfish interests in an enlightened manner. They weigh the rewards and sanctions, costs and benefits, that alternative courses of action represent for them. In conflict situations, as in all other choice situations, their own prior preferences and history, their predispositions, as well as the group structures and influence processes they are caught up in, determine their choices. Indeed, many are bullied and coerced into choices that are contrary to their predispositions. The resource management approach can account for these processes in a routine way. (Oberschall, 1973:28–29)*

According to Oberschall, two conditions are necessary to mobilize for group conflict: a minimum consensus on objects of hostility and/or grievances and a preexisting basis for organization. Tilly saw groups as

> *forming and dissolving, mobilizing and demobilizing, formulating and making claims, acting collectively and ceasing to act, gaining and losing power, in response to changes in five sets of variables: (1) articulated group interests, (2) prevailing standards of justice, (3) resources controlled by groups and their members, (4) resources controlled by other groups (especially governments), and (5) costs of mobilization and collective action. (1973:6–7)*

In the same vein, Ronald Aminzade (1973:6) believed that collective actions are "conceptualized as organizational phenomena which occur, not merely because of widespread discontent with war, unemployment, or whatever, but because organizations exist which make possible the channeling and expression of that discontent into concerted social action."

According to Alain Touraine (1992) social movements are situated at the level of class conflict because they are antagonistic to the existing social and political order. They represent certain forms of social life. However, not all movements are representative of society and they do not speak for all its members.

Gamson (1990:14) distinguished between three distinct concepts of "target" for challenging groups: (1) the target of influence, (2) the target of mobilization, and (3) the target of benefits. By target of influence, Gamson means that "set of individuals, groups, or social institutions [which] must alter their decisions or policies . . . to which the challenging group objects." For example, anti-abortion advocates challenge the constitutionality of abortion by targeting not only the Supreme Court but all those groups and institutions that condone abortion, including politicians, liberals, clinics, and doctors who perform abortions. The target of mobilization, wrote Gamson (1990:15), includes all "those individuals or groups whose resources and energy the group seeks in carrying out its efforts at change, called here the group's constituency." The concept of mobilization involves both the "activation of commitment and the creation of commitment." The former refers to efforts to move those who "possess some degree of commitment to take a specific action." The latter entails a change from low generalized readiness out to a high generalized readiness to act collectively" (Gamson, 1990:15).

Critics argue that social mobilization theories rely on simplistic, rational, and economic models and overemphasize the importance of formal organizations, elites, and leaders while failing to address the stakes involved in struggles. Social mobilization theorists, critics assert, should take a more comparative approach by examining different societies and different social movements.

Finally, by target of benefits Gamson (1990:16–17) refers to all those "individuals or groups whom the challenging group hopes will be affected positively by the changes that it seeks from its antagonist." Gamson calls this target "the group's beneficiary." According to him (1990:16–17) a challenging group must seek (1) "the mobilization of an unmobilized constituency" and (2) its antagonist must lie outside of its constituency. In most instances, constituency and the beneficiary of the group are identical but this is not always the case. Changes may affect everyone whether one is a member of a constituency or not.

Research on Social Movements

Research on social movements was stimulated by the disorders and social unrest of the 1960s. In the United States the work by Anthony Oberschal, William Gamson, Charles Tilly, Frances F. Piven, Richard Cloward and a host of others contributed to an avalanche of writings on social movements. While research on social movements was carried out by a number of social scientists in many parts of the world, it was in the United States and certain parts of western Europe that such research was proliferated.

Research on social movements in Europe were not only directed against the capitalist state but against political parties and interest groups as well. The French Marxists, for example, stressed the importance of urban movements including students movements in mobilization for social change. Both European and American research on social movements began to converge on a number of issues. The most important of which were: (1) the idea of political opportunity and political motivation of collective action and (2) the cyclical nature of protest and the relationship between protest and reform. Using data from the Dutch peace mobilization movement, Klandermans and Oegema (1987) identified four stages in social mobilization: formation of mobilization potentials, formation and activation of recruitment networks, arousal of motivation to participation, and removals of barriers to participation. On the basis of these four dimensions, the authors distinguished four major steps in participation in social movements: becoming part of the mobilization potentials, becoming a target of mobilization attempts, becoming motivated to participate, and overcoming barriers to participation.

In the United States research on social movements became the most popular among sociologists in general and political sociologists in particular. Unlike earlier psychological theories of social movements and collective behavior, the new research mobilization perspective was the dominant paradigm and stressed the role of organizations and collectivities in social movements rather than the individuals. William Gamson (1990) stressed the various strategies of political alliances and state actions that contributed to the success or failure of challenging groups. He found that: (a) groups with single demands were more successful than those having multiple demands (b) users of violence were more successful than recipients of violence and (c) centralized bureaucratic challenging groups, free of factionalism, were more successful social movements than decentralized, nonbureaucratic, and factionalism prove.

During the 1980s the emphasis on research in social movements was somewhat shifted from the resource mobilization to the political process model. McAdam (1982: 43), for example, criticized the resource mobilization model for failing to account for the role of people and political opportunities for the emergence of sociopolitical movements, including: the narrowing of power discrepancy between elites and challenging groups, the existence of established organizations to take advantage of political opportunities for such movements, favorable conditions for political action, and the level of social control by elites. Indeed, both European and American social researchers increasingly stressed the "political process model" in social movements by linking collective action and conventional politics. Studies using the "political process model" included: (1) McAdam's work on civil rights and Black protest of the 1950s and 1960s who concluded that it was a combination of "expanding political opportunities: including a more responsive federal government and Black organizational strength and not feelings of deprivation and strain". Similarly, studies by Browing, Marshal, and Tabb's (1986) on minority urban politics and Jenkin's research (1983) on the farm workers adopted a "political process model" in their research on social movements.

During the 1990s social movements were re-conceptualized as vehicles of "cultural renovation" and "renewal" rather than efforts by organized groups to attain political objectives and power. Drawing from her early experiences as an activist and feminist in the 1960s, Barbara Epstein (1991) looked at the roots of movements such as pacifism, anti-war activism, radical feminism, and environment activism. She saw these diverse movements as expressive rather than instrumental. An expressive as opposed to instrumental movement is based on various cultural and artistic innovations and ideas of renewal rather than economic gains and political power. Somewhat similarly, Ron Fyerman and Andrew Jamison (1991) argued along the same line as Epstein. According to them social movements are best understood as frameworks for cultural renovation rather than political or material attainment.

How to Understand and Analyze Social Movements

Social movements can be analyzed along a set of standard dimensions, such as ideology, strategy and tactics, social base and geographic scope, structure and process, and finally leadership and entrepreneurship. Empirical applications of resource mobilization theory in a number of studies of the women's movement (Carden, 1978), the farm worker's movement (Walsh, 1978), the antibusing movement (Useem, 1975), and the antinuclear movement (Walsh, 1981; Walsh & Warland, 1983) have found ideology to be an important variable in resource mobilization processes. The ideology of an organization provides the framework of meaning for identifying and evaluating the legitimacy of various types of resources, strategies, tactics, and leadership.

Strategy and tactics exist as two separate phenomena but are highly interdependent. *Strategy* refers to both short- and long-range objectives and goals, while tactics involve the methods, programs, and actions used to carry out the goals and objectives of the social movement. If strategy is the "what," tactics is the "how." Tactics vary according to the nature and type of social movement. For example, tactics may include violent or nonviolent means, including psychological manipulation, propaganda, and both direct and indirect forms of coercion and power.

The dimension of social base addresses the issue of who supports a particular movement, or what kind of groups and collectivities (including ethnic, racial, religious, age, gender, generational, cultural, class, and organizational groups) join the movement. The dimension of geographic scope refers to the local, the national, and the international dimensions of recruitment or organization. Another issue that can be used to analyze social movements is exclusiveness, or whether an organization is open to everybody or limited to a particular type of individual or group.

Social base or recruitment of new members is crucial in the continuity and success of the objectives of social movements. Prahl et al., (1991) have developed a mathematical model of recruitment strategy of participants in a collective action campaign. Elements of the model include: (1) the reach of the strategy or the number of people recruited (2) the selectivity of the strategy or the extent to which a particular strategy focuses on recruitment efforts on those with the greatest interest and resource levels (3) interdependence or the extent to which the actions of recruits affect the actions of others and (4) the production function or what is the relationship between the total amount recruits contribute to the campaign to the amount of the collective good that is achieved. In other words, the type of strategy employed in recruitment of new members helps the outcome of a collective action campaign.

A related issue to recruitment and social support is the importance of social networks. Social networks are especially significant in explaining social movements and political protest (Curtis and Zurcher, 1974; McAdam and Paulsen, 1991). Personal networks are also relevant for mobilizing citizens to actively participate in protest movements (Opp, 1988; McAdam and Paulsen, 1991). Oliver (1984) believed that social integration of a neighborhood is an essential element in a collective response to some threat (Opp and Gern, 1993:659). Also, Marwell et al., (1988) found that centralization of network ties always has a positive effect on collective action.

Structure and process is an exceedingly important dimension used in the analysis of social movements. Structure refers to group and organizational aspects of a movement, including such issues as temporality, or how long a movement can hold personnel. How structured or centralized is the power? Is there a single center or multiple centers of power? Movements are structures that change as their objectives change, and they go through phases. *Process,* then, refers to the dynamics of movement's internal structures and of the external environment in which movements take place. As the external environment (e.g., government policies or public opinion) changes, the strategy and tactics of a movement change as well.

Leadership and entrepreneurship are extremely important in generating and sustaining movements. The dimension of leadership deals with the ability of a movement to find the appropriate individuals to lead it to success. Despite the fact that there is no agreement among social scientists as to what constitutes an effective leader or leadership, one cannot deny its importance in social movements. Leadership is, above all, a quality. An effective leader is group-oriented and has the ability and charisma needed to lead. Democratic leaders are not appointed "from above" but emerge "from below." A democratic leader must be accepted by the people and enjoy the public trust. An authoritarian leader is imposed from above. He or she does not leave room for discourse. An entrepreneur is someone who makes things happen or someone who takes advantage of an opportunity or a situation. In the context of social movements, an entrepreneur is the initiator of a movement. He or she is the one who creates or uses resources, including ideas, people, organizations, and ideologies, to spearhead the movement.

All these elements are found in most social movements. Despite the fact that they are analytically distinct, all are interdependent. Ideology, for example, varies with social base, structure and process, strategy and tactics, and leadership and entrepreneurship. Likewise, social support varies according to other dimensions.

The Civil Rights Movement of the 1960s

The Civil Rights movement of the 1960s was a catalyst for social change, because it profoundly affected American society and its institutions. Even today, it captures our imagination. Literature on the various issues of the Civil Rights movement is extensive. Issues such as quality education, equal justice, equal opportunity, recognition of

African cultural heritage, the fight against racial prejudice, and institutional racism are still very important not only to African Americans but most Americans.

The 1954 United States Supreme Court's decision of "separate but equal" as unconstitutional by their ruling in Brown v. Board of Education became one of the most important landmarks of racial integration and contributed to the 1960 Civil Rights movement. The Brown decision succeeded to portray segregation as evil and laid the groundwork for massive attack upon Jim Crow itself (Blumberg, 1991:42). Jim Crow refers to the discriminatory laws against African Americans in the South. The Brown v. Board of Education court decision was a reversal of the "separate but equal" clause in Plessy v. Ferguson of 1896. Bloom (1987:87–89, 187) argued that the Federal government joined along with the African American and the southern merchant leadership to overcome the entrenched interests of the traditional southern rural and landlord class. From approximately 1955 to 1965, the Civil Rights Movement succeeded in ending segregation in the South and in generating sweeping civil rights legislation during President Lyndon Johnson's administration.

Running parallel to the Civil Rights movement was the student protest movement against the United States involvement in the war against Vietnam. These movements had different agendas and goals—one to end the war and the other to end institutional racism in the United States. The deep South responded with massive resistance, intimidation, arrests of civil rights workers, beatings, jail, and killings. Riots erupted in the urban ghettoes of the North from 1964 to 1968. Dr. Martin Luther King, of the Southern Christian Leadership Conference and a Baptist theologian, was one of the major leaders and advocates of non-violence. Later, he received a Nobel prize for peace and non-violence. His philosophy of non-violence was based on the teachings of Jesus Christ, Henry David Thoreau (1862–1917), and Mahatma Gandhi. Gandhi led a similar movement against the British for his country's independence from England in the 1940s.

Martin Luther King's integration policy and non-violence also sought to forge a coalition of progressive middle class whites with African Americans and other minorities, including Puerto Rican Americans, Mexican Americans, and Appalachians. But by the late 1960s, the Civil Rights coalition began to fall apart (Bloom, 1987:182–87; Blumberg, 1991:-90). Two factions surfaced: one espousing an Integrationist philosophy advocated by Martin Luther King, using the strategy and tactics of non-violence; the other called the Black Power nationalist movement which rejected integration and White American culture and advocated separation and Black nationalism. The nationalist strain among African Americans has been present throughout the history of the Blacks; for example, Marcus Garvey who came from Jamaica, formed the Back to Africa Movement in the 1920s.

Black nationalism in the United States was reinforced by the African liberation movements against western European colonialism for the creation of independent nation states. The ideology of Black nationalism was expressed in the writings and speeches by a member of African American intellectuals and leaders including Malcolm X, Stokely Carmichael, Harold Cruse, and Nathan Hare and by African intellectuals and political leaders such as Frantz Fanon, Julius Nyerere, and Kwame Nkrumah. The writings of both African Americans and those from African countries were available and widely discussed among African Americans.

The Rev. Jesse Jackson's movement and his candidacy for president of the United States during the 1980s must be seen as a continuation of Martin Luther King's legacy of the Civil Rights movement. In addition, Rev. Jesse Jackson, who was a follower of Martin Luther King and organized PUSH (People United to Save Humanity), attempted to bring together both the Black nationalist and integrationist strands of the Civil Rights movement. At the same time, he appealed to the poor groups of different backgrounds, including farmers, workers, students, Blacks, Hispanics, and gays, to form what he called a "rainbow coalition."

In conclusion, the Civil Rights movement of the 1960s was a sociopolitical oriented reform movement. Its ideology was articulated by the various African American leaders and Black organizations. Its social base and its geographical scope were wide, covering most Black social classes and most regions of the United States along the local, state, and national levels.

Summary and Conclusion

In this chapter a number of issues on social and political movements were discussed. In general social movements are organized collectivities aiming at some social change or resisting that change. We can distinguish between politically oriented social movements and culturally oriented social movements. Most movements combine elements of both. Some movements aim at the restructuring of society or individuals. Political movements aim at changes in power arrangements.

One way to understand the nature of social and political movements is to compare them with the more institutionalized forms of politics—political parties. While political parties are more formalized, hierarchical, and highly specialized, social movements tend to be more fluid. What distinguishes social movements from political parties is their relative lack of direct power in the government. This lack of power causes them to rely heavily on unconventional tactics including demonstrations and protest activities. Another way to understand social movements is to contrast them with other forms of collective behavior including riots, crowds, mobs, panics and the like. Compared to collective behavior, social movements tend to be more organized, more goal-oriented, last longer, and seek or oppose social change.

Social movements were classified in terms of their direction, degree of change, and geographical scope. They can be classified as reactionary, conservative, reformist, revolutionary, escapist, and expressive. A number of explanations of social movements were suggested. For a long time social movements were explained as symptoms of psychological aberration and social pathology. Researchers stressed such ideas as irrationality, discontent, deprivation and the like. More recently, however, attempts were made to explain social movements using breakdown models. The breakdown model states that collective protest movements automatically and spontaneously occur when "things go wrong."

Five perspectives on social and political movements were briefly examined including: Marx's view, Weber's view, the collective behavior view, the mass social view, and the relative deprivation view. These perspectives were contrasted with the resource mobilization perspective and its three subcategories—rational action, organizational, entrepreneurial, and political process.

The resource mobilization and organizational models along with the work of its major practitioners on research in social and political movements were discussed both in the United States and western Europe. Finally, how to analyze social movements were suggested by looking at a number of dimensions such as ideology, strategy and tactics, social base and geographic scope, structure and process, leadership and entrepreneurship. A brief analysis of the Civil Rights Movement of the 1960s was also examined as an illustration of a sociopolitical movement.

Endnotes

1. Such movements against colonialism include Algeria against France, 1950s; Vietnam against France 1950s and later against the United States, late 1960s and early 1970s; Angola against Portugal, 1960s and 1970s; Congo against Belgium during 1970s; Indonesia against Holland, 1960s; and Cyprus against Britain 1960s. Coupled with these nationalist movements were the Chinese Revolution in 1949 and the Cultural Revolution in the 1960s, the Hungarian Revolt in 1956, the Cuban Revolution in 1959, the Palestinian Movement and the Panafricanism Movement in the 1960s, the French Student Revolt in 1968, the Prague Spring Revolt in 1968, the Solidarity Movement in Poland in the 1980s, and, in the United States, the Civil Rights Movement and the feminist, ecological, peace, antinuclear, and religious fundamentalist movements. More recently we have seen the resurgence of nationalist movements in the former Soviet Union, the former Yugoslavia and other parts of the world.

2. *Collective behavior* refers to unstructured patterns of behavior exhibited by individuals or categories of people responding to some stimulus or common influence. Forms of collective behavior include various types of crowd behavior, such as riots, panics, publics, fads, fashions, and public opinion; some researchers include social and political movements as well. Earlier studies on social and political movements considered them as forms of collective behavior. Originally, the emphasis of study concerning collective behavior was on irrationality, emotionalism contagious behavior, lack of structure and leadership. More recent studies concerning social and political movements view them as more organized, purposeful, and rational forms of behavior similar to the more conventional patterns of political participation.

3. Marx's and Weber's specific views on sociopolitical movements will not be discussed here. Suffice it to say that Marx is well known for his ideas of revolution, class struggle, alienation, ideology, and praxis (action), which can be construed as aspects of social and political movements (especially revolutionary and radical movements). Weber, on the other hand, stressed the more conventional or traditional aspects of politics including bureaucratization, rationalization, tradition, status, and party. His analysis of charisma and charismatic authority is an important contribution to the understanding of charismatic leaders and the role they play in sociopolitical movements.

References

Aminzade, Ronald. 1973. *Revolution and Collective Political Violence: The Case of the Working Class of Marseille, France 1830–1871.* Working paper #86. Center for Research on Social Organization. Ann Arbor: University of Michigan (October).

Arendt, Hannah. 1963. *On Revolution.* New York: Viking.

Bloom, Jack 1987. *Class, Race, and the Civil Rights Movement.* Bloomington: Indiana University Press

Blumberg, Rhoda Lois 1991. "Rediscovering Women Leaders of the Civil Rights Movement" in *Dream and Reality: The Modern Black Struggle* for *Freedom and Equality* ed. Jeanine Swift. Westport, Conn.: Greenwood Press.

Bottomore, Tom. 1993. *Political Sociology.* Minneapolis: University of Minnesota Press.

Braungart, Richard, and Margaret Braungart. 1990. "Political Generational Themes in the American Student Movements of the 1930s and 1960s." *Journal of Political and Military Sociology.* Vol. 18, no. 2:177–230.

Brinton, Crane. 1956. *The Anatomy of Revolution.* New York: Vintage Books.

Browning, Rufus P., Marshall, Dale Rogers, Tabb, David H. 1986. "Protest is Not Enough: The Struggle of Blacks and Hispanics for Equality in Urban Politics" *Urban Affairs Quarterly* Vol. 22, (Dec.): 350–356. (Chapter 10)

Cameron, William Bruse. 1966. *Modern Social Movements: A Sociological Outline.* New York: Random House.

Carden, Maren Lockwood. 1978. "The Proliferation of a Social Movement: Ideology and Individual Incentives in the Contemporary Feminist Movement." *Research in Social Movements, Conflicts and Change.* Vol. 1:179–96.

Curtis, Russell L. and Louis A. Zurcher 1974. "Social Movements: An Analytical Exploration of Organizational Forms" *Social Problems,* Vol. 21, No. 3 Pp. 356–370.

Davies, James C. 1962. "Toward a Theory of Revolution." *American Sociological Review.* Vol. 27 (February):5–19.

Epstein, Barbara 1991. *Political Protest and Cultural Revolution: Nonviolent Direct Action in the 1970s and 1980s* Berkeley: University of California Press

Eyerman, Ron and Andrew Jamison 1991. *Social Movements: A Cognitive Approach.* University Park: Pennsylvania State University

Ferree, Myra Marx, and Fred D. Miller. 1985. "Mobilization and Meaning: Toward an Integration of Social Psychological and Resource Perspectives on Social Movements." *Sociological Inquiry.* Vol. 55, no. 1:38–61.

Feuer, Lewis S. 1969. *The Conflict of Generations: The Character and Significance of Student Movements.* New York: Basic Books.

Foss, Daniel A., and Ralph Larkin. 1986. *Beyond Revolution.* South Hadley, MA: Bergin and Garvey.

Gamson, William. 1990. *The Strategy of Social Protest,* 2nd ed. Belmont, MA: Wordsworth.

Goode, Erich. 1992. *Collective Behavior.* New York: Harcourt Brace Jovanovich.

Gurr, Ted Robert. 1970. *Why Men Rebel.* Princeton: Princeton University Press.

Hoffer, Eric. 1951. *The True Believer.* New York: Harper & Row.

Hofstadter, Richard. 1963. "The Pseudo-Conservative Revolt." In *The Radical Right,* ed. Daniel Bell, 63–80. Garden City, NY: Doubleday.

Jenkins, Craig J. 1983. "Resources Mobilization Theory and the Study of Social Movements." *Annual Review of Sociology.* Vol. 9:527–53.

———. 1981. "Sociopolitical Movements." In *Handbook of Political Behavior.* Vol. 4, ed. L. L. Samuel, 81–153. New York: Plenum.

Klandermans, Bert and Dirk Oegema 1987 "Potentials, Networks, Motivations, and Barriers: Steps Towards Participation in Social Movements" *American Sociological Review* Vol. 52 (Aug.): 519–531 (Chapter References)

Klandermans, P. B., and S. Tarrow. 1988. "Mobilization into Social Movements: Synthesizing European and American Approach." In *From Structure to Action: Comparing Social Movement Research Across Cultures,* ed. B. Klandermans, H. Kriesi, and S. Tarrow. Greenwich, New Jersey: JAI Press.

Kornhauser, William. 1959. *The Politics of Mass Society.* New York: Free Press.

Kourvetaris, George A., and Betty A. Dobratz. 1980. *Society and Politics.* Dubuque: Kendall/Hunt.

Leggett, John. 1964. "Economic Insecurity and Working Class Consciousness." *American Sociology Review* Vol. 29 (April):223–26.

Lenski, Gerhard. 1954. "Status Crystallization: A Nonvertical Dimension of Social Status." *American Sociological Review.* Vol. 19 (August):405–13.

Lipset, Seymour Martin. 1981. *Political Man.* Baltimore: Johns Hopkins University Press.

Lipset, Seymour M., and Earl Raab. 1970. *The Politics of Unreason: Right-Wing Extremism in America, 1790–1970.* New York: Harper & Row.

Marwell, Gerald, Pamela Oliver, and Ralph Prahl 1988. "Social Networks and Collective Action:

A Theory of the Critical Mass" *American Journal of Sociology* Vol. 94, No. 3 (Nov.): 502–534.

Marx, Gary T. 1967. *Protest and Prejudice: A Study of Belief in the Black Community.* New York: Harper and Row.

McAdam, D. 1982. *Political Process and the Development of Black Insurgency.* Chicago: University of Chicago Press.

McCarthy, John D., and Mayer N. Zald. 1977. *The Trend of Social Movements in America: Professionalization and Resource Mobilization.* Morristown, N.J.: General Learning.

Mizzuchi, Ephraim H. 1983. *Regulating Society.* New York: Free Press.

Morris, A., and C. Herring. 1987. "Theory and Research in Social Movements: A Critical Review." *Annual Review of Political Science.* Vol. 2:138–98.

Neidhardt, Friedhelp, and Dieter Rucht. 1991. "The Analysis of Social Movements: The State of the Art and Some Perspectives for Further Research." In *Research on Social Movements,* ed. Dieter Rucht, Pp. ___. Boulder, CO: Westview Press.

Oberschall, Anthony. 1973. *Social Conflict and Social Movement.* Englewood Cliffs, NJ: Prentice-Hall.

Olson, Mancur Jr. 1965. *The Logic of Collective Action.* Cambridge: Harvard University Press.

Orum, Anthony M., and Amy Orum. 1968. "The Class and Status Bases of Negro Student Protest." *Sociological Science Quarterly.* Vol. 49 (Dec.):521–33.

Petras, James, and Maurice Zeitlin. 1968. "Miners and Agrarian Radicalism." In *Latin American Revolution or Reform?,* ed. James Petras and Maurice Zeitlin, 235–48. Greenwich, CT: Fawcett.

Pinard, Maurice. 1968. "Mass Society and Political Movements: A New Formulation." *American Journal of Sociology.* Vol. 73 (May):682–90.

Portes, Alejandro. 1970. "Leftist Radicalism in Chile: A Test of Three Hypotheses." *Comparative Politics.* Vol. 2 (January):251–74.

Prahl, Ralph, Gerald Marwell and Pamela Oliver 1991. "Reach and Selectivity as Strategies of Recruitment for Collective Action: A Theory of the Critical Mass" *Journal of Mathematical Sociology* Vol. 16, No. 2 (137–164).

Opp, Karl-Dieter and Christiane Gern 1993. "Dissident Groups, Personal Networks, and Spontaneous Cooperation: The East German Revolution of 1989" *American Sociological Review* Vol. 58 (Oct) 659–680.

Reiter, Howard, 1993. "The Rise of the 'New Agenda' and the Decline of Partisanship." In *West European Politics,* vol. 16, no. 2 (April):89–104.

Rejai, Mostafa, L. Masey, D. D. Beller. 1971 (ed.) *Decline of Ideology?* Chicago and New York: Aldine-Atherton, Pp. 268–85.

Rosenthal, Naomi, and Michael Schwartz. 1989. "Spontaneity and Democracy in Social Protest." In *Organizing for Change: Social Movement Organizations in Europe and the U.S.,* Vol. 5, Greenwich, N.J.: JAI Press.

Tarrow, Sidney. 1988. "National Politics and Collective Action: Recent Theory and Research in Western Europe and the United States." *Annual Review of Sociology.* Vol. 14:421–40.

Taylor, Verta. 1989. "Social Movement Continuity: The Women's Movement In Abeyance." *American Sociological Review.* Vol. 54 (October): 761–775.

Tilly, Charles. 1978. *From Mobilization to Revolution.* Reading, MA: Addison-Wesley.

Touraine, Alain. 1992. "Beyond Social Movements?" *Theory Culture and Society.* Vol. 9: 125–45.

Useem, Michael. 1975. *Protest Movements in America.* Indianapolis: Bobbs-Merrill.

Walsh, Edward. 1978. "Mobilization Theory Vis-à-vis Mobilization Process: The Case of the United Farm Workers' Movement." *Research in Social Movements, Conflicts and Change.* Vol. 1:55–77.

Walsh, Edward. 1981. "Resource Mobilization and Citizen Protest in Communities Around Three Mile Island." *Social Problems.* Vol. 29: 1–21.

Walsh, Edward J., and Rex H. Warland. 1983. "Social Movement Involvement in the Wake of a Nuclear Accident: Activists and Free Riders in the TMI Area." *American Sociology Review* Vol. 48:764–80.

Zald, Mayer, Roberta Ash, and John McCarthy. 1966. "Social Movement Organizations: Growth, Decay, and Change." *Social Forces.* Vol. 44:327–41.

Zeitlin, Maurice. 1966. "Economic Insecurity and the Political Attitudes of Cuban Workers." *American Sociological Review.* Vol. 31 (February):31–51.

Democratization and Development

The processes of democratization and development have always been of theoretical and empirical interest to political sociologists and social scientists. To sociologists, the term *democratization* usually means the extent to which a country allows pluralistic institutions, including political parties, to compete openly for political power. A democratic regime includes, at minimum, free elections, freedom of speech, freedom of assembly, and a renewal of political parties in government. The term *development* refers to the level of political, economic, and social "modernization" or "growth" (as generally defined in the West); technological, scientific, and bureaucratic development are measured using such indices as per capita income, education, mass communication, industrial output, and political culture. Social scientists generally believe that the democratic road to development is slower than but preferable to the authoritarian road because it leads toward independence from arbitrary shows of power by governments and, in theory, provides safety for civil, constitutional, and human rights.

The recent expansion of democracy, which first occurred in Greece, Spain, and Portugal in the mid-1970s, in Argentina, Brazil and the Philippines in the early 1980s, and, most recently, in Eastern Europe and the former Soviet Union in the late 1980s and in South Africa in the early 1990s, has again stimulated the study of democratization and development. By the end of 1993, 99 of 186 countries had competitive elections (Lipset, 1994). According to Seymour Lipset, democracy remains weakest in Islamic countries (e.g., Iran, Pakistan, and Albania) and in parts of Africa (e.g., Somalia, Nigeria, and South Africa). Furthermore, although not fully democratic, "more than 30 African countries are in the process of transition from an authoritarian civilian or military government to one that is more pluralistic" (quoted in Lipset, 1994:1; Diamond, 1992:38–39, 1993:3–4; Schneidman, 1992).

The collapse of the Communist regimes in Eastern Europe and the Soviet Union opened the way for a new wave of neonationalisms and ethnocracies (the rule of one ethnic group over others), which has resulted in mass brutality and social and political uncertainty. The transition from socialism to Western-type market economies has raised a number of questions for political sociologists and political scientists. The most frequently asked is whether democracy is feasible in these "fledgling" countries which, emerging from a long tradition of Communist authoritarian rule, have little or no experience with democratic institutions.

How do we deal, for example, with Eastern European countries which have strong national cultures but lack experience in pluralistic and democratic politics? Can or should we see the reemergence of nationalisms and ethnocracies as steps toward democracy? What are the conditions under which democracy emerges and sustains itself? Conversely, under what conditions do democratic regimes collapse? What are the prospects of democracy? What are some of the long-standing explanations of democratization and development, and to what extent can they be applied to the newly independent countries?

Democracy, Democratization, and Development: Conceptual Clarification

Since the time of Herodotus (484?–425? B.C.), a Greek historian, it has been customary to classify governments as either monarchies (the rule of one ruler), oligarchies (the rule of a few), or democracies (the rule of the many). Throughout the ages, democracy has been more of an ideal than a reality. For instance, even in the United States, the "liberties" of democracy were until relatively recently limited to white male citizens. Modern definitions of democracy are inclusive of all members of the adult population who are citizens. Although many nations speak of themselves as democracies, a relatively few are really democracies. What, then, is an operational definition of democracy?

To Aristotle, democracy meant "a constitution in which the free-born and poor control the government—being at the same time a majority" (Aristotle, 1961:164). To James Bryce (1921), democracy was that political system in which the will of a whole people prevails. Karl Popper (1977: vol. 1, 124) offered a more descriptive definition of democracy by distinguishing between two main forms of government: "The first type consists of governments which we can get rid of without bloodshed by way of general elections," while the second type "consists of governments which the ruled cannot get rid of except by way of a successful revolution—that is to say, in most cases, not at all." The first type is democracy. Joseph Schumpeter (1950:250) defined democracy as that "institutional arrangement for arriving at political decisions in which individuals acquire the power to decide by means of competitive struggle for the people's vote."

Robert A. Dahl (1956/1968) believed that democracy concerns itself with "processes by which ordinary citizens exert a relatively high degree of influence over leaders." He recognized three types of democracy: Madisonian democracy, populist democracy, and polyarchal democracy. By Madisonian democracy, he meant a compromise between the power of majorities and the power of minorities by placing constitutional restraints upon the former. A populist democracy is based on the notion of popular sovereignty and political equality, while polyarchal democracy focuses on the social prerequisites of democracy. Dahl (1971, 1982) identified two components of democratization: (1) public contestation or political competition, which includes the right to oppose and (2) the right to participate, or the idea of inclusiveness, by which everybody is included in the political process. He (1971:2–9) defined contestation as the "existence of institutional guarantees" for a people's right to express and communicate political preferences and noted that while contestation is a necessary condition for democracy, it is not a sufficient one: inclusiveness is also necessary.

Lipset (1994:3) concentrated on the centrality of political culture in democracy. In his words, "democracy requires a supportive culture, the acceptance by the citizenry and political elites of principles underlying freedom of speech, media, assembly, religion, the rights of opposition parties, the rule of law, human rights, and the like." Other political sociologists (Diamond et al., 1986:3, 1988a:xvi) have viewed democracy as that political system that meets three criteria: (1) a meaningful and extensive competition among organized groups and organized individuals, (2) a high degree of political participation in selecting leaders and policies, and (3) a level of civil liberties that allows political competition and participation. Lipset (1994) believed that to be successful, democracies must be institutionalized, consolidated, and legitimized. Political stability in a democracy cannot rely on force; it must rely on legitimacy, which is best gained through the Weberian types of traditional, legal, and charismatic authority discussed in Chapter 2.

Measures of Democratization[1]

Measures of democratization are as diverse as definitions of democracy. Indices of democratization include political participation, political competition, level of political culture, level of economic and political development, degree of social and political equality, civil liberties, and electoral politics. Marvin E. Olsen (1968) developed an index of democratization based on five dimensions: executive functioning, legislative functioning, party organization, power diversification, and citizen influence. W. Flanigan and E. Fogelman (1971) constructed a somewhat similar index of democratization based on four main components of democracy: electoral or parliamentary succession, political competition, popular electoral participation, and absence of suppression. Kenneth A. Bollen (1979, 1980, 1983) and Bollen and B. D. Granjean (1981) used two dimensions of democratization in their measure—popular sovereignty and political liberties—and constructed a six-point index of democracy including three measures of popular sovereignty (fairness of elections, effective executive selection, and legislative selection) and three measures of political liberties (freedom of the press, freedom of group opposition, and government sanctions).

The Concepts of Development and Modernization

The concepts of development and modernization can be traced to major social changes that took place in western Europe during the Industrial Revolution. In modern times *development* came to signify a form of stage-by-stage social progress toward the more economically and technologically advanced societies of western Europe. For example, following World War II those Third World countries that had been colonies of western European industrial nations were perceived to be either underdeveloped economically or as undergoing the process of political and economic development.

During the 1950s and 1960s an entirely new field of regional studies emerged which placed emphasis on, for instance, Latin American studies, Middle Eastern studies, Southeast Asian studies, West African studies, and Mediterranean studies. Many of those studying these regions argued for allowance of different routes to democratization and development based on each region's peculiarities and particular history and culture. For example, Clark Neher and Ross Maclay (1995) described the political systems of these regions as "semi-democratic," that is, having elements of both Western-type liberal democracy and authoritarianism. Similarly, Dwight King (1994, written communication) believed that "the developmental state" and "neo-authoritarianism" in Southeast Asia are compatible with rapid economic development and economic liberalism.[2] Such regional studies were especially attractive to social scientists who had comparative and interdisciplinary approaches to such disciplines as economics, sociology, political science, public administration, anthropology, civil engineering, agronomy, and urban planning. Students of comparative politics and sociology sought to identify obstacles to social, economic, and political development in developing countries and used various interpretations, concepts, and theories to understand and explain the notions of development and modernization.

During the late 1960s and 1970s the concepts of modernization and development came under severe criticism from "dependency" and "underdevelopment" advocates, especially André Gunder Frank (1969) and T. Dos Santos (1973). Yet during the 1980s and 1990s the concepts of development and modernization once again sustained social scientific interest because they were associated with democratization and disengagement of military regimes from civilian politics and with the reemergence of new democracies, semi-democracies, and/or ethnocracies, not only in previously socialist and Communist states, but also in many African and Asian countries.

By the early 1990s there was a global crisis in which ecological, economic, social, and spiritual factors led to political leadership challenges. According to David Ray Griffin and Richard Falk (1993:1–16), the global crisis and political leadership problems were caused by the very notion of modernity itself, which they believed had become irrelevant to most of the world. Griffin and Falk (1993:4) used the notion of "postmodern politics" to mean "a new world order" based on "wholeness," which included both humankind and the life of the planet as a whole.

Theoretical Explanations of Democratization and Development

Theories of democratization deal primarily with the conditions necessary for the creation and survival of democracy. Aristotle pointed out that democracy is closely related to social equality. Montesquieu and Tocqueville linked democracy with social equality or equality of conditions. To them, democracy required certain economic, political, and cultural factors, such as electoral politics, political parties, equality in the distribution of land and free forms of governance. More recently such pioneer social scientists as Karl W. Deutch (1961), D. Lerner, and Lipset (1981, 1994) have undertaken research on the requisites of democracy. Lerner (1958/ 1968:46–64), for example, linked democracy with urbanization, modernization, education, mass media exposure, and political and economic participation. Similarly, Schumpeter (1950) believed that "historically, modern democracy rose along with capitalism, and in causal connection with it." Dietrich Rueschemeyer and colleagues argued that although capitalist economic development and democracy were positively correlated,

> *capitalist development was associated with democracy, because it transforms the class structure, strengthening the working and middle classes, and weakening the landed upper class. It was not the capitalist market nor the capitalists as the new dominant force, but rather the contradictions of capitalism that advanced the cause of democracy. (Rueschemeyer et al., 1992:7)*

In other words, democracy advanced primarily due to the opening of the class structure which, in turn, led to class mobility and gave many people the opportunity to achieve a middle- and working-class status.

Lipset offered one of the most influential explanatory theories of democracy. Influenced by the writings of Aristotle, Schumpeter, and Weber, Lipset linked democracy to economic development. In his words, "the more well-to-do a nation, the greater the chances that it will sustain democracy" (Lipset, 1981:31). Lipset examined a number of countries in Europe and Latin America. He concluded that countries that scored higher in the indices of wealth (measured by per capita income, thousands of persons per physician, and number of motor vehicles, telephones, radios, media), industrialization (measured in terms of proportion of males employed in agriculture and per capita energy consumption), education (measured in terms of enrollment in primary, secondary, and higher education), and urbanization (measured in terms of proportion of people living in cities and urban areas) were more likely to be democratic. A flaw in Lipset's study was that he simply accepted the notion that Anglo-Saxon countries in western Europe were more democratic and that countries in Latin America were more authoritarian. In his more recent work, however, Lipset (1994) expanded the number of conditions necessary for democratization in the emerging new democracies or semi-democracies by examining political, cultural, institutional, and civic conditions in addition to the economic conditions he stressed in his earlier work. However, new democracies, Lipset argued, must attain both legitimacy and efficacy in the economic arena as well as in the political arena.

Competing Theoretical Approaches to Modernization and Development

The most important theoretical approaches to the study of modernization and development are modernization theory and dependency theory. Modernization theory has its roots in classical sociology in the distinction between "traditional" and "modern" societies. Classical sociologists such as Emile Durkheim, Georg Simmel, Ferdinand Toennies, and Max Weber used this dichotomy to interpret historical transformations of European societies in the aftermaths of three major revolutions in Europe: the Enlightenment (1700s), the French Revolution (1789), and the Industrial Revolution (1850–1900s). Modernization theorists applied notions of development cross-culturally within developing societies or between them on the one hand and among the economically and technologically developed western European societies on the other (Gilbert & Muñoz, 1992:711–712). Modernization theory was the dominant paradigm of development until the early 1960s. In brief, it was based on the evolutionary notions of late nineteenth- and early twentieth-century social Darwinism and laissez-faire classical economic liberalism, which held that societies and polities, like biological organisms, go through a number of stages of development—birth, maturation, and decay.

Modernization theory, like evolutionary theory, is a stage-by-stage explanation of development. Advocates of modernization theory argued that the West had reached its zenith of democracy and development; now the rest of the world must emulate it (Bauzon, 1992:36). Indeed, the most influential post–World War II modernization theorist, Walt W. Rostow (1960), argued that development in societies follows five distinct stages: (1) traditional, (2) the take-off, (3) the drive to maturity, (4) mass consumption, and (5) post–mass consumption. Several other theorists focused on various indigenous factors as obstacles to development. For example, Gabriel A. Almond and Sidney Verba (1963) believed that democracy and development were highly correlated with the state of a polity's "civic culture." Deutsch (1966), Alex Inkeles and David H. Smith (1974), Lerner (1958/1968), and David C. McClelland (1961) focused on a number of psychological, political, social, and cultural factors. McClelland, for example, stressed the "need for achievement." Inkeles and Smith believed that if development was to take place, modern man had to embrace a set of new values, such as "readiness for new experience," "belief in human efficacy," "faith in science and technology," and a "disposition to form and hold opinions." Everett E. Hagen (1962), along with Lerner, emphasized "modern personality" as key to development. Lucien Pye (1971) stressed the necessity of mass communication, and Lipset offered, as discussed earlier, a set of social and economic conditions, including education, industrialization, mass media, and political participation. Other theorists examined traditional and cultural values and norms, such as regionalism, superstition, ethnocentrism, pride, dignity, honor, fatalism, and the like as cultural barriers to development and modernization (Foster, 1973; McNall, 1971).

One critique of modernization theory focused on its unilinear view of development as well as on its ethnocentric, pro-capitalist, and pro-Western bias. Bauzon (1992:38) listed five reasons for the ultimate failure of modernization theory: (1) The mistaken belief that all societies followed a unilinear path to the same level of development. In most instances, when we refer to modernization, we tend to compare non-Western societies with a Western model of industrial and socioeconomic development. We often ignore the historical and cultural factors that may have impeded the development and modernization of a country. (2) The assumption that development is primarily a function of factors (for example, the economy, politics, education, culture, and demographic resources) that are internal to a particular society. Many external influences on a country, such as international relations, regional conflicts, and international trade also directly affect development and modernization. (3) The assumption that the state is a reflection of a community-wide consensus. It can be argued that government is not always representative of a people. Decisions are not always made by the people. In fact, many countries are ruled by dictatorships or governments that violate the human rights of their own citizens. (4) Modernization theory's teleological orientation, which ignores conflictual processes. Many governments tend to ignore or to overlook the various social cleavages and conflicts that take place among ethnic and racial groups, social classes, genders, and religions. Often, in their efforts to modernize and to become more technologically advanced, governments violate the human and democratic rights of their citizens. (5) The alienation and disaffection of a large segment of the population from the political system. In most countries, including the most industrialized, large segments of the citizenry, especially the poor and the lower classes, do not participate in politics. In essence, they have given up on the idea of affecting the political system and do not feel a significant part of it. They fail to see the relevance of politics or government to their everyday lives. Lamenting modernization theory's apparent paralysis, Albert Hirschman (1981:1), one of its long-time exponents, offered a retrospective explanation. He wrote that the "old liveliness is no longer there,. . . new ideas are ever harder to come by and . . . the field is not adequately reproducing itself." In short, modernization theory has serious problems.

By the early 1970s it was clear that the dominant modernization approach to development was inoperative. Critics of modernization theory questioned the belief that development in Third World countries would occur simply as a result of the introduction of ideas and institutions from more developed and advanced Western societies. A number of writers, especially in Latin America, influenced by a blend of nationalism, Marxism, and liberalism, called themselves *dependendistas,* or dependency theorists. It was they who first offered the alternative dependency theory. Thus, while modernization theory was conceived and constructed in the United States and exported to Latin America and other countries of the Third World, dependency theory was primarily a Latin American product exported to the United States (Gilbert & Muñoz, 1992:713).

Dependency theory advocates argued that the obstacle to development was the very dependency of the less developed nations on the more developed ones. Closely related to the world system theory, dependency theory argued that the major reason some countries were described as "underdeveloped" was because they played a minor, or peripheral, role in the world market economy. In order to produce finished products and for their economic advantage alone, dependency theorists believed that the core industrialized nations penetrated the less developed peripheral countries by means of multinational corporations and investments in these countries and, as a result, drained the resources of these underdeveloped countries. The link between the core industrialized countries and those in the periphery or semi-periphery was thus the main reason for the peripheral nations' underdevelopment. Albert Szymanski (1976), for example, suggested two interpretations of this link. One view held that capital flowed from the more industrialized, capitalist societies to the less developed countries, resulting in the poorer countries' relative growth and industrialization. Opposed to this "trickle-down" ideology, the other, more contemporary, view maintained that dependency resulted in the siphoning of resources through multinationals from the less developed to the more developed nations.

A number of studies have examined the link between economic development and dependency, including income inequality, political democracy, and dependency. Bollen (1983), in his test of the dependency and democracy hypothesis, which used empirical data concerning a hundred nations, concluded that political democracy, as measured by political liberties and popular sovereignty, positively correlated with economic development and greater dependency. In a more recent study, of fifty countries, Edward Muller (1988) found that democracy and democratic stability were correlated with income inequality. He found that the more stable the democratic regime, the less income inequality; conversely, the greater the income inequality, the greater the political instability. This relationship of dependency, development, and political democracy is illustrated in Fig. 11.1.

In a review of the literature on dependency in Latin American countries, Dennis Gilbert and Braulio Muñoz (1992:71c) summarized the main points made by dependency theorists: (1) Latin American economies were largely dependent on their positions within the world division of labor and their economic links with the advanced capitalist economies. (2) Latin American capitalists, while collaborating with foreign capitalists and traditional rural elites, were incapable of dynamic economic independence. (3) Latin American states were, as a rule, weak, because they were dominated by foreign capitalists and the governments of advanced capitalist countries. They were thus unable to promote independent national development. (4) Within the existing system of dependent capitalism, Latin American economies and political systems could grow only in a distorted way that was limited to a privileged few and contrary to the interests of all people. Presently, while dependency theory is not as dominant as it once was, it continues to generate interest and research because no other school of thought in development studies has yet emerged.

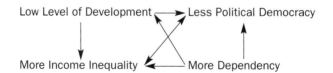

Figure 11.1   Macro-Processes and Income Inequality

Source: Charles E. Hurst, *Social Inequality* (1992:30); reprinted here by permission of Allyn and Bacon.

Studies on the Social Requisites of Democracy and Development

Contemporary research on the social requisites of democracy can be traced to the pioneering studies and hypotheses of such scholars as Lerner and Lipset. Lerner (1958/1968) argued that the passing of traditional society leads to urbanization, followed by increased literacy, media exposure, and economic and political participation. In his view, democratization historically arrived late and usually appeared in the process of citizen participation. Drawing from Aristotle's *Politics,* especially Aristotle's view of the middle class as a stabilizing force in political regimes, Lipset (1981:31) hypothesized that "democracy is related to economic development." In general, Lipset believed that political culture, legitimacy, religious tolerance, competitive politics, equalitarian ethos, efficacy, economic efficiency, and economic growth are essential elements of democratization and development.

Surveying the literature on the theme of capitalist development and democracy, Rueschemeyer and his colleagues (1992:269) concluded that a number of comparative studies confirmed the importance of three clusters of power—"class power, state power, and transnational structures of power—for the development (and demise) of democracy in the process of capitalist development in the advanced countries of Europe, Latin America, Central America, and the Caribbean." More specifically, they found class to be central to the process of democratization in most of these countries. They believed that, with a few exceptions, the working class was of major importance in the development of democracy in most regions of the world and that democracy could be consolidated only if landlords were not a significant force, did not depend on cheap labor, and did not control the state (Rueschemeyer et al., 1992:270). The labor-intensive agriculture practices and presence of large landlords in South and Central America and in other countries in the periphery of the world system tended to retard the processes of democratization and development because the landowners often used the military dictatorships to suppress democracy. Furthermore, capitalist development, the authors argued, weakened the landed upper classes and strengthened the working and other subordinate classes. Thus, the link between capitalist development and democracy took place in terms of changes in the balance of class power. Because the working class was not strong enough to bring about democracy alone, it relied on the middle class to bring it to fruition.

In a study of despotism, democracy, and economic development, Charles Kurzman (1993) found that, contrary to the common assumption that they contribute to modernization, authoritarian regimes were not associated with economic growth and development. In fact, democracy was positively correlated to economic development. Kurzman (1993:16) found that "Third World dictatorships performed no better economically than Third World democracies in the period 1953–1982."

With class power, state and multinational power play equally important roles in consolidating democracy in many countries. Authoritarian military elites permeated the state power structure and contributed to the erosion of democracy in Greece, Spain, and Portugal. In Latin America, the state played an antidemocratic role through involvement of the military in civilian politics, which was used as an instrument by the dominant, landed classes to suppress the peasants and keep the lower classes from gaining power and equality. The antidemocratic role of the state in Latin America has been emulated by Third World countries in Africa, the Middle East, and Southeast Asia. George A. Lopez and Michael Stohl (1989) argued that ample evidence exists of the relationship between repression and economic and political factors that binds states together in international politics. State repression must be seen in the context of local political culture and elite decisions within particular states. The overwhelming conclusion of these studies is that economic development is many times achieved at the expense of human rights and freedom. Most authoritarian and Communist regimes, like China, stress development and modernization at the expense of democracy, human rights, and freedom.

A major issue related to development is the power wielded by multinational corporations (MNCs). In the past, multinational corporations have subverted many governments and supported authoritarian regimes in many countries of the Third World in order to further their own profits. The term *multinational* (or *transnational) corporation* generally refers to any corporation in which ownership, management, production, and marketing extend over several countries. The "home country" is the nation where the MNC has its official headquarters, while the "host countries" are the nations where the foreign branches and subsidiaries of the MNC operate. Home countries tend to be more industrially developed, core nations, while host countries are usually less developed countries (LDCs). MNCs make direct investments in host countries so that they will be able to establish major permanent economic relationships with them. A major question concerning the growth and development of MNCs is how much power they really have in home and host countries. This issue is complex because MNCs are found in many nations rather than in just a few and because, for a variety of reasons, it is usually difficult to obtain reliable information from either MNCs or the governments concerned. More multinational corporations are headquartered in the United States than anywhere else in the world. By the 1980s most MNCs were concentrated in the core "triad" countries of the world system, the United States, Japan, and the European Community (Jones & Schröter, 1993:3).

C. Fred Bergsten and his colleagues (1978) have identified four broad frameworks used to examine multinational power. Two of these frameworks view MNCs as junior partners of their home countries; this partnership exercises power at the expense of the MNCs host countries. The other two frameworks see MNCs as an important source of power. The first framework is the *neoimperialist,* which suggests that MNCs are the agents of exploitation (they are usually viewed as extensions of U.S. capitalism) and that less developed countries are exploited by MNCs. The neoimperialist view also states that certain local elites in these LDCs do well, but at the expense of the general population. Despite the advantages that accrue to LDC elites, the center of power remains in the more industrialized nations, and the LDCs are dependent on them. At the same time, the neoimperialist framework argues that U.S. corporations always need a means to invest their surplus capital and thus need the foreign markets and natural resources of the LDCs. Michael Kimmel (1975–

1976) maintained that increasing MNC penetration into the economies of peripheral nations has reduced the political importance of peripheral states and has created an international managerial elite.

The second framework that emphasizes the power of the MNC and the home country is the *neomercantilist* model. This interpretation sees the nation-state (rather than the capitalist class) as actively trying to maximize its power at the cost of other nation-states. MNCs, are thus seen as tools used to promote national interests rather than corporate interests (Kumar, 1979:292–293).

The third and fourth frameworks view MNCs as independent sources of power rather than as mere extensions of the power of the home country. The third framework is the *sovereignty-at-bay* (Vernon, 1977) or liberal *diffusionist* interpretation (Kumar, 1979). According to this interpretation, MNCs work to the benefit of both the home and the host countries. Viewed this way, MNCs are apolitical institutions that help LDCs by bringing capital and skills desperately needed in these nations. Yet it can be argued that the more industrialized nations benefit most because they receive consumer goods, natural resources, new business, and profits (Kumar, 1979:292). Raymond Vernon (1977) believed that the home country, host countries, and MNCs are each powerful in their own right, but that each also has a relatively distinct domain of power.

In opposition to the sovereignty-at-bay view is the *global reach* or *dependencia* perspective, which sees MNCs as operating at the expense of nation-states, especially developing host countries that are dependent on MNCs. According to this view, MNCs stifle competition and monopolize world markets, worsen the pattern of income distribution, and create poverty. MNCs are seen as responsible for exporting jobs from the home countries because they seek cheaper sources of labor abroad. Furthermore, dependencia perspective advocates believe that MNCs destroy jobs (especially those provided by small businesses) and exploit the natural resources in host countries. Richard Barnet and Ronald E. Muller (1974) stressed the power of MNCs as oligopolies in terms of (1) knowledge and technology of production, (2) marketing, and (3) manipulation of finance capital. They believed that MNCs depleted rather than contributed to local finance capital.

Consumer activist Ralph Nader (1975) believed that it is difficult to find any poor country where MNCs have contributed to a pattern of intensive job development and broad economic growth. In many ways, MNCs contribute to single-cash-crop development, and they build up elite classes and authoritarian regimes that do not consider the interests of the poor. For example, Brazil's pharmaceuticals industry is dominated by multinational drug firms which account for more than three-fourths of all drug sales in Brazil (Ledogar, 1975:7). Although in the 1970s three-fourths of the people in Brazil died before the age of fifty, the drug companies made most of their money by selling their products to the rich and the urban middle classes, who could afford to buy them. After examining numerous case studies, Robert J. Ledogar (1975:5) concluded that the advantages created by the MNCs went to a minority while the majority, who most needed their drugs, seemed to get little of them. The situation may have improved somewhat but the overall conditions remain the same (Zirker, 1994).

The research on world systems, multinationals, and nation-states shows inconsistent and sometimes contradictory support for these various frameworks. To evaluate each one, we may need to develop measurements that are more consistent with each theory. We may also need to specify each theory in greater detail. Additional comparative studies of countries within the core or semiperiphery as well as studies of countries in different world positions, may help advance our knowledge concerning what conditions best explain a nation's position in the world system and, more specifically, what powers a nation-state or an MNC wields. It is essential that such explanations consider both the possibilities of change and the dynamics of these relationships.

Prospects for Democracy and Development

For many the collapse of the Soviet Union and the disintegration of Yugoslavia are examples of the expansion of democracy and of self-determination by oppressed people; for others, however, the reemergence of ethnocracies in the former Soviet Union and former Yugoslavia signal a resurgence of extreme nationalism bordering on fascism. In the words of Michael Ignatieff (1993), "[w]e even thought for a while, that the democratic current in the East might sweep through our own exhausted oligarchies in the West." Ignatieff, however, revealed the irony of such hopeful events: "We soon found out how wrong we were. The repression has returned, and its name is nationalism." Given this irony, what are the prospects for democracy in the newly independent countries of the former Soviet Union, Eastern Europe, and former Yugoslavia? And how will democracy fare in developing countries in Latin America, Africa, and Southeast Asia?

While it is difficult to predict how the story of democratization and development will unfold in the years ahead, one can offer a tentative model for a global system of peace, democracy, and development based on a set of five, general, interrelated propositions organized as a set of the sociopolitical variables of inequality, national interest, system closure, dependency, and property rights (see Table 11.1).[3]

These variables can be operationalized as major causes and effects of conflict, including wars at both the national and international levels. The extent to which these variables exist contributes to the likelihood of social, political, and ethnic conflict, while their absence or lessening may contribute to democracy and peace. These five propositions constitute what political sociologists refer to as the power conflict perspective. This perspective is more likely to be held by the nations located in the periphery or semiperiphery in the world system, while the core or corporate-military-industrial nations are more likely to endorse a functionalist perspective. In other words, while periphery and semi-periphery nations stress social change, the core nations stress stability. We find the same tendencies within most societies or cultures. For example, the corporate, military, and political elites stress consensus, order, and stability, while the lower socioeconomic classes and racial minority groups stress change.

Table 11.1 High Likelihood of Conflict/War
vs. High Likelihood of Peace/Democracy

Social Inequality	Social Equality
Prejudice, Racism, Sexism	Lessening of Prejudice, Racism, Sexism
from National Interests	to Human International Interests
from Bureaucratization and/or Closed World System	to Democratization and Open World System
from Dependency	to Interdependency
from Property Rights	to Human Rights

Source: George A. Kourvetaris, "Beyond the Arms Race" (1991: 233–252).

Functionalists explain stratification and social inequality as inevitable and compatible with social harmony and societal stability, while conflict theorists explain them as the cause and the consequence of conflict within and across societies and cultures. Functionalists stress the unequal marketability and different importance of occupations and professions, while conflict theorists try to minimize such distinctions.

While the conflict perspective is difficult to prove empirically, it is not to be dismissed. It is a powerful explanation of much of the unrest and tension that occurs in countries. At the same time, while conflict theory explains social change and accepts the existence of a dominant, unified ruling class, it does not adequately explain the persistence of order and stability across societies and cultures. Furthermore, conflict does not always lead to change, as Marxist theory, a subtype of conflict theory, proposed.

In general, those societies that stress increasing social equality (including sex and race equality) are more likely to experience less conflict and war. In addition, those nations that operate on the old "realist model," which places national interest before human international interests, dependency before interdependency between nations, property rights before human rights, and a rigid, closed world system before an open one, will continue to experience conflict.

What are the prospects for democracy in the future? It seems that social scientists can offer no definite answers. While democratization and development will advance somewhat in the years ahead, such advancement will be slow and uneven in many parts of the world.

Summary and Conclusion

In this chapter an effort was made to clarify the concepts of democratization and development in the light of new possibilities of democratization and development in certain regions of the world. By the early 1990s almost two hundred countries had competitive elections. At the same time a new wave of neonationalism has emerged following the collapse of former Yugoslavia and the former Soviet Union.

Both historically and conceptually the concepts of democracy, democratization, and development were briefly examined. For democracy and democratization to emerge certain conditions and prerequisites are necessary including: equality of opportunity, a political culture, education, political competition, economic development, freedom of speech, the rule of law, human rights, and the like. Along with the conceptual clarification of democracy, measures of democratization were also explored by looking at such indices as political participation, political competition, level of political culture, level of economic and political development, degree of social and political equality, civil liberties, and electoral politics. A number of political sociologists have suggested a number of indices of democratization including such dimensions as: electoral competition, citizen participation, popular sovereignty, political liberties, fairness of elections, freedom of the press, freedom of group opposition and the like.

The concepts of development and modernization were briefly analyzed in the context of an entirely new field of regional studies which emerged during the 1950s and 1960s. These regional studies cover areas such as Latin America, the Middle East, South East Asia, West Africa, and the Eastern Mediterranean to name only a few.

Theoretical and competing explanations of democratization, development, and modernization were also briefly examined by looking at some basic issues in a comparative analysis. Modernization theory like evolutionary theory was treated as a stage-by-stage development. A number of modernization and development theorists have advanced various versions of development and modernization theories including dependency theory, economic theories, psychological, cultural, and political theories of development. A number of researchers have focused on various stages of a unilinear western model of modernization and development. Both the positive and negative aspects of these theories and approaches were discussed.

Finally, a number of studies on the social requisites and prospects of democracy and development were delineated. In these last sections issues such as democracy, equalitarianism, economic efficiency, economic growth, competitive politics, multinational corporations, political efficacy, and interdependence were briefly assessed for future prospects of democracy and development in many parts of the world.

Endnotes

1. Among the most important works concerning measures of democracy are Banks and Textor (1963), Cutright (1963), Gastil (1988), Lerner (1958/1968), Lipset (1981), and Weiner and Ozbudun (1987).

2. See also Augustinos (1991) on Southeastern Europe, Mouzelis (1978) on Greece, and Theobald

(1990) on corruption and development. Many who study development and democratization talk about different varieties of development and democracy and semi-democracy.

3. Most of this section is based on the author's article, "Beyond the Arms Race: A Search for a New Paradigm for a Peaceful World" (1991:233-252).

References

Almond, Gabriel A., and Sidney Verba. 1963. *The Civic Culture: Political Attitudes and Democracy in Five Nations.* Princeton: Princeton University Press.

Aristotle. 1961. *The Politics of Aristotle,* trans. E. Barker. Oxford: Clarendon.

Augustinos, Gerasimos, ed. 1991. *Diverse Paths to Modernity in Southeastern Europe: Essays in National Development.* Westport, Conn: Greenwood.

Banks, A. S., and R. B. Textor. 1963. *A Cross-Polity Survey.* Cambridge, Mass: Institute of Technology.

Barnet, Richard, and Ronald E. Muller. 1974. *Global Reach: The Power of the Multinational Corporations.* New York: Simon and Schuster.

Bauzon, Kenneth E. 1992. "Development Studies: Contending Approaches and Research Trends." In *Development and Democratization in the Third World,* ed. Kenneth E. Bauzon, pp. 35–52. Washington, DC: Crane Russak.

Bergsten, C. Fred, Thomas Horst, and Theodore Moran. 1978. *American Multinationals and American Interests.* Washington, DC: Brookings Institute.

Bollen, Kenneth A. 1980. "Issues in the Comparative Measurement of Political Democracy." *American Sociological Review.* Vol. 45:370–390.

———. 1979. "Political Democracy and the Timing of Development." *American Sociological Review.* Vol. 44:572–587.

———. 1983. "World System Position, Dependency and Democracy." *American Sociological Review.* Vol. 48:468–479.

Bollen, K. A., and B. D. Grandjean. 1981. "The Dimension(s) of Democracy: Further Issues in the Measurement and Effects of Political Democracy." *American Sociological Review.* Vol. 46:651–659.

Bryce, James. 1921. *Modern Democracies.* London: Macmillan.

———. 1982. *Dilemmas of Pluralist Democracy. Autonomy vs. Control.* New Haven: Yale University Press.

Cutright, P. 1963. "National Political Development: Measurement and Analysis." *American Sociological Review.* Vol. 28:253–264.

Dahl, Robert A. 1971 and 1982. *Polarchy: Participation and Opposition.* New Haven: Yale University Press.

———. 1956/1968. *A Preface to Democratic Theory.* Chicago: University of Chicago.

Deutsch, Karl W. 1966. *Nationalism and Social Communication: An Inquiry into the Foundations of Nationality.* Cambridge: MIT Press.

———. 1961. "Social Mobilization and Political Development." *American Political Science Review.* Vol. 60, no. 3:493–514.

Diamond, Larry., J. J. Linz, and S. M. Lipset, 1986 "Developing and Sustaining Democratic Government in the Third World" presented at the 1986 Annual Meeting of the American Political Science Association August 28–31, Washington, D.C.

———. 1988a. Democracy in *Developing Countries.* Africa, Vol. 2; Asia, Vol. 3, Boulder: Lynne Rienner.

Diamond, Larry. 1992. "The Second Liberation." *African Report.* Vol. 37:38–41.

Dos Santos, T. 1973. "The Crisis of Development Theory and the Problem of Dependence in Latin America." In *Underdevelopment and Development: The Third World Today,* 2nd ed., H. Bernstein, pp. 57–80. Harmondsworth: Penguin.

Flanigan, W., and E. Fogelman. 1971. "Patterns of Political Development and Democratization: A Quantitative Analysis." In *Macro-Quantitative Analysis: Conflict, Development, and Democratization,* ed. J. V. Gillespie and B. A. Nesvold, pp. 441–473. Beverly Hills: Sage.

Foster, George M. 1973. *Traditional Societies in Technological Change,* 2nd ed. New York: Harper and Row.

Frank, André Gunder. 1969. *Latin America: Underdevelopment or Revolution: Essays on the Development of Underdevelopment and the Immediate Enemy.* New York: Monthly Review Press.

Gastil, R. D. 1988. *Freedom in the World, Political Rights, and Civil Liberties 1987–1988.* New York: Freedom House.

Gilbert, Dennis, and Braulio Muñoz. 1992. "Sociology: An Essay." In *Latin America and the Caribbean,* ed. Paula H. Covington, pp. 711–719. Westport, Conn: Greenwood.

Griffin, David Ray, and Richard Falk, eds. 1993. *Postmodern Politics for a Planet in Crisis.* New York: State University of New York Press.

Hagen, Everett E. 1962. *On the Theory of Social Change.* Homewood, Illinois: Dorsey.

Hirschman, Albert. 1981. *Essays in Trespassing: Economics to Politics and Beyond.* New York: Cambridge University Press.

Huntington, Samuel P. 1991. *The Third Wave: Democratization in the Late Twentieth Century.* Norman: University of Oklahoma Press.

Hurst, Charles E. 1992. *Social Inequality: Forms, Causes, and Consequences.* Boston: Allyn and Bacon.

Ignatieff, Michael. 1993. *Blood and Belonging: Journeys into the New Nationalism.* New York: Farrar, Straus and Giroux.

Inkeles, Alex, and David H. Smith. 1974. *Becoming Modern: Individual Change in Six Developing Countries.* Cambridge: Harvard University Press.

Jones, Geoffrey, and Harm G. Schröter, eds. 1993. *The Rise of Multinationals in Continental Europe.* England: Edward Edgar.

Kimmel, Michael. 1975–1976. "The Negation of National Sovereignty: The Multinational Corporation and the World Economy." *Berkeley Journal of Sociology.* Vol. 20:91–111.

Kourvetaris, George A. 1991. "Beyond the Arms Race: The Search for a New Paradigm of a Peaceful World." *Journal of Political and Military Sociology.* Vol. 19 (Winter):233–252.

Kumar, Krishna. 1979. "Review Essay: Multinational Corporations and Transnational Relations." *Journal of Political and Military Sociology.* Vol. 7 (Fall):291–304.

Kurzman, Charles. 1993. "Despotism, Democracy, and Economic Development," presented American Society of Management Association, Miami, Florida.

Ledogar, Robert J. 1975. *Hungry for Profits: U.S. Food and Drug Multinations in Latin America.* New York: International Documentation.

Lerner, D. 1958/1968. *The Passing of Traditional Society: Modernizing the Middle East.* New York: Free Press.

Lipset, Seymour M. 1981. *Political Man,* updated ed. Baltimore: Johns Hopkins University Press.

———. 1994. "The Social Requisites of Democracy Revisited: Presidential Address." *American Sociological Review.* Vol. 59, no. 1:1–22.

———. 1959. "Some Social Requisites of Democracy: Economic Development and Political Legitimacy." *American Political Science Review.* Vol. 53, no. 1:69–105.

Lopez, George A., and Michael Stohl, eds. 1989. *Dependence, Development and State Repression.* Westport, Conn.: Greenwood Press.

McClelland, David C. 1961. *Achieving Society.* New York: Free Press.

McNall, Scott. 1971. *The Greek Peasant.* Washington, D.C.: American Sociological Association, The Arnold Rose Monographs.

Mouzelis, Nicos P. 1978. *Modern Greece: Facets of Underdevelopment.* London: Macmillan.

Muller, Edward. 1988. "Democracy, Economic Development, and Income Inequality." *American Sociological Review.* Vol. 53:50–68.

Nader, Ralph. 1975. Introduction. In *Hungry for Profits,* ed. Robert Ledogar, vii–x. New York: International Documentation.

Neher, Clark. 1994. *The Winds of Change.* Unpublished manuscript.

Olsen, Marvin E. 1968. "Multivariate Analysis of National Political Development." *American Sociological Review.* Vol. 33, no. 5:699–712.

Popper, Karl. 1977. *The Open Society and Its Enemies,* London: Routledge and Kegan Paul.

Pye, Lucien. 1971. "The Concept of Political Development." In *Political Development and Social Change,* ed. Jason L. Finkle and Richard W. Gable, pp. 43–51. New York: John Wiley and Sons.

Rostow, Walt W. 1960. *The Stages of Economic Growth: A Non-Communist Manifesto.* Cambridge: Cambridge University Press.

Rueschemeyer, Dietrich, Evelyne H. Stephens, and John D. Stephens. 1992. *Capitalist Development and Democracy.* Chicago: University of Chicago Press.

Schneidman, W. W. 1992. "Africa's Transition to Pluralism: Economic and Investment Implications." *CSIS Africa Notes.* (November):1–7.

Schumpeter, Joseph. 1950. *Capitalism, Socialism and Democracy,* 3rd ed. New York: Harper and Row.

Szymanski, Albert. 1976. "Dependence, Exploitation and Economic Growth." *Journal of Political and Military Sociology.* Vol. 4 (Spring):53–65.

Theobald, Robin. 1990. *Corruption, Development and Underdevelopment.* Durham: Duke University Press.

Vernon, Raymond. 1977. *Storm over the Multinationals.* Cambridge: Harvard University Press.

Weiner, Myron, and Ergun Ozbudun, eds. 1987. *Competitive Elections in Developing Countries.* Washington, DC: American Institute Books.

Zirker, Dan. 1994. "Written Communication" to me in Department of *Political Science.* (Spring). University of Idaho.

Chapter 12
Social Conflict and Ethnic Nationalism

Social conflict permeates and shapes all aspects of human interaction and helps to explain how societies, organizations, and social systems, from the most basic to the most advanced, struggle for personal or group values and interests. Social theorists look at conflict and competition as social processes and aspects of intergroup relations. Social conflict theory historically stems from the writings of Thucydides (471–400? B.C.), Machiavelli (1469–1527), and Hobbes (1588–1679). The early classical European and U.S social scientists, such as Karl Marx, Robert Park (1864–1944), Georg Simmel (1858–1918), Albion Small (1854–1926), and William Sumner (1840–1910), dealt extensively with the notion of social conflict. Marx, for example, stressed the economic and material aspects underlying all forms of social conflict, such as class struggles and property relations. Other conflict theorists, such as Gustav Ratzenhofer (1842–1904), Ludwig Gumplowitz (1838–1909), Herbert Spencer (1820–1903), and Jacques Novicov (1849–1912), explained conflict in evolutionary terms and emphasized group struggle for existence. They also viewed military power and ethnic interests as bases for conquest and conflict.

Since the 1960s the conflict perspective has become the dominant paradigm used in sociology and political sociology for analyzing social conflict. Many conflict theorists draw from the rich Marxist and neo-Marxist tradition, while other conflict theorists offer distinct non-Marxist analyses of social conflict. Ralf Dahrendorf (1959) and Randal Collins (1975) are examples of non-Marxist interpreters of conflict: Dahrendorf believed that authority relations, not property relations, underlie social conflict, while Collins found coercion and violence, at both the interpersonal and the social-structural levels, to be important aspects of control and conflict. In general, most conflict theorists stress (e.g., class, status, or power) inequality as the primary cause of social conflict. More recently, however, more theorists have argued that the escalation of conflict in many parts of the world is due to the reemergence of ethnic nationalism. Also, while most studies in the past focused on the emergence of conflict, more recent analyses emphasize deescalation and conflict management

(Kleidman, 1993; Kriesberg, 1992; Kriesberg & Thorson, 1991; Patchen, 1988; Ziegenhagen & Koutsoukis, 1992).[1]

Few regions of the world remain that have not been touched by some form of ethnic, religious, or racial conflict and violence. The ethnic problems that many thought had been resolved through the processes of assimilation, accommodation, and modernization have rematerialized. Indeed since World War II the intensity of ethnic conflicts and communal violence throughout the world has increased. The first instance of major ethnic conflict took place in 1947 during the partition of the Indian subcontinent between Moslem Pakistan and Hindu India. This was followed by many more ethnic conflicts, including the secession of Biafra from Nigeria; the ongoing struggles involving the Basque separatists in Spain and Eritrean separatists in Ethiopia; the conflict between Roman Catholics and Protestants in Northern Ireland; the conflict between Christians, Moslems, and Jews in Lebanon; and the quest by ethnic Kurds in Turkey, Iraq, Iran, and Syria for autonomy.

What are the roots of ethnic conflict and of ethnicity itself? James McKay (1982) looked at ethnic phenomena from two basic perspectives. First, there is a primordial view that focuses on emotional bonds of solidarity among ethnic groups. Second, there is the "mobilization perspective," which sees ethnic conflict as resulting from a conscious effort on the part of individuals and groups to mobilize around ethnic symbols, such as history, language, traditions, and religion, in order to obtain social, political, and economic advantages, and thus to advance their own ethnic interests. In many respects, the primordial perspective of ethnicity has ignored the dynamics of social, political, and economic change. While most writers see these two approaches as mutually exclusive, McKay argued that both perspectives are involved in most ethnic conflicts.

Most countries are multiethnic, multiracial, multireligious, and multicultural in nature. When diverse ethnic groups interact, and their goals, values, and interests clash with each other, the likelihood of conflict increases. Because of its inherent destabilizing forces, ethnic conflict has political, economic, ideological, and social consequences for a society and polity. It destroys the social bond that is essential for cohesiveness and unity.

In addition, ethnic conflict in one region of the world can create international tensions in others. In some cases, ethnic conflict provokes military intervention by outside powers. Somalia is a case in point. The military war lords and tribal divisions in Somalia contributed to mass starvation in that country. This provoked the United Nations to send troops to Somalia to maintain peace and distribute food. Tensions arose among United Nations member countries concerning their responsibilities and long-term strategies in Somalia. And the loss of U.S. troops there came to affect U.S. domestic politics.

While ethnic conflicts are often used as pretexts for military intervention by one country into another's affairs, they are also used as excuses for irredentist policies. Irredentism is the policy of incorporation of or expansion into a territory that is historically or ethnically related to one political unit but under the political control of another. For example, in 1974 Turkey invaded Cyprus, an independent island republic, under the pretext of a threat to its Turkish Cypriot minority by the Greek Cypriot majority. Turkey invaded the island twice and displaced two hundred thousand Greek Cypriots from their homes, splitting the island in two. In 1983, the Turkish Cypriot Muslim minority, with the support of Turkish troops, declared the northern part of Cyprus an independent state; however, no nation except Turkey recognizes this state.

Ethnic Conflict and Mobilization: A World Perspective

Even a casual observer of world events will notice the extent to which many parts of the world have been touched by ethnic, racial, and religious violence. Those who commit terrorism, assassinations, bombings, "ethnic cleansing," or hijacking usually justify their actions politically or ideologically but underpinning such violent activity is often ethnic, religious, and/or racial animosity. Genocide, the systematic extermination of an entire ethnic group by the state, is an example of an extreme form of violence directed by one ethnic group against another, examples include Turkish attempts to eliminate Armenians and Hitler's efforts to destroy Jews.

It can be argued that no human society or nation can survive if it experiences continuous societal conflict. Not all social conflict, however, is considered dysfunctional. Conflicts can often assist us in identifying some of society's problems, and, as a result, can point to necessary policy changes in our institutions and society. For example, the Civil Rights Movement, the anti–Vietnam war movement, and the Women's Movement brought about many changes in U.S. institutions and in our views about ethnic relations, war, and gender roles.

Ethnic mobilization is the process by which social groups organize around some aspect of ethnic identity, such as religion, race, nationality, language, or region, to pursue some collective goal. Walker Connor (1991) defined ethnic nationalism as subnational movements for autonomy or independence organized along linguistic, religious, or cultural lines. Ethnic nationalism can thus be seen as one form of ethnic mobilization. Other forms include ethnic rights movements, movements for autonomy, interethnic conflict, and civil war (Nagel, 1993:111).

Racial and ethnic conflict and mobilization in the United States can be explained by what political sociologists call order and power-conflict theories. Order theories tend to stress progressive adaptation and assimilation into the dominant Anglo-Saxon model, which emphasizes stability in intergroup relations. Power-conflict theories focus on the outcomes of continuing dominance of minorities by majorities. Functionalism is, more or less, a combination of order and power-conflict theories: functionalists perceive ethnic groups as social subsystems performing many complementary functions for the entire social system. In the functionalist view, ethnic groups gradually lose their identities and merge into the more universal culture by adopting and internalizing the values and norms of the dominant culture.

Another important dimension of ethnic conflict and mobilization is ethnic stratification. By social stratification, sociologists are referring to the ranking of individuals. This rank is based on objective criteria such as income, education, and occupation. The higher one's income, education, and occupation the higher the social status or social standing in the community. Similarly by ethnic stratification, sociologists mean the classification of ethnic groups in terms of categories of people who conceive of themselves as being of a kind, or they are defined by others as being different on the basis of physical, cultural, religious, linguistic, regional, national origins or a combination of these. When the horizontal classification of various ethnic groups is ranked vertically as higher or lower then it becomes ethnic stratification. For example, when color or ethnicity becomes the basis of one's social standing in the society we speak of ethnic stratification. In this way, people perceive certain ethnic groups as higher or lower in social status depending on certain ascriptive criteria such as sex, race, ethnicity, age and so on. We can also speak of sex stratification, race or ethnic stratification, age stratification and so on. For example, one form of ethnic stratification in the United States conforms to the Anglo-Saxon model: any incoming group ultimately has to adopt the dominant cultural and political values. The majority of European immigrants to the United States surrendered most of their ethnic subcultures and adopted the Anglo-Saxon core values over two or three generations. European ethnic groups maintained only some of their in-group ethnic ties, particularly those pertaining to family ties, religion, or what George A. Kourvetaris (1994) has called the "dionysian"[2] or symbolic, aspects of their ethnic subcultures. The majority of these European ethnics strove for equality with the dominant groups by conforming to the dominant values of old-stock Euro-Americans, who came primarily from northwestern Europe. Ethnic conflict was minimized so long as the immigrant groups adopted the dominant values.

One outcome of initial ethnic stratification is a roughly egalitarian inclusion of the ethnic groups in the dominant culture. However, ethnic groups in this pluralist model retain certain cultural and primary group distinctions, including religious, marital, and kinship patterns. This outcome suggests an ideal model in which all ethnic groups are treated equally within a multiculturalist framework and an equalitarian, inclusive culture. While the descendants of ethnic and ethnoreligious groups, mostly from southern, eastern, and central Europe, achieve political and economic equality, and in some instances surpass the dominant Anglo-Saxon groups or old-stock European Americans, they remain symbolically Jewish, Greek, Italian, or Irish (Gans, 1979).

But another outcome of ethnic stratification may be continuing intergroup conflict, such as a persistent subordination of some racial and/or ethnic groups and thus a permanent ethnic stratification. The political, economic, and social inequality between dominant white ethnic groups and nonwhites was so great in the past that it was described by a number of scholars as internal colonialism (Blauner, 1972). In this form of ethnic stratification, the nature of ethnic intergroup relationships is explained in terms of subordinate versus dominant ethnic relations.

Stanley Lieberson (1961) described the situation of ethnic minority populations that results from conquest as "migrant superordination." For example, British and other northwestern European settlers conquered and subordinated Native Americans. However, new immigrants who came to the United States from southern or central Europe or Asia were subordinate to the old-stock European immigrants and their progeny. Here, functionalism and power-conflict theory differ in that the functionalist perspective corresponds to the "migrant subordination" view while the power-conflict perspective fits more with "migrant superordination." But the integrationist and conflict perspectives are not mutually exclusive. There are times when integration can occur only through conflict (Schermerhorn, 1970:57–58).

At the international level, ethnic conflict and mobilization can arise as a result of social and political change or from an identity crisis occurring in the process of historical and political transformation of nations. For instance, symbolic forms of communication, such as rituals, ceremonies, myths, festivities, art, literature, ideologies, parades, and ethnic celebrations, are ways by which an ethnic community or a nation-state organizes the intellectual and emotional activities of its members, reinforces its values, and legitimizes its national identity and international existence. The recognition of the new nation-states of the former Soviet Union and the former Yugoslavia by international organizations such as the United Nations and the European Economic Community are cases in point: All these new emerging nation-states had developed their own symbols of national identity or borrowed symbols such as flags, national anthems, and myths from other cultures or histories. The state of Israel is a perfect example of ethnic symbolism and nation building. Zionism,[3] as a political and cultural secular movement, succeeded in establishing an independent state of Israel in the promised land of biblical Palestine. Palestine was a symbol that the Jews of the diaspora identified with the land of their ancestors.

Interethnic Conflicts and Ethnic Violence Around the World

During the Cold War many violent interethnic conflicts erupted, particularly in the European colonies in Asia and Africa. Some of these conflicts were underwritten by East-West competition for economic and geopolitical advantages. On the other hand, present ethnic conflicts in the former Yugoslavia and the former Soviet Union are rooted in ethnic rivalries that lay dormant during the Cold War.

Three basic forces seem to generate ethnic conflict: ethnic heterogeneity, retribalization of the world, and ethnic diaspora (dispersion). Only a handful of nations are culturally and ethnically homogenous; obviously, ethnic homogeneity affords the opportunity for ethnic conflicts to arise. The collapse of the strong, cross-ethnic Communist regimes in the Soviet Union and Eastern Europe—which suppressed ethnic identification in order to promote ideological identification—has strengthened the forces of ethnic nationalism and ethnic fragmentation, or retribalization. Finally, ethnic diasporas lead to the establishment of ethnic minority groups in countries whose "native" ethnic groups may react negatively. For instance, Rita Jalali and Seymour Martin Lipset (1992–1993:586) have noted that only 16 percent of all Jews live in Israel. Arabs are found in thirty-seven states and Kurds in six. In Europe 40 percent of all Albanians live outside Albania and 23 percent of Hungarians live outside Hungary. These groups have frequently encountered hostility in their new homelands.

Ethnic conflict is likely to increase in the years ahead. Daniel Patrick Moynihan has predicted that in the next fifty years another fifty states will be riddled with ethnic conflict (cited in Djilas, 1993). David Binder and Barbara Crossette (1993) listed forty-eight trouble spots in the world in which the major players are tribes or ethnic groups. As of December 1994, the United Nations had peacekeeping forces in 17 countries to prevent domestic insurrection and civil strife (United Nations, Public Information Bulletin, 1996:7).

The resurgence of ethnic nationalism has been facilitated by a number of factors and developments, including (1) democratization, (2) concern for human rights, (3) desire for self-determination (for ethnic minorities), (4) modernization and development, and (5) the emergence of regional powers. One can argue that the trend toward democratization in recent years has contributed to the reemergence of ethnic nationalism in a number of countries. Democratization demands that ethnic minorities be free to express themselves both politically and economically. Violation of the human rights of ethnic minorities by ethnic majorities also fosters separatist ethnic movements. For example, the Kurds, one of the largest Middle Eastern ethnic groups, have struggled for years for their own separate state. Primarily because of this, their basic human rights have been denied both by Turkey and by Iraq, which in turn has strengthened their commitment to separation.

Self-determination, which was affirmed after World War I by the League of Nations and later by the United Nations, means that every nationality or ethnic group has the right to pursue its own destiny and independence. However, self-determination has lost its original democratic meaning, that there should be political equality among individuals irrespective of their ethnic, religious, or social status. It has instead increasingly become a political and ideological weapon for the gain of power advantages of one ethnic group over another; the establishment of such gain is commonly known as ethnocracy. Most secessionist movements justify themselves by referring to the principle of self-determination (Premdas et al., 1990).

The fourth factor that fosters ethnic consciousness and nationalism is modernization. Jalali and Lipset (1992–1993), Joane Nagel (1993), and Susan Olzak (1983) argued persuasively that modernization increases levels of competition for jobs and housing among ethnic groups. This increased ethnic competition exacerbates ethnic conflicts and social movements based on ethnic boundaries. The literature on the economic basis of ethnic nationalism lends support to this economic competition thesis of ethnic mobilization.

Finally, the emergence of regional powers can reinforce ethnic nationalism.

Ethnic Nationalism

Ethnic nationalism has become part of the political landscape not only in many Third World countries, but also in many western European industrialized countries. To understand the causes of interethnic conflict and polarization within various multiethnic and multiracial societies, we must look not only at the "nationalist-subnationalist dialectic," but also at the role of supranational forces such as historical colonialism, multinationalism, modern militarism, and arms sales. While a state is a legal or territorial entity, a nation is a sociological, or social group, entity. When nations or social groups in a state develop a "sense of peoplehood" or "consciousness of kind" as distinct ethnic groups, they become "ethnicized" (Premdas et al., 1990:16). Thus, ethnicity and nationalism are interrelated phenomena.

In many places, ethnic nationalism has at various times been kept in check by the rival ideologies of Communism and capitalism. Communism discourages ethnic diversity and ethnic nationalism. Instead, it stresses class consciousness and transnational proletarian rule. Capitalism, on the other hand, while it allows ethnic diversity, especially in terms of religion, does not always favor ethnic nationalism if it endangers a capitalist nation's economic and geopolitical interests. In fact, most peoples of Africa, Asia, and other regions of the world have had to struggle against the capitalist-colonialist powers for their independence.

Before ethnic nationalist movements become secessionist movements, they usually develop five major characteristics, according to Ralph R. Premdas and colleagues (1990:14–16): (1) *An organized struggle.* This means that any ethnic group within a multiethnic nation state whose members share primordial ethnic ties organizes, mobilizes, and struggles for territorial autonomy and independence. (2) *Territorial self-government.* For example, an ethnic group participating in a secessionist movement seeks a territorial base that it calls its "homeland," as the Palestinians in the West Bank and Gaza Strip in Israel have. (3) *Primordial and secondary factors.* Primordial ties are "mythical claims" of ethnic identity and "ethnic consciousness," which may lack historical objectivity and authenticity. Secondary claims may include feelings of discrimination or oppression on the part of minorities who pursue territorial self-government. These two factors are believed to facilitate ethnic identification with a secessionist movement. (4) *The doctrine of self-determination.* Self-determination is the idea that every nation has a God-given, natural right to pursue its own destiny through self-rule and independence. (5) *International recognition.* Recognition by other nations is essential for the success and legitimacy of a secessionist movement.

Nagel (1993: 103–11) identified two major types of "ethnic nationalism"—historical ethnic nationalism, or anticolonialism, and ethnic subnationalism, or secessionist movements. The first wave of ethnic nationalism, also known as decolonization, can be traced to various indigenous ethnic groups in Asian and African countries organizing against the western European colonial powers. The colonial powers carved out many "artificial states" without regard to ethnic demography; these borders fractured many indigenous nations and forced separate ethnic groups into uncomfortable proximity. The first, ethnic secessionist movements aimed to remove the colonizers and were designated by the colonial powers as Indian nationalism, Ghanian nationalism, Nigerian nationalism, and so on. Ted R. Gurr views the second, ethnic subnationalist movements as "peoples against states." Many of these movements stem from the imposition of the arbitrary colonial borders. According to Gurr (1994: 350), "all but five of the twenty-three wars being fought in 1994 [were] based on communal rivalries and ethnic challenges to states."

Subnationalist ethnic movements have sometimes been more violent than the first ethnic secessionist movements. For instance, the Tamil separatist movement in Sri Lanka has been going on for years. In the Philippines, the minority Muslim Moros want to gain independence from the dominant, Roman Catholic Filipinos. And the southern Sudanese have rebelled against the northern Sudanese (the cleavage in Sudan is based on both religion and class).

An Analysis of Ethnic Subnationalism in the Former Yugoslavia

The resurgence of ethnic nationalism in the former Soviet republics and former Yugoslavia are among the most severe expressions of ethnic subnationalism (Vujacic & Zaslavsky, 1991:121; Sekulic et al., 1994). In the Soviet Union, Marxism and ethnic nationalism were seen as ideologically incompatible. Although the Bolsheviks, including Lenin himself, and Marxists in general saw the political potential of ethnic nationalism in the Soviet Union and elsewhere, the nationality policy of the Soviets was predicated on the assumption of the transitory nature of nationalism (Vujacic & Zaslavsky, 1991:121). Prior to the Bolshevik revolution of 1917, the Bolsheviks did not spell out a clear nationality policy or the rights of various nationalities to self-determination. Nationality policy, however, became one of the major components of their political strategy.

The successful manipulation of various ethnic minorities helped to insure the Bolsheviks' victory in the 1917–1921 civil war (Vujacic & Zaslavsky, 1991:121). This manipulation was influenced by Stalin's definition of the concept of nation, which linked language, culture, ethnicity, territory, and political administration. The Soviet Union was the first modern state to accept the nationality principle as the basis of its federal structure (Vujacic & Zaslavsky, 1991:122): the Soviet Union was seen as a collection of sovereign nation-states controlled by a strong center. The purpose of Soviet federalism was to accommodate various nationalities within an all-Soviet framework, giving each Soviet republic a role in the centralized Communist party, state administration, cadre selection, and central planning. All Soviet republics had similar bureaucratic and educational structures, and this "structural isomorphism" appealed to ethnic middle classes. Despite structural isomorphism, however, preferential treatment of nationalities was a Soviet policy of ethnic stratification. The Soviet quota system favored indigenous populations and ethnic groups having developed senses of nationhood. Indeed, the Russians, the largest ethnic and religious group (Russian Orthodox), were dominant in the former Soviet republics.

Yugoslavia, originally a Soviet client state, was also a multiethnic and multireligious society. As Russians were dominant in the Soviet Union, the Serbs were—and still are—the dominant ethnic group in Yugoslavia. The success of the partisans led by the Communist Josip Tito in repelling the Nazis during World War II appealed to many ethnic minorities, who were promised national self-determination after the war (Burks, 1961). Indeed, the Communists promised to put an end to prewar "greater Serbian hegemony." Centralism and the state along the Soviet model were to be recognized. Thus the 1946 Yugoslav constitution, based on the 1936 Stalinist institutionalization of federalism, divided the country into six republics, one autonomous province (Vojvodina, the northern autonomous province of Serbia), and one autonomous region (Kosovo). Both of these autonomous subunits were located within Serbia, the largest republic, and were designed to contain centralist Serbian aspirations. At least one republic, Bosnia-Herzegovina, was created as a compromise between Serbs and Croats—the two largest ethnic groups—because it did not have a clear titular nationality. Yugoslav republics were thus designed as "homelands" for the indigenous nationalities residing within them.

Tito's charismatic and authoritarian personality and the centralized structure of the Communist party created what seemed to be a nation-state. However, Yugoslavia was a federation of ethnic and religious groups rather than a democracy built on people's identification as Yugoslavian citizens. By maintaining their distinct identities, the ethnic and religious federal units failed to develop a common, core, universalistic Yugoslav identity that could transcend ethnic and religious particularities. Using survey data from 1985 and 1989, just prior to Yugoslavia's collapse into ethnic hostility, Dusko Seculic and colleagues (1994:83) found that those having urban backgrounds, the young, those of mixed parentage, Communist Party members, and those from minority nationalities were more likely to espouse a common Yugoslav identity. This identity, however, was not strong enough to stop the rising tide of ethnic nationalism.

Following the demise of the Soviet Union and the collapse of Soviet-dominated Eastern European regimes, Yugoslavia disintegrated. Within a short period, four of the six Yugoslav federal units demanded complete national independence and sovereignty: Slovenia, Croatia, Macedonia,[4] and Bosnia-Herzegovina. The other two, Serbia and Montenegro, formed a federation and called themselves Yugoslavia. In addition, the Albanian ethnic minority (about one million in 1991) is concentrated in Kosovo, an autonomous province in Serbian territory. Kosovo also seeks independence, but Serbia currently refuses to accept this.

The disintegration of Yugoslavia appears to be the result of certain weaknesses it shared with the Soviet Union—the failure of modernization and restructuring of the economy, the problem of redistribution of social and political power, the rise of ethnic subnationalism, and the failure of nationality policies in socialist-type societies (Sekelj, 1993; Sekulic et al., 1994; Vujacik & Zaslavskey, 1991). The roots of the crisis can be traced back to 1945–1946 and the Sovietization of Yugoslav society (Sekelj, 1993:2). Yugoslavia was the first European country to establish a dictatorship of the proletariat along the Soviet-Stalinist model. Due to Yugoslavia's anti-fascist struggle during the war and the achievements of its Communist Party, there was no Soviet push for intervention in its internal affairs. Initially, the Communist Party elite established an equalitarian society and enjoyed broad popular support. However, starting in 1948, the Yugoslav leadership, through its party-state organ, forced collectivization and nationalization of the economy. It eliminated the last remnants of bourgeois society and established a Stalinist order (Sekelj, 1993:3).

Yugoslavism and socialism gave way to both ethnic nationalism and ethnic mobilization. The anti-Yugoslav demonstrations by ethnic Albanians in Kosovo in 1968 and 1980 and later the waves of political ethnic nationalism in Slovenia and Croatia reflected more than casual grievances. These disturbances were the manifestation of deep-rooted historical ethnic cleavages which socialism and Yugoslavism had failed to heal. Indeed, the constitution of 1974 recognized neither the concept of Yugoslav citizenship nor the Yugoslav political community. The only recognized entities in Yugoslavia were the separate ethnic nationalities that occupied different territories. For instance, an ethnic Albanian living in Kosovo developed a distinct ethnic identity but had no psychological and historical ties with Yugoslavia as a federal state. Ethnic Albanians living in Yugoslavia are not integrated into the Yugoslav society. Federalism failed to function under the Communist system in either Yugoslavia or the Soviet Union because it lacked the principles of liberal political and economic democracy. Instead of a common political national identity, a creed based on citizenship, and a common constitution, Yugoslavia and the Soviet Union were organized around ethnicity, religion, and language—a recipe for ethnic tribalism and militant ethnic nationalism.

In a sense, ethnic mobilization and primordial nationalisms replaced collectivism in post-Communist Yugoslavia and in the former Soviet Union. Thus Serbs, Croats, Slovenians, and Bosnians became strangers and enemies in their own state. While during the summer and fall of 1990 the Yugoslav Social Science Institute reported that 61 percent of a representative sample of persons all over Yugoslavia were against the creation of independent national states, by 1993 only 5 percent of the population identified themselves as Yugoslavians (Sekelj, 1993:277). This revealed how shallow and volatile Yugoslavism and socialism as forms of collective identity were. (See Table 12.1.)

Despite the diverse ethnic composition of a federation, for such a multinational liberal federal state to function, it must be based on the same liberal principles as are nation-states. These include economic integration with a unified market, protection of individual and collective human rights, a common defense and foreign policy, and a balance of power between federalism and constituent federal units. The multinational state and its constitution should not be based on nationality, religion, race, or a combination of these but on political and legal principles of citizenship similar to

Table 12.1   Percentages of Adult Population of Yugoslavia Identifying Themselves as Yugoslavs in Yugoslavia and within Each Republic and Province: 1961, 1971, and 1981

| | Percentage Identifying as Yugoslav | | | |
Geographic Area	1961	1971	1981	Predominant Nationality in 1981
All of Yugoslavia	1.7	1.3	5.4	36.3% Serbian
Republics and Provinces				
Croatia	.4	1.9	8.2	75.1% Croatian
Serbia	.2	1.4	4.8	85.4% Serbian
Bosnia/Herzegovina	8.4	1.2	7.9	39.5% Moslem
Kosovo	.5	.1	.1	77.4% Albanian
Macedonia	.1	.2	.7	67.0% Macedonian
Montenegro	.3	2.1	5.3	68.3% Montenegro
Slovenia	.2	.4	1.4	90.5% Slovenian
Vojvodina	.2	2.4	8.2	54.3% Serbian

Source: Dusko Sekulic et al., "Who Were the Yugoslavs?" (1994:85); adapted and reprinted by permission from the *American Sociological Review.*

those of the United States. The absence of a representative democracy and the resurgence of ethnocracies in its place made civil war in the former Yugoslavia inevitable. The Yugoslav crisis had its roots in the structural failure of the Communist nationality policy and the collapse of state Communism in general. The linkage between territory, language, administration, and ethnicity and the overlap between regional, economic, and ethnic interests resulted in ethnic mobilization for political and economic advantages (Vujacic & Zaslavsky, 1991:137).

Finally, interethnic conflicts and historical cleavages led to ethnic homogenization in the republics of Yugoslavia by means of "ethnic cleansing" and transfers. According to Veljko Vujacic and Victor Zaslasvsky (1991:138), Yugoslavia exemplified the inherent difficulties associated with the simultaneous pursuit of marketization and democratization of multinational Soviet-type societies. These two processes, in this type of society, are somewhat incompatible, for while marketization exacerbates tensions between more and less developed regions, democratization leads the way to self-determination for nationalist parties pursuing separatist goals. In such a state of affairs the superimposition of economic, ethnic, and political conflicts favors the disintegration of the state. State socialism and authoritarian rule, whether by the left or the right, have not been viable alternatives to liberal democracy and market capitalism.

Are ethnonationalism, ethnic identity, and belonging always undesirable? Both negative and positive consequences seem to result from such concepts. Louis Kriesberg and his colleagues (1992:43) listed three negative aspects of ethnonationalism: parochialism, oppression, and violence. *Parochialism* refers to members of the same ethnic or racial group or collectivity who look primarily at the interests of its own collectivity. This inward or intraethnic concern quite often hampers large-scale cooperation in society. Oppression is cruel treatment of one group by another, taking such forms as slavery, imperialism, institutional racism, discrimination, exploitation, and domination. Finally, the most brutal consequence of ethnic nationalism is physical violence committed by one group against another, which includes genocide, pogroms, and massacres. Rwanda, Bosnia, and Lebanon are only a few recent examples showing that oppression and violence occur jointly. The perceived virtues of one group or in-group and the perceived vices of the out-group seem to justify for some dehumanization, oppression, and violence.

Although the negative aspects of ethnic identity are the most salient, positive aspects do exist. Ethnic identity gives an individual a sense of belonging to a larger entity. In a real sense, we are all members of various groups based on attributes such as ethnicity, religion, race, gender, and class. These social distinctions in themselves are not necessarily problematic. Problems and conflicts arise when one collectivity dominates and oppresses another collectivity because of its difference.

Another positive aspect of ethnocultural diversity, or multiculturalism, is that it is compatible with the ideas and values of liberalism and market capitalism. Ethnic diversity has survival value, and ethnocultures can provide solutions to our problems. Because ethnonationalism also has a progressive quality, it facilitates popular participation and contributes to democratization and ethnic mobilization for genuine and constructive social change.

Summary and Conclusion

Historically the study of social conflict was traced in the writings of some classical and modern social and political theorists (including Thucidides, Machiavelli, Hobbes, Marx, Simmel, Sumner, Small and others). Since the 1960s the conflict perspective has become the dominant paradigm in sociology. Political sociologists draw from both the Marxist and non-Marxist traditions of social conflict. The escalation of conflict in many parts of the world was due in part to the reemergence of ethnic nationalism

Since World War II, the intensity of ethnic conflicts and communal violence have increased. Many more social scientists thought that ethnic conflicts could be resolved through the processes of assimilation and modernization, which did not happen. There are two basic perspectives dealing with ethnic phenomena and ethnic conflict. One, there is a primordial view that focuses on emotional bonds of solidarity among diverse ethnic groups and two, there is the ethnic mobilization perspective. The latter sees ethnic conflict as resulting from a conscious effort on the part of ethnic groups to mobilize around ethnic symbols in order to obtain social, political, and economic advantages. Both perspectives are involved in most ethnic conflict.

The ethnic conflict and mobilization were treated both historically and in contemporary terms. Ethnic nationalism, along with ethnic stratification were also analyzed as aspects of ethnic conflict and ethnic mobilization. In the United States ethnic conflict is explained in terms of ethnic stratification and intergroup dominant (white) versus subordinate (non-white) intergroup relations. At the international level ethnic conflict and mobilization arise as a result of social and political change. The re-emergence of ethnic nationalism and ethnic conflict have been facilitated by a number of developments including—democratization, modernization, the desire for self-determination, the rise of regional powers, and concern for human rights.

The nature of ethnic nationalism was examined both historically, in terms of nationalist movements of national independence from colonialism at the end of World War II, and as secessionist movements after independence and in more modern times. The factors contributing to secessionist movements were also discussed including factors such as an organized struggle, territorial self-government, primordial attachment, self-determination, and international factors. Finally, an in depth analysis of the ethnic subnationalism (secessionist) movement in former Yugoslavia was discussed with references to the former Soviet Union. In order to understand the disintegration of former Yugoslavia one has to look at the multi-ethnic and multi-religious nature of former Yugoslavia as well as the historical, political, economic, and cultural aspects of the Balkans in general.

Endnotes

1. A useful, annotated historical bibliography on conflict and conflict resolution is Porter (1982).

2. Kourvetaris has proposed a distinction between dionysian and appollonian aspects of ethnic subcultures. By dionysian he means the more external or symbolic aspects of ethnic subculture pertaining to such things as food, dance, religious rituals, and ethnic parades; he takes the term from

Dionysus, the god of ecstasy, emotional festivities, and good times in Greek mythology. The apollonian aspects (after Apollo, the god of sobriety, rationality, music, harmony, and symmetry) are the more esoteric or internal and substantive aspects of ethnic subculture, such as spirituality, literature, and ethnic and religious identity (ethnic nationalism).

3. Zionism is a nationalist, political, cultural ideology and movement initiated by Jews of the diaspora for the establishment of a Jewish state in Palestine. It started around 1896 and its main goal was to urge Jews from other countries to go back to what is now known as Israel. Israel became a country in 1947. Palestine was divided among Jews and Palestinian Arabs, but during the Arab-Israel wars, Israel captured most of Palestine and still occupies it. The cause of the conflict between Arabs and Jews is who controls the land. The Jews used the biblical argument to claim the territory of Palestine now called Israel. After so many wars between Israel and its Arab neighbors, Israel has signed peace treaties with Egypt, Jordan, and now negotiates a peace treaty with Syria. The Palestinians have negotiated peace with Israel and they gained self-rule in West-Bank and Gaza Strip, the predominantly Palestinian settlements.

4. Although it accepts the independence of the former Yugoslav republic, Greece objects vehemently to the use of the name Macedonia because it fears future territorial claims on Greek Macedonia, the northern province of Greece. International recognition of Macedonia awaits a compromise on this issue.

References

Binder, David, and Barbara Crossette. 1993. "As Ethnic Wars Multiply, U.S. Strives for a Policy." *New York Times.* (February 7):

Blauner, Robert. 1972. *Racial Oppression in America.* New York: Harper and Row.

Burks, R. V. 1961. *The Dynamics of Communism in Eastern Europe.* Princeton: Princeton University Press.

Collins, Randal. 1975. *Conflict Sociology.* New York: Academic Press.

Connor, Walker. 1991. "What Is a Nation?" *Ethnic and Racial Studies.* Vol. 13 (January):92–103.

Dahrendorf, Ralf. 1959. *Class and Class Conflict in Industrial Society.* New York: The Free Press.

Djilas, Aleksa. 1993. "A Review Essay in the Ending of Yugoslavia." *New Republic.* Vol. 208 No. 4 (January 25): 38.

Gans, Herbert J. 1979. "Symbolic Ethnicity: The Future of Ethnic Groups and Cultures." In *On the Making of Americans,* ed. Herbert Gans, University of Pennsylvania Press.

Gurr, Ted R. 1994. "Peoples against States: Ethnopolitical Conflict and the Changing World System." *International Studies Quarterly.* Vol. 38: 347–377.

Jalali, Rita, and Seymour M. Lipset. 1992–1993. "Racial and Ethnic Conflicts: A Global Perspective." *Political Science Quarterly.* Vol. 107, no. 4:588–606.

Kleidman, Robert. 1993. *Organizing for Peace: Neutrality, the Test Ban, and the Freeze.* Syracuse: Syracuse University Press.

Kourvetaris, George A. 1994. "The Apollonian and Dionysian Dimensions of Ethnicity: A Convergence Model." Paper presented at the Illinois Sociological Association, Peoria, Illinois (April).

Kriesberg, Louis. 1992. *International Conflict Resolution.* New Haven: Yale University Press.

Kriesberg, Louis, Terrell A. Northru, and Stuart J. Thorson, eds. 1989. *Intractable Conflicts and Their Transformation.* Syracuse: Syracuse University Press.

Kriesberg, Louis, and Stuart J. Thorson, eds. 1991. *Timing the De-escalation of International Conflicts.* Syracuse: Syracuse University Press.

Lieberson, Stanley. 1961. "A Societal Theory of Race and Ethnic Relations." *American Sociological Review* Vol. 26 (December):902–20.

Mach, Zdzislaw. 1993. *Symbols, Conflict and Identity.* New York: State University of New York Press.

McKay, James. 1982. "An Exploratory Synthesis of Primordial and Mobilization Approaches of Ethnic Phenomena." *Ethnic and Racial Studies.* Vol. 5, no. 4:395–420.

Nagel, Joane. 1993. "Ethnic Nationalisms: Politics, Ideology, and the World Order." *International*

Journal of Comparative Sociology. Vol. 34, nos. 1–2:103–112.

Olzak, Susan, 1983. "Contemporary Ethnic Mobilization." *Annual Review of Sociology* Vol. 9: 355–374.

Patchen, Martin. 1988. *Resolving Disputes Between Nations: Coercion or Conciliation.* Durham: Duke University Press.

Porter, Jack Nusan. 1982. *Conflict and Conflict Resolution.* New York: Garland.

Premdas, Ralph R., S. W. R. de A. Samarasinghe, and Alan B. Anderson. 1990. *Secessionist Movements in Comparative Perspective.* New York: St. Martin's.

Schermerhorn, R. A. 1970. *Comparative Ethnic Relations.* New York: Random House.

Sekelj, Laslo. 1993. *Yugoslavia: The Process of Disintegration,* Vera Vukelic (trans.). Highland Lakes, NJ. District of Columbia University Press.

Sekulic, Dusko, Garth Massey, and Randy Hodson. 1994."Who Were the Yugoslavs? Failed Sources of a Common Identity in the Former Yugoslavia." *American Sociological Review* Vol. 59, no. 1:83–97.

United Nations 1996 "Peace-Keeping: Answers at Your Fingertips." p. 7 New York: United Nations.

Vujacic, Veljko, and Victor Zaslavsky. 1991. "The Causes of Disintegration in the USSR and Yugoslavia." *Telos.* No. 88: (Summer): 120–140.

Ziegenhagen, Edward A., and Kleomenis S. Koutsoukis. 1992. *Political Conflict in Southern Europe.* Westport Conn.: Praeger.

C h a p t e r **13**

Politics and Society in the Post–Cold War Era

Despite the euphoria ushered in by the end of the Cold War, the closing decade of the twentieth century has witnessed an assortment of hostilities between nation-states. With the end of the Cold War, what is the emerging structure of the international system? Is there a new world order, and, if so, how can we conceptualize it? Who are the major players in the new international system? What is the role of the United States in such a system? What are some possible scenarios in the post–Cold War era?

The International System of Nation-States

An international system of sovereign states is epitomized by the United Nations organization, which was founded at the end of World War II to promote world peace. System implies an organization of or interdependence between political units or states that recognize each other as independent nations. Nation-states, existing in an international environment, seek recognition and legitimation from other nation-states or from organizations of nation-states, such as the United Nations (UN) and the European Economic Community (EEC). Like individuals and groups, nation-states compete for resources and power such as land, influence, knowledge, and technology. Sometimes one nation-state tries to take advantage of another by means of war or the threat of war. Questions such as what is the nature of the nation state in global politics and how does a nation-state behave vis-à-vis other nation-states are especially important today.

Due to the proliferation of states in the world, a number of analysts, like Hedley Bull (1977), view the international system of states as anarchic. In an anarchic or chaotic society, the rule of law breaks down, and those in charge are incapable of maintaining order, engendering a normlessness that allows individuals or groups to take the law into their own hands. In an international system of sovereign nation-states, no higher form of government than the nation-state itself exists. It is thus possible that stronger nations may dominate weaker ones. Is it possible to maintain order and justice in the absence of a world government?

Most theories concerning nation-states in international politics use a political economy or a neo-Marxist global perspective and present nation-states as economic, political, military, and ideological units competing among themselves in world politics. R.W. Cox, for example, viewed nations as historically constructed and continually reconstructed entities maintaining both global and domestic social, political, economic, and ideological relations:

> *The world can be represented as a pattern of interacting social forces in which states play an intermediate though autonomous role between the global structure of social forces and local configurations of social forces within particular countries. This may be called a political economy perspective of the world: power is seen as emerging from social processes rather than taken as given in the form of accumulated material capabilities, that is as the result of these processes. (Cox, 1981:194)*

Similarly, Mark E. Rupert (1990:431) viewed states as processes of historical construction linking institutional state building, capital accumulation, class formation, conflict, interstate competition, and warfare.[1] In other words, states are historical constructs that emerge out of institutional differentiation and nation building. This means that economic, political, and military resources and capabilities facilitate the process of state formation.

Another non-Marxist interpretation of nation-states was offered by Harry Redner (1990:648–650), who distinguished between five types of modern nation-states: autonomous, community, client, satellite, and independent states. Redner wrote that *autonomous states* are those that internally and externally command resources and possess the capability to stand on their own. With the demise of the Soviet Union, the only remaining nation-state that qualifies for autonomous status is the United States. While China and India are the largest nations, they lack the economic, technological, and organizational resources needed to be autonomous, modern nation-states. Neither can Japan be regarded as a fully autonomous state because of its reliance on foreign markets, its lack of resources, and its military dependence on the United States. Competing with these fully or partially autonomous states are a number of *community states* which, because independent nation-states act in concert with one another, can become autonomous and economically powerful. At present there are two such communities—the EEC and the Association of Southeast Asian Nations (ASEAN). In the future we may see more such potentially autonomous community states.

Client states are those that depend both economically and militarily on other more powerful states. Israel, for example, greatly depends on the United States for both military and economic aid. In fact, Israel is the largest recipient of U.S. economic and military assistance. States under the military control of other states are defined as *satellite states*. All the Eastern European countries of the Warsaw Pact could be characterized as satellite states before the demise of state socialism. Finally, there is a residual category of nation-states which are *independent* or neutral, such as Sweden and Switzerland.

It must be kept in mind that these five types of modern states are not mutually exclusive. One state can be independent in some respects, a client in others, and a potential or actual member of a state community. Redner (1990:659) applied three internal criteria derived from a Marxian and Weberian model of the state— (1) expropriation of power (the action of the state taking or modifying the property rights of an individual); (2) monopoly of the means of violence; (3) legitimacy, or rational-legal, authority—to the five types of state discussed above. He argued that the United States as an autonomous nation-state has high levels of expropriation and militarization and a low level of need for legitimacy. He also argued that the Soviet Union had a high level of expropriation, militarization, and need for legitimacy; that Japan has a high level of expropriation but low levels of militarization and need for legitimacy; that China has a high level of expropriation, a middle level of militarization, and a high level of need for legitimacy; and that India has many diverse kinds of expropriation, a middle level of militarization, and a high level of need for legitimacy. Indeed, the world system, which is of late synonymous with the capitalist system, is highly intertwined with property rights or forms of economic power, organized forms of violence (which are embodied in its military establishment), and the need for political legitimation.

Perspectives and Visions of the New International System

Since the end of the Cold War, we have been witnessing a debate among academicians, mass media specialists, and foreign-policy makers concerning the nature and structure of the emerging new world order and international politics. A number of social scientists and political sociologists (Cosgrove, 1992; Mearsheimer, 1992; Nye, 1992) have proposed new visions of a new world order, while another group of researchers (Headley, 1991; Hudson, 1992; Kourvetaris, 1991 MacEwan, 1991; Sanders, 1991) have advanced scenarios critical of the unipolar model of the new world order. Joseph S. Nye (1992) foresees five different versions of a new world order: return to bipolarity, multipolar, economic blocks, unipolar (or *Pax Americana*), and multilevel interdependence. According to Nye, a return to bipolarity will happen if democratization and market reforms in the former Soviet Union republics and in the rest of the socialist societies fail (he thinks this is unlikely) and if the countries move toward the right or toward supernationalism. The sizable vote for the supernationalist Vladimir Zhirinovsky, indicative of an anti-reform and anti-Yeltsin movement in Russia, gave some weight to some analysts' views that Russia may shift to the right.

The multipolar model refers to a world order in which no one country or group of countries will dominate world politics. The economic blocks model refers to groups of nations that join together as economic partners, such as EEC and the United States, Canada, and Mexico, which signed the North American Free Trade Agreement (NAFTA). The unipolar, or *Pax Americana*, model refers to the dominance of the United States, which is now the only country enjoying superpower status. The multilevel interdependence model refers to cooperation among different nations on different levels or in different spheres, including the economic, political, cultural, military, and technological spheres.

In support of the multipolar vision, Jeremy Brecher et al. (1993) argued that global corporations and multinationals are using international institutions such as the General Agreement on Tariffs and Trade (GATT), the World Bank, and the International Monetary Fund and agreements such as NAFTA to create a new, highly centralized and authoritarian governing structure for the global economy. In such a global, highly competitive economy, economically weak nations will be unable to compete. As a result, the core nations will dominate those nations in the periphery and semiperiphery.

B.S. Chimni (1993) outlined four major perspectives on international law and world order: the realist approach advanced by Hans Morgenthau, the McDougal-Laswell approach, the Richard Falk transdisciplinary jurisprudence approach, and the Marxist approach. The realist approach, which we discussed in Chapter 1, pays more attention to the structure and function of international politics. Realists believe that nations pursue their own national interests, which are defined in terms of power. Morgenthau defined the realist model as a "struggle for power." In his words, "whatever the ultimate aims of international politics, power is always the immediate aim" (Morgenthau, 1985:31).

However, some classical realists, such as A.F.K. Organski and Jacek Kugler (1978) think that balance of power among states is more likely to lead to war and anarchy. In their view, order is more likely to be maintained if one state is the strongest. In this type of international system the strongest nation is less likely to be challenged by less powerful states (Nye, 1992:4). Organski and Kugler's model fits the present international system in which the United States is the only military superpower. However, order and power do not always bring peace and stability. Order is a necessary condition for peace, but is not sufficient alone; other essential components are justice, international law, and fairness.

The chief criticism of the realist view of international politics is that it takes on a form of Machiavellian statecraft in which the stronger nation dominates the weaker one by any means necessary. Their critics argue that realists do not always recognize the diversity of national interests and social structures of states and societies. It has been argued that realists often have little respect for legal and moral norms for resolving conflicts among nations (Chimni, 1993: 40, 47, 55, 61). For realists, international law and international morality are useless unless backed up by strong military power. For Myres McDougal (1960), however, law was of paramount importance in the international legal system of rules through which some actions are allowed while others are not (Chimni, 1993:83). Law is important not only in the international system of states but within states, as well. The realist approach to international politics is a rather simplistic and monocausal view of an everchanging and complex international system of states and societies.

The McDougal-Laswell model is basically a policy-oriented approach, interdisciplinary in nature, and comprehensive in scope. McDougal criticized the realist approach for failing to understand the role law plays in international power relations in maintaining the values of a free, peaceful, and abundant world society (Chimni, 1993:142). McDougal's conception of law was aptly stated by W.L. Morrison (1976:3–78):

> *Law is conceived as a social process of authoritative and controlling decision.... Social Process refers to interactions among participants in a context which maintain relatively stable, but not necessarily formally organized, patterns of value shaping and sharing. Decisions are taken to be commitments attended by threats of severe deprivation or extremely high indulgence. These are said to be authoritative when they are, in a stipulated degree, in accordance with community expectation about who is to make them, about the criteria in accordance with which they should be made, and about the situations in which, and the procedures by which, they are to be made. They are said to be controlling when the outcome sought is in fact realized to a significant degree.*

In addition, McDougal saw law as a "dynamic social process" linked to community values and human dignity. In his view there is a relationship between law and policy. As facts and social contexts change, so do policies. He favored the contextual approach (taking circumstances, significant objectives, values, and strategies into account) in interpreting the law and was against rigidity and formalism (Chimni, 1993:82). McDougal spelled out five ingredients of a policy-oriented model of jurisprudence: "These are: clarification of goal values, the description of past trends in decision, the analysis of conditions affecting decision, the projection of future trends in decision, the invention and evaluation of policy alternatives" (Chimni, 1993:119). This means that decisions and policies must be viewed within a social context and not within a vacuum.

A third approach in the field of international law and politics is what Richard A. Falk (1970: 41–60) referred to as the "intermediate view of legal theory" in international society. His middle-of-the-road approach ought to promote "a simultaneous need for '*minimum stability*' among sovereign states and a '*minimum social change*' between the more advantaged and less disadvantaged societies and polities." Falk has been associated with the World Order Models Project (WOMP). WOMP is a part of world order studies representing a non-Marxist, interdisciplinary, and prescriptive or normative policy approach to international politics.

Since its inception in the 1970s, WOMP[2] has produced more than six volumes dealing with preferred worlds for the 1990s, while another series of WOMP's studies deals with a just world order theme. These latter studies examine the way things should be on the world stage instead of the way things are at various stages. WOMP has stressed law and institution building, preferred worlds or diverse images of world order, and the struggle of the oppressed (Kim, 1984:83–86). The major thrust of WOMP studies is to transform the structure of international relations by diminishing the role of sovereign states (Falk, 1982:160), which, in reality, is not happening. Briefly, WOMP has raised four major issues: war systems or militarism, overpopulation, depletion of the earth's resources, and ecological concerns. According to Falk, state systems have failed to address these global problems because each state pursues its own selfish national interests.

S. Mendlovitz (1981), a law professor and director of WOMP studies, wrote about the long range goals of WOMP: "We set out to do normative social research that was at one and the same time oriented to the future, interdisciplinary, and focused on the design of social change actions, policies, and institutions." With its architectonic, globalist, and future-oriented conception and design, the WOMP study group wants to change the present course of nation-states competing for power and advantage in the international system. In addition, WOMP offers a holistic and interdisciplinary view of the world, emphasizing national interest and the state system and based primarily on universal values and principles of peace, economic welfare, social justice, and ecological balance. According to Christine Sylvester (1981:104), WOMP's mission is

> *a) To combine a theory of populist struggle with a vision of world order and expression with concerns of oppressed peoples. b) To redefine security as a human need and develop a campaign against all forms of militarism worldwide. c) To review cultural foundations of political and moral order so as to understand emerging global society and guide it toward humanistic ends. d) To develop a methodology of individual learning based on thinking, feeling, and acting as a global citizen. e) To explore the notion of governance in order to redirect world order inquiry away from the formal constitutional thrust of the Preferred Worlds series toward concern for humane governance. f) To engage in more penetrating analysis of interrelations between global and local politics. g) To reexamine world authority as a vehicle for coordinating complexity.*

An alternative strategy of transition to a just future world order is the idea of the central guidance system suggested by Falk (1975: 226). Here, an element of utopianism surfaces in Falk's blueprint, for it postulated a relationship between the political-legal superstructure and its constituent sociological elements on the one hand and rules and policies on the other. Falk did not clearly spell out these elements, although he referred to them collectively as a "Grotian[3] quest for a just world order." Despite its shortcomings, however, this new paradigm for international legal order is relevant to the emerging interdependent world in which "common good" is stressed over "national interest." It views the transitional spirit of the age in terms of legal principles, international law, order, and justice. Yet, WOMP predictions and normative analysis have not been vindicated: the reemergence of nationalism has meant that the role of the state system has increased rather than decreased.

The Marxist approach to international relations is an economic theory of imperialism which is the basis of all Marxist thought. According to this theory all political phenomena and power relations are the reflection of economic forces. Lenin and his followers defined imperialism as an advance stage of capitalism (quoted in Hans J. Morgenthau, 1985: 61–62). In general, extreme Marxists equate capitalism and imperialism (Morgenthau, 1985: 63). Another view of international politics is known as the liberal or neoliberal perspective. According to this view, order comes not from the distribution or balance of power in the international system but from the fostering of pluralistic values and institutions. Michael Doyle (1983:205–235) and William J. Dixon (1994:14–32) argued that it is difficult to find a democracy or pluralistic political system fighting other democracies. In other words, democracy and democratic values have the potential to be the best guarantee of order and peace in the world. For example, a democratic Russia can be a source of order and stability in the former Soviet Union. The European community of democratic nations, as a regional international system of states, is also a source of order and peace in Europe, which has in the past been the theater of major conflicts.

The End of the Cold War and the Process of Globalization

Through history, at the end of each major conflict or transformation, the more powerful nations have tried to establish a new world order. After the Napoleonic wars and the failure of France to unite Europe under its hegemony, there was a new distribution of power. Following the defeat of Napoleon Britain became the "mistress of the seas" and the most powerful nation in Europe, indeed, the world, with its overseas colonies. During World War II Nazi Germany and its allies tried to set up a new world order under its hegemony, but fascism was defeated. With the end of World War II the structure of international politics changed. Both France and England lost their superpower status. World politics became bipolar as the United States and the Soviet Union, allies during the war, became ideological adversaries. Due to this adversarial "balance," for almost half a century—although there were a number of regional wars in the Third World—there was no major world war. Following World War II, the longest known general peace in history rested on two basic policies: bipolarity and nuclear deterrence (Waltz, 1993:44). With the end of the Cold War came the end of bipolarity. The end of bipolarity has created a more unstable world.

What triggered the end of the Cold War and the end of bipolarity? During the late 1980s Paul Kennedy (1988), a historian, advanced a popular thesis by arguing that the decline of superpowers is due to "an imperial overstretch." Simply put, this theory argues that as a superpower extends itself militarily and politically overseas to protect its economic and strategic interests, it tends to undermine its social infrastructure, including its economy at home, which begins to decline. Historians make the same argument concerning the decline of past civilizations and empires. Those who accept the overstretch thesis of the decline of superpowers apply the same argument to explain the end of bipolarity between the United States and the Soviet Union.

Indeed, both superpowers overstretched themselves militarily in many regions of the world. The advocates of the overstretch and militarism thesis argue that the domestic needs of the people in both nations led to a condition of social deterioration at home resulting in poverty, class polarization, homelessness, health crisis, violence, crime, unemployment, pollution, and community disorganization. The economy, the decline advocates argue, was, and still is, geared toward expensive military and defense technologies. Others, however, argue that while in a general sense the over-stretch thesis sounds plausible, it is more applicable to the Soviet Union than to the United States.

Edward Shevardnadze, the secretary of state in the Soviet Union who served under the general secretary of the Communist Party, Mikhail Gorbachev, and who later became the president of Georgia, a republic in the former Soviet Union, "told the 18th party Congress in 1990 that twenty-five percent of the Soviet Gross National Product went to defense" (Nye, 1992:7). According to Nye (1992), the United States, even during conservative Republican administrations, which tradi-tionally support military spending, spent only five to six percent of Gross National Product on the military.

The rise of Gorbachev to power in 1985 and his policies of democratic reform, epitomized in the concepts of *perestroika* and *glasnost*, brought about a new thinking in international politics in the Soviet Union. This new thinking, or openness, directly challenged the legitimacy of Russian power and domination over various nationalities at home, which were dissatisfied both economically and politically with the central-ized Soviet Communist system, and Russia's hegemony over Eastern Europe.[5] Even-tually this new thinking brought about the planned demise of the Soviet Union.

The end of bipolarity has reinforced existing political globalization trends. George Modelski (1974) provided a model of globalization of politics. Modelski's model distinguishes between two forms of political interaction: (1) interstate or international relations (2) transnational relations. International or interstate rela-tions are defined as the official relationships and diplomatic interactions between national governments. International relations are defined as the process or processes of conflict and cooperation between sovereign nations, including the participation of international organizations if governments decide to include them in negotiations (McGrew et al., 1992:5). International politics is understood in terms of conflict and cooperation between independent nation-states, which represent the major actors in a global interstate system.

The concept of nation-state has become the dominant form of political organi-zation at the world level. We speak of the globalization of the nation-states or of a global political system. This means that different nations are engaged in competition in a global economy and in a world of politics within a world capitalist system. Bull (1977:20–21) argued that, "What is chiefly responsible for the degree of interaction among political systems in all continents of the world, sufficient to make it possible for us to speak of a world political system, has been the expansion of the European state system all over the globe, and its transformation into a state system of global dimension." In addition (1977:291–92),

> *it is no accident that . . . it is the countries of . . . the Third World that are most insistent on the preservation of state sovereignty. . . . They regard the institution of sovereignty as one which provides safeguard against the attempts of more powerful states to wrest from them control of the eco-nomic resources they now enjoy. It has been by creating sovereign states in*

defiance of the colonial powers, and by defending these sovereign states against the intrusion and penetration of them by the so-called 'neo-colonial' powers, that the poorer and the weaker nations have been able to achieve for themselves some measure of international justice and, in some cases, of human justice for their inhabitants. (Bull, 1977:291–292)

However, it must be emphasized that the process of globalization does not necessarily lead to global integration or to a world order marked by the development of a homogeneous society and politics. Globalization can generate forces of both unification and disintegration. In positive terms, globalization implies two distinct phenomena. First, there is the realization that political, economic, and social activity is worldwide in scope. Second, it suggests that there is an increase of interaction and interconnectedness within and among states and societies (McGrew et al., 1992:1–28).

The emergence of a global nation-states system has been reinforced by two major post–World War II political developments, the decolonization process and the eclipse of bipolarity. Yet within such a multi-nation-state system, policies pursued by one nation-state are bound to interfere with the interests and policies of another nation-state. For example, the recognition of the former Yugoslav republic of Macedonia by a number of countries as a sovereign nation state has aggravated Greece.

In Modelski's model *transnational relations* refers to all those relationships and networks that cut across national societies and cultures by creating linkages between individuals, groups, organizations, communities, or movements among various nation-states. These transnational relationships bypass the government and operate within the societal domain, going beyond direct state control (McGrew et al., 1992:7). Two major components of transnational relations are transnational politics and transnational organizations. The former is defined by Anthony G. McGrew and colleagues (1992:7) as all those relationships and organizations that cut across cultures and societies and intervene either intentionally or unintentionally in both domestic and foreign politics. Transnational organizations are nongovernmental groups that operate across national boundaries and seek to establish linkages between national societies, cultures, politics, and segments of these societies (Bull, 1977:270). Examples of transnational organizations are multinational or transnational corporations such as International Business Machines, Nestlé SA, and the Shell Oil Company. In addition, there are other types of transnational organizations or associations that concentrate on a specific activity or issue; these include political bodies (interparliamentary groups), ecological or environmental pressure groups (Greenpeace and Friends of the Earth), professional associations (the International Sociological Association), religious organizations (the World Council of Churches), as well as sports, welfare, and scientific organizations. Since the turn of the century there has been a tremendous increase in the number of transnational organizations. Transgovernmental relations involve networks of various departments or bureaucracies within different national governments. For example, direct contacts exist between various police or paramilitary departments or agencies, like Interpol, to track down criminals or intercept drug traffic across national states and societies. Military alliances such as NATO are also part of transgovernmental relations.

Perspectives Concerning World Order

The concepts order, world order, and new world order are somewhat ambiguous. Conservative political ideologists use the term *order* to indicate stability or the power of the state. Liberal ideologists believe that order is inseparable from justice because, according to them, only a just order can bring peace. In general, order is a means to an end, not an end in itself. Order is essential for development but not sufficient for the growth and nourishment of democracy. It can be argued, for instance, that some governments preserve order only as a means of denying their own citizens' human rights. Similarly, stronger nations may use their military, political, and economic power to impose their will or their own version of world order on weaker nations or groups.

We also speak of *social order, economic order,* and *political order,* and we associate the terms with social institutions or societal structures designed to maintain continuity and stability in society. These include the economic, political, kinship, religious, or educational institutions. In short, the idea of order is functionalist. In this context, society and polity are viewed as a functional whole in which concepts such as structure, stability, consensus, harmony, equilibrium, balance, convergence, hierarchy, and stratification are linked to the notion of social or political order. Indeed, a functionalist perspective of society is a theory of social order.

The opposites of order are disorder, conflict, instability, divergence, diversity, and dissent. Democracy, by definition, is not always an orderly political system; autocracy or authoritarianism are more orderly. For instance, from the beginning, the United States found itself in a dilemma, having to choose between American nationalism, which stresses unity within conformity and order along an assimilationist Anglo-Saxon model, and American liberalism/capitalism, which emphasizes unity within cultural diversity (or what is now called multiculturalism) along ethnic, racial, nationality, religious, and gender dimensions. The idea of unity within conformity is a more conservative view of world order while unity within diversity is a more liberal view. The former model is more predictable and stable, while the latter is more unpredictable and unstable yet allows more freedom, creativity, individuality, and democracy to flourish.

Order is also associated with the notion of peace, which refers not only to the absence of war, but also to the well-being of people who are happy with what they are doing in a society that provides opportunities for individuals to pursue worthwhile goals and to satisfy their aspirations. In a peaceful society, people have a sense of security and freedom, and they are not afraid to walk the streets alone at night. Peace also means that people have a sense of purpose in their lives, find meaning in what they are doing, and feel a sense of accomplishment. However, when society is fractured by economic disparities and social inequality that is aggravated by ethnic, religious, and racial cleavages and conflicts, that society or nation is not at peace.

World order is not a new concept. Samuel S. Kim (1984:61–62) examined the rhetorical and contending images of world order, namely the reactionary, the globalist/hegemonic, and the apocalyptic/eschatological views. The reactionary view is exemplified by the slogan "law and order," which does not raise the issue of justice. A just world order is based on normative and/or empirical images and values such as peace, well-being, justice, and ecological integrity and balance in nature. Normative definitions of justice are difficult to find because what is justice for one nation may not be for another. Philosophers and jurists have spent lifetimes trying to define justice and international law but have come to no consensus.

The globalist/hegemonic view sees world order as a globalizing form of ideology promulgated by a superpower that finds itself in hegemonic decline. Countries in the periphery or semiperiphery are suspicious of the globalist or hegemonic images of the world due to their bitter experience with past models of world order. For some, the term *world order* has an apocalyptic or eschatological ring to it that suggests that the world will come to an end unless something very dramatic takes place.

The concerns of most nations are national in scope, not global. Their main global interests principally concern survival in a world of powers competing for economic, political, and military advantages. For the last half century, world order was principally the concern of the two superpowers, who were engaged in a balance of terror based on the theory of deterrence, which has robbed the world and depleted the resources of our ecosystem.

Contending Global Images of World Order

During the 1970s there was a proliferation of contending images of world order. These global images were classified under three basic rubrics: system-maintaining, system-reforming, and system-transforming approaches (Falk, 1982:146–174). Drawing on Falk's (1982) and Anthony J. Dolman's (1981:49–60) work, Kim (1984:63–68) elaborated on these three types of images. A system-maintaining image of world order seeks to maintain the existing patterns of stratification and stability in a rapidly changing world. It is a functionalist and hegemonic model. This means that wherever there is disruption or breakdown of the world order, those countries on the top of the stratification system of power and domination in the world system act or react to preserve their authority and dominance. As long as their interests are not affected by changes of world order, the powerful nations do not intervene. The Trilateral Commission;[4] academic, defense, cultural, corporate, and political elites; think tanks; national security managers; Pentagonists; and foreign relations policy makers support the existing world order. In general, the core countries in the world system try to maintain a stratified and hierarchical structure of the world. Policies made by the United States, its Western allies, and the seven most industrialized nations seek to maintain military and economic hegemony. The present world order is thus supported by the industrialized, capitalist nations in the world system. With the exception of Japan, the United States, and Canada, the "Big Seven" nations are European. The United States and its western European partners represent the Euro-American and Anglo-Saxon world order.

Those espousing a system-reforming image of the world order support the existing capitalist structure of the world but advocate functional interdependence and cooperation between those countries in the core, periphery, and semiperiphery. This model is supported principally by the countries of the Third World and by international organizations such as the United Nations General Assembly, the Third World Caucus, and RIO (Reshaping the International Order). These groups seek to encourage dialogue among nations, scientists, and world order specialists.

Finally, there is the system-transforming image of the world order. While one can argue that a transformation of the present world capitalist system into something more equitable and equalitarian is desirable, reality in the mid-1990s makes it seem unlikely. The neo-Marxist world system model, as formulated by Immanuel Wallerstein's (1974, 1979) historical investigations, can also be considered a system-transforming image of world order. In view of the demise of the Soviet Union and the crisis of world Communism as an ideology in general, the global socialist transformation as promulgated by Marxists and neo-Marxists is a rather remote possibility. In general, the system-maintenance, system-reform, and system-transformation images of the world order share a number of common concerns about the future of the world, including the depletion of the earth's resources, the world economy, world hunger, violence, and overpopulation.

Whenever the present Eurocentric or Euro-American world order is challenged, the Western industrialized nations—Germany, France, United States, England, Italy, Canada, and now Japan—meet to discuss the state of the world economy. China and India, the most populous countries in Asia, which contain almost half of the earth's population, are not yet part of this elite power structure. However, China and India are likely to compete for superpower status in the twenty-first century. Japan and Germany, although part of the elite power structure, are not likely to achieve military superpower status because of their histories and the restrictions imposed on their militaries by the Allies after World War II. The former Soviet Union is still a great power, but it has lost its superpower status since it lost its continental empire and its hegemony over Eastern Europe and because of its domestic economic failure to provide both guns and butter (Martellaro, 1987).

Contending Models for the Post–Cold War Era

One model for the post–Cold War era sees the decline of military technology and the rise of economic power blocs as the most important basis of the new world order—there will be an Asian economic bloc led by Japan, a European Union economic bloc, and a North American economic bloc like, for example, the bloc encouraged by NAFTA. Another vision of the post–Cold War era is what is called the Unipolar Movement, which is associated with the *Pax Americana*. Nye (1992) refuted this vision, arguing that the United States cannot exercise a hegemonic role because the world economy is tripolar (the poles are Europe, Japan, and the United States) and because of the diffusion nuclear weapons capability to small countries and transnational groups. North Korea's nuclear program, for instance, could destabilize the Southeast Asian region and challenge U.S. hegemony there.

William K. Tabb (1992) introduced the term *vampire capitalism* to refer to the new world order. According to Tabb, vampire capitalism is a strategy of growth based on coercion, military force, and the political and ideological domination of the world. He suggested that an index of vampire capitalism is the continuation of the United States military-industrial complex in a post–Cold War world for the purpose of military intervention or coercion. Tabb argued that the strategy of vampire capitalism is to neutralize three forces that oppose the United States elite dominance: rival capitalist forces (Japan and Germany), the domestic working class, and developing nations dependent on United States aid.

Michael C. Hudson (1992:301–316) also raised the issue of a U.S.-led new world order by suggesting four scenarios: a new stable order, a new chaotic order, an old order with relative stability, and an old order with chaos. Hudson believed that the fourth outcome is most likely—there will be little change in order but heightened instability. Here a new stable order means that the present capitalist system will continue to be dominated by the economic and commercial interests of the United States around the world. A new chaotic order would involve a series of regional conflicts or disputes between nations or groups of nations following the end of the Cold war (the conflict in the former Yugoslavia would be an example). An old order with relative stability is again capitalist in nature but has its ups and downs without a major threat to the present existing capitalist order occurring. The old order with chaos is what is more evident at present. I tend to agree with Hudson's old order with chaos scenario for it seems that the new world order is an old wine, so to speak, in new bottles, the new bottles being the new problems occurring as emerging nations assert themselves and pursue their self-determination and independence from the paternalism of the dominant nations. The new force driving chaos is no longer the "menace of communism" or the "evil empire" but the reemergence of nationalism as a worldwide phenomenon.

Another model of the new world order is what is known as a postmodernist approach (Griffin & Falk, 1993). According to this view, postmodernism must supplant modernity as a world view. Modernity threatens the very survival of life on our planet, and the crisis involves ecological, economic, social, and spiritual dimensions. Postmodern politics are based on the notion of wholeness, veering away from the concept of modernity with its two destructive elements: "the drive to subdue nature and the profit-making ethos" (Griffin & Falk, 1993:6).

A postmodern world view is one of interdependence and harmony between nature and the human race. Education, for example, is seen as based not on national interest, self-interest, and careerism but on "wonder, interest, confidence, compassion, courage, social feeling, a sense for beauty, and reverence for life" (Sloan, 1993:7). Generally speaking, postmodern politics repudiates the modern, passive democracy in favor of a participatory and more active democracy. A postmodernist new world order is genuinely new if it is based on a sustainable relationship between the human enterprise, as a whole, and the rest of the ecosystem. A new world order should not be based on military, political, and economic domination but on what Lester Milbrath (1989) referred to as a value structure for a sustainable society and the world. Milbrath's proposed value structure envisions a number of systems and structures that provide health, peace, order, equality, freedom, a sense of belonging, knowledge, fulfilling work and leisure, and goods and services for a sustainable society and life in a viable ecosystem (Milbrath, 1989).

David Held (1992:10–39) proposed a cosmopolitan democratic model of the new international order in which there is a genuine development of multiple and overlapping networks of power. The emphasis is on the creation of new global institutions and on the broadening of existing ones. Some of the key features of this model, and both the short term and the long range objectives, (1) the notion of self-determination and commitment to a democratic international legal order; (2) law making and law enforcement at national, regional, and international levels; (3) the principle of noncoercive settling of disputes among nations according to democratic principles of international law; (4) the application of principles of social justice in the production, distribution, and exploitation of resources; (5) the broadening of the United Nations Security Council to give the countries in the periphery a more significant voice; (6) the future creation of a global parliament connected to regions, nations, and localities may be desirable; (7) a new charter of rights and duties interconnected with a global legal system; (8) the establishment of a small, but effective, international military force having as its long-term aim demilitarization and transcendence of the present war and military system attached to the state system; (9) the enhancement of nonstate and nonmarket solutions to world problems, along with the creation of self-regulating associations and groups; and (10) the limitation of private ownership of key public institutions such as the media. These ideas of cosmopolitanism can be achieved in the next century. In short, according to Held, the new post–Cold War era must see the institution of a set of universal values, human rights, and standards of international law, order, and justice.

Related to the global cosmopolitan model is the transnational public law model. According to Harold H. Koh (1991), transnational public law litigation seeks to vindicate public rights and values through the judicial process. Beginning with the 1946 war crimes trials at Nuremberg and Tokyo, nation-states have brought claims against one another based on treaty or international law before international tribunals. The vast field of international human rights law includes such treaties as the genocide convention of December 9, 1948, which condemns the systematic extermination of groups of people by the state as a crime against humanity; the European covenant on civil and political fundamental freedoms of November 4, 1950; and the Helsinki Accords of August 1, 1975, on security and cooperation in Europe. All these international laws and judicial procedures are critical of the power of nation-states. Given the anarchy of the world system, the only safeguard against state power and the violation of human rights by states against their own citizens is some kind of international system of jurisprudence having the power to maintain peace and order with law and justice.

In conclusion, we can say that the new world order is not as new as many would like to believe. Both the Cold War and bipolarity have provided an artificial stability and a world order imposed by the two superpowers for the last half century. In many ways, both superpowers have failed the world, having robbed the earth's resources and drained the economies of other nation-states by engaging in the arms race at the expense of human betterment. The new world in the next century must be navigated by commitment to social justice, social equality, and the peaceful coexistence of all the people of the world, irrespective of race, religion, region, or national origins. It is ironic that the demise of Communism and the end of the Cold War have opened a Pandora's box of ethnic nationalism and racism in some parts of the world while, in others, it has brought people closer. Held's cosmopolitan democratic model and Huntington's third wave of democratization will be utopian visions in the next century if we continue to operate using current principles concerning the national interests of nation-states and power politics.

Summary and Conclusion

In this last chapter on the "politics and society in the post cold war era" some key issues in the sociology of international relations were raised using the international system of nation states as a framework. Some political sociologists have advanced new visions of a new world order while others have proposed scenarios critical of the unipolar model of the new world order. Joseph Nye introduced five different versions of a new world order: return to bipolarity, multipolar, economic blocs, unipolar, and multi-level interdependence. B. S. Chimni outlined four major perspectives on international law and world order: the realist approach advanced originally by Morgenthau, the McDougal-Laswell approach, the Richard Falk transdisciplinary jurisprudence approach, and the Marxist approach.

A brief background analysis about the end of the Cold War and the process of globalization were discussed focusing on the re-emergence of the nation-state as the dominant form of political organization of the international system. The expansion of the European state system has contributed to its transformation into a system of global dimension. This globalization process of the state system has contributed to both integration and disintegration of the world order. In positive terms, globalization has contributed (a) to an increased interaction and interconnectedness among nations and (b) to a worldwide social, political, and economic activity both at the governmental level and at the societal level.

The concepts of order, world order and new world order were defined and discussed within the context of functionalist and conflict sociological perspectives and the conservative versus liberal political ideologies.

In addition, the rhetorical and contending images of world order were briefly examined. Samuel Kim proposed three major rhetorical images: the reactionary as exemplified in the slogan "law and order," the globalist/hegemonic view promulgated by a superpower that finds itself in decline, and the apocalyptic/eschatological view that suggests the world is coming to an end unless something very dramatic takes place. In conjunction with the aforementioned images three additional approaches were discussed: system-maintaining, system-reforming, and system-transforming.

Finally, a number of contending models for the post-Cold War Era were briefly articulated. Michael Hudson has suggested four scenarios of the new world order: a new stable order, a new chaotic order, an old order with relative stability, and an old order with chaos. Another view of a new world is the post modernist approach to politics, based on the notion of wholeness and away from the "profit-making ethos." Lester Milbrath proposed a value structure for a sustainable society and the world.

Somewhat related to that of Milbrath is the cosmopolitan democratic model of the new international order suggested by David Held and the transnational public law based on public rights and valued through the judicial process proposed by Harold Koh.

In short, the new world order is not as new as many would like to believe. The Cold War Era and bipolarity (1954–1989) have provided an artificial sense of stability and a world order by the two superpowers for the last half century. In many ways, both superpowers have failed the world by engaging in the arms race, robbed the earth's resources, and drained the economies of other nations at the expense of human betterment. It will be highly desirable if the new world order in the next century is going to be navigated by a commitment to the ideals of social justice, social equality, and peaceful coexistence of all the people of the world, irrespective of religion, region, or national origins.

Endnotes

1. For more extensive treatment of the origins, structure, and impact of the modern state see *The Political Sociology of the State,* edited by Richard G. Braungart and Margaret M. Braungart (Greenwich: JAI Press, 1990).

2. For an analysis of WOMP see Dolman (1981), Falk (1981), Kim (1981), and Oakes and Stunkel (1981).

3. Falk referred to Hugo Grotius (1583–1645), a Dutch jurist and the father of international law. He wrote the first "comprehensive and system-atic treatise on international law." He carried out the spirit of Westphalia and advanced the normative basis of an emerging world order (Chimni, 1993: 227).

4. The Trilateral Commission was a nongovernmental group of individuals from western Europe, the United States, and Japan representing Europe, North America, and Asia. It had an elitist and hegemonic agenda for the emerging new world order. It started during the 1970s. Former president Jimmy Carter was a member of this commission.

References

Brecher, Jeremy, John Childs and Jill Cutler, 1993, *Global Visions: Beyond the New World Order.* Boston: South End Press.

Bull, Hedley. 1977. *The Anarchical Society: A Study of Order in World Politics.* New York: Columbia University Press.

Chimni, B. S. 1993. *International Law and World Order: A Critique of Contemporary Approaches.* New Delhi: Sage.

Cosgrove, Denis. 1992. "Orders and a New World: Cultural Geography 1990–91." *Progress in Human Geography.* Vol. 16, no. 2:272–80.

Cox, R. W. 1981. "Social Forces, States, and World Order: Beyond International Relations." *Millennium.* Vol. 10:126–55.

Dixon, William J. 1994. "Democracy and the Peaceful Settlement of International Conflict." *American Political Science Review* Vol. 88, no. 1:14–32.

Dolman, Anthony J. 1981. *Resources, Regimes, World Order.* New York: Pergamon.

Doyle, Michael. 1983. "Kant, Liberal Legacies, and Foreign Affairs." *Philosophy and Public Affairs.* Vol. 12 (Summer):205–235.

Falk, Richard A. 1982. "Contending Approaches to World Order." In *Toward a Just World Order,* ed. Richard A. Falk, Samuel S. Kim, and Saul H. Mendlovitz, Boulder: Westview. pp. 146–174.

———. 1981. "In Search of WOMP" a Comment By Richard Falk, In Support of the "WOMP" research published in the *Journal of Political and Military Sociology* vol. 9 no. 1 (Spring): 121–122.

———. 1975. *The Study of Future Worlds*. New York: Free Press.

———. 1970. *The Status of Law in International Society*. Princeton: Princeton University Press.

Griffin, David R., and Richard Falk, eds. 1993. *Postmodern Politics for a Planet in Crisis*. New York: State University of New York Press.

Headley, Bernard D. 1991. "The New World Order and the Persian Gulf War." *Humanity and Society*. Vol. 15, no. 3:317–324.

Held, David, ed. 1992. "Prospects for Democracy." *Political Studies*. Vol. 40:5–160.

Hudson, Michael C. 1992. "The Middle East Under Pax Americana: How New, How Orderly?" *Third World Quarterly*. Vol. 13, no. 2:301–16.

Kennedy, Paul. 1988. *The Rise and Fall of the Great Powers*. New York: Random House.

Kim, Samuel S. 1984. *The Quest for a Just World Order*. Boulder: Westview.

———. 1981. "The World Order Models Project and Its Strange Critics." *Journal of Political and Military Sociology* Vol. 7 (spring):109–15.

Koh, Harold H. 1991. "Transnational Public Law Litigation." *Yale Law Journal*. Vol. 100, no. 8: 2347–402.

Kourvetaris, George A. 1991. "Beyond the Arms Race: The Search for a New Paradigm of a Peaceful World." *Journal of Political and Military Sociology* Vol. 19, no. 2:233–52.

MacEwan, Arthur. 1991. *Still Out of Order: Bush's New World Order Won't Restore Us Economic Might*. Boston: University of Massachusetts.

Martellaro, Joseph A. 1987. "The Post–World War II Soviet Economy: The Case of Butter and Guns." *Journal of Political and Military Sociology* Vol. 15 (Summer):83.

McGrew, Anthony G., Paul G. Lewis, et al. 1992. *Global Politics: Globalization and the Nation State*. England: Polity.

Mearsheimer, John. 1992. "Why We Will Soon Miss The Cold War." In *The New World Order: Rethinking America's Global Role*, ed. Carol Rae Hansen and with editorial assistance

by Robert Scott Jastar and Shirley Kew Jastar, 51–73.

Mendlovitz, S. 1981. "A Comment." 1981 in Kim, S. "The World Order Project and its Strange Critics" in *Journal of Political and Military Sociology* Vol. 7 (Spring):109–115.

Milbrath, Lester. 1989. *Envisioning a Sustainable Society*. New York: State University of New York Press.

Modelski, George. 1974. *Principles of World Politics*. New York: Free Press.

Morganthau, Hans. 1985. *Politics among Nations: The Struggle for Power and Peace*, rev. Kenneth W. Thompson. New York: McGraw-Hill.

Morrison, W. L. 1976. "Myres S. McDougal and Twentieth Century Jurisprudence: A Comparative Essay." In *Toward World Order and Human Dignity; Essays in Honor of Myres S. McDougal*, ed. M. W. Reisman and B. H. Westoy, 3–78. New York: Free Press.

Neher, Clark D. and Ross Marlay 1995. *Democracy and Development in Southeast Asia: The Winds of Change* Boulder, Colorado: Westview Press.

Nye, Joseph S. 1992. "Is There a New World Order?" In *The New World Order: Rethinking America's Global Role*, ed. Carol Roe Hansen, 3–18 Flagstaff: Arizona Honors Academy Press.

Oakes, Guy, and Kenneth Stunkel. 1981. "In Search of World Order Models Project (WOMP)." *Journal of Political and Military Sociology* Vol. 9 (Spring):83–99.

Organski, A. F. K., and Jacek Kugler. 1978. "Davids and Goliaths: Predicting the Outcomes of International Wars." *Comparative Political Studies*. Vol. 11:141–80.

Redner, Harry. 1990. "Beyond Marx-Weber: A Diversified and International Approach to the State." *Political Studies*. Vol. 38:638–653.

Rupert, Mark E. 1990. "Producing Hegemony." *International Studies Quarterly*. Vol. 34:433–435.

Sanders, Terry W. 1991. "The Gulf War and Bush's Folly." *Peace Review*. Vol. 3, no. 2:27–35.

Sloan, Douglas. 1993. "A Postmodern Vision of Education for a Living Planet." In David Griffin and Richard Falk. (eds.) *Postmodern Poli-*

tics for a Planet in Crisis, New York: State University, New York Press.

Sylvester, Christine. 1981. "In Defence of the World Order Models Project: A Behavioralist's Response." *Journal Political and Military Sociology* Vol. 9 (Spring):101–108.

Tabb, William K. 1992. "Vampire Capitalism." *Socialist Review.* Vol. 22, no. 1:81–93.

Wallerstein, Immanuel. 1974. *The Modern World System: Capitalist Agriculture and the Origins of the European World-Economy in the Sixteenth Century.* New York: Academic Press.

———. 1979. *The Capitalist World-Economy.* New York: Cambridge University Press.

Waltz, Kenneth N. 1993. "The Emerging Structure of International Politics." *International Security."* Vol. 18, no. 2 :44–79.

Index

ABC. *See* American Broadcasting Corporation (ABC)

Abrahamsson, Bengt, 119

absolutist state, 68–69

accommodation (and political ideology), 192

Adamic, Louis, 22

Adams, Gordon, 122

administration (as element of state), 59–60

Africa, 88, 126, 159, 228. *See also names of specific countries*

African Americans
  Civil Rights Movement and. *See* Civil Rights Movement, factions within; participants in
  Clarence Thomas nomination and, 44, 139
  nationalism by, 212–213
  political participation by, 63, 136, 148, 150, 200
  racial discrimination against, 10–11, 82–83
  representation in Congress by, 139
  status inconsistency among, 148
  voting by, 63, 136

Age of Reason. *See* Enlightenment

agenda setting (by mass media), 107–109

Alford, Robert R., 60, 73, 135

alignment (of political parties), 169, 171, 172

Althusser, Louis, 38, 184

American Academy of Arts and Sciences, 94

American Academy of Engineering, 94

American Association for Labor, 72

American Broadcasting Corporation (ABC), 103, 105–106

American Dilemma, An (Myrdal, 1944), 11

American Federation of Labor, 72

American Medical Association, 163

American Revolution, 159, 203

American Sociological Association, 200

Aminzade, Ronald, 207–208

Anderson, Cösta-Esping, 68

Andreski, Stanislaw, 122

anticolonialism, 240

antiestablishment movement (1960s). *See also* Civil Rights Movement; Vietnam War
  effect on political sociology, 23–24
  events/issues behind, 52, 149, 181
  opposition to, 175
  political participation and, 149, 150, 152, 181
  resource mobilization theory and, 206

AP. *See* Associated Press (AP)

Apter, David E., 188

Argentina, 128, 188, 217

aristocracy, 61, 65, 68

aristocratic/feudal model (of military), 118

Aristotle, 3, 21, 50, 60–61, 88–89, 136, 218, 220, 221, 225

arms. *See* weapons

arms race. *See* Cold War; nuclear arms

Aron, Raymond, 193–194

ASEAN. *See* Association of Southeast Asian Nations (ASEAN)

Asia, 126, 159. *See also names of specific countries*

assimilation, 21, 22

Associated Press (AP), 106

Association of Southeast Asian Nations (ASEAN), 249

Ataturk, Mustafa, 188

attitudinal/behavioral model (of political ideology), 186–187

authoritarianism
  decline of, 88
  definition of, 61–62
  development under, 225–226
  examples of, 62
  media control under, 109
  political socialization under, 152
  social/political order under, 257

authority (as form of power), 49–52